CBSE Term II
2022

Applied Mathematics

Class
XI

CBSE Term II
2022

Applied Mathematics

Class XI

- Theory Covering Whole Syllabus
- Case Based Questions
- Short/Long Answer Type Questions
- 3 Practice Papers with Explanations

Author
Brijesh Kumar Dwevedi

arihant
ARIHANT PRAKASHAN (School Division Series)

ARIHANT PRAKASHAN (School Division Series)

ॐ **Administrative & Production Offices**

Regd. Office

'Ramchhaya' 4577/15, Agarwal Road, Darya Ganj, New Delhi -110002
Tele: 011- 47630600, 43518550

ॐ **Head Office**

 Kalindi, TP Nagar, Meerut (UP) - 250002, Tel: 0121-7156203, 7156204

ॐ **Sales & Support Offices**

Agra, Ahmedabad, Bengaluru, Bareilly, Chennai, Delhi, Guwahati, Hyderabad, Jaipur, Jhansi, Kolkata, Lucknow, Nagpur & Pune.

ॐ **ISBN :** 978-93-25796-74-4

ॐ **PRICE :** ₹200.00

PO No : TXT-XX-XXXXXXX-X-XX

Published by Arihant Publications (India) Ltd.

For further information about the books published by Arihant, log on to www.arihantbooks.com or e-mail at info@arihantbooks.com

Follow us on    

Contents

Syllabus

CBSE Term II Class XI

Theory - 40 Marks | | **Duration - 2 hrs**

No	Units	Marks
II	Algebra (Continued)	06
IV	Calculus (Continued)	06
V	Probability	08
VI	Basics of Financial Mathematics	15
VII	Coordinate Geometry	05
	Total	**40**

Sl.No.	Contents	Learning Outcomes Students Will Be Able To	Notes/ Explanations
Permutations and Combinations			
2.15	Factorial	• Define factorial of a number • Calculate factorial of a number	• Definition of factorial: $n! = n(n-1)(n-2)\ldots3.2.1$ Usage of factorial in counting principles
2.16	Fundamental Principle of Counting	• Appreciate how to count without counting	• Fundamental Principle of Addition • Fundamental Principle of Multiplication
2.17	Permutations	• Define permutation • Apply the concept of permutation to solve simple problems	• Permutation as arrangement of objects in a definite order taken some or all at a time • Theorems under different conditions resulting in $^{n}P_{r} = \dfrac{n!}{(n-r)!}$ or n^{r} or $\dfrac{n!}{n_1!\, n_2!\ldots n_k!}$ arrangements

SI.No.	Contents	Learning Outcomes Students Will Be Able To	Notes/ Explanations
2.20	Combinations	• Define combination • Differentiate between permutation and combination • Apply the formula of combination to solve the related problems	• The number of combinations of n different objects taken r at a time is given by $^nC_r = \dfrac{n!}{r!(n-r)!}$ Some results on combinations: • $^nC_0 = 1 = {}^nC_n$ • $^nC_a = {}^nC_b \Rightarrow a = b$ or $a + b = n$ • $^nC_r = {}^nC_{n-r}$ • $^nC_r + {}^nC_{r-1} = {}^{n+1}C_r$

UNIT - 4 CALCULUS

SI.No.	Contents	Learning Outcomes Students Will Be Able To	Notes/ Explanations
4.5	Concepts of limits and continuity of a function	• Define limit of a function • Solve problems based on the algebra of limits • Define continuity of a function	• Left hand limit, Right hand limit, Limit of a function, Continuity of a function
4.6	Instantaneous rate of change	• Define instantaneous rate of change	• The ratio $\dfrac{\Delta y}{\Delta x} = \dfrac{f(x + \Delta x) - f(x)}{\Delta x}$ as instantaneous rate of change, where Δy is change in y and Δx is change in x at any instant
4.7	Differentiation as a process of finding derivative	• Find the derivative of the functions	• Derivatives of functions (non- trigonometric only)
4.8	Derivatives of algebraic functions using Chain Rule	• Find the derivative of function of a function	• If $y = f(u)$ where $u = g(x)$ then differential coefficient of y w.r.t. x is $\dfrac{dy}{dx} = \dfrac{dy}{du}\,\dfrac{du}{dx}$

UNIT - 5 PROBABILITY

SI.No.	Contents	Learning Outcomes Students Will Be Able To	Notes/ Explanations
5.1	Introduction	• Appreciate the use of probability in daily life situations	• Probability as quantitative measure of uncertainly • Use of probability in determining the insurance premium, weather forecasts etc.

Sl.No.	Contents	Learning Outcomes Students Will Be Able To	Notes/ Explanations
5.2	Random experiment and sample space	• Define random experiment and sample space with suitable examples	• Sample space as set of all possible outcomes
5.3	Event	• Define an event • Recognize and differentiate different types of events and find their probabilities	• Types of Event: Impossible and sure event, Independent and dependent event, mutually exclusive and exhaustive event
5.4	Conditional Probability	• Define the concept of conditional probability • Apply reasoning skills to solve problems based on conditional probability	• Conditional Probability of event E given that F has occurred is: $P(E/F) = \dfrac{P(E \cap F)}{P(F)}, P(F) \neq 0$
5.5	Total Probability	• Interpret mathematical information and identify situations when to apply total probability • Solve problems based on application of total probability	• Total Probability: Let $E_1 E_2, \dots E_n$ be a partition of the sample space S, then probability of an event A associated with S is: $P(A) = \Sigma_{j=1}^{n} P(E_j) P(A|E_j)$
5.6	Bayes' Theorem	• State Bayes' theorem • Solve practical problems based on Bayes' Theorem	• Bayes' Theorem: If $E_1 E_2, \dots E_n$ be n non empty events which constitute a partition of a sample space S and A be any event with non zero probability, then: $P(E_1|A) = \dfrac{P(E_i)P(A|F_i)}{\Sigma_{j=1}^{n} P(E_j) P(A|E_j)}$

UNIT - 7 FINANCIAL MATHEMATICS

Sl.No.	Contents	Learning Outcomes Students Will Be Able To	Notes/ Explanations
7.1	Interest and Interest Rates	• Define the concept of Interest Rates • Compare the difference between Nominal Interest Rate, Effective Rate and Real Interest Rate • Solve Practical applications of interest rate	• Impact of high interest rates and low interest rates on the business

Sl.No.	Contents	Learning Outcomes Students Will Be Able To	Notes/ Explanations
7.2	Accumulation with simple and compound interest	• Interpret the concept of simple and compound interest • Calculate Simple Interest and Compound Interest	• Meaning and significance of simple and compound interest • Compound interest rates applications on various financial products
7.3	Simple and compound interest rates with equivalency	• Explain the meaning, nature and concept of equivalency • Analyze various examples for understanding annual equivalency rate	• Concept of Equivalency • Annual Equivalency Rate
7.4	Effective rate of interest	• Define with examples the concept of effective rate of interest	• Effective Annual Interest Rate $= (1 + i/n)^n - 1$ where: i = Nominal Interest Rate n = Number of Periods
7.5	Present value, net present value and future value	• Interpret the concept of compounding and discounting along with practical applications • Compute net present value • Apply net present value in capital budgeting decisions	• Formula for Present Value: $PV = CF/(1 + r)^n$ Where: CF = Cash Flow in Future Period r = Periodic Rate of return or Interest (also called the discount rate or the required rate of return) n = Number of periods • Use of PVAF, FVAF tables for practical purposes • Solve problems based on Application of net present value
7.6	Annuities, Calculating value of Regular Annuity	• Explain the concept of Immediate Annuity, Annuity due and Deferred Annuity • Calculate General Annuity	• Definition, Formulae and Examples
7.7	Simple applications of regular annuities (upto 3 period)	• Calculate the future value of regular annuity, annuity due • Apply the concept of Annuity in real life situations	• Examples of regular annuity: Mortgage Payment, Car Loan Payments, Leases, Rent Payment, Insurance payouts etc.

SI.No.	Contents	Learning Outcomes Students Will Be Able To	Notes/ Explanations
7.8	Tax, calculation of tax, simple applications of tax calculation in Goods and service tax, Income Tax	• Explain fundamentals of taxation • Differentiate between Direct and indirect tax • Define and explain GST • Calculate GST • Explain rules under State Goods and Services Tax (SGST) Central Goods and Services Tax (CGST) and Union Territory Goods and Services Tax (UTGST)	• Computation of income tax Add Income from Salary, house property, business or profession, capital gain, other sources, etc. Less deductions PF, PPF, LIC, Housing loan, FD, NSC etc. • Assess the Individuals under Income Tax Act • Formula for GST Different Tax heads under GST
7.9	Bills, tariff rates, fixed charge, surcharge, service charge	• Describe the meaning of bills and its various types • Analyze the meaning and rules determining tariff rates • Explain the concept of fixed charge	• Tariff rates- its basis of determination • Concept of fixed charge service charge and their applications in various sectors of Indian economy
7.10	Calculation and interpretation of electricity bill, water supply bill and other supply bills	• To interpret and analyze electricity bills, water bills and other supply bills • Evaluate how to calculate units consumed under electricity bills/water bill	• Components of electricity bill/water supply and other supply bills: i) overcharging of electricity ii) water supply bills iii) units consumed in electricity bills

UNIT 8 COORDINATE GEOMETRY

SI.No.	Contents	Learning Outcomes Students Will Be Able To	Notes/ Explanations
8.1	Straight line	• Find the slope and equation of line in various form • Find angle between the two lines • Find the perpendicular from a given point on a line • Find the distance between two parallel lines	• Gradient of a line • Equation of line: Parallel to axes, point-slope form, two-points form, slope intercept form, intercept form • Application of the straight line in demand curve related to economics problems

Sl.No.	Contents	Learning Outcomes Students Will Be Able To	Notes/ Explanations
8.2	Circle	• Define a circle • Find different form of equations of a circle • Solve problems based on applications of circle	• Circle as a locus of a point in a plane • Equation of a circle in standard form, central form, diameter form and general form
8.3	Parabola	• Define parabola and related terms • Define eccentricity of a parabola • Derive the equation of parabola	• Parabola as a locus of a point in a plane. • Equation of a parabola in standard form: • Focus, Directrix, Axis, Latusrectum, Eccentricity

Internal Assessment:

The weightage of internal assessment may be as under:

Term	Area and Weightage	Assessment Area	Marks allocated
Term 2	Practical	Performance of practical and record	05
		Term-end test of any one practical + Viva	05
		Total	**10**

CBSE Circular

Exam Scheme Term I & II

केन्द्रीय माध्यमिक शिक्षा बोर्ड

(शिक्षा मंत्रालय, भारत सरकार के अधीन एक स्वायत संगठन)

CENTRAL BOARD OF SECONDARY EDUCATION

(An Autonomous Organisation under the Ministryof Education, Govt. of India)

CBSE/DIR (ACAD)/2021

Date: July 05, 2021

Circular No: Acad-51/2021

All the Heads of Schools affiliated to CBSE

Subject: Special Scheme of Assessment for Board Examination Classes X and XII for the Session 2021-22

COVID 19 pandemic caused almost all CBSE schools to function in a virtual mode for most part of the academic session of 2020-21. Due to the extreme risk associated with the conduct of Board examinations during the second wave in April 2021, CBSE had to cancel both its class X and XII Board examinations of the year 2021 and results are to be declared on the basis of a credible, reliable, flexible and valid alternative assessment policy. This, in turn, also necessitated deliberations over alternative ways to look at the learning objectives as well as the conduct of the Board Examinations for the academic session 2021-22 in case the situation remains unfeasible.

CBSE has also held stake holder consultations with Government schools as well as private independent schools from across the country especially schools from the remote rural areas and a majority of them have requested for the rationalization of the syllabus, similar to last year in view of reduced time permitted for organizing online classes. The Board has also considered the concerns regarding differential availability of electronic gadgets, connectivity and effectiveness of online teaching and other socio-economic issues specially with respect to students from economically weaker section and those residing in far flung areas of the country. In a survey conducted by CBSE, it was revealed that the rationalized syllabus notified for the session 2020-21 was effective for schools in covering the syllabus and helped learners in achieving learning objectives in a less stressful manner.

In the above backdrop and in line with the Board's continued focus on assessing stipulated learning outcomes by making the examinations competencies and core concepts based, student-centric, transparent, technology-driven, and having advance provision of alternatives for different future scenarios, the following schemes are introduced for the Academic Session for Class X and Class XII 2021-22.

Special Scheme for 2021-22

A. Academic session to be divided into 2 Terms with approximately 50% syllabus in each term:

The syllabus for the Academic session 2021-22 will be divided into 2 terms by following a systematic approach by looking into the interconnectivity of concepts and topics by the Subject Experts and the Board will conduct examinations at the end of each term on the basis of the bifurcated syllabus. This is done to increase the probability of having a Board conducted classes X and XII examinations at the end of the academic session.

B. The syllabus for the Board examination 2021-22 will be rationalized similar to that of the last academic session to be notified in July 2021. For academic transactions, however, schools will follow the curriculum and syllabus released by the Board vide Circular no. F.1001/CBSE-Acad/Curriculum/2021 dated 31 March 2021. Schools will also use alternative academic calendar and inputs from the NCERT on transacting the curriculum.

C. Efforts will be made to make Internal Assessment/ Practical/ Project work more credible and valid as per the guidelines and Moderation Policy to be announced by the Board to ensure fair distribution of marks.

Details of Curriculum Transaction

- Schools will continue teaching in distance mode till the authorities permit in-person mode of teaching in schools.
- **Classes IX-X: Internal Assessment** (throughout the year-irrespective of Term I and II) would include the *3 periodic tests, student enrichment, portfolio and practical work/ speaking listening activities/ project.*
- **Classes XI-XII: Internal Assessment** (throughout the year-irrespective of Term I and II) would include end of topic or unit tests/ exploratory activities/ practicals/ projects.
- Schools would create a student profile for all assessment undertaken over the year and retain the evidences in digital format.
- CBSE will facilitate schools to upload marks of Internal Assessment on the CBSE IT platform.
- Guidelines for Internal Assessment for all subjects will also be released along with the rationalized term wise divided syllabus for the session 2021-22.The Board would also provide additional resources like sample assessments, question banks, teacher training etc. for more reliable and valid internal assessments.

केन्द्रीय माध्यमिक शिक्षा बोर्ड

(शिक्षा मंत्रालय, भारत सरकार के अधीन एक स्वायत संगठन)

CENTRAL BOARD OF SECONDARY EDUCATION

(An Autonomous Organisation under the Ministryof Education, Govt. of India)

Term I Examinations:

- At the end of the first term, the Board will organize **Term I Examination** in a flexible schedule to be conducted between November-December 2021 with a window period of 4-8 weeks for schools situated in different parts of country and abroad. Dates for conduct of examinations will be notified subsequently.

- The Question Paper will have Multiple Choice Questions (MCQ) including case-based MCQs and MCQs on assertion-reasoning type. Duration of test will be **90 minutes** and it will cover only the rationalized syllabus of **Term I only** (i.e. approx. 50% of the entire syllabus).

- Question Papers will be sent by the CBSE to schools along with marking scheme.

- The exams will be conducted under the supervision of the External Center Superintendents and Observers appointed by CBSE.

- The responses of students will be captured on OMR sheets which, after scanning may be directly uploaded at CBSE portal or alternatively may be evaluated and marks obtained will be uploaded by the school on the very same day. The final direction in this regard will be conveyed to schools by the Examination Unit of the Board.

- Marks of the **Term I** Examination will contribute to the final overall score of students.

Term II Examination/ Year-end Examination:

- At the end of the second term, the Board would organize **Term II or Year-end Examination** based on the rationalized syllabus of Term II only (i.e. approximately 50% of the entire syllabus).

- This examination would be held around **March-April 2022** at the examination centres fixed by the Board.

- The paper will be of **2 hours duration** and have questions of different formats (case-based/ situation based, open ended- short answer/ long answer type).

- In case the situation is not conducive for normal descriptive examination **a 90 minute MCQ based exam** will be conducted at the end of the Term II also.

- Marks of the Term II Examination would contribute to the final overall score.

केन्द्रीय माध्यमिक शिक्षा बोर्ड

(शिक्षा मंत्रालय, भारत सरकार के अधीन एक स्वायत संगठन)

CENTRAL BOARD OF SECONDARY EDUCATION

(An Autonomous Organisation under the Ministryof Education, Govt. of India)

Assessment / Examination as per different situations

A. In case the situation of the pandemic improves and students are able to come to schools or centres for taking the exams.

Board would conduct Term I and Term II examinations at schools/centres and the theory marks will be distributed equally between the two exams.

B. In case the situation of the pandemic forces complete closure of schools during November-December 2021, but Term II exams are held at schools or centres.

Term I MCQ based examination would be done by students online/offline from home - in this case, the weightage of this exam for the final score would be reduced, and weightage of Term II exams will be increased for declaration of final result.

C. In case the situation of the pandemic forces complete closure of schools during March-April 2022, but Term I exams are held at schools or centres.

Results would be based on the performance of students on Term I MCQ based examination and internal assessments. The weightage of marks of Term I examination conducted by the Board will be increased to provide year end results of candidates.

D. In case the situation of the pandemic forces complete closure of schools and Board conducted Term I and II exams are taken by the candidates from home in the session 2021-22.

Results would be computed on the basis of the Internal Assessment/Practical/Project Work and Theory marks of Term-I and II exams taken by the candidate from home in Class X / XII subject to the moderation or other measures to ensure validity and reliability of the assessment.

In all the above cases, data analysis of marks of students will be undertaken to ensure the integrity of internal assessments and home based exams.

Dr. Joseph Emmanuel
Director (Academics)

Permutation and Combination

In this Chapter...

- Fundamental Principles of Counting
- Factorial Notation
- Permutations
- Restricted Permutations
- Combinations

Fundamental Principles of Counting

There are two fundamental principles of counting which are the base of permutations and combinations.

Fundamental Principle of Multiplication (FPM)

If an event can occur in m different ways, another event can occur in n different ways, then the total number of occurrence of the events in the given order is $m \times n$.

In other words, if there are two operations say E and F such that E can be performed in m ways and associated with each way of performing operation E, operation F can be performed in n ways. Then, the two operations in succession can be performed in $m \times n$ ways.

e.g. In a school, there are 200 boys and 150 girls. The teacher wants to select a boy and a girl to represent the school in inter school competition.

Here, the teacher can select a boy in 200 ways and a girl in 150 ways. So, by principle of multiplication, the teacher can select a boy and a girl in $200 \times 150 = 30000$ ways.

Note *The above principle can be extended to any finite number of events (or operations) as stated below :*

If there are n events, say $E_1, E_2, \ldots, E_n$ such that E_1 can occur in m_1 ways, E_2 can occur in m_2 ways, E_3 can occur in m_3 ways and so on, then the total number of ways in which all the events can be occurred in the stated order is $m_1 \times m_2 \times m_3 \times \ldots \times m_n$.

Fundamental Principle of Addition (FPA)

If there are two events such that they can be performed independently in m and n ways respectively, then either of the two events can be occurred in $(m + n)$ ways.

In other words, if an operation can be performed in m different ways and another operation which is independent of the first operation , can be performed in n different ways. Then, either of the two operations can be performed in $(m + n)$ ways.

Factorial Notation

n Factorial

Many times, we come across the products of the form $1 \times 2, 1 \times 2 \times 3, 1 \times 2 \times 3 \times 4, \ldots$. For our convenience, we use a special notation instead of writing all the factors of such a product. We write

$$1! = 1$$
$$2! = 2 \times 1$$
$$3! = 3 \times 2 \times 1$$
$$\vdots \quad \vdots$$
$$n! = n(n-1)(n-2)\ldots 3 \cdot 2 \cdot 1$$

Thus, the notation $n!$ represent the product of first n natural numbers. We read this notation as 'n factorial' and it is also denoted by $n!$.

Clearly, for a natural number n,

$$n! = n(n-1)!$$
$$= n(n-1)(n-2)! \qquad \text{[provided } n \geq 2]$$
$$= n(n-1)(n-2)(n-3)! \qquad \text{[provided } n \geq 3]$$
$$\vdots \qquad \vdots$$
$$= n(n-1)(n-2)(n-3)\ldots 3 \cdot 2 \cdot 1$$

e.g. $\quad 5! = 5 \times 4 \times 3 \times 2 \times 1 = 120$

and $\quad 8! = 8 \times (7)! = 8 \times 7 \times (6!)$

Zero Factorial

It does not make any sense to define $0!$ as product of the integers from 1 to 0. So, we define $0! = 1$.

Note *Factorial of proper fractions or negative integers are not defined. $n!$ is defined only for whole numbers, i.e. for non-negative integers.*

Permutations

A permutation is an arrangement of objects in a definite order. Arrangement can be made by taking some or all objects at a time. e.g. If there are three objects say A, B and C, then the permutations of these three objects taking two at a time are AB, BA, AC, CA BC, CB and the permutations of these three objects taking all at a time are ABC, ACB, BAC, BCA, CAB, CBA.

Here, in each case, number of permutations is 6.

Note that the order of arrangement is important. Because when the order is changed, then different permutation is obtained.

Permutations, When All the Objects are Distinct

When all given objects are distinct, then we can find the number of permutations with the help of following theorem

Theorem 1 The number of permutations of n different objects taken r at a time, where $0 < r \leq n$ and the objects do not repeat, is $n(n-1)(n-2)\ldots(n-r+1)$, which is denoted by ${}^nP_r$ or $P(n, r)$.

i.e. $\quad P(n, r) = {}^nP_r = \dfrac{n!}{(n-r)!}, \ 0 \leq r \leq n$

Proof We know that

$$P(n, r) = {}^nP_r = n(n-1)(n-2)(n-3)\ldots[n-(r-1)]$$

On multiplying numerator and denominator by $(n-r)(n-r-1)\ldots 3 \times 2 \times 1$, we get

$${}^nP_r = \dfrac{\begin{bmatrix} n(n-1)(n-2)\ldots(n-(r-1)) \\ \times(n-r)(n-(r+1))\ldots 3 \cdot 2 \cdot 1 \end{bmatrix}}{(n-r)(n-(r+1))\ldots 3 \cdot 2 \cdot 1}$$

$$= \dfrac{n(n-1)(n-2)\ldots 3 \cdot 2 \cdot 1}{(n-r)(n-r-1)\ldots 3 \cdot 2 \cdot 1}$$

$$= \dfrac{n!}{(n-r)!}$$

where, $0 \leq r \leq n$

In Particular,

(i) When $r = 0$, then ${}^nP_0 = \dfrac{n!}{(n-0)!} = \dfrac{n!}{n!} = 1$

(ii) When $r = n$, then ${}^nP_n = \dfrac{n!}{(n-n)!} = \dfrac{n!}{0!} = n!$ $\quad [\because 0! = 1]$

Note *Number of permutations of n different things taken all at a time $= n!$*

Permutations with Repetitions

When repetition of objects is allowed, then number of permutations can be obtained with the help of following theorem.

Theorem 2 The number of permutation of n different objects taken r at a time, when each may be repeated any number of times in each arrangement, is n^r (permutation with repetitions).

Note *The number of permutations of n different objects, all at a time, when each may be repeated any number of times in each arrangement, is n^n.*

Permutations When all the Objects are not Distinct Objects

When all the objects are not distinct, i.e. some objects are of same kind, then we can find the number of permutations with the help of following theorems (without proof).

Theorem 3 The number of permutations of n objects, where p objects are of the same kind or identical and other are distinct, is given by $\dfrac{n!}{p!}$.

Theorem 4 The number of permutations of n objects, where p_1 objects are of one kind, p_2 are of second kind, $\ldots p_k$ are of kth kind and the rest if any, are of different kind is $\dfrac{n!}{p_1! \, p_2! \ldots p_k!}$.

Restricted Permutations

Here, we shall discuss permutations of objects under certain conditions, e.g. permutation when certain objects occur together, when position of particular objects are fixed, when a particular object occurs in every arrangement etc.

Some Important Results

(i) If r particular things out of n different things are to be together, then we count these r particular things as one things and remaining $(n-r)$ things as separate things.

Then, total number of things $= (n-r) + 1$

$$= n - r + 1.$$

Since, these are different things, therefore number of permutations of these things $= (n-r+1)!$.

But, r particular things can also be arrange among themselves in $r!$ ways.

$\therefore$ Required number of permutations $= (n-r+1)! \, r!$

Note *If r particular things are identical, then required number of permutations $= (n-r+1)!$*

(ii) The number of permutations of n objects taken r at a time, when a particular object is taken in each arrangement, is $r \cdot {}^{n-1}P_{r-1}$.

(iii) The number of permutations of n objects taken r at a time, when a particular object is never taken in each arrangement, is ${}^{n-1}P_r$.

(iv) The number of permutations of n different objects taken r at a time in which two specific objects always occur together, is $2!(r-1) \cdot {}^{n-2}P_{r-2}$.

Combinations

The word **combination** means selection.

Each of the different selection, which is made by taking some or all of a number of different objects at a time, irrespective of their arrangements is called a combination.

e.g. The different combinations formed from three letters A, B, C taking two at a time are AB, AC, BC.

Difference between Permutations and Combinations

The process of selecting objects is called combination and that of arranging objects is called permutation.

If we have 4 objects A, B, C and D, the possible selection (or combination) and arrangement (or permutation) of 3 objects out of 4 are given below.

This will help you to understand clearly the difference between permutations and combinations.

Selection ↓ Combination	Arrangement ↓ Permutation
ABC	ABC, ACB, BAC, BCA, CAB, CBA
ABD	ABD, ADB, BAD, BDA, DAB, DBA
ACD	ACD, ADC, CAD, CDA, DAC, DCA
BCD	BCD, BDC, CBD, CDB, DBC, DCB
Total 4 combinations	24 permutations

Meaning of ${}^nC_r$

The number of combinations of n different things taken r at a time is meant the number of groups of r things which can be formed from n things and generally it is denoted by symbol ${}^nC_r$ or $C(n, r)$.

Combinations of n Different Things Taken r at a Time

The number of combinations of n distinct objects taken r at a time is given by ${}^nC_r = \dfrac{n!}{r!(n-r)!}$.

Some Important Theorems

Theorem 1 ${}^nP_r = {}^nC_r \cdot r!, \, 0 < r \le n$

Proof The number of combinations of n distinct objects taken r at a time is ${}^nC_r$. In these combinations, r things can be arranged among themselves in $r!$ ways. So, we have $r!$ permutations.

Therefore, the total number of permutations of n different things taken r at a time is ${}^nC_r \times r!$, which is equal to ${}^nP_r$.

$$\therefore \qquad {}^nP_r = r! \times {}^nC_r, \, 0 < r \le n \qquad \text{Hence proved.}$$

Theorem 2 ${}^nC_r = {}^nC_{n-r}, \, 0 \le r \le n$

Note This theorem is used to simplify the calculation when r is large.

Theorem 3 ${}^nC_r + {}^nC_{r-1} = {}^{n+1}C_r$

Proof LHS $= {}^nC_r + {}^nC_{r-1} = \dfrac{n!}{r!(n-r)!} + \dfrac{n!}{(r-1)!(n-r+1)!}$

$$= \dfrac{n!(n-r+1)}{r!(n-r+1)(n-r)!} + \dfrac{n!r}{r(r-1)!(n-r+1)!}$$

$$= \dfrac{n!(n-r+1)}{r!(n-r+1)!} + \dfrac{n!r}{r!(n-r+1)!}$$

$$= n!\left[\dfrac{n-r+1+r}{r!(n-r+1)!}\right]$$

$$= \dfrac{(n+1)n!}{r!(n+1-r)!} = \dfrac{(n+1)!}{r!(n+1-r)!}$$

$$= {}^{n+1}C_r = \text{RHS} \qquad \text{Hence proved.}$$

Theorem 4 If ${}^nC_x = {}^nC_y$, then either $x = y$ or $x + y = n$.

Solved Examples

Example 1. A room has 11 doors. In how many ways can a man enter the room through one door and come out through a different door?

Sol. Here, we need to perform two operations :

    (i) Selecting a door to enter.

    (ii) Selecting a door to come out.

Clearly, the man can enter the room through anyone of the seven doors. So, there are eleven ways of entering into the room. Note that the man can come out through anyone of the remaining ten doors. So, he can come out through a different door in 10 ways.

Hence, by fundamental principle of counting, required number of ways = $11 \times 10 = 110$

Example 2. If $\dfrac{1}{11!} + \dfrac{1}{12!} = \dfrac{x}{13!}$, then find x.

Sol. Given, $\dfrac{1}{11!} + \dfrac{1}{12!} = \dfrac{x}{13!}$

$\Rightarrow \dfrac{1}{11!} + \dfrac{1}{12 \times 11!} = \dfrac{x}{13 \times 12 \times 11!}$

$\Rightarrow \dfrac{1}{11!}\left(1 + \dfrac{1}{12}\right) = \dfrac{x}{13 \times 12 \times 11!}$

$\Rightarrow \dfrac{13}{12} = \dfrac{x}{13 \times 12}$

$\Rightarrow x = 13 \times 13$

$\Rightarrow x = 169$

Example 3. How many 5-digit telephone numbers can be constructed using the digits 0 to 9, if each number starts with 67 and no digit appears more than once?

Sol. Since, telephone number start with 67, so two digits is already fixed. Now, we have to do arrangement of three digits from remaining eight digits.

$\therefore$ Possible number of ways $= {}^8 P_3$

$$= \dfrac{8!}{(8-3)!} = \dfrac{8!}{5!}$$

$$= 8 \times 7 \times 6 = 336 \text{ days}$$

Example 4. If ${}^{2n+1}P_{n-1} : {}^{2n-1}P_n = 3:5$, then find the value of n.

Sol. Given, ${}^{2n+1}P_{n-1} : {}^{2n-1}P_n = 3:5$

$\Rightarrow \dfrac{(2n+1)!}{(n+2)!} \times \dfrac{(n-1)!}{(2n-1)!} = \dfrac{3}{5}$

$\Rightarrow \dfrac{(2n+1)\,2n}{(n+2)\,(n+1)\,n} = \dfrac{3}{5}$

$\Rightarrow 10(2n+1) = 3(n^2 + 3n + 2)$

$\Rightarrow \quad 3n^2 - 11n - 4 = 0$

$\Rightarrow \quad (3n+1)(n-4) = 0$

$\therefore \qquad n = 4 \qquad \left[n \neq -\dfrac{1}{3}\right]$

Example 5. Find the number of different words that can be formed from the letters of the word 'TRIANGLE', so that no vowels are together.

Sol. Number of letters in the word 'TRIANGLE' = 8, out of which 5 are consonants and 3 are vowels.

If vowels are not together, then we have following arrangement.

V	C	V	C	V	C	V	C	V	C	V

Consonants can be arranged in $= 5! = 120$ ways and vowels can occupy at 6 places.

The 3 vowels can be arranged at 6 place in ${}^6 P_3$ ways

$$= \dfrac{6!}{(6-3)!} = \dfrac{6!}{3!}$$

$$= \dfrac{6 \times 5 \times 4 \times 3!}{3!} = 120$$

Total number of arrangement $= 120 \times 120 = 14400$

Example 6. Determine n, if ${}^{2n}C_2 : {}^n C_2 = 9:2$.

Sol. Given, ${}^{2n}C_2 : {}^n C_2 = 9:2$

$\Rightarrow \dfrac{{}^{2n}C_2}{{}^n C_2} = \dfrac{9}{2}$

$\Rightarrow \dfrac{(2n)!}{2!(2n-2)!} \times \dfrac{2!(n-2)!}{n!} = \dfrac{9}{2}$

$\Rightarrow \dfrac{(2n)(2n-1)(2n-2)!}{2(2n-2)!} \times \dfrac{2(n-2)!}{n(n-1)(n-2)!} = \dfrac{9}{2}$

$\Rightarrow \dfrac{2(2n-1)}{n-1} = \dfrac{9}{2}$

$\Rightarrow 4(2n-1) = 9(n-1)$

$\Rightarrow 8n - 4 = 9n - 9$

$\Rightarrow 9n - 8n = -4 + 9$

$\therefore \qquad n = 5$

Example 7. If ${}^n C_{r-1} = 36$, ${}^n C_r = 84$ and ${}^n C_{r+1} = 126$, then find the value of ${}^r C_2$.

Sol. Given, $\quad {}^n C_{r-1} = 36 \qquad \qquad \text{...(i)}$

$\Rightarrow \qquad {}^n C_r = 84 \qquad \qquad \text{...(ii)}$

$\Rightarrow \qquad {}^n C_{r+1} = 126 \qquad \qquad \text{...(iii)}$

On dividing Eq. (i) by Eq. (ii), we get

$$\frac{{}^nC_{r-1}}{{}^nC_r} = \frac{36}{84} \qquad \left[\because {}^nC_r = \frac{n!}{r!(n-r)!} \text{ and } n! = n\,(n-1)!\right]$$

$$\Rightarrow \quad \frac{n!}{(r-1)!\{n-(r-1)\}!} \cdot \frac{r!(n-r)!}{n!} = \frac{3}{7}$$

$$\Rightarrow \quad \frac{1}{(r-1)!(n-r+1)!} \cdot \frac{r(r-1)!(n-r)!}{1} = \frac{3}{7}$$

$$\Rightarrow \quad \frac{1 \cdot r}{(n-r+1)(n-r)!} \cdot (n-r)! = \frac{3}{7}$$

$$\Rightarrow \quad \frac{r}{n-r+1} = \frac{3}{7}$$

$$\Rightarrow \quad 7r = 3n - 3r + 3$$

$$\Rightarrow \quad 10r - 3n = 3 \qquad \text{...(iv)}$$

On dividing Eq. (ii) by Eq. (iii), we get

$$\frac{{}^nC_r}{{}^nC_{r+1}} = \frac{84}{126}$$

$$\Rightarrow \quad \frac{n!}{r!(n-r)!} \cdot \frac{(r+1)!(n-r-1)!}{n!} = \frac{14}{21}$$

$$\Rightarrow \quad \frac{1}{r!(n-r)(n-r-1)!} \cdot \frac{(r+1)\,r!(n-r-1)!}{1} = \frac{2}{3}$$

$$\Rightarrow \quad \frac{r+1}{n-r} = \frac{2}{3}$$

$$\Rightarrow \quad 3r + 3 = 2n - 2r$$

$$\Rightarrow \quad 2n - 5r = 3 \qquad \text{...(v)}$$

On multiplying Eq. (iv) by 2 and Eq. (v) by 3, we get

$$20r - 6n = 6 \qquad \text{...(vi)}$$
$$6n - 15r = 9 \qquad \text{...(vii)}$$

On adding Eqs. (vi) and (vii),

$$5r = 15 \quad \Rightarrow \quad r = 3$$

From Eq. (v), $\quad 2n = 3 + 15$

$$\Rightarrow \quad 2n = 18 \quad \Rightarrow \quad n = 9$$

$$\therefore \quad {}^rC_2 = {}^3C_2 = \frac{3!}{2!1!} = \frac{3 \times 2!}{2!} = 3$$

Example 8. In how many ways can 5 prizes be distributed among four students when every student can take one or more prizes?

Sol. Clearly, first prize can be distributed among 4 students in

$${}^4C_1 = 4 \text{ ways}$$

and second prize can be distributed among 4 students in

$${}^4C_1 = 4 \text{ ways}$$

Similarly 3rd, 4th and 5th prize can be distributed in 4 ways each.

Hence, by fundamental principle of counting, the total number of ways $= 4 \times 4 \times 4 \times 4 \times 4 = 4^5 = 1024$

Example 9. We wish to select 6 person from 8 but, if the person A is chosen, then B must be chosen. In how many ways can selections be made?

Sol. Total number of person $= 8$

Number of person to be selected $= 6$

It is given that, if A is chosen then, B must be chosen. Therefore, following cases arise.

Case I When A is chosen, B must be chosen.

Number of ways $= {}^{8-2}C_{6-2} = {}^6C_4$

Case II When A is not chosen.

Then, B may be chosen.

$\therefore$ Number of ways $= {}^{8-1}C_6 = {}^7C_6$

Hence, required number of ways $= {}^6C_4 + {}^7C_6$

$$= 15 + 7 = 22$$

Example 10. Find the number of four-letter words that can be formed (the words need not be meaningful) using the letters of the word 'MEDITERRANEAN' such that the first letter is E and the last letter is R.

Sol. Word 'MEDITERRANEAN' has 2A, 3E, 1D, 1I, 1M, 2N, 2R, 1T.

Out of four letters E and R is fixed and rest of the two letters can be chosen in following ways:

Case I Both letters are of same kind i.e. ${}^3C_2$ ways, therefore

number of words $= {}^3C_2 \times \dfrac{2!}{2!} = 3$

Case II Both letters are of different kinds i.e. ${}^8C_2$ ways, therefore number of words $= {}^8C_2 \times 2! = 56$

Hence, total number of words $= 56 + 3 = 59$

Chapter Practice

Objective Questions

• Multiple Choice Questions

1. If $\dfrac{1}{9!} + \dfrac{1}{10!} = \dfrac{x}{11!}$, then x is equal to
   - (a) 81
   - (b) 100
   - (c) 121
   - (d) None of these

2. If $(n+1)! = 12 \times (n-1)!$, then n is equal to
   - (a) 4
   - (b) 3
   - (c) 2
   - (d) 1

3. If $\dfrac{(2n)!}{3!(2n-3)!}$ and $\dfrac{n!}{2!(n-2)!}$ are in the ratio 44 : 3, then n is equal to
   - (a) 1
   - (b) 2
   - (c) 4
   - (d) 6

4. If $P(n, 4) = 20 \times P(n, 2)$, then n is equal to
   - (a) 7
   - (b) 6
   - (c) 5
   - (d) 4

5. If $^{n}P_{r} = 720$ and $^{n}C_{r} = 120$, then r is equal to
   - (a) 1
   - (b) 2
   - (c) 3
   - (d) 4

6. If $^{n}C_{15} = {^{n}C_{8}}$, then the value of $^{n}C_{21}$ is
   - (a) 252
   - (b) 253
   - (c) 254
   - (d) 255

7. If $^{m}C_{1} = {^{n}C_{2}}$, then
   - (a) $2m = n$
   - (b) $2m = n(n+1)$
   - (c) $2m = n(n-1)$
   - (d) $2n = m(m-1)$

8. Mohan has 3 pants and 2 shirts. The number of different pairs of a pant and shirt he can wear are
   - (a) 5
   - (b) 6
   - (c) 7
   - (d) None of these

9. Sabnam has 2 school bags, 3 tiffin boxes and 2 water bottles. In how many ways can she carry these items (choosing one each)?
   - (a) 11
   - (b) 12
   - (c) 13
   - (d) 14

10. A telegraph has 5 arms and each arm is capable of 4 distincts positions, including the position of rest. The total number of signals that can be made is
    - (a) 1024
    - (b) 1023
    - (c) 1022
    - (d) 1021

11. A sequence is a ternary sequence, if it contains digits 0, 1 and 2. The total number of ternary sequences of length 9 which either begin with 210 or end with 210, is
    - (a) 1458
    - (b) 1431
    - (c) 729
    - (d) 707

12. The number of ways in which 3 prize can be distributed to 4 childrens, so that no child gets all the three prizes, are
    - (a) 64
    - (b) 62
    - (c) 60
    - (d) None of these

13. The number of 5-digit telephone numbers having atleast one of their digits repeated is
    - (a) 90000
    - (b) 10000
    - (c) 30240
    - (d) 69760

14. The sum of all the numbers that can be formed with the digits 2, 3, 4, 5 taken all at a time, is
    - (a) 93321
    - (b) 93322
    - (c) 93323
    - (d) 93324

15. The number of arrangements can be made with the letters of the word 'MATHEMATICS' in which all vowels are together, is
    - (a) 120920
    - (b) 120930
    - (c) 120940
    - (d) 120960

16. How many number lying between 999 and 10000 can be formed with the help of the digits 0, 2, 3, 6, 7, 8, when the digits are not be repeated?
    - (a) 100
    - (b) 200
    - (c) 300
    - (d) 400

17. The number of ways a team of 2 players can be formed out of a group of 3 lawn tennis players X, Y, Z is

(a) 7   (b) 6   (c) 3   (d) 4

18. If $n = {}^mC_2$, then the value of ${}^nC_2$ is

(a) ${}^{m+1}C_4$ (b) ${}^{m-1}C_4$

(c) ${}^{m+2}C_4$ (d) $3 \times {}^{m+1}C_4$

19. ${}^{15}C_8 + {}^{15}C_9 - {}^{15}C_6 - {}^{15}C_7$ is equal to ....

(a) 0   (b) 2

(c) 1   (d) 3

• Case Based MCQs

20. The number of mutually distinguishable permutations of n things, taken all at a time, of which p are alike of one kind, q are alike of second such that $p + q = n$ is $\dfrac{n!}{p!\,q!}$.

Now, consider a word "INDEPENDENCE".

On the basis of above information, answer the following questions.

(i) The number of total words that can be formed with the letters of the given word, is

(a) 12600   (b) 1646400

(c) 1663200   (d) 138600

(ii) The number of words that start with P, is

(a) 138600   (b) 12600

(c) 1646400   (d) None of these

(iii) The number of words in which all the vowels always occur together, is

(a) 1646400   (b) 12600

(c) 16800   (d) None of these

(iv) The number of words in which vowels never occur together, is

(a) 1646400   (b) 12600

(c) 16800   (d) None of these

(v) The number of words that begin with I and end in P, is

(a) 1646400   (b) 12600

(c) 16800   (d) None of these

21. The number of all combinations of n distinct objects, taken r at a time is given by

$$ {}^nC_r = \frac{n!}{(n-r)!\,r!} $$

Pawan select 4 cards from a pack of 52 playing cards. Then, the number of ways in

(i) Four cards are of the same suit, is

(a) 2860   (b) 495

(c) 105625   (d) 29900

(ii) Four cards belong to four different suits is

(a) 2860   (b) 495

(c) 28561   (d) 105625

(iii) Four cards are face cards, is

(a) 485   (b) 495

(c) 505   (d) None of these

(iv) Two are red cards and two are black cards, is

(a) 106625   (b) 105625

(c) 104625   (d) None of these

(v) Cards are of the same colour, is

(a) 29900

(b) 29800

(c) 29700

(d) 29600

PART 2
Subjective Questions

• Short Answer Type Questions

1. A room has 6 doors. In how many ways can a man enter the room through one door and come out through a different door?

2. How many numbers are there between 100 and 1000 such that every digit is either 2 or 9?

3. A gentleman has 6 friends to invite. In how many ways can he send invitation cards to them, if he has three servants to carry the cards?

4. How many 3-digit even numbers can be formed from the digits 1, 2, 3, 4, 5 and 6, if the digits can be repeated?

5. In how many ways 5 rings of different types can be worn in 4 fingers?

6. Prove that $P(n-1, r) + r \cdot P(n-1, r-1) = P(n, r)$.

7. How many different signals can be made by 5 flags from 8 flags of different colours?

8. In how many ways can 6 persons stand in a queue?

9. A polygon has 44 diagonals. Find the number of its sides.

10. If ${}^8C_r - {}^7C_3 = {}^7C_2$, then find r.

11. If there are 10 persons in a party and, if each two of them shake hands with each other, how many handshakes happen in the party?

12. In how many ways can 6 persons occupy 4 vacants seats?

13. How many permutations of the letters of the words 'INDIA' are there?

14. Evaluate $\sum_{r=1}^{5} {}^5C_r$.

• Long Answer Type Questions

15. Find the number of positive integers greater than 6000 and less than 7000 which are divisible by 5, provided that no digit is to be repeated.

16. Find the number of different words that can be formed from the letters of the word 'TRIANGLE', so that
   (i) all vowels occur together.
   (ii) all vowels do not occur together.

17. If ${}^{n-1}C_r : {}^nC_r : {}^{n+1}C_r = 6:9:13$, then find the values of n and r.

18. In an examination, Yamini has to select 4 questions from each part. There are 6, 7 and 8 questions in part I, part II and part III, respectively. What is the number of possible combinations in which she can choose the questions?

19. A committee of 10 is to be formed from 8 gentlemen and 9 ladies. In how many ways this can be done, if atleast five ladies have to be included in a committee? In how many of these committees
   (i) the ladies are in majority?
   (ii) the gentlemen are in majority?

20. How many different words can be formed by using all the letters of the word 'ALLAHABAD'? In how many of them, vowels occupy the even position?

21. There are 10 points in a plane, no three of which are in the same straight line, excepting 4 points, which are collinear. Find
   (i) the number of straight lines obtained from the pairs of these points.
   (ii) the number of triangles that can be formed with the vertices as these points.

22. How many four-letter words can be formed using the letters of the word 'FAILURE', so that
   (i) F is included in each word?
   (ii) F is not included in any word?

• Case Based Questions

23. Hanuman wants to find the number of lines, diagonals, triangles etc. When some points are given.

Vicky suggested Hanuman that using concept of combination, you can do it easily. He explained him, the number of combination of selecting r items from n items is given by ${}^nC_r$. Also, ${}^nC_r = \dfrac{n!}{(n-r)!\,r!}$.

On the basis of above information, answer the following questions.
   (i) How many triangles can be formed by joining the vertices of a hexagon?
   (ii) How many diagonals are there in a polygon with n sides?
   (iii) A polygon has 44 diagonals. Find the number of its sides.
   (iv) How many chords can be drawn through 21 points on a circle?
   (v) How many lines can be drawn from 10 points of which only 4 points are collinear.

SOLUTIONS

Objective Questions

1. (c) We have, $\dfrac{1}{9!} + \dfrac{1}{10!} = \dfrac{x}{11!}$

$\Rightarrow \quad \dfrac{1}{9!} + \dfrac{1}{10 \times 9!} = \dfrac{x}{11 \times 10 \times 9!}$

$\Rightarrow \quad 1 + \dfrac{1}{10} = \dfrac{x}{110}$

$\Rightarrow \quad \dfrac{11}{10} = \dfrac{x}{110} \Rightarrow x = 121$

2. (b) We have, $(n+1)! = 12 \times (n-1)!$

$\Rightarrow \quad (n+1)\, n(n-1)! = 12 \times (n-1)!$

$\Rightarrow \quad (n+1)\, n = 12$

$\Rightarrow \quad (n+1)\, n = 4 \times 3$

$\therefore \quad n = 3$

3. (d) We have, $\dfrac{(2n)!}{3!(2n-3)!} : \dfrac{n!}{2!(n-2)!} = 44:3$

$\Rightarrow \quad \dfrac{(2n)! \times 2! \times (n-2)!}{3! \times (2n-3)! \times n!} = \dfrac{44}{3}$

$\Rightarrow \quad \dfrac{2n(2n-1)(2n-2)(2n-3)! \times 2! \times (n-2)!}{3 \times 2! \times (2n-3)! \times n(n-1)(n-2)!} = \dfrac{44}{3}$

$\Rightarrow \quad \dfrac{2n(2n-1)(2n-2)}{3 \times n(n-1)} = \dfrac{44}{3}$

$\Rightarrow \quad \dfrac{4n(2n-1)(n-1)}{3n(n-1)} = \dfrac{44}{3}$

$\Rightarrow \quad 2n - 1 = 11$

$\Rightarrow \quad n = 6$

4. (a) We have, $P(n, 4) = 20 \times P(n, 2)$

$\Rightarrow \qquad {}^nP_4 = 20 \times {}^nP_2$

$\Rightarrow \qquad \dfrac{n!}{(n-4)!} = 20 \times \dfrac{n!}{(n-2)!}$

$\Rightarrow \qquad (n-2)! = 20 \times (n-4)!$

$\Rightarrow (n-2)(n-3)(n-4)! = 20 \times (n-4)!$

$\Rightarrow \qquad (n-2)(n-3) = 5 \times 4$

$\Rightarrow \qquad n-2 = 5$

$\Rightarrow \qquad n = 7$

5. (c) We know that, ${}^nC_r = \dfrac{{}^nP_r}{r!}$

$\Rightarrow \qquad 120 = \dfrac{720}{r!}$

$\Rightarrow \qquad r! = 6$

$\Rightarrow \qquad r! = 3!$

$\Rightarrow \qquad r = 3$

6. (b) We have, ${}^nC_{15} = {}^nC_8$

$\Rightarrow \qquad n = 15 + 8 = 23$

$$[\because {}^nC_x = {}^nC_y \Rightarrow n = x + y]$$

$\therefore \qquad {}^nC_{21} = {}^{23}C_{21}$

$\qquad\qquad = {}^{23}C_2 \qquad [\because {}^nC_r = {}^nC_{n-r}]$

$\qquad\qquad = \dfrac{23 \times 22}{2 \times 1}$

$\qquad\qquad = 253$

7. (c) We have, ${}^mC_1 = {}^nC_2,$

$\Rightarrow \qquad \dfrac{m}{1} = \dfrac{n(n-1)}{2}$

$\Rightarrow \qquad 2m = n(n-1)$

8. (b) Number of different pairs of a pant and shirt $= 3 \times 2$

$\qquad\qquad\qquad\qquad\qquad\qquad\qquad = 6$

9. (b) Number of ways she can carry the 3 items $= 2 \times 3 \times 2$

$\qquad\qquad\qquad\qquad\qquad\qquad\qquad\qquad = 12$

10. (b) Since, each arm can be kept in 4 positions and a signal is possible when all the 5 arms are simultaneously placed in positions.

$\therefore$ Total number of ways placing the arms $= 4^5$

But, this includes one inadmissible case, when all the arms are in the position of rest and then no signal can be made.

Hence, the required number of signals $= 4^5 - 1$

$\qquad\qquad\qquad\qquad\qquad\qquad = 1023$

11. (b) Since, each digit in a ternary sequence of length 9 can be filled in 3 ways.

Therefore, the number of nine-digit ternary sequence beginning with 210 is 3^6

and number of nine-digit ternary sequence ending with 210 is also 3^6.

The number of ternary sequence of 9 digits which begin and end with 210 is 3^3.

$\therefore$ Required number of such numbers $= 3^6 + 3^6 - 3^3 = 1431$

12. (c) $\therefore$ Total number of ways of distributing prizes

$\qquad\qquad\qquad\qquad\qquad\qquad = 4 \times 4 \times 4 = 64$

Number of ways in which one child gets all prizes $= 4$

$\therefore$ Number of ways in which no child gets all the three prizes

$\qquad\qquad\qquad\qquad\qquad\qquad = 64 - 4 = 60$

13. (d) If all the digits repeated, then number of 5 digit telephone numbers can be formed in 10^5 ways and if no digit repeated, then 5-digit telephone numbers can be formed in ${}^{10}P_5$ ways.

$\therefore$ Required number of ways $= 10^5 - {}^{10}P_5$

$\qquad\qquad\qquad = 100000 - 30240 = 69760$

14. (d) Total number of numbers formed with the digits 2, 3, 4, 5 taken all at a time

$\qquad =$ Number of arrangement of 4 digits, taken all at a time

$\qquad = {}^4P_4 = 24$

Consider the digits in the unit's places in all these numbers. Each of the digit 2, 3, 4, 5 occurs in $3! (= 6)$ times in the unit's place.

So, total for the digits in the unit's place in all the numbers

$= (2 + 3 + 4 + 5) \times 3! = 84$.

Since, each of the digits 2, 3, 4, 5 occurs 3! times in any one of the remaining places.

So, the sum of the digits in the ten's, hundred's, thousand's places in all the numbers $= (2 + 3 + 4 + 5) \times 3! = 84$

$\therefore$ Sum of all the numbers $= 84 (10^0 + 10^1 + 10^2 + 10^3)$

$\qquad\qquad\qquad\qquad = 93324$

15. (d) Considering these four vowels as one letter we have 8 letters (M, T, H, M, T, C, S and one letter obtained by combining all vowels), out of which M occurs twice, T occurs twice and the rest all different. These 8 letters can be arranged in $\dfrac{8!}{2! \times 2!}$ ways. But the four vowel, (A, E, A, I) can be put together in $\dfrac{4!}{2!}$ ways.

Hence, total number of arrangements in which vowels are always together $= \dfrac{8!}{2! \times 2!} \times \dfrac{4!}{2!} = 120960$

16. (c) The number of 4-digit numbers formed by digits 0, 2, 3, 6, 7, 8 is ${}^6P_4 = 360$.

But here those numbers are also involved which begin from 0. So, we take those numbers as three-digit numbers.

Taking initial digit 0, the number of ways to fill remaining 3 places from five digits 2, 3, 6, 7, 8 are ${}^5P_3 = 60$.

So, the required numbers $= 360 - 60 = 300$

17. (c) There are only 3 possible ways in which the team could be constructed.

These are XY, YZ and ZX.

18. (d) We have, $n = {}^{m}C_2 = \dfrac{m(m-1)}{2}$

$\therefore \quad {}^{n}C_2 = \dfrac{n(n-1)}{2} = \dfrac{m(m-1)}{4}\left\{\dfrac{m(m-1)}{2} - 1\right\}$

$\qquad\qquad = 3\left\{\dfrac{1}{24}(m+1)\,m\,(m-1)\,(m-2)\right\}$

[multiplying and dividing by 3]

$\qquad\qquad = 3 \times {}^{m+1}C_4$

19. (a) ${}^{15}C_8 + {}^{15}C_9 - {}^{15}C_6 - {}^{15}C_7$

$\qquad = {}^{15}C_{15-8} + {}^{15}C_{15-9} - {}^{15}C_6 - {}^{15}C_7 \qquad [\because {}^{n}C_r = {}^{n}C_{n-r}]$

$\qquad = {}^{15}C_7 + {}^{15}C_6 - {}^{15}C_6 - {}^{15}C_7 = 0$

20. (i) (c) In the word 'INDEPENDENCE', there are 12 letters of which 3 are N's, 4 are E's and 2 are D's.

Therefore, total number of arrangements $= \dfrac{12!}{3!\,4!\,2!}$

$\qquad\qquad\qquad\qquad\qquad\qquad = 1663200$

(ii) (a) After fixing the letter P at the extreme left position, there are 11 letters consisting of 3 N's, 4E's and 2D's.

These 11 letters can be arranged in $\dfrac{11!}{3!\,4!\,2!} = 138600$

Number of words beginning with P $= \dfrac{11!}{3!\,4!\,2!} = 138600$

(iii) (c) There are 5 vowels in the given word of which 4 are E's and one I. These vowels can be put together in $\dfrac{5!}{4!\,1!}$ ways. Considering these 5 vowels are one letter there are 8 letters (taking 7 remaining letters), which can be arranged in $\dfrac{8!}{3!\,2!}$ ways (as, there are 3 N's and 2D's). Since, corresponding to each arrangement of 5 vowels there are $\dfrac{8!}{3!\,2!}$ ways of arranging remaining 7 letters and one letter formed by 5 vowels.

Hence, by fundamental principle of multiplication, the required number of arrangements is

$$\dfrac{8!}{3!\,2!} \times \dfrac{5!}{4!\,1!} = 16800$$

(iv) (a) The required number of arrangements

$\qquad = $ The total number of arrangements

$\qquad\qquad - $ The number of arrangements in which

$\qquad\qquad\qquad\qquad$ all the vowels occur together

$\qquad = 1663200 - 16800 = 1646400$

(v) (b) Let us fix I at the extreme left end and P at the extreme right end.

Now, we are left with 10 letters of which 3 are N's, 4 are E's and 2 are D's. These ten letters can be arranged in $\dfrac{10!}{4!\,3!\,2!}$ ways.

Hence, required number of arrangements $= \dfrac{10!}{4!\,3!\,2!}$

$\qquad\qquad\qquad\qquad\qquad\qquad = 12600$

21. (i) (a) There are four suits (diamond, spade, club and heart) of 13 cards each. Therefore, there are ${}^{13}C_4$ ways of choosing 4 diamond cards, ${}^{13}C_4$ ways of choosing 4

club cards, ${}^{13}C_4$ ways of choosing 4 spade cards and ${}^{13}C_4$ ways of choosing heart cards.

$\therefore$ Required number of ways

$\qquad = {}^{13}C_4 + {}^{13}C_4 + {}^{13}C_4 + {}^{13}C_4$

$\qquad = 4 \times {}^{13}C_4 = 4 \times \dfrac{13!}{9!\,4!} = 2860$

(ii) (c) There are 13 cards in each suit. Four cards drawn belong to four different suits means one card is drawn from each suit. Out of 13 diamond cards, one card can be drawn in ${}^{13}C_1$ ways.

Similarly, there are ${}^{13}C_1$ ways of choosing one club card, ${}^{13}C_1$ ways of choosing one spade card and ${}^{13}C_1$ ways of choosing one heart card.

$\therefore$ Number of ways of selecting one card from each suit

$\qquad = {}^{13}C_1 \times {}^{13}C_1 \times {}^{13}C_1 \times {}^{13}C_1 = 13^4 = 28561$

(iii) (b) There are 12 face cards out of which 4 cards can be chosen in ${}^{12}C_4$ ways.

$\therefore$ Required number of ways $= {}^{12}C_4 = \dfrac{12!}{4!\,8!} = 495$

(iv) (b) There are 26 red cards and 26 black cards. Therefore, 2 red cards can be chosen in ${}^{26}C_2$ ways and 2 black cards can be chosen in ${}^{26}C_2$ ways.

Hence, 2 red and 2 black cards can be chosen in

$${}^{26}C_2 \times {}^{26}C_2 = \left(\dfrac{26!}{24!\,2!}\right)^2 = (325)^2 = 105625 \text{ ways.}$$

(v) (a) Out of 26 red cards, 4 red cards can be chosen in ${}^{26}C_4$ ways. Similarly, 4 black cards can be chosen in ${}^{26}C_4$ ways.

Hence, 4 red or 4 black cards can be chosen in

$${}^{26}C_4 + {}^{26}C_4 = 2 \times {}^{26}C_4 = 2 \times \dfrac{26!}{4!\,22!} = 29900 \text{ ways.}$$

Subjective Questions

1. Clearly, a person can enter the room through any one of the six doors. So, there are six ways of entering into the room. After entering into the room, the man can come out through any one of the remaining five doors. So, he can come out through a different door in 5 ways.

Hence, the number of ways in which a man can enter a room through one door and come out through a different door

$$= 6 \times 5 = 30$$

2. Every number between 100 and 1000 consists of three digits. So, we have to determine the total number of three digit numbers such that every digit is either 2 or 9.

Clearly, each one of the unit's, ten's and hundred's place can be filled in 2 ways.

So, the total number of required numbers $= 2 \times 2 \times 2 = 8$.

3. Since, a card can be sent by any one of the three servants, so the number of ways of sending the invitation card to the first friend $= 3$. Similarly, invitation cards can be sent to each of the six friends in 3 ways.

So, the required number of ways $= 3 \times 3 \times 3 \times 3 \times 3 \times 3$

$$= 3^6 = 729$$

4. For a number to be even, we must have 2, 4 and 6 at the unit's place. So, there are 3 ways to fill in the unit's place. Since, digits can be repeated, so each of the ten's and hundred's place can be filled in 6 ways.

Hence, required number of numbers = $3 \times 6 \times 6 = 108$.

5. The first ring can be worn in any of the 4 fingers. So, there are 4 ways of wearing it. Similarly, each one of the other rings can be worn in 4 ways.

Hence, the required number of ways = $4 \times 4 \times 4 \times 4 \times 4$
$$= 4^5$$

6. We have, $P(n-1, r) + r \cdot P(n-1, r-1)$

$$= \frac{(n-1)!}{(n-1-r)!} + r \times \frac{(n-1)!}{(n-1-r+1)!}$$

$$= \frac{(n-1)!}{(n-r-1)!} + r \times \frac{(n-1)!}{(n-r)!}$$

$$= \frac{(n-1)!}{(n-r-1)!} + r \times \frac{(n-1)!}{(n-r)(n-r-1)!}$$

$$= \frac{(n-1)!}{(n-r-1)!} \left[1 + \frac{r}{n-r} \right]$$

$$= \frac{(n-1)!}{(n-r-1)!} \times \frac{n-r+r}{n-r}$$

$$= \frac{n(n-1)!}{(n-r)(n-r-1)!}$$

$$= \frac{n!}{(n-r)!}$$

$$= P(n, r)$$

7. The total number of signals is the number of arrangements of 8 flags by taking 5 flags at a time.

Hence, required number of signals = $^8P_5$

$$= \frac{8!}{(8-5)!}$$

$$= \frac{8!}{3!}$$

$$= \frac{8 \times 7 \times 6 \times 5 \times 4 \times 3!}{3!}$$

$$= 6720$$

8. The number of ways in which 6 persons can stand in a queue is same as the number of arrangements of 6 different things taken all at a time.

Hence, the required number of ways = $^6P_6 = 6!$
$$= 720.$$

9. Let there be n sides of the polygon. Then, it is given that
Number of diagonals = 44

$$\Rightarrow \quad ^nC_2 - n = 44$$

$$\Rightarrow \quad \frac{n(n-1)}{2} - n = 44$$

$$\Rightarrow \quad \frac{n(n-3)}{2} = 44$$

$$\Rightarrow \quad n(n-3) = 88$$

$$\Rightarrow \quad n(n-3) = 11 \times 8$$

$$\Rightarrow \quad n = 11$$

10. We have, $^8C_r - ^7C_3 = ^7C_2$

$$\Rightarrow \quad ^8C_r = ^7C_3 + ^7C_2$$

$$\Rightarrow \quad ^8C_r = ^8C_3 \qquad [\because \ ^nC_r + ^nC_{r-1} = ^{n+1}C_r]$$

$$\Rightarrow \quad r = 3 \text{ or } r + 3 = 8$$

$$[\because \text{ if } ^nC_x = ^nC_y, \text{ then } x + y = n \text{ or } x = y]$$

$$\Rightarrow \quad r = 3, 5$$

11. It is to note here that, when two persons shake hands, it is counted as one handshake, not two. The total number of handshakes is same as the number of ways of selecting 2 persons among 12 persons.

i.e. $\qquad ^{12}C_2 = \frac{12 \times 11}{2 \times 1} = 66$

12. Required number of ways is same as number of permutations of 6 different things taken 4 at a time.

Hence, required number of ways = $^6P_4$

$$= \frac{6!}{(6-4)!}$$

$$= \frac{6!}{2!}$$

$$= 6 \times 5 \times 4 \times 3$$

$$= 360$$

13. Here, we have 5 letters, two of which are of the same kind and others are different.

∴ Required number of permutations (or arrangements)

$$= \frac{5!}{2!} = 5 \times 4 \times 3 = 60$$

14. We have, $\sum\limits_{r=1}^{5} {}^5C_r = {}^5C_1 + {}^5C_2 + {}^5C_3 + {}^5C_4 + {}^5C_5$

$$= {}^5C_1 + {}^5C_2 + {}^5C_2 + {}^5C_1 + {}^5C_0$$

$$[\because \ ^nC_r = ^nC_{n-r}]$$

$$= 2 \times {}^5C_1 + 2 \times {}^5C_2 + {}^5C_0$$

$$= 2 \times 5 + 2 \times \frac{5 \times 4}{2 \times 1} + 1$$

$$= 10 + 20 + 1$$

$$= 31$$

15. We know a number will be divisible by 5, if either 0 or 5 is at unit place.

∴ Number of ways to fill the unit's place = 2

Also note that, for number to be greater than 6000 and less than 7000, digit 6 should be fixed at thousand's place.

∴ Number of ways to fill the thousand's place = 1

Now, we left with 8 digits. So hundred's place can be filled in 8 ways and ten's place can be filled in 7 ways.

Thousand's place	Hundred's place	Ten's place	Unit's place
6			0 or 5
↓	↓	↓	↓
1 way	8 ways	7 ways	2 ways

∴ Total number of numbers = $1 \times 8 \times 7 \times 2 = 112$

16. There are 8 distinct letters in the word TRIANGLE, out of which 3 are vowels, namely A, E, I and 5 are consonants, namely T, R, N, G, L.

(i) Since, the vowels have to occur together, so let us assume them as a single object (AEI).

$$\boxed{A\ E\ I}\ T, R, N, G, L$$

Now, this single object together with 5 remaining letters will be counted as 6 objects and these can be arrange in $^6P_6 = 6!$ ways.

Corresponding to each of these permutations, we have $3! = 6$ permutations of the three vowels A, E and I taken all at a time.

Hence, by fundamental principle of multiplication, the required number of words $= 6! \times 3! = 4320$

(ii) Clearly, required number of words

$\qquad$ = Number of all possible arrangements of 8 letters

$\qquad\qquad$ taken all at a time – Number of permutation

$\qquad\qquad\qquad$ in which the vowels are always together

$$= {}^8P_8 - 6! \times 3! = 8! - 6! \times 3!$$

$$= 8 \times 7 \times 6! - 6! \times 3!$$

$$= 6!\,(56 - 6)$$

$$= 720 \times 50$$

$$= 36000$$

17. We have, $\qquad\qquad \dfrac{^{n-1}C_r}{^nC_r} = \dfrac{6}{9}$

$$\Rightarrow \qquad \frac{\dfrac{(n-1)!}{r!\,(n-1-r)!}}{\dfrac{n!}{r!\,(n-r)!}} = \frac{2}{3}$$

$$\Rightarrow \qquad \frac{(n-1)!}{(n-(r+1))!} \times \frac{(n-r)!}{n!} = \frac{2}{3}$$

$$\Rightarrow \quad \frac{(n-1)!}{(n-(r+1))!} \times \frac{(n-r)(n-(r+1))!}{n(n-1)!} = \frac{2}{3}$$

$$\Rightarrow \qquad\qquad\qquad \frac{n-r}{n} = \frac{2}{3}$$

$$\Rightarrow \qquad\qquad\qquad 3n - 3r = 2n$$

$$\Rightarrow \qquad\qquad\qquad n - 3r = 0 \qquad \ldots\text{(i)}$$

Also, we have $\qquad\qquad \dfrac{^nC_r}{^{n+1}C_r} = \dfrac{9}{13}$

$$\Rightarrow \qquad \frac{n!}{r!\,(n-r)!} \times \frac{r!\,(n+1-r)!}{(n+1)!} = \frac{9}{13}$$

$$\Rightarrow \qquad \frac{n!}{(n-r)!} \times \frac{(n-(r-1))!}{(n+1)n!} = \frac{9}{13}$$

$$\Rightarrow \qquad \frac{(n-(r-1))(n-r)!}{(n-r)!\,(n+1)} = \frac{9}{13}$$

$$\Rightarrow \qquad\qquad \frac{n-r+1}{n+1} = \frac{9}{13}$$

$$\Rightarrow \qquad\qquad 13n - 13r + 13 = 9n + 9$$

$$\Rightarrow \qquad\qquad 4n - 13r = -4 \qquad \ldots\text{(ii)}$$

On solving Eqs. (i) and (ii), we get
$$n = 12 \text{ and } r = 4$$

18.

Name of parts and number of questions in the parts	Number of questions selected by Yamini
Part I = 6	4
Part II = 7	4
Part III = 8	4

Clearly, total number of ways of selection

= Number of ways of selecting 4 questions from 6 questions

$\times$ Number of ways of selecting 4 questions from 7 questions

$\times$ Number of ways of selecting 4 questions from 8 questions

$$= {}^6C_4 \times {}^7C_4 \times {}^8C_4 \qquad\qquad [\because {}^nC_r = {}^nC_{n-r}]$$

$$= {}^6C_2 \times {}^7C_3 \times {}^8C_4$$

$$= \frac{6 \times 5}{2 \times 1} \times \frac{7 \times 6 \times 5}{3 \times 2 \times 1} \times \frac{8 \times 7 \times 6 \times 5}{4 \times 3 \times 2 \times 1}$$

$$= 15 \times 35 \times 70 = 36750 \text{ ways}$$

Hence, the total number of possible combination in which she can choose the questions is 36750 ways.

19. There are 9 ladies and 8 gentlemen. We have to form a committee of 10, consisting of atleast 5 ladies.

This can be formed by selecting

(a) 5 ladies and 5 gentlemen (b) 6 ladies and 4 gentlemen
(c) 7 ladies and 3 gentlemen (d) 8 ladies and 2 gentlemen
(e) 9 ladies and 1 gentleman

Now, the number of ways of forming a committee

$$= {}^9C_5 \times {}^8C_5 + {}^9C_6 \times {}^8C_4 + {}^9C_7 \times {}^8C_3$$
$$+ {}^9C_8 \times {}^8C_2 + {}^9C_9 \times {}^8C_1$$

$$= {}^9C_4 \times {}^8C_3 + {}^9C_3 \times {}^8C_4 + {}^9C_2 \times {}^8C_3$$
$$+ {}^9C_1 \times {}^8C_2 + {}^9C_0 \times {}^8C_1 \; [\because {}^nC_r = {}^nC_{n-r}]$$

$$= \frac{9 \times 8 \times 7 \times 6}{4 \times 3 \times 2 \times 1} \times \frac{8 \times 7 \times 6}{3 \times 2 \times 1} + \frac{9 \times 8 \times 7}{3 \times 2 \times 1}$$

$$\times \frac{8 \times 7 \times 6 \times 5}{4 \times 3 \times 2 \times 1} + \frac{9 \times 8}{2 \times 1} \times \frac{8 \times 7 \times 6}{3 \times 2 \times 1} + 9 \times \frac{8 \times 7}{2 \times 1} + 1 \times 8$$

$$= 126 \times 56 + 84 \times 70 + 36 \times 56 + 9 \times 28 + 8$$

$$= 7056 + 5880 + 2016 + 252 + 8 = 15212$$

(i) Clearly, ladies are in majority in (b), (c), (d) and (e) cases as discussed above.

$\therefore$ Number of committees in which ladies are in majority
$$= 15212 - {}^9C_5 \times {}^8C_5$$
$$= 15212 - 7056 = 8156$$

(ii) Clearly, gentlemen are not in majority in the cases discussed above.

Thus, there is no committee in which gentlemen are in majority. Hence, number of such committee = 0.

20. There are 9 letters in the word ALLAHABAD. In these letters, A occurs 4 times, L occurs twice and rest all are different.

$\therefore$ Total number of words $= \dfrac{9!}{4!\,2!} = 7560$

Now, consider the case, where vowels occupy the even position.

Since, the word ALLAHABAD contains 4 vowels, A, A, A and A, and there are 4 even places, therefore 4 vowels can be arranged in 4 even places.
This can be done in

$$^4P_4 \times \frac{1}{4!} = 4! \times \frac{1}{4!} = 1 \text{ way.}$$

Now, we left with 5 places and 5 letters, which can be arranged in $^5P_5 \times \frac{1}{2!} = \frac{5!}{2!}$ ways.

$$[\because \text{ out of 5 letters, 2 are alike}]$$

Hence, the number of words in which vowels occupy the even position $= \frac{5!}{2!} = 60.$

21. (i) Number of straight lines formed joining the 10 points, taking 2 at a time $= {}^{10}C_2$

$$= \frac{10!}{2!8!} = 45$$

Number of straight lines formed by joining the 4 points, taking 2 at a time $= {}^4C_2 = \frac{4!}{2!2!} = 6$

But, 4 collinear points, when joined pairwise give only one line.

$\therefore$ Required number of straight lines $= 45 - 6 + 1 = 40$

(ii) Number of triangles formed by joining the points, taking 3 at a time $= {}^{10}C_3 = \frac{10!}{3!7!} = 120$

Number of triangles formed by joining the 4 points, taken 3 at a time $= {}^4C_3 = {}^4C_1 = 4.$

But, 4 collinear points cannot form a triangle, when taken 3 at a time.

So, required number of triangles $= 120 - 4 = 116.$

22. There are 7 letters in the word 'FAILURE'.

(i) To include F in every 4 letter word, we first select four letters from the 7 letters of the word 'FAILURE' such that F is included in every selection. This can be done by selecting three letters from the remaining 6 letters i.e. A, I, L, U, R, E in $^6C_3$ ways. Now, there are 4 letters in each of $^6C_3$ selections. Consider one of these $^6C_3$ selections. This selection contains 4 letters, which can be arranged in 4! ways. Thus, each of $^6C_3$ selections provides 4! words.

Hence, the total number of words $= {}^6C_3 \times 4! = 480.$

(ii) If F is not to be included in any word, then we first select 4 letters from the remaining 6 letters. This can be

done in $^6C_4$ ways. Now, every selection has 4 letters which can be arranged in a row in 4! ways.

Hence, the total number of words $= {}^6C_4 \times 4! = 360$

23. (i) There are 6 vertices of a hexagon. One triangle is formed by selecting a group of 3 vertices from given 6 vertices. This can be done in $^6C_3$ ways.

$\therefore$ Number of triangles $= {}^6C_3 = \frac{6!}{3!3!} = 20$

(ii) A polygon of n sides has n vertices. By joining any two vertices of a polygon, we obtain either a side or a diagonal of the polygon. Number of line segments obtained by joining the vertices of an n sided polygon taken 2 at a time.

$$= \text{Number of ways of selecting 2 out of } n$$
$$= {}^nC_2 = \frac{n(n-1)}{2}$$

Out of these lines, n lines are the sides of the polygon.

$\therefore$ Number of diagonals of the polygon $= \frac{n(n-1)}{2} - n$

$$= \frac{n(n-3)}{2}$$

(iii) Let there be n sides of the polygon. We know that the number of diagonals of n sided polygon is $\frac{n(n-3)}{2}$.

$$\therefore \qquad \frac{n(n-3)}{2} = 44 \Rightarrow n^2 - 3n - 88 = 0$$

$$\Rightarrow (n-11)(n+8) = 0$$

$$\Rightarrow \qquad n = 11 \qquad [\because n > 0]$$

Hence, there are 11 sides of the polygon.

(iv) A chord is obtained by joining any two points on a circle. Therefore, total number of chords drawn through 21 points is same as the number of ways of selecting 2 points out of 21 points. This can be done in $^{21}C_2$ ways.

Hence, total number of chords $= {}^{21}C_2 = \frac{21!}{19!2!}$

$$= 21 \times 10 = 210$$

(v) A line is obtained by joining two points. But, from collinear points only one line can be formed.

Hence, total number of lines $= {}^{10}C_2 - {}^4C_2 + 1$

$$= \frac{10 \times 9}{2 \times 1} - \frac{4 \times 3}{2 \times 1} + 1$$

$$= 45 - 6 + 1$$

$$= 40$$

Chapter Test

Multiple Choice Questions

1. If $^nC_r + {}^nC_{r+1} = {}^{n+1}C_x$, then x is equal to

    (a) r (b) $r - 1$
    (c) n (d) $r + 1$

2. The number of ways to arrange the letters of the word 'CHEESE' are

    (a) 120   (b) 240
    (c) 720   (d) 6

3. The value of $2P(n, n - 2)$ is

    (a) n (b) $n!$
    (c) $(n - 1)!$ (d) $(n - 2)!$

4. The number of ways in which three different rings can be worn in four fingers with at most one in each finger is

    (a) 6   (b) 12
    (c) 18   (d) 24

5. If $P(n, 5) = 20 . P(n, 3)$, then n is equal to

    (a) 8   (b) 6
    (c) 4   (d) 3

Case Based MCQs

6. Each of the arrangements, which can be made by taking some or all of a number of things is called a permutation.

If n and r are positive integers such that $1 \le r \le n$, then the number of all permutations of n distinct things, taken r at a time is denoted by the symbol $P(n, r)$ or ^nP_r.

Also, $^nP_r = \dfrac{n!}{(n - r)!}$

On the basis of above information, answer the following questions.

(i) The number of signals that can be made by 5 flags from 8 flags of different colours is

    (a) 6710   (b) 6720
    (c) 6730   (d) 6740

(ii) If $P(5, r) = P(6, r - 1)$, then r is equal to

    (a) 1   (b) 2
    (c) 3   (d) 4

(iii) The number of four-digit numbers with distinct digit is

    (a) 4516   (b) 4526
    (c) 4536   (d) 4546

(iv) If $P(n - 1, 3) : P(n, 4) = 1 : 9$, then n is equal to

    (a) 8   (b) 9
    (c) 10   (d) 11

(v) If $^{56}P_{r+6} : {}^{54}P_{r+3} = 30800 : 1$, then r is equal to

    (a) 41   (b) 40
    (c) 39   (d) 38

Short Answer Type Questions

7. Prove that $\dfrac{(2n)!}{n!} = \{1 \cdot 3 \cdot 5 \dots (2n - 1)\}2^n$.

8. If $P(9, r) = 3024$, find r.

9. How many 3-digit numbers can be formed by using the digits 1 to 9, if no digit is repeated?

10. Evaluate $^nC_r + 2 \cdot {}^nC_{r-1} + {}^nC_{r-2}$.

11. The English alphabet has 5 vowels and 21 consonants. How many words with 2 different vowels and 2 different consonants can be formed from the alphabet?

Long Answer Type Questions

12. Determine the number of natural numbers smaller than 10^4, in the decimal notation of which all the digits are distinct.

13. Find the value of the expression $^{47}C_4 + \sum\limits_{j=1}^{5} {}^{52-j}C_3$.

14. There are 10 professors and 20 students out of whom a committee of 2 professors and 3 students is to be formed. Find the number of ways in which this can be done. Further find in how many of these committees

(i) a particular professors is included?

(ii) a particular student is included?

(iii) a particular student is excluded?

Answers

1. (d)   *2.* (a)   *3.* (b)   *4.* (d)   *5.* (a)

6. (i) (b) (ii) (d) (iii) (c) (iv) (b) (v) (a)

8. 4   *9.* 504   *10.* $^{n+2}C_r$ *11.* 50400   *12.* 5274

13. 270725   *14.* (i) 10260 (ii) 7695 (iii) 43605

For Detailed Solutions

Scan the code

CHAPTER 02

Limits and Continuity

In this Chapter...

- Definition of Limit
- Limits of Rational Functions
- Continuity of a Function at a Point

Definition of Limit

If $f(x)$ approaches to a real number l, when x approaches to a (through lesser or greater values to a) i.e. if $f(x) \to l$ when $x \to a$, then l is called limit of the function $f(x)$.

In symbolic form, it can be written as

$$\lim_{x \to a} f(x) = l$$

Left Hand Limit

A real number l_1 is the left hand limit of function $f(x)$ at $x = a$, if the values of $f(x)$ can be made as close as l_1 at points closed to a and on the left of a.

Symbolically, it is written as

$$\text{LHL} = \lim_{x \to a^-} f(x) = l_1$$

Right Hand Limit

A real number l_2 is the right hand limit of function $f(x)$ at $x = a$, if the values of $f(x)$ can be made as close as l_2 at points closed to a and on the right of a.

Symbolically, it is written as

$$\text{RHL} = \lim_{x \to a^+} f(x) = l_2$$

Existence of Limit

If the right hand limit and left hand limit coincide (i.e. same), then we say that limit exists and their common value is called the limit of $f(x)$ at $x = a$ and denoted it by $\lim_{x \to a} f(x)$.

Limits of Rational Functions

A function f is said to be a rational function, if $f(x) = \dfrac{g(x)}{h(x)}$, where $g(x)$ and $h(x)$ are polynomial functions such that $h(x) \neq 0$.

Then,

$$\lim_{x \to a} f(x) = \lim_{x \to a} \frac{g(x)}{h(x)}$$

$$= \frac{\lim_{x \to a} g(x)}{\lim_{x \to a} h(x)}$$

$$= \frac{g(a)}{h(a)}$$

However, if $h(a) = 0$, then there are two cases arise,

(i) $g(a) \neq 0$ (ii) $g(a) = 0$.

In the first case, we say that the limit does not exist.

In the second case, we can find limit.

Limit of a rational function can be find with the help of following methods

Direct Substitution Method

In this method, we substitute the point, to which the variable tends to in the given limit. If it gives us a real number, then the number so obtained is the limit of the function and if it does not give us a real number, then use other methods.

Rationalisation Method

If we get $\dfrac{0}{0}$ form and numerator or denominator or both have radical sign, then we rationalise the numerator or denominator or both by multiplying their conjugate to remove $\dfrac{0}{0}$ form and then find limit by direct substitution method.

By using Some Standard Limits

If the given limit is of the form $\lim\limits_{x \to a} \dfrac{x^n - a^n}{x - a}$, then we can find the limit directly by using the following theorem

Theorem Let n be any positive integer. Then,

$$\lim_{x \to a} \frac{x^n - a^n}{x - a} = n\, a^{n-1}$$

Proof We know that, $x^n - a^n$

$$= (x - a)(x^{n-1} + ax^{n-2} + \ldots + a^{n-2}x + a^{n-1})$$

On dividing both sides by $(x - a)$, we get

$$\frac{x^n - a^n}{x - a} = x^{n-1} + ax^{n-2} + \ldots + a^{n-2}x + a^{n-1}$$

Thus, $\lim\limits_{x \to a} \dfrac{x^n - a^n}{x - a}$

$$= \lim_{x \to a}(x^{n-1} + ax^{n-2} + \ldots + a^{n-2}x + a^{n-1})$$

$$= a^{n-1} + a\,(a^{n-2}) + \ldots + a^{n-2}\,a + a^{n-1}$$

$$= a^{n-1} + a^{n-1} + \ldots + a^{n-1} + a^{n-1} \qquad [n \text{ terms}]$$

$$= na^{n-1}$$

Continuity of a Function at a Point

A function $f(x)$ is said to be continuous at a point $x = a$, if the value of function at $x = a$ is equal to the limit of the function at $x = a$.

i.e. $f(x)$ is continuous at $x = a$, if

$$(\text{LHL})_{x=a} = (\text{RHL})_{x=a} = f(a)$$

A function $f(x)$ is said to be **discontinuous** at $x = a$, if it is not continuous
at $x = a$, i.e.

- $\lim\limits_{x \to a} f(a)$ does not exist.

- Left hand limit and right hand limit are not equal.

- $\lim\limits_{x \to a} f(x) \neq f(a)$

Solved Examples

Example 1. Evaluate $\lim\limits_{x \to 3} \dfrac{x^2 - 9}{x - 3}$.

Sol. Given, $\lim\limits_{x \to 3} \dfrac{x^2 - 9}{x - 3} = \lim\limits_{x \to 3} \dfrac{x^2 - (3)^2}{x - 3}$

$$= \lim\limits_{x \to 3} \dfrac{(x + 3)(x - 3)}{(x - 3)}$$

$$= \lim\limits_{x \to 3} (x + 3)$$

$$= 3 + 3 = 6$$

Example 2. Evaluate $\lim\limits_{x \to a} \dfrac{(2 + x)^{5/2} - (a + 2)^{5/2}}{x - a}$.

Sol. Given, $\lim\limits_{x \to a} \dfrac{(2 + x)^{5/2} - (a + 2)^{5/2}}{x - a}$

$$= \lim\limits_{x \to a} \dfrac{(2 + x)^{5/2} - (a + 2)^{5/2}}{(2 + x) - (a + 2)}$$

$$= \dfrac{5}{2}(a + 2)^{\frac{5}{2} - 1} \qquad \left[\because \lim\limits_{x \to a} \dfrac{x^n - a^n}{x - a} = n a^{n-1} \right]$$

$$= \dfrac{5}{2}(a + 2)^{3/2} \qquad [\because x \to a \Rightarrow x + 2 \to a + 2]$$

Example 3. Find the value of $\lim\limits_{x \to 2} \dfrac{5}{\sqrt{2} - \sqrt{x}}$.

Sol. $\text{LHL} = \lim\limits_{x \to 2^-} \dfrac{5}{\sqrt{2} - \sqrt{x}}$

$$= \lim\limits_{h \to 0} \dfrac{5}{(\sqrt{2} - \sqrt{2 - h})} \times \dfrac{(\sqrt{2} + \sqrt{2 - h})}{(\sqrt{2} + \sqrt{2 - h})}$$

$$= \lim\limits_{h \to 0} \dfrac{5(\sqrt{2} + \sqrt{2 - h})}{2 - 2 + h} = \infty$$

$\text{RHL} = \lim\limits_{x \to 2^+} \dfrac{5}{\sqrt{2} - \sqrt{x}}$

$$= \lim\limits_{h \to 0} \dfrac{5}{\sqrt{2} - \sqrt{2 + h}} \times \dfrac{(\sqrt{2} + \sqrt{2 + h})}{(\sqrt{2} + \sqrt{2 + h})}$$

$$= \lim\limits_{h \to 0} \dfrac{5(\sqrt{2} + \sqrt{2 + h})}{2 - 2 - h} = -\infty$$

$\therefore \text{LHL} \neq \text{RHL}$

Hence, limit does not exist.

Example 4. Evaluate $\lim\limits_{x \to \sqrt{2}} \dfrac{x^4 - 4}{x^2 + 3\sqrt{2}x - 8}$.

Sol. Given, $\lim\limits_{x \to \sqrt{2}} \dfrac{x^4 - 4}{x^2 + 3\sqrt{2}x - 8} = \lim\limits_{x \to \sqrt{2}} \dfrac{(x^2)^2 - (2)^2}{x^2 + 3\sqrt{2}x - 8}$

$$= \lim\limits_{x \to \sqrt{2}} \dfrac{(x^2 - 2)(x^2 + 2)}{x^2 + 4\sqrt{2}x - \sqrt{2}x - 8}$$

$$= \lim\limits_{x \to \sqrt{2}} \dfrac{(x - \sqrt{2})(x + \sqrt{2})(x^2 + 2)}{x(x + 4\sqrt{2}) - \sqrt{2}(x + 4\sqrt{2})}$$

$$= \lim\limits_{x \to \sqrt{2}} \dfrac{(x - \sqrt{2})(x + \sqrt{2})(x^2 + 2)}{(x - \sqrt{2})(x + 4\sqrt{2})}$$

$$= \lim\limits_{x \to \sqrt{2}} \dfrac{(x + \sqrt{2})(x^2 + 2)}{(x + 4\sqrt{2})}$$

$$= \dfrac{(\sqrt{2} + \sqrt{2})[(\sqrt{2})^2 + 2]}{(\sqrt{2} + 4\sqrt{2})}$$

$$= \dfrac{2\sqrt{2}(2 + 2)}{5\sqrt{2}}$$

$$= \dfrac{8}{5}$$

Example 5. Evaluate $\lim\limits_{x \to 1} \dfrac{x^7 - 2x^5 + 1}{x^3 - 3x^2 + 2}$.

Sol. Given, $\lim\limits_{x \to 1} \dfrac{x^7 - 2x^5 + 1}{x^3 - 3x^2 + 2} \qquad \left[\dfrac{0}{0} \text{ form} \right]$

$$= \lim\limits_{x \to 1} \dfrac{x^7 - x^5 - x^5 + 1}{x^3 - x^2 - 2x^2 + 2}$$

$$= \lim\limits_{x \to 1} \dfrac{x^5(x^2 - 1) - 1(x^5 - 1)}{x^2(x - 1) - 2(x^2 - 1)}$$

On dividing numerator and denominator by $(x - 1)$, then

$$= \lim\limits_{x \to 1} \dfrac{\dfrac{x^5(x^2 - 1)}{(x - 1)} - \dfrac{1(x^5 - 1)}{(x - 1)}}{\dfrac{x^2(x - 1)}{(x - 1)} - \dfrac{2(x^2 - 1)}{(x - 1)}}$$

$$= \dfrac{\lim\limits_{x \to 1} x^5(x + 1) - \lim\limits_{x \to 1}\left(\dfrac{x^5 - 1}{x - 1}\right)}{\lim\limits_{x \to 1} x^2 - \lim\limits_{x \to 1} 2(x + 1)}$$

$$= \dfrac{1 \times 2 - 5 \times (1)^4}{1 - 2 \times 2}$$

$$= \dfrac{2 - 5}{1 - 4}$$

$$= \dfrac{-3}{-3} = 1$$

Example 6. Evaluate $\lim\limits_{h \to 0} \dfrac{\sqrt{x+h} - \sqrt{x}}{h}$.

Sol. Given, $\lim\limits_{h \to 0} \dfrac{\sqrt{x+h} - \sqrt{x}}{h} = \lim\limits_{h \to 0} \dfrac{(x+h)^{1/2} - (x)^{1/2}}{x+h-x}$

$$= \lim\limits_{h \to 0} \dfrac{(x+h)^{1/2} - (x)^{1/2}}{(x+h) - x}$$

$$\left[\because \lim\limits_{x \to a} \dfrac{x^n - a^n}{x - a} = na^{n-1} \right]$$

$$= \frac{1}{2} x^{\frac{1}{2} - 1} = \frac{1}{2} x^{-1/2}$$

$$[\because h \to 0 \Rightarrow x + h \to x]$$

$$= \frac{1}{2\sqrt{x}}$$

Example 7. Evaluate $\lim\limits_{x \to 0} \dfrac{(x+2)^{1/3} - 2^{1/3}}{x}$.

Sol. Given, $\lim\limits_{x \to 0} \dfrac{(x+2)^{1/3} - 2^{1/3}}{x} = \lim\limits_{x \to 0} \dfrac{(x+2)^{1/3} - 2^{1/3}}{(x+2) - 2}$

$$= \frac{1}{3} \times 2^{\frac{1}{3} - 1}$$

$$\left[\because \lim\limits_{x \to a} \dfrac{x^n - a^n}{x - a} = na^{n-1} \right]$$

$$= \frac{1}{3} \times (2)^{-2/3}$$

$$= \frac{1}{3(2)^{2/3}}$$

$$[\because x \to 0 \Rightarrow x + 2 \to 2]$$

Example 8. Discuss the continuity of the function $f(x)$ at $x = 1/2$, when $f(x)$ is defined as follows.

$$f(x) = \begin{cases} 1/2 + x, & 0 \le x < 1/2 \\ 1, & x = 1/2 \\ 3/2 + x, & 1/2 < x \le 1 \end{cases}$$

Sol. Given function is

$$f(x) = \begin{cases} \dfrac{1}{2} + x, & 0 \le x < \dfrac{1}{2} \\ 1, & x = \dfrac{1}{2} \\ \dfrac{3}{2} + x, & \dfrac{1}{2} < x \le 1 \end{cases}$$

We have to check continuity of $f(x)$ at $x = \dfrac{1}{2}$.

Now, $\text{LHL} = \lim\limits_{x \to \frac{1}{2}^-} f(x) = \lim\limits_{x \to \frac{1}{2}^-} \left(\dfrac{1}{2} + x \right)$

$$= \lim\limits_{h \to 0} \left(\dfrac{1}{2} + \dfrac{1}{2} - h \right)$$

$$\left[\text{put } x = \dfrac{1}{2} - h; \text{ when } x \to \dfrac{1}{2}^-, \text{ then } h \to 0 \right]$$

$$= \lim\limits_{h \to 0} (1 - h) = 1$$

and $\text{RHL} = \lim\limits_{x \to \frac{1}{2}^+} f(x)$

$$= \lim\limits_{x \to \frac{1}{2}^+} \left(\dfrac{3}{2} + x \right)$$

$$= \lim\limits_{h \to 0} \left(\dfrac{3}{2} + \dfrac{1}{2} + h \right)$$

$$\left[\text{put } x = \dfrac{1}{2} + h; \text{ when } x \to \dfrac{1}{2}^+, \text{ then } h \to 0 \right]$$

$$= \lim\limits_{h \to 0} (2 + h) = 2$$

$\because \qquad \text{LHL} \ne \text{RHL at } x = 1/2.$

$\therefore$ $f(x)$ is discontinuous at $x = \dfrac{1}{2}$.

Example 9. Find the value of k, so that the following function is continuous at $x = 2$.

$$f(x) = \begin{cases} \dfrac{x^3 + x^2 - 16x + 20}{(x-2)^2}, & x \ne 2 \\ k, & x = 2 \end{cases}$$

Sol. Let $f(x) = \begin{cases} \dfrac{x^3 + x^2 - 16x + 20}{(x-2)^2}, & x \ne 2 \\ k, & x = 2 \end{cases}$

is continuous at $x = 2$.

Now, we have, $f(2) = k$

and $\lim\limits_{x \to 2} f(x) = \lim\limits_{x \to 2} \dfrac{x^3 + x^2 - 16x + 20}{(x-2)^2}$

$$= \lim\limits_{x \to 2} \dfrac{(x-2)(x^2 + 3x - 10)}{(x-2)^2}$$

$$= \lim\limits_{x \to 2} \dfrac{(x-2)(x+5)(x-2)}{(x-2)^2}$$

$$= \lim\limits_{x \to 2} (x+5) = 2 + 5 = 7$$

Since, $f(x)$ is continuous at $x = 2$.

$\therefore \qquad \lim\limits_{x \to 2} f(x) = f(2)$

$\Rightarrow \qquad 7 = k$

$\Rightarrow \qquad k = 7$

Example 10. Find all points of discontinuity of f, where f is defined as follows.

$$f(x) = \begin{cases} |x| + 3, & x \le -3 \\ -2x, & -3 < x < 3 \\ 6x + 2, & x \ge 3 \end{cases}$$

Sol. Given function is

$$f(x) = \begin{cases} |x| + 3, & x \le -3 \\ -2x, & -3 < x < 3 \\ 6x + 2, & x \ge 3 \end{cases} = \begin{cases} -x + 3, & x \le -3 \\ -2x, & -3 < x < 3 \\ 6x + 2, & x \ge 3 \end{cases}$$

First, we verify continuity at $x = -3$ and then at $x = 3$.

Continuity at $x = -3$

$$\text{LHL} = \lim_{x \to (-3)^-} f(x)$$

$$= \lim_{x \to (-3)^-} (-x + 3)$$

$$\Rightarrow \quad \text{LHL} = \lim_{h \to 0} [-(-3 - h) + 3]$$

$$= \lim_{h \to 0} (3 + h + 3)$$

[put $x = -3 - h$; when $x \to -3^-$, then $h \to 0$]

$$= 3 + 3 = 6$$

and $\quad \text{RHL} = \lim_{x \to (-3)^+} f(x)$

$$= \lim_{x \to (-3)^+} (-2x)$$

$$\Rightarrow \quad \text{RHL} = \lim_{h \to 0} [-2(-3 + h)]$$

[put $x = -3 + h$; when $x \to -3^+$, then $h \to 0$]

$$= \lim_{h \to 0} (6 - 2h)$$

$$\Rightarrow \quad \text{RHL} = 6$$

Also, $f(-3) = $ value of $f(x)$ at $x = -3$

$$= -(-3) + 3$$

$$= 3 + 3 = 6$$

$\because \quad \text{LHL} = \text{RHL} = f(-3)$

$\therefore \quad f(x)$ is continuous at $x = -3$.

So, $x = -3$ is the point of continuity.

Continuity at $x = 3$

$$\text{LHL} = \lim_{x \to 3^-} f(x)$$

$$= \lim_{x \to 3^-} [-(2x)]$$

$$\Rightarrow \quad \text{LHL} = \lim_{h \to 0} [-2(3 - h)]$$

[put $x = 3 - h$; when $x \to 3^-$, then $h \to 0$]

$$= \lim_{h \to 0} (-6 + 2h)$$

$$\Rightarrow \quad \text{LHL} = -6$$

and $\quad \text{RHL} = \lim_{x \to 3^+} f(x)$

$$= \lim_{x \to 3^+} (6x + 2)$$

$$\Rightarrow \quad \text{RHL} = \lim_{h \to 0} [6(3 + h) + 2]$$

[put $x = 3 + h$; when $x \to 3^+$, then $h \to 0$]

$$= \lim_{h \to 0} (18 + 6h + 2)$$

$$\Rightarrow \quad \text{RHL} = 20$$

$\because \quad \text{LHL} \ne \text{RHL}$

$\therefore \ f(x)$ is discontinuous at $x = 3$.

Now, as $f(x)$ is a polynomial function for $x < -3$, $-3 < x < 3$ and $x > 3$, so it is continuous in these intervals.

Hence, only $x = 3$ is the point of discontinuity of $f(x)$.

Example 11. Find the relationship between a and b, so that the function f defined by

$$f(x) = \begin{cases} ax + 1, & \text{if } x \le 3 \\ bx + 3, & \text{if } x > 3 \end{cases} \text{ is continuous at } x = 3.$$

Sol. Here, $f(x) = \begin{cases} ax + 1, & \text{if } x \le 3 \\ bx + 3, & \text{if } x > 3 \end{cases}$

$$\text{LHL} = \lim_{x \to 3^-} f(x) = \lim_{x \to 3^-} (ax + 1)$$

Putting $x = 3 - h$ as $x \to 3^-$, $h \to 0$

$\therefore \ \lim_{h \to 0} [a(3 - h) + 1] = \lim_{h \to 0} (3a - ah + 1) = 3a + 1$

$$\text{RHL} = \lim_{x \to 3^+} f(x)$$

$$= \lim_{x \to 3^+} (bx + 3)$$

Putting $x = 3 + h$ as $x \to 3^+$, $h \to 0$

$\therefore \ \lim_{h \to 0} [b(3 + h) + 3] = \lim_{h \to 0} (3b + bh + 3) = 3b + 3$

Also, $f(3) = 3a + 1$ $\qquad\qquad [\because f(x) = ax + 1]$

Since, $f(x)$ is continuous at $x = 3$.

$\therefore \qquad \text{LHL} = \text{RHL} = f(3)$

$\Rightarrow \qquad 3a + 1 = 3b + 3$

$\Rightarrow \qquad 3a = 3b + 2$

$$\Rightarrow \qquad a = b + \frac{2}{3}$$

Example 12. Find the value of a for which

$$f(x) = \begin{cases} ax + 5, & \text{if } x \le 2 \\ x - 1, & \text{if } x > 2 \end{cases} \text{ is continuous at } x = 2.$$

Sol. Given, $f(x) = \begin{cases} ax + 5, & \text{if } x \le 2 \\ x - 1, & \text{if } x > 2 \end{cases}$

At $x = 2$, $f(2) = a(2) + 5 = 2a + 5$

$$\text{LHL} = \lim_{x \to 2^-} f(x)$$

$$= \lim_{x \to 2^-} (ax + 5)$$

$$= \lim_{h \to 0} [a(2 - h) + 5]$$

$$= \lim_{h \to 0} (2a - ah + 5) = 2a + 5$$

$$\text{RHL} = \lim_{x \to 2^+} f(x) = \lim_{x \to 2^+} (x - 1)$$

$$= \lim_{h \to 0} [(2 + h) - 1]$$

$$= \lim_{h \to 0} (1 + h) = 1$$

Since, $f(x)$ is continuous at $x = 2$.

$\therefore \qquad \text{LHL} = \text{RHL} = f(2)$

$\Rightarrow \qquad 2a + 5 = 1 = 2a + 5$

$\therefore \qquad 2a + 5 = 1$

$\Rightarrow \qquad 2a = -4$

$\Rightarrow \qquad a = -2$

Hence, the required value of a is -2, for which $f(x)$ is continuous at $x = 2$.

Chapter Practice

Objective Questions

• Multiple Choice Questions

1. If $f(x) = \begin{cases} x^2 - 1, & x \leq 1 \\ -x^2 - 1, & x > 1 \end{cases}$, then

(a) $\text{LHL} \neq \text{RHL}$, at $x = 1$
(b) $\text{LHL} = \text{RHL} = -2$, at $x = 1$
(c) $\text{LHL} = \text{RHL} = -1$, at $x = 1$
(d) None of the above

2. If $f(x) = \begin{cases} \dfrac{x}{|x|}, & x \neq 0 \\ 0, & x = 0 \end{cases}$, then

(a) $\text{LHL} = \text{RHL} = 1$, at $x = 0$ (b) $\text{LHL} = \text{RHL} = -1$, at $x = 0$
(c) $\text{LHL} \neq \text{RHL}$, at $x = 0$ (d) None of these

3. Suppose, $f(x) = \begin{cases} a + bx, & x < 1 \\ 4, & x = 1 \\ b - ax, & x > 1 \end{cases}$

and if $\lim\limits_{x \to 1} f(x) = f(1)$, then
(a) $a = 4$ and $b = 0$ (b) $a = 0$ and $b = 4$
(c) $a = 0$ and $b = 0$ (d) $a = 4$ and $b = 4$

4. Let $a_1, a_2, a_3, \ldots\ldots, a_n$ be fixed real numbers and define a function,
$f(x) = (x - a_1)(x - a_2)\ldots\ldots(x - a_n)$, then
(a) $\lim\limits_{x \to a_1} f(x) = 0$

(b) $\lim\limits_{x \to a} f(x) = (a - a_1)(a - a_2)\ldots\ldots(a - a_n)$,
for some $a \neq a_1, a_2, a_3, \ldots\ldots, a_n$
(c) Both (a) and (b) are true
(d) Either (a) or (b) is true

5. If $f(x) = \begin{cases} |x| + 1, & x < 0 \\ 0, & x = 0 \\ |x| - 1, & x > 0 \end{cases}$, then $\lim\limits_{x \to a} f(x)$ exists for all

(a) $a \neq 1$ (b) $a \neq 0$
(c) $a \neq -1$ (d) $a \neq 2$

6. If $f(x) = \begin{cases} mx^2 + n, & x < 0 \\ nx + m, & 0 \leq x \leq 1, \text{ then} \\ nx^3 + m, & x > 1 \end{cases}$

(a) $\lim\limits_{x \to 0} f(x)$ exists, when $m = n$
(b) $\lim\limits_{x \to 1} f(x)$ exists for any integral value of m and n
(c) Both (a) and (b) are true
(d) Either (a) or (b) is true

7. $\lim\limits_{x \to 2} \left[\dfrac{1}{x - 2} - \dfrac{2(2x - 3)}{x^3 - 3x^2 + 2x} \right]$ is equal to

(a) $\dfrac{1}{2}$ (b) $\dfrac{-1}{2}$

(c) 1 (d) -2

8. $\lim\limits_{x \to 0} \dfrac{\sqrt{2 + x} - \sqrt{2}}{x}$ is equal to

(a) $\dfrac{1}{2}$ (b) $\dfrac{1}{\sqrt{2}}$

(c) $\dfrac{1}{2\sqrt{2}}$ (d) $\sqrt{2}$

9. $\lim\limits_{n \to \infty} \dfrac{1 + 2 + 3 + \ldots\ldots + n}{n^2}$, $n \in N$ is equal to

(a) 0 (b) 1

(c) $\dfrac{1}{2}$ (d) $\dfrac{1}{4}$

10. The function $f(x) = \begin{cases} \dfrac{x^2 - x - 6}{x + 2}, & \text{if } x \neq -2 \\ -5, & \text{if } x = -2 \end{cases}$ at $x = -2$
is
(a) continuous (b) not continuous
(c) $f(-2) = 5$ (d) None of these

11. The function f, where f is defined by
$f(x) = \begin{cases} -2, & \text{if } x \leq -1 \\ 2x, & \text{if } -1 < x < \infty \end{cases}$ is

(a) not continuous at $x = 1$
(b) not continuous at $x = -1$
(c) not continuous at R
(d) continuous at R

12. The function $f(x) = \begin{cases} 1, & \text{if } x \neq 0 \\ 2, & \text{if } x = 0 \end{cases}$ is not continuous at

(a) $x = 0$ (b) $x = 1$
(c) $x = -1$ (d) None of these

13. The point of discontinuity of the function
$f(x) = \begin{cases} 2x + 3, & \text{if } x \leq 2 \\ 2x - 3, & \text{if } x > 2 \end{cases}$ is

(a) $x = 0$ (b) $x = 1$
(c) $x = 2$ (d) None of these

14. If $f(x) = 2x$ and $g(x) = \dfrac{x^2}{2} + 1$, then which of the following can be a discontinuous function?

(a) $f(x) + g(x)$ (b) $f(x) - g(x)$
(c) $f(x) \cdot g(x)$ (d) $\dfrac{g(x)}{f(x)}$

15. The function defined by $g(x) = x - [x]$ is discontinuous at

(a) all rational points (b) all irrational points
(c) all integer points (d) None of these

16. The $f(x) = x + |x|$ is continuous for

(a) $x \in (-\infty, \infty)$ (b) $x \in (-\infty, \infty) - \{0\}$
(c) only $x > 0$ (d) no value of x

17. Find the value of k, for which the function
$f(x) = \begin{cases} \dfrac{x^2 - 2x - 3}{x + 1}, & x \neq -1 \\ k, & x = -1 \end{cases}$ is continuous at $x = -1$.

(a) 4 (b) −4
(c) 2 (d) −3

• Case Based MCQs

18. For a function $f(x)$, at $x = a$

$\text{LHL} = \lim\limits_{x \to a^-} f(x)$ and $\text{RHL} = \lim\limits_{x \to a^+} f(x)$.

When LHL = RHL, then $\lim\limits_{x \to a} f(x)$ exists.

On the basis of the above information, answer the following questions.

(i) $\lim\limits_{x \to 3^-} |x - 3|$ is

(a) 0 (b) 1
(c) −1 (d) does not exist

(ii) $\lim\limits_{x \to 3^+} |x - 3|$ is

(a) 0 (b) 1
(c) −1 (d) does not exist

(iii) $\lim\limits_{x \to 8^+} \dfrac{2x}{x + 8}$ is

(a) −1 (b) 1
(c) 2 (d) does not exist

(iv) $\lim\limits_{x \to 0} \dfrac{x - 4}{x + 2}$ is

(a) 2 (b) − 2
(c) 1 (d) −1

(v) $\lim\limits_{x \to 3} |x - 3|$ is

(a) 0 (b) 1
(c) − 1 (d) does not exist

19. Suppose, $f(x) = \begin{cases} 2a + bx, & x < 1 \\ 3, & x = 1 \\ b + ax, & x > 1 \end{cases}$ and $\lim\limits_{x \to 1} f(x) = f(1)$.

On the basis of above information, answer the following questions.

(i) $\lim\limits_{x \to 1^-} f(x)$ is

(a) $2a + b$ (b) 3
(c) $b + a$ (d) None of these

(ii) $\lim\limits_{x \to 1^+} f(x)$ is

(a) $2a + b$ (b) 3
(c) $b + a$ (d) None of these

(iii) $f(1)$ is

(a) $2a + b$ (b) 3
(c) $b + a$ (d) None of these

(iv) a is

(a) 0 (b) 1
(c) 2 (d) 3

(v) b is

(a) 0 (b) 1
(c) 2 (d) 3

20. Every polynomial function, constant functions are continuous everywhere. Also, for a function to be continuous at $x = a$, $\lim\limits_{x \to a} f(x) = f(a)$.

On the basis of above information, answer the following questions.

(i) If $f(x) = \begin{cases} 3x, & \text{for } x \leq 0 \\ 0, & \text{for } x > 0 \end{cases}$, then at $x = 0$

(a) $f(x)$ is continuous
(b) $f(x)$ is not continuous
(c) $f(x)$ does not exist
(d) None of the above

(ii) If $f(x) = |x - 2|$, $x \in R$, then at $x = 2$

(a) $f(x)$ is not continuous
(b) $f(x)$ is continuous
(c) $f(x)$ does not exist
(d) None of the above

(iii) $f(x) = x^2 + 3x$

(a) continuous at $x = 3$ (b) discontinuous at $x = 3$
(c) does not exist at $x = 3$ (d) None of these

(iv) If $f(x) = x + 3$, then at $x = 1$, $f(x)$ is

    (a) continuous   (b) discontinuous

    (c) can't say anything   (d) None of these

(v) If $f(x) = \begin{cases} kx + 3, & x < 1 \\ x + 2, & x \geq 1 \end{cases}$ is continuous at $x = 1$, then

    k is equal to

    (a) 0   (b) 1

    (c) 2   (d) 3

PART 2
Subjective Questions

• Short Answer Type Questions

1. Evaluate the left hand and right hand limits of the following function at $x = 2$.
$$f(x) = \begin{cases} 2x + 3, \text{ if } x \leq 2 \\ x + 5, \text{ if } x > 2 \end{cases}$$
Does $\lim_{x \to 2} f(x)$ exist?

2. Evaluate the left hand and right hand limits of the function defined by
$$f(x) = \begin{cases} 1 + x^2, \text{ if } 0 \leq x \leq 1 \\ 2 - x^2, \text{ if } x > 1 \end{cases} \text{ at } x = 1.$$
Also, show that $\lim_{x \to 1} f(x)$ does not exist.

3. If $f(x) = \begin{cases} \dfrac{x - |x|}{x}, & \text{ if } x \neq 0 \\ 2, & \text{ if } x = 0 \end{cases}$, then show that $\lim_{x \to 0} f(x)$ does not exist.

4. Evaluate $\lim_{x \to \frac{1}{2}} \dfrac{4x^2 - 1}{2x - 1}$.

5. Evaluate $\lim_{x \to 2} \left[\dfrac{x^2 - 4}{x^3 - 4x^2 + 4x} \right]$.

6. Evaluate $\lim_{x \to 0} \dfrac{\sqrt{2 + x} - \sqrt{2}}{x}$.

7. Evaluate $\lim_{x \to 1} \dfrac{(2x - 3)(\sqrt{x} - 1)}{2x^2 + x - 3}$.

8. Evaluate $\lim_{x \to 2} \dfrac{x^5 - 32}{x^3 - 8}$.

9. Evaluate $\lim_{x \to 0} \dfrac{(1 + x)^6 - 1}{(1 + x)^2 - 1}$.

10. If $\lim_{x \to b} \dfrac{x^3 - b^3}{x - b} = \lim_{x \to 1} \dfrac{x^4 - 1}{x - 1}$, find all possible values of b.

11. Evaluate $\lim_{x \to 1} \left(\dfrac{2}{1 - x^2} + \dfrac{1}{x - 1} \right)$.

12. Let $f(x)$ be a function defined by
$$f(x) = \begin{cases} 6x - 6, & \text{ if } x \leq 3 \\ 2x - k, & \text{ if } x > 3 \end{cases}.$$
Find the value of k, if $\lim_{x \to 3} f(x)$ exists.

13. Find the value of a, so that
$$f(x) = \begin{cases} ax + 5, & \text{ if } x \leq 2 \\ x - 1, & \text{ if } x > 2 \end{cases} \text{ is continuous at } x = 2.$$

14. Show that the function $f(x) = 2x - |x|$ is continuous at $x = 0$.

15. Find the value of λ. If $f(x) = \begin{cases} \lambda(x^2 - 2x), & x \leq 0 \\ 4x + 1, & x > 0 \end{cases}$ is continuous at $x = 0$.

• Long Answer Type Questions

16. Evaluate $\lim_{x \to a} \dfrac{\sqrt{a + 2x} - \sqrt{3x}}{\sqrt{3a + x} - 2\sqrt{x}}$.

17. Evaluate $\lim_{x \to 1} \dfrac{x^n + x^{n-1} + x^{n-2} + \ldots + x^2 + x - n}{x - 1}$.

18. Find the values of a and b such that the function defined by $f(x) = \begin{cases} 5, \text{ if } x \leq 2 \\ ax + b, \text{ if } 2 < x < 10 \\ 21, \text{ if } x \geq 10 \end{cases}$
is continuous function.

19. If $f(x) = \begin{cases} \dfrac{\sqrt{1 + kx} - \sqrt{1 - kx}}{x}, & \text{ for } -1 \leq x < 0 \\ 2x^2 + 3x - 2, & \text{ for } 0 \leq x \leq 1 \end{cases}$ is continuous at $x = 0$, then find the value of k.

20. If $f(x) = \begin{cases} ax + 3, & x \leq 2 \\ a^2x - 1, & x > 2 \end{cases}$, then find the values of a for which f is continuous for all values of x.

21. Find all the points of discontinuity of the function f defined by $f(x) = \begin{cases} 3, & \text{ if } 0 \leq x \leq 1 \\ 4, & \text{ if } 1 < x < 3 \\ 5, & \text{ if } 3 \leq x \leq 10 \end{cases}.$

• Case Based Questions

22. If $P(x)$ and $Q(x)$ are two polynomials of degree m and n, then we have

$$\lim_{x \to \infty} \frac{P(x)}{Q(x)}$$

$$= \begin{cases} \dfrac{\text{Coefficient of highest power in } P(x)}{\text{Coefficient of highest power in } Q(x)}, & \text{if } m = n \\ 0, & \text{if } m < n \\ \infty, & \text{if } m > n \end{cases}$$

On the basis of above information, answer the following questions.

(i) Evaluate $\displaystyle\lim_{n \to \infty} \dfrac{1^2 + 2^2 + 3^2 + \ldots + n^2}{n^3}$

(ii) Evaluate $\displaystyle\lim_{n \to \infty} \dfrac{n!}{(n+1)! - n!}$

(iii) Evaluate $\displaystyle\lim_{x \to \infty} (\sqrt{x^2 + 7x} - x)$

23. A function $f(x)$ is said to be continuous at a point $x = a$ of its domain, if $\displaystyle\lim_{x \to a} f(x) = f(a)$.

On the basis of above information, answer the following questions.

(i) Show that, $f(x) = \begin{cases} 5x - 4, & \text{if } 0 < x \leq 1 \\ 4x^3 - 3x, & \text{if } 1 < x < 2 \end{cases}$ is continuous at $x = 1$.

(ii) Find the value of 'a', if the function $f(x)$ defined by $f(x) = \begin{cases} 2x - 1, & x < 2 \\ a, & x = 2 \\ x + 1, & x > 2 \end{cases}$ is continuous at $x = 2$.

(iii) Find the value of 'k', if the function $f(x)$ defined by $f(x) = \begin{cases} \dfrac{x^2 - 25}{x - 5}, & x \neq 5 \\ k, & x = 5 \end{cases}$ is continuous at $x = 5$.

SOLUTIONS

Objective Questions

1. (a) Given, $f(x) = \begin{cases} x^2 - 1, & x \leq 1 \\ -x^2 - 1, & x > 1 \end{cases}$

At $x = 1$,

$\text{RHL} = \displaystyle\lim_{x \to 1^+} f(x) = \lim_{h \to 0} f(1 + h)$

$\quad = \displaystyle\lim_{h \to 0} -(1 + h)^2 - 1 \qquad [\because \text{put } x = 1 + h]$

$\quad = -(1 + 0)^2 - 1$

$\quad = -1 - 1 = -2$

$\text{LHL} = \displaystyle\lim_{x \to 1^-} f(x) = \lim_{h \to 0} f(1 - h) \qquad [\because \text{put } x = 1 - h]$

$\quad = \displaystyle\lim_{h \to 0} (1 - h)^2 - 1$

$\quad = (1 - 0)^2 - 1$

$\quad = 1 - 1 = 0$

$\Rightarrow \quad \text{RHL} \neq \text{LHL}$

Hence, at $x = 1$, limit doesn't exist.

2. (c) Given, $f(x) = \begin{cases} \dfrac{x}{|x|}, & x \neq 0 \\ 0, & x = 0 \end{cases}$

At $x = 0$,

$\text{RHL} = \displaystyle\lim_{x \to 0^+} f(x) = \lim_{h \to 0} f(0 + h)$

$\quad = \displaystyle\lim_{h \to 0} \dfrac{0 + h}{|0 + h|}$

$\quad = \displaystyle\lim_{h \to 0} \dfrac{0 + h}{(0 + h)} = 1$

$\text{LHL} = \displaystyle\lim_{x \to 0^-} f(x)$

$\quad = \displaystyle\lim_{h \to 0} f(0 - h)$

$\quad = \displaystyle\lim_{h \to 0} \dfrac{(0 - h)}{|0 - h|}$

$\quad = \displaystyle\lim_{h \to 0} \dfrac{(0 - h)}{-(0 - h)} = -1$

$\Rightarrow \quad \text{RHL} \neq \text{LHL}$

Hence, at $x = 0$ limit does not exist.

3. (b) We have, $f(x) = \begin{cases} a + bx, & x < 1 \\ 4, & x = 1 \\ b - ax, & x > 1 \end{cases}$

Given, $\displaystyle\lim_{x \to 1} f(x) = f(1)$

i.e. $\quad \text{RHL} = \text{LHL} = f(1)$

$\Rightarrow \quad \displaystyle\lim_{x \to 1^+} f(x) = \lim_{x \to 1^-} f(x) = 4$

$\Rightarrow \quad \displaystyle\lim_{h \to 0} f(1 + h) = \lim_{h \to 0} f(1 - h) = 4$

$\Rightarrow \quad \displaystyle\lim_{h \to 0} b - a(1 + h) = \lim_{h \to 0} a + b(1 - h) = 4$

$\Rightarrow \quad b - a(1 + 0) = a + b(1 - 0) = 4$

$\Rightarrow \quad b - a = a + b = 4$

$\Rightarrow \quad b - a = 4 \qquad \ldots\text{(i)}$

and $\quad b + a = 4 \qquad \ldots\text{(ii)}$

On solving Eqs. (i) and (ii), we get

$\quad b = 4 \text{ and } a = 0.$

4. (c) Given, $f(x) = (x - a_1)(x - a_2) \ldots (x - a_n)$

$$\therefore \quad \lim_{x \to a_1} f(x) = \lim_{x \to a_1} (x - a_1)(x - a_2) \ldots (x - a_n)$$

$$= (a_1 - a_1)(a_1 - a_2) \ldots (a_1 - a_n)$$

$$= 0 \times (a_1 - a_2) \ldots (a_1 - a_n) = 0$$

Again, $\lim_{x \to a} f(x) = \lim_{x \to a} (x - a_1)(x - a_2) \ldots (x - a_n)$

$$= (a - a_1)(a - a_2) \ldots (a - a_n)$$

5. (b) Given, $f(x) = \begin{cases} |x| + 1, & x < 0 \\ 0, & x = 0 \\ |x| - 1, & x > 0 \end{cases} = \begin{cases} -x + 1, & x < 0 \\ 0, & x = 0 \\ x - 1, & x > 0 \end{cases}$

Let us first, check the existence of limit of $f(x)$ at $x = 0$.
At $x = 0$,

$$\text{RHL} = \lim_{x \to 0^+} f(x) = \lim_{h \to 0} f(0 + h) = \lim_{h \to 0} (0 + h) - 1$$

$$= \lim_{h \to 0} h - 1 = 0 - 1 = -1$$

$$\text{LHL} = \lim_{x \to 0^-} f(x) = \lim_{h \to 0} f(0 - h)$$

$$= \lim_{h \to 0} -(0 - h) + 1$$

$$= \lim_{h \to 0} h + 1 = 0 + 1 = 1$$

$\Rightarrow \text{RHL} \neq \text{LHL}$

$\Rightarrow$ At $x = 0$, limit does not exist.

Note that for any $a < 0$ or $a > 0$, $\lim_{x \to a} f(x)$ exists, as for

$a < 0$, $\lim_{x \to a} f(x) = \lim_{x \to a} -x + 1 = -a + 1$ exists and for

$a > 0$, $\lim_{x \to a} f(x) = \lim_{x \to a} x - 1 = a - 1$ exists.

Hence, $\lim_{x \to a} f(x)$ exists for all $a \neq 0$.

6. (c) $\because$ At $x = 0$, limit exists.

Therefore, $\qquad \text{RHL} = \text{LHL}$

$\Rightarrow \qquad \lim_{x \to 0^+} f(x) = \lim_{x \to 0^-} f(x)$

$\Rightarrow \qquad \lim_{h \to 0} f(0 + h) = \lim_{h \to 0} f(0 - h)$

$\Rightarrow \quad \lim_{h \to 0} n(0 + h) + m = \lim_{h \to 0} m(0 - h)^2 + n$

$\Rightarrow \qquad n(0 + 0) + m = m(0 - 0)^2 + n$

$\Rightarrow \qquad\qquad m = n \qquad\qquad\qquad \ldots\text{(i)}$

Again, at $x = 1$ limit exists.

$\Rightarrow \qquad\qquad \text{RHL} = \text{LHL}$

$\Rightarrow \qquad\quad \lim_{x \to 1^+} f(x) = \lim_{x \to 1^-} f(x)$

$\Rightarrow \qquad \lim_{h \to 0} f(1 + h) = \lim_{h \to 0} f(1 - h)$

$\Rightarrow \quad \lim_{h \to 0} n(1 + h)^3 + m = \lim_{h \to 0} n(1 - h) + m$

$\Rightarrow \qquad n(1 + 0)^3 + m = n(1 - 0) + m$

$\Rightarrow \qquad\qquad n + m = m + n \qquad\qquad \ldots\text{(ii)}$

Hence, from Eqs. (i) and (ii), we get $\lim_{x \to 0} f(x)$ exist, when

$m = n$ and $\lim_{x \to 1} f(x)$ exists for any integral value of m and n.

7. (b) We have,

$$\lim_{x \to 2} \left[\frac{1}{x - 2} - \frac{2(2x - 3)}{x^3 - 3x^2 + 2x} \right] = \lim_{x \to 2} \left[\frac{1}{x - 2} - \frac{2(2x - 3)}{x(x - 1)(x - 2)} \right]$$

$$= \lim_{x \to 2} \left[\frac{x(x - 1) - 2(2x - 3)}{x(x - 1)(x - 2)} \right]$$

$$= \lim_{x \to 2} \left[\frac{x^2 - 5x + 6}{x(x - 1)(x - 2)} \right]$$

$$= \lim_{x \to 2} \left[\frac{(x - 2)(x - 3)}{x(x - 1)(x - 2)} \right]$$

$$(x - 2 \neq 0)$$

$$= \lim_{x \to 2} \left[\frac{x - 3}{x(x - 1)} \right] = \frac{-1}{2}$$

8. (c) Put $y = 2 + x$, so that when $x \to 0$, $y \to 2$.

Then, $\quad \lim_{x \to 0} \dfrac{\sqrt{2 + x} - \sqrt{2}}{x} = \lim_{y \to 2} \dfrac{y^{\frac{1}{2}} - 2^{\frac{1}{2}}}{y - 2}$

$$= \frac{1}{2}(2)^{\frac{1}{2} - 1} = \frac{1}{2} \cdot 2^{-\frac{1}{2}} = \frac{1}{2\sqrt{2}}$$

9. (c) We have, $\lim_{n \to \infty} \dfrac{1 + 2 + 3 + \ldots + n}{n^2}$

$$= \lim_{n \to \infty} \frac{n(n + 1)}{2n^2} = \lim_{n \to \infty} \frac{1}{2}\left(1 + \frac{1}{n}\right) = \frac{1}{2}$$

10. (a) We have, $f(x) = \begin{cases} \dfrac{x^2 - x - 6}{x + 2}, & \text{if } x \neq -2 \\ -5, & \text{if } x = -2 \end{cases}$

At $x = -2$,

$$\lim_{x \to -2} f(x) = \lim_{x \to -2} \frac{x^2 - x - 6}{x + 2}$$

Now, factorising the numerator, we get

$$\lim_{x \to -2} f(x) = \lim_{x \to -2} \frac{(x - 3)(x + 2)}{(x + 2)}$$

$$= \lim_{x \to -2} (x - 3) = -2 - 3 = -5$$

Also, at $x = -2$, $f(x) = -5$ i.e. $f(-2) = -5$

Thus, $\lim_{x \to -2} f(x) = f(-2)$

Hence, $f(x)$ is continuous at $x = -2$.

11. (d) We have, $f(x) = \begin{cases} -2, & \text{if } x \leq -1 \\ 2x, & \text{if } -1 < x < \infty \end{cases}$

Since, $f(x)$ is a polynomial function, so it is continuous everywhere except at $x = -1$.

So, we have to check the continuity at $x = -1$ only.

At $x = -1$, $\quad f(-1) = -2$

$\text{LHL} = \lim_{x \to -1^-} f(x) = \lim_{x \to -1^-} (-2) = -2$

$\text{RHL} = \lim_{x \to -1^+} f(x)$

$$= \lim_{x \to -1^+} 2x = \lim_{h \to 0} 2(-1 + h)$$

$$[\because \text{put } x = -1 + h; \text{ when } x \to -1^+, \text{ then } h \to 0]$$

$$= \lim_{h \to 0} (-2 + 2h) = -2$$

Thus, $f(-1) = \text{LHL} = \text{RHL}$

$\therefore f(x)$ is continuous at $x = -1$.

Hence, $f(x)$ is continuous for every value of x.

12. (a) Given, function $f(x) = \begin{cases} 1, & \text{if } x \neq 0 \\ 2, & \text{if } x = 0 \end{cases}$

At $x = 0$,

Value of function, $f(0) = 2$

And $\qquad \lim\limits_{x \to 0} f(x) = 1$

$\because \qquad \lim\limits_{x \to 0} f(x) \neq f(0)$

or $\qquad \lim\limits_{x \to a} f(x) \neq$ value of function

$\therefore$ Function $f(x)$ is not continuous at $x = 0$.

13. (c) At $x = 2$,

$\text{LHL} = \lim\limits_{x \to 2^-} (2x + 3) = 2 \times 2 + 3 = 7$

$\text{RHL} = \lim\limits_{x \to 2^+} (2x - 3) = 2 \times 2 - 3 = 1$

$\because \text{LHL} \neq \text{RHL}$

$\therefore$ Point of discontinuity of the function is $x = 2$.

14. (d) We know that, if f and g be continuous functions, then

(a) $f + g$ is continuous

(b) $f - g$ is continuous.

(c) fg is continuous

(d) $\dfrac{f}{g}$ is continuous at those points, where $g(x) \neq 0$.

Here, $\dfrac{g(x)}{f(x)} = \dfrac{\dfrac{x^2}{2} + 1}{2x} = \dfrac{x^2 + 2}{4x}$,

which is discontinuous at $x = 0$.

15. (c) $g(x) = x - [x]$

Let $f(x) = [x]$

$\because f(x)$ is discontinuous at every integer.

$\therefore g(x) = x - [x]$ is discontinuous at all the integers.

16. (a) Given, $f(x) = x + |x|$

$\therefore \qquad f(x) = \begin{cases} 2x, & x \geq 0 \\ 0, & x < 0 \end{cases}$

It is clear from the graph of $f(x)$ is continuous for every value of x.

17. (b) $\lim\limits_{x \to -1} f(x) = \lim\limits_{x \to -1} \dfrac{x^2 - 2x - 3}{x + 1}$

$\lim\limits_{x \to -1} \dfrac{(x - 3)(x + 1)}{x + 1} = \lim\limits_{x \to -1} (x - 3)$

$\qquad\qquad\qquad = -1 - 3 = -4$

For continuity at $x = -1$, we must have

$\lim\limits_{x \to -1} f(x) = f(-1)$

$\Rightarrow \qquad k = -4$

18. (i) (a) $\lim\limits_{x \to 3^-} |x - 3| = \lim\limits_{h \to 0} |3 - h - 3|$

$\qquad\qquad = \lim\limits_{h \to 0} h = 0$

(ii) (a) $\lim\limits_{x \to 3^+} |x - 3| = \lim\limits_{h \to 0} |3 + h - 3|$

$\qquad\qquad = \lim\limits_{h \to 0} h = 0$

(iii) (b) $\lim\limits_{x \to 8^+} \dfrac{2x}{x + 8} = \lim\limits_{h \to 0} \dfrac{2(8 + h)}{8 + h + 8}$

$\qquad\qquad = \dfrac{16}{16} = 1$

(iv) (b) $\lim\limits_{x \to 0} \dfrac{x - 4}{x + 2} = \dfrac{-4}{2} = -2$

(v) (a) Since, $\lim\limits_{x \to 3^-} |x - 3| = \lim\limits_{x \to 3^+} |x - 3| = 0$

$\therefore \qquad \lim\limits_{x \to 3} |x - 3| = 0$

19. (i) (a) $\lim\limits_{x \to 1^-} f(x) = \lim\limits_{x \to 1^-} (2a + bx)$

$\qquad\qquad = \lim\limits_{h \to 0} [2a + b(1 - h)]$

$\qquad\qquad = 2a + b$

(ii) (c) $\lim\limits_{x \to 1^+} f(x) = \lim\limits_{x \to 1^+} (b + ax)$

$\qquad\qquad = \lim\limits_{h \to 0} [b + a(1 + h)]$

$\qquad\qquad = b + a$

(iii) (b) $f(1) = 3$

Since, $\lim\limits_{x \to 1} f(x) = f(1)$

$\therefore \quad \lim\limits_{x \to 1^-} f(x) = \lim\limits_{x \to 1^+} f(x) = f(1)$

$\Rightarrow \qquad 2a + b = b + a = 3$

$\therefore \qquad 2a + b = b + a \Rightarrow a = 0$

and $\qquad b + a = 3 \Rightarrow b = 3$

(iv) (a) $a = 0$

(v) (d) $b = 3$

20. (i) (a) Given, function $f(x) = \begin{cases} 3x, & \text{for } x \leq 0 \\ 0, & \text{for } x > 0 \end{cases}$

Continuity at $x = 0$,

$\text{LHL} = \lim\limits_{h \to 0} f(0 - h) = \lim\limits_{h \to 0} 3(0 - h)$

$\qquad\qquad = \lim\limits_{h \to 0} -3h = -3 \times 0 = 0$

$\text{RHL} = \lim\limits_{h \to 0} f(0 + h) = \lim\limits_{h \to 0} 0 = 0$

and value of the function at $x = 0$, $f(0) = 3 \times 0 = 0$

$\because \text{LHL} = \text{RHL} = f(0)$

$\therefore$ The given function $f(x)$ is continuous at $x = 0$.

(ii) (b) Given function, $f(x) = |x - 2|$, $x \in R$

$$f(x) = \begin{cases} -(x-2), & \text{for } x \le 2 \\ +(x-2), & \text{for } x > 2 \end{cases}$$

$$f(x) = \begin{cases} 2 - x, & x \le 2 \\ x - 2, & x > 2 \end{cases}$$

Continuity at $x = 2$,

$\text{LHL} = \lim\limits_{h \to 0} f(2-h) = \lim\limits_{h \to 0} [2-(2-h)]$

$= \lim\limits_{h \to 0} h = 0$

$\text{RHL} = \lim\limits_{h \to 0} f(2+h) = \lim\limits_{h \to 0} [(2+h) - 2]$

$= \lim\limits_{h \to 0} h = 0$

Value of function at $x = 2$

$f(2) = 2 - 2 = 0$

$\because \text{LHL} = \text{RHL} = f(2)$

$\therefore f(x)$ is continuous at $x = 2$.

(iii) (a) Given, function

$$f(x) = x^2 + 3x$$

Continuity at $x = 3$,

$\text{LHL} = \lim\limits_{h \to 0} f(3-h)$

$= \lim\limits_{h \to 0} [(3-h)^2 + 3(3-h)]$

$= \lim\limits_{h \to 0} (9 + h^2 - 6h + 9 - 3h)$

$= \lim\limits_{h \to 0} (h^2 + 18 - 9h) = 18$

$\text{RHL} = \lim\limits_{h \to 0} f(3+h)$

$= \lim\limits_{h \to 0} [(3+h)^2 + 3(3+h)]$

$= \lim\limits_{h \to 0} (9 + h^2 + 6h + 9 + 3h)$

$= \lim\limits_{h \to 0} (h^2 + 18 + 9h) = 18$

Value of function at $x = 3$,

$f(3) = 3^2 + 3 \times 3 = 18$

$\because \text{LHL} = \text{RHL} = f(3)$

$\therefore f(x)$ is continuous at $x = 3$.

(iv) (a) Given, function $f(x) = x + 3$. At $x = 1$,

$\text{LHL} = \lim\limits_{x \to 1^-} f(x) = \lim\limits_{x \to 1^-} (x+3)$

$= \lim\limits_{h \to 0} (1 - h + 3) = 4$

$\text{RHL} = \lim\limits_{x \to 1^+} f(x) = \lim\limits_{x \to 1^+} (x+3)$

$= \lim\limits_{h \to 0} (1 + h + 3) = 4$

and $f(1) = 1 + 3 = 4$

$\because \text{LHL} = \text{RHL} = f(1)$

$\therefore f(x)$ is continuous at $x = 1$.

(v) (a) Since, $f(x)$ is continuous at $x = 1$, then

$$\lim\limits_{x \to 1} f(x) = f(1)$$

$\Rightarrow \quad \lim\limits_{x \to 1} (kx + 3) = 1 + 2$

$\Rightarrow \quad k + 3 = 3 \Rightarrow k = 0$

Subjective Questions

1. Given, $f(x) = \begin{cases} 2x + 3, & \text{if } x \le 2 \\ x + 5, & \text{if } x > 2 \end{cases}$

$\text{LHL} = \lim\limits_{x \to 2^-} f(x) = \lim\limits_{x \to 2^-} 2x + 3$

$\qquad [\because f(x) = 2x + 3, \text{ if } x \le 2]$

$= \lim\limits_{h \to 0} [2(2-h) + 3]$

$= 2(2 - 0) + 3$

[putting $x = 2 - h$ and when $x \to 2^-$, then $h \to 0$]

$= 4 + 3 = 7$

and $\quad \text{RHL} = \lim\limits_{x \to 2^+} f(x)$

$= \lim\limits_{x \to 2^+} (x + 5) \qquad [\because f(x) = x + 5, \text{ if } x > 2]$

$= \lim\limits_{h \to 0} (2 + h + 5) = 2 + 0 + 5 = 7$

[putting $x = 2 + h$ and $x \to 2^+$, then $h \to 0$]

$\because \text{LHL of } f(\text{at } x = 2) = \text{RHL of } f(\text{at } x = 2)$

$\therefore \lim\limits_{x \to 2} f(x)$ exists and it is equal to 7.

2. We have, $f(x) = \begin{cases} 1 + x^2, & \text{if } 0 \le x \le 1 \\ 2 - x^2, & \text{if } x > 1 \end{cases}$

At $x = 1$, $\text{LHL} = \lim\limits_{x \to 1^-} f(x)$

$= \lim\limits_{x \to 1^-} (1 + x^2) \quad [\because f(x) = 1 + x^2, \text{ if } 0 \le x \le 1]$

$= \lim\limits_{h \to 0} [1 + (1-h)^2] = 1 + (1 - 0)^2 = 2$

[putting $x = 1 - h$ and when $x \to 1^-$, then $h \to 0$]

$\text{RHL} = \lim\limits_{x \to 1^+} f(x) = \lim\limits_{x \to 1^+} (2 - x^2) \quad [\because f(x) = 2 - x^2, \text{ if } x > 1]$

$= \lim\limits_{h \to 0} [2 - (1 + h)^2]$

[putting $x = 1 + h$ and when $x \to 1^+$, then $h \to 0$]

$= 2 - 1 = 1$

Since, $\text{LHL} \ne \text{RHL}$

Therefore, $\lim\limits_{x \to 1} f(x)$ does not exist.

3. $\text{RHL} = \lim\limits_{x \to 0^+} f(x) = \lim\limits_{x \to 0^+} \dfrac{x - |x|}{x}$

$= \lim\limits_{h \to 0} \dfrac{(0 + h) - |0 + h|}{0 + h}$

$= 0$

$\text{LHL} = \lim\limits_{x \to 0^-} f(x)$

$= \lim\limits_{x \to 0^-} \dfrac{x - |x|}{x}$

$= \lim\limits_{h \to 0} \dfrac{(0 - h) - |(0 - h)|}{0 - h}$

$= \lim\limits_{h \to 0} \dfrac{-h - h}{-h} = 2$

$\therefore \text{LHL} \ne \text{RHL}$.

So, $\lim\limits_{x \to 0} f(x)$ does not exist.

4. On putting $x = \dfrac{1}{2}$, we get the form $\dfrac{0}{0}$.

So, let us first factorise it.

Consider, $\displaystyle\lim_{x \to \frac{1}{2}} \dfrac{4x^2 - 1}{2x - 1} = \lim_{x \to \frac{1}{2}} \dfrac{(2x + 1)(2x - 1)}{(2x - 1)}$

$\qquad\qquad\qquad$ [using factorisation method]

$\qquad = \displaystyle\lim_{x \to \frac{1}{2}} (2x + 1)$

$\qquad = 2\left(\dfrac{1}{2}\right) + 1 = 2$

5. On putting $x = 2$, we get the form $\dfrac{0}{0}$. So, let us first factorise it.

Consider, $\displaystyle\lim_{x \to 2} \dfrac{x^2 - 4}{x^3 - 4x^2 + 4x} = \lim_{x \to 2} \dfrac{(x + 2)(x - 2)}{x(x - 2)^2}$

$\qquad = \displaystyle\lim_{x \to 2} \dfrac{(x + 2)}{x(x - 2)}$

$\qquad = \dfrac{2 + 2}{2(2 - 2)} = \dfrac{4}{0}$,

which is not defined.

$\therefore \quad \displaystyle\lim_{x \to 2}\left[\dfrac{x^2 - 4}{x^3 - 4x^2 + 4x}\right]$ does not exist.

6. When $x = 0$, then the expression $\dfrac{\sqrt{2 + x} - \sqrt{2}}{x}$ becomes of the form $\dfrac{0}{0}$. So, we will rationalising the numerator by multiplying and dividing its conjugate i.e. $\sqrt{2 + x} + \sqrt{2}$.

$\therefore \displaystyle\lim_{x \to 0} \dfrac{\sqrt{2 + x} - \sqrt{2}}{x} = \lim_{x \to 0} \dfrac{(\sqrt{2 + x} - \sqrt{2})(\sqrt{2 + x} + \sqrt{2})}{x(\sqrt{2 + x} + \sqrt{2})}$

$\qquad\qquad$ [multiplying numerator and
$\qquad\qquad$ denominator by $\sqrt{2 + x} + \sqrt{2}$]

$\qquad = \displaystyle\lim_{x \to 0} \dfrac{2 + x - 2}{x(\sqrt{2 + x} + \sqrt{2})}$

$\qquad = \displaystyle\lim_{x \to 0} \dfrac{1}{\sqrt{2 + x} + \sqrt{2}}$

$\qquad = \dfrac{1}{2\sqrt{2}}$

$\qquad\qquad$ [using direct substitution method]

7. When $x = 1$, then expression $\dfrac{(2x - 3)(\sqrt{x} - 1)}{2x^2 + x - 3}$ becomes of the form $\dfrac{0}{0}$. So, rationalising $(\sqrt{x} - 1)$ in the numerator by multiplying and dividing its conjugate i.e. $\sqrt{x} + 1$.

We have, $\displaystyle\lim_{x \to 1} \dfrac{(2x - 3)(\sqrt{x} - 1)}{2x^2 + x - 3}$

$\qquad = \displaystyle\lim_{x \to 1} \dfrac{(2x - 3)(\sqrt{x} - 1)(\sqrt{x} + 1)}{(\sqrt{x} + 1)(2x^2 + x - 3)}$

$\qquad = \displaystyle\lim_{x \to 1} \dfrac{(2x - 3)(x - 1)}{(\sqrt{x} + 1)(2x^2 + x - 3)} \qquad \left[\dfrac{0}{0} \text{form}\right]$

$\qquad = \displaystyle\lim_{x \to 1} \dfrac{(2x - 3)(x - 1)}{(\sqrt{x} + 1)(2x + 3)(x - 1)}$

$\qquad = \displaystyle\lim_{x \to 1} \dfrac{2x - 3}{(\sqrt{x} + 1)(2x + 3)}$

$\qquad = -\dfrac{1}{10}$

8. $\displaystyle\lim_{x \to 2} \dfrac{x^5 - 32}{x^3 - 8} = \lim_{x \to 2} \dfrac{x^5 - 2^5}{x^3 - 2^3} \qquad [\because 2^5 = 32 \text{ and } 2^3 = 8]$

$\qquad = \displaystyle\lim_{x \to 2} \dfrac{\dfrac{x^5 - 2^5}{x - 2}}{\dfrac{x^3 - 2^3}{x - 2}}$

$\qquad\qquad$ [dividing numerator and denominator by $(x - 2)$]

$\qquad = \displaystyle\lim_{x \to 2} \dfrac{x^5 - 2^5}{x - 2} \div \lim_{x \to 2} \dfrac{x^3 - 2^3}{x - 2}$

$\qquad \left[\because \displaystyle\lim_{x \to a} \dfrac{f(x)}{g(x)} = \lim_{x \to a} f(x) \div \lim_{x \to a} g(x)\right]$

$\qquad = 5 \times 2^{5-1} \div 3 \times 2^{3-1} \qquad \left[\because \displaystyle\lim_{x \to a} \dfrac{x^n - a^n}{x - a} = na^{n-1}\right]$

$\qquad = 5 \times 2^4 \div 3 \times 2^2$

$\qquad = \dfrac{5 \times 2^4}{3 \times 2^2}$

$\qquad = \dfrac{5}{3} \times 2^2 = \dfrac{5}{3} \times 4 = \dfrac{20}{3}$

9. Put $1 + x = y$, then $y \to 1$ as $x \to 0$

$\therefore \displaystyle\lim_{x \to 0} \dfrac{(1 + x)^6 - 1}{(1 + x)^2 - 1} = \lim_{y \to 1} \dfrac{y^6 - 1}{y^2 - 1}$

$\qquad = \displaystyle\lim_{y \to 1} \left(\dfrac{\dfrac{y^6 - 1}{y - 1}}{\dfrac{y^2 - 1}{y - 1}}\right)$

$\qquad\qquad$ [dividing numerator and denominator by $y - 1$]

$\qquad = \displaystyle\lim_{y \to 1} \dfrac{y^6 - 1}{y - 1} \div \lim_{y \to 1} \dfrac{y^2 - 1}{y - 1}$

$\qquad = \dfrac{6(1)^{6 - 1}}{2(1)^{2 - 1}}$

$\qquad = \dfrac{6}{2} = 3 \qquad \left[\because \displaystyle\lim_{x \to a} \dfrac{x^n - a^n}{x - a} = na^{n - 1}\right]$

10. We have, $\displaystyle\lim_{x \to b} \dfrac{x^3 - b^3}{x - b} = \lim_{x \to 1} \dfrac{x^4 - 1}{x - 1}$

$\Rightarrow \qquad 3(b)^{3 - 1} = 4(1)^{4 - 1} \qquad \left[\because \displaystyle\lim_{x \to a} \dfrac{x^n - a^n}{x - a} = na^{n - 1}\right]$

$\Rightarrow \qquad 3b^2 = 4$

$\Rightarrow \qquad b^2 = \dfrac{4}{3}$

$\Rightarrow \qquad b = \pm \dfrac{2}{\sqrt{3}}$

11. We have, $\lim\limits_{x \to 1}\left(\dfrac{2}{1-x^2}+\dfrac{1}{x-1}\right)=\lim\limits_{x \to 1}\left(\dfrac{2}{1-x^2}-\dfrac{1}{1-x}\right)$

$$=\lim\limits_{x \to 1}\left(\dfrac{2-(1+x)}{1-x^2}\right)$$

$$=\lim\limits_{x \to 1}\dfrac{1-x}{(1-x)(1+x)}$$

$$=\lim\limits_{x \to 1}\dfrac{1}{1+x}$$

$$=\dfrac{1}{2}$$

12. We have, $f(x)=\begin{cases} 6x-6, & \text{if } x \le 3 \\ 2x-k, & \text{if } x > 3 \end{cases}$

Now, at $x = 3$,

$$\text{LHL}=\lim\limits_{x \to 3^-} f(x)$$

$$=\lim\limits_{x \to 3^-}(6x-6)$$

$$=\lim\limits_{h \to 0}[6(3-h)-6]=12$$

and　　$\text{RHL}=\lim\limits_{x \to 3^+} f(x)$

$$=\lim\limits_{x \to 3^+}(2x-k)$$

$$=\lim\limits_{h \to 0}[2(3+h)-k]=6-k$$

Since, $\lim\limits_{x \to 3} f(x)$ exist.

$\therefore$　　　$\text{LHL}=\text{RHL}$

$\Rightarrow$　　　$12=6-k$

$\Rightarrow$　　　$k=-6$

13. Given, $f(x)=\begin{cases} ax+5, & \text{if } x \le 2 \\ x-1, & \text{if } x > 2 \end{cases}$

and at $x = 2$, $f(x)$ is continuous.
Here, a is an unknown constant.
At $x = 2$, $f(2)=a(2)+5=2a+5$

$$\text{LHL}=\lim\limits_{x \to 2^-} f(x)$$

$$=\lim\limits_{x \to 2^-}(ax+5)$$

$$=\lim\limits_{h \to 0}[a(2-h)+5]$$

$$=\lim\limits_{h \to 0}(2a-ah+5)=2a+5$$

$$\text{RHL}=\lim\limits_{x \to 2^+} f(x)=\lim\limits_{x \to 2^+}(x-1)$$

$$=\lim\limits_{h \to 0}[(2+h)-1]=\lim\limits_{h \to 0}(1+h)=1$$

Since, $f(x)$ is continuous at $x = 2$.
At $x = 2$, $\text{LHL}=\text{RHL}=f(2)$

$\Rightarrow$　　　$2a+5=1=2a+5$

$\therefore$　　　$2a+5=1$

$\Rightarrow$　　　$2a=-4$

$\Rightarrow$　　　$a=-2$

Hence, the required value of a is -2, for which $f(x)$ is continuous at $x = 2$.

14. The given function is $f(x)=2x-|x|$.

$\therefore\quad f(x)=\begin{cases} 2x-x, & \text{if } x \ge 0 \\ 2x-(-x), & \text{if } x < 0 \end{cases}$　$\left[\because |x|=\begin{cases} x, & \text{if } x \ge 0 \\ -x, & \text{if } x < 0 \end{cases}\right]$

i.e. $f(x)=\begin{cases} x, & \text{if } x \ge 0 \\ 3x, & \text{if } x < 0 \end{cases}$

At $x = 0$, $\text{LHL}=\lim\limits_{x \to 0^-} f(x)$

$$=\lim\limits_{x \to 0^-} 3x=3\times 0=0$$

and　　$\text{RHL}=\lim\limits_{x \to 0^+} f(x)=\lim\limits_{x \to 0^+} x=0$

Also,　　$f(0)=0$

Thus,　　$\text{LHL}=\text{RHL}=f(0)$

Hence, $f(x)$ is continuous function at $x = 0$.

15. Here, $f(x)=\begin{cases} \lambda(x^2-2x), & \text{if } x \le 0 \\ 4x+1, & \text{if } x > 0 \end{cases}$

At $x = 0$, $\text{LHL}=\lim\limits_{x \to 0^-} f(x)=\lim\limits_{x \to 0^-}\lambda(x^2-2x)$

$$\therefore\ \text{LHL}=\lim\limits_{h \to 0}\lambda[(0-h)^2-2(0-h)]$$

$$=\lim\limits_{h \to 0}[\lambda(h^2+2h)]=0$$

$$[\text{put } x=0-h; \text{ when } x \to 0^-, \text{ then } h \to 0]$$

$$\text{RHL}=\lim\limits_{x \to 0^+} f(x)=\lim\limits_{x \to 0^+}(4x+1)$$

$$\therefore\ \text{RHL}=\lim\limits_{h \to 0}[4(0+h)+1]=\lim\limits_{h \to 0}[4h+1]=0+1=1$$

$$[\text{put } x=0+h; \text{ when } x \to 0^+, \text{ then } h \to 0]$$

$\therefore\ \text{LHL} \ne \text{RHL}$

Thus, $f(x)$ is not continuous at $x = 0$ for any value of λ.

16. We have, $\lim\limits_{x \to a}\dfrac{\sqrt{a+2x}-\sqrt{3x}}{\sqrt{3a+x}-2\sqrt{x}}$

$$=\lim\limits_{x \to a}\dfrac{\sqrt{a+2x}-\sqrt{3x}}{\sqrt{3a+x}-2\sqrt{x}}\times\dfrac{\sqrt{a+2x}+\sqrt{3x}}{\sqrt{a+2x}+\sqrt{3x}}$$

[multiplying numerator and denominator by $\sqrt{a+2x}+\sqrt{3x}$]

$$=\lim\limits_{x \to a}\dfrac{a+2x-3x}{(\sqrt{3a+x}-2\sqrt{x})(\sqrt{a+2x}+\sqrt{3x})}$$

$$[\because (A-B)(A+B)=A^2-B^2]$$

$$=\lim\limits_{x \to a}\dfrac{(a-x)(\sqrt{3a+x}+2\sqrt{x})}{(\sqrt{a+2x}+\sqrt{3x})(\sqrt{3a+x}-2\sqrt{x})(\sqrt{3a+x}+2\sqrt{x})}$$

[multiplying numerator and denominator by $\sqrt{3a+x}+2\sqrt{x}$]

$$=\lim\limits_{x \to a}\dfrac{(a-x)[\sqrt{3a+x}+2\sqrt{x}]}{(\sqrt{a+2x}+\sqrt{3x})(3a+x-4x)}$$

$$=\lim\limits_{x \to a}\dfrac{(a-x)(\sqrt{3a+x}+2\sqrt{x})}{(\sqrt{a+2x}+\sqrt{3x})(3a-3x)}$$

$$=\dfrac{\sqrt{3a+a}+2\sqrt{a}}{3(\sqrt{a+2a}+\sqrt{3a})}=\dfrac{4\sqrt{a}}{3\times 2\sqrt{3}\sqrt{a}}$$

$$=\dfrac{2}{3\sqrt{3}}=\dfrac{2\sqrt{3}}{9}$$

17. $\displaystyle\lim_{x \to 1} \frac{x^n + x^{n-1} + x^{n-2} + \ldots + x^2 + x - n}{x - 1}$

$= \displaystyle\lim_{x \to 1} \frac{(x^n - 1) + (x^{n-1} - 1) + \ldots + (x^2 - 1) + (x - 1)}{(x - 1)}$

$$[\because n = 1 + 1 + 1 + \ldots \text{ to } n \text{ terms}]$$

$= \displaystyle\lim_{x \to 1} \frac{x^n - 1^n}{x - 1} + \lim_{x \to 1} \frac{x^{n-1} - 1^{n-1}}{x - 1}$

$\qquad\qquad + \ldots + \displaystyle\lim_{x \to 1} \frac{x^2 - 1^2}{x - 1} + \lim_{x \to 1} \frac{x - 1}{x - 1}$

$= n\,(1)^{n-1} + (n-1)\,(1)^{n-2} + \ldots + 2\,(1)^{2-1} + 1$

$$\left[\because \lim_{x \to a} \frac{x^n - a^n}{x - a} = na^{n-1} \right]$$

$= n + (n-1) + \ldots + 2 + 1 = \dfrac{n\,(n+1)}{2} \quad \left[\because \Sigma n = \dfrac{n(n+1)}{2} \right]$

18. Here, $f(x) = \begin{cases} 5, & \text{if } x \leq 2 \\ ax + b, & \text{if } 2 < x < 10 \\ 21, & \text{if } x \geq 10 \end{cases}$

At $x = 2$, $\text{LHL} = \displaystyle\lim_{x \to 2^-} f(x) = \lim_{x \to 2^-} (5) = 5$

and $\qquad \text{RHL} = \displaystyle\lim_{x \to 2^+} f(x) = \lim_{x \to 2^+} (ax + b)$

$\therefore \qquad \text{RHL} = \displaystyle\lim_{h \to 0} [a(2 + h) + b]$

$\qquad\qquad$ [put $x = 2 + h$; when $x \to 2^+$, then $h \to 0$]

$\qquad = \displaystyle\lim_{h \to 0} (2a + ah + b) = 2a + b$

Also, $f(2) = 5$

Since, $f(x)$ is continuous at $x = 2$.

$\therefore \quad \text{LHL} = \text{RHL} = f(2) \Rightarrow 2a + b = 5 \qquad\qquad \ldots(i)$

Now, at $x = 10$,

$\quad \text{LHL} = \displaystyle\lim_{x \to 10^-} f(x) = \lim_{x \to 10^-} (ax + b)$

$\therefore \quad \text{LHL} = \displaystyle\lim_{h \to 0} [a(10 - h) + b] = \lim_{h \to 0} (10a - ah + b)$

$\qquad\qquad$ [put $x = 10 - h$; when $x \to 10^-$, then $h \to 0$]

$\qquad = 10a + b$

and $\text{RHL} = \displaystyle\lim_{x \to 10^+} f(x) = \lim_{x \to 10^+} (21) = 21$

Also, $f(10) = 21$.

Since, $f(x)$ is continuous at $x = 10$.

$\therefore \quad \text{LHL} = \text{RHL} = f(10)$

$\Rightarrow \quad 10a + b = 21 \qquad\qquad\qquad\qquad \ldots(ii)$

On subtracting Eq. (i) from Eq. (ii), we get

$$8a = 16 \Rightarrow a = 2$$

On putting $a = 2$ in Eq. (i), we get

$$2 \times 2 + b = 5 \Rightarrow b = 1$$

Hence, the values of a and b are 2 and 1, respectively.

19. At $x = 0$,

$\text{LHL} = \displaystyle\lim_{x \to 0^-} \frac{\sqrt{1 + kx} - \sqrt{1 - kx}}{x} \times \frac{\sqrt{1 + kx} + \sqrt{1 - kx}}{\sqrt{1 + kx} + \sqrt{1 - kx}}$

$= \displaystyle\lim_{x \to 0^-} \frac{2kx}{x(\sqrt{1 + kx} + \sqrt{1 - kx})}$

$= \dfrac{2k}{\sqrt{1 + 0} + \sqrt{1 - 0}} = k$

$\text{RHL} = \displaystyle\lim_{x \to 0^+} (2x^2 + 3x - 2) = -2$

$f(0) = -2$

$\because$ It is given that $f(x)$ is continuous at $x = 0$.

$\therefore \qquad \text{LHL} = \text{RHL} = f(0) \Rightarrow k = -2$

20. Given, $f(x) = \begin{cases} ax + 3, & x \leq 2 \\ a^2 x - 1, & x > 2 \end{cases}$

Continuity at $x = 2$,

$\text{LHL} = \displaystyle\lim_{x \to 2^-} f(x) = \lim_{x \to 2} (ax + 3) = 2a + 3$

$\text{RHL} = \displaystyle\lim_{x \to 2^+} f(x) = \lim_{x \to 2} (a^2 x - 1) = 2a^2 - 1$

Since, $f(x)$ is continuous for all values of x.

$\therefore \qquad\qquad \text{LHL} = \text{RHL}$

$\Rightarrow \qquad\qquad 2a + 3 = 2a^2 - 1$

$\Rightarrow \qquad\quad 2a^2 - 2a - 4 = 0$

$\Rightarrow \qquad\qquad a^2 - a - 2 = 0$

$\Rightarrow \qquad\quad a^2 - 2a + a - 2 = 0$

$\Rightarrow \quad a(a - 2) + 1(a - 2) = 0$

$\Rightarrow \qquad\quad (a + 1)(a - 2) = 0$

$\therefore \qquad\qquad\qquad a = -1, 2$

21. Here, $f(x) = \begin{cases} 3, & \text{if } 0 \leq x \leq 1 \\ 4, & \text{if } 1 < x < 3 \\ 5, & \text{if } 3 \leq x \leq 10 \end{cases}$

For $0 \leq x \leq 1$, $f(x) = 3$, $1 < x < 3$, $f(x) = 4$ and $3 \leq x \leq 10$, $f(x) = 5$ are constant functions, so it is continuous in the given interval, so we have to check the continuity at $x = 1, 3$.

At $x = 1$, $\text{LHL} = \displaystyle\lim_{x \to 1^-} f(x) = \lim_{x \to 1^-} (3) = 3$,

$\qquad\qquad \text{RHL} = \displaystyle\lim_{x \to 1^+} f(x) = \lim_{x \to 1^+} (4) = 4$

$\therefore \qquad\qquad \text{LHL} \neq \text{RHL}$

Thus, $f(x)$ is discontinuous at $x = 1$.

At $x = 3$, $\text{LHL} = \displaystyle\lim_{x \to 3^-} f(x) = \lim_{x \to 3^-} (4) = 4$,

$\qquad\qquad \text{RHL} = \displaystyle\lim_{x \to 3^+} f(x) = \lim_{x \to 3^+} (5) = 5$

$\therefore \qquad\qquad \text{LHL} \neq \text{RHL}$

Thus, $f(x)$ is discontinuous at $x = 3$.

Hence, $f(x)$ is continuous everywhere except at $x = 1, 3$.

22. (i) We have,

$\quad \displaystyle\lim_{n \to \infty} \frac{1^2 + 2^2 + 3^2 + \ldots + n^2}{n^3}$

$= \displaystyle\lim_{n \to \infty} \frac{n(n + 1)(2n + 1)}{6n^3} \left[\because \Sigma n^2 = \frac{n(n+1)(2n+1)}{6} \right]$

$= \displaystyle\lim_{n \to \infty} \frac{2n^3 + 3n^2 + n}{6n^3}$

$= \dfrac{2}{6} = \dfrac{1}{3}$

(ii) We have,

$$\lim_{n \to \infty} \frac{n!}{(n+1)! - n!} = \lim_{n \to \infty} \frac{n!}{(n+1)n! - n!}$$

$$= \lim_{n \to \infty} \frac{1}{n+1-1}$$

$$= \lim_{n \to \infty} \frac{1}{n}$$

$$= 0$$

(iii) We have,

$$\lim_{x \to \infty} (\sqrt{x^2 + 7x} - x)$$

$$= \lim_{x \to \infty} \left[\sqrt{x^2 + 7x} - x \times \frac{\sqrt{x^2 + 7x} + x}{\sqrt{x^2 + 7x} + x} \right]$$

$$= \lim_{x \to \infty} \frac{x^2 + 7x - x^2}{\sqrt{x^2 + 7x} + x}$$

$$= \lim_{x \to \infty} \frac{7x}{\sqrt{x^2 + 7x} + x}$$

$$= \frac{7}{\sqrt{1} + 1} = \frac{7}{2}$$

23. (i) We have, at $x = 1$

$$\text{LHL} = \lim_{x \to 1^-} f(x)$$

$$= \lim_{x \to 1} (5x - 4)$$

$$= 5 - 4 = 1$$

$$\text{RHL} = \lim_{x \to 1^+} f(x)$$

$$= \lim_{x \to 1} (4x^3 - 3x) = 4 - 3 = 1$$

and $f(1) = 5 \times 1 - 4 = 1$

$$\therefore \lim_{x \to 1^-} f(x) = \lim_{x \to 1^+} f(x) = f(1)$$

So, $f(x)$ is continuous at $x = 1$.

(ii) We have, at $x = 2$

$$\text{LHL} = \lim_{x \to 2^-} f(x)$$

$$= \lim_{x \to 2} (2x - 1) = 2 \times 2 - 1 = 3$$

$$\text{RHL} = \lim_{x \to 2^+} f(x)$$

$$= \lim_{x \to 2} (x + 1) = 2 + 1 = 3$$

and $f(2) = a$

Since, $f(x)$ is continuous at $x = 2$, then

$$\text{LHL} = \text{RHL} = f(2)$$

$$\therefore \quad a = 3$$

(iii) We have, $f(x)$ is continuous at $x = 5$, then

$$\lim_{x \to 5} f(x) = f(5)$$

$$\Rightarrow \qquad \lim_{x \to 5} \frac{x^2 - 25}{x - 5} = k$$

$$\Rightarrow \qquad \lim_{x \to 5} \frac{(x - 5)(x + 5)}{x - 5} = k$$

$$\Rightarrow \qquad \lim_{x \to 5} (x + 5) = k$$

$$\Rightarrow \qquad 5 + 5 = k$$

$$\Rightarrow \qquad k = 10$$

Multiple Choice Questions

1. $\lim\limits_{x \to \infty} \dfrac{\sqrt{x^2 - 1}}{2x + 1}$ is equal to

(a) 1   (b) 0

(c) -1 (d) $\dfrac{1}{2}$

2. If $\lim\limits_{x \to 1} \dfrac{x + x^2 + x^3 + \ldots + x^n - n}{x - 1} = 5050$, then n is equal to

(a) 10   (b) 100

(c) 150   (d) 200

3. $\lim\limits_{x \to 0} \dfrac{\sqrt{1 + x} - 1}{x}$ is equal to

(a) $\dfrac{1}{2}$ (b) 2

(c) 0   (d) 1

4. $f(x) = \begin{cases} \dfrac{\sqrt{1 + px} - \sqrt{1 - px}}{x}, & -1 \le x < 0 \\ \dfrac{2x + 1}{x - 2}, & 0 \le x < 1 \end{cases}$ is continuous in

the interval $[-1, 1]$, then p is equal to

(a) -1 (b) $-\dfrac{1}{2}$

(c) $\dfrac{1}{2}$ (d) 1

5. The points of discontinuity of the function

$$f(x) = \begin{cases} \dfrac{1}{5}(2x^2 + 3), & x \le 1 \\ 6 - 5x, & 1 < x < 3 \\ x - 3, & x \ge 3 \end{cases}$$ is (are)

(a) $x = 1$ (b) $x = 3$

(c) $x = 1, 3$ (d) None of these

Case Based MCQs

6. Sometimes, the factorisation of a given polynomial is not easy, so we can't calculate the limit using factorisation. Instead of factorisation, we use the formula given,

$$\lim_{x \to a} \dfrac{x^n - a^n}{x - a} = na^{n-1}$$

On the basis of above information, answer the following questions.

(i) $\lim\limits_{x \to 2} \dfrac{x^9 - 512}{x - 2}$ is equal to

(a) 1024   (b) 2304

(c) 3304   (d) 4024

(ii) $\lim\limits_{x \to 0} \dfrac{(1 - x)^n - 1}{x}$ is equal to

(a) n (b) 1

(c) $-n$ (d) 0

(iii) $\lim\limits_{x \to 4} \dfrac{x^3 - 64}{x^2 - 16}$ is equal to

(a) 4   (b) 6

(c) 8   (d) 10

(iv) If $\lim\limits_{x \to 3} \dfrac{x^n - 3^n}{x - 3} = 108$, then n is equal to

(a) 4   (b) 3

(c) 2   (d) 1

(v) $\lim\limits_{x \to 1} \dfrac{x^{100} - 1}{x^{10} - 1}$ is equal to

(a) 1   (b) 5

(c) 10   (d) 100

Short Answer Type Questions

7. Show that $\lim\limits_{x \to 0} \dfrac{e^{\frac{1}{x}} - 1}{e^{\frac{1}{x}} + 1}$ does not exist.

8. Evaluate $\lim\limits_{x \to 3} \left(\dfrac{1}{x - 3} - \dfrac{2}{x^2 - 4x + 3} \right)$.

9. Evaluate $\lim\limits_{x \to 1} \dfrac{\sqrt{3 + x} - \sqrt{5 - x}}{x^2 - 1}$.

10. If $\lim\limits_{x \to a} \dfrac{x^5 - a^5}{x - a} = 405$, find all possible values of a.

11. Discuss the continuity of the given function

$$f(x) = \begin{cases} 2x, & x < 0 \\ 0, & 0 \le x \le 1 \\ 4x, & x > 1 \end{cases}$$

Long Answer Type Questions

12. Evaluate $\lim\limits_{x \to \sqrt{10}} \dfrac{\sqrt{7 - 2x} - (\sqrt{5} - \sqrt{2})}{x^2 - 10}$.

13. If $f(x) = \begin{cases} x^2 a, & 0 \le x < 1 \\ a, & 1 \le x < \sqrt{2} \\ \dfrac{2b^2 - 4b}{x^2}, & \sqrt{2} \le x < \infty \end{cases}$

is continuous for $0 \le x < \infty$, then find the value of a and b, if $a + b = 0$.

Answers

1. (d)   **2.** (b)   **3.** (a)   **4.** (b)   **5.** (b)

6. (i) (b)   (ii) (c)   (iii) (b)   (iv) (a)   (v) (c)

8. $\dfrac{1}{2}$ **9.** $\dfrac{1}{4}$ **10.** ± 3

12. $-\left(\dfrac{\sqrt{5} + \sqrt{2}}{6\sqrt{10}} \right)$ **13.** $a = -1, b = 1$

For Detailed Solutions

Scan the code

CHAPTER 03

Differentiation

In this Chapter...

- Derivative at a Point
- First Principle of Derivative
- Algebra of Derivative of Functions
- Derivative of Composite Functions

Derivative at a Point

Suppose f is a real valued function and a is a point in its domain. Then, derivative of f at a is defined by

$$\lim_{h \to 0} \frac{f(a+h) - f(a)}{h}$$

provided this limit exists.

The derivative of $f(x)$ at a is denoted by $f'(a)$.

First Principle of Derivative

Suppose f is a real valued function, the function defined by $\lim_{h \to 0} \frac{f(x+h) - f(x)}{h}$, wherever the limit exists, is defined to be the derivative of f at x and is denoted by $f'(x)$.

This definition of derivative is called the first principle of derivative.

Thus,
$$f'(x) = \lim_{x \to 0} \frac{f(x+h) - f(x)}{h}$$

Sometimes $f'(x)$ is denoted by $\frac{d}{dx}[f(x)]$ or if $y = f(x)$, then it is denoted by $\frac{dy}{dx}$ and referred to as derivative of $f(x)$ or y with respect to x. It is also denoted by $D[f(x)]$.

Note Derivative of f at $x = a$ is also given by substituting $x = a$ in $f'(x)$ and it is denoted by

$$\frac{d}{dx} f(x)\Big|_a \text{ or } \frac{df}{dx}\Big|_a \text{ or } \left(\frac{df}{dx}\right)_{x=a}.$$

Algebra of Derivative of Functions

Let f and g be two functions such that their derivatives are defined in a common domain.

Then,

(i) Derivative of sum of two functions is sum of the derivatives of the functions.
$$\frac{d}{dx}[f(x) + g(x)] = \frac{d}{dx} f(x) + \frac{d}{dx} g(x)$$

(ii) Derivative of difference of two functions is difference of the derivatives of the functions.
$$\frac{d}{dx}[f(x) - g(x)] = \frac{d}{dx} f(x) - \frac{d}{dx} g(x)$$

(iii) Derivative of product of two functions is given by the following product rule.
$$\frac{d}{dx}[f(x) \cdot g(x)] = f(x)\frac{d}{dx} g(x) + g(x)\frac{d}{dx} f(x)$$

This is also known as Leibnitz product rule of derivative.

(iv) Derivative of quotient of two functions is given by the following quotient rule.

$$\frac{d}{dx}\left[\frac{f(x)}{g(x)}\right] = \frac{g(x)\dfrac{d}{dx}f(x) - f(x)\dfrac{d}{dx}g(x)}{[g(x)]^2}, \, g(x) \neq 0$$

Note $\dfrac{d}{dx}[c \cdot f(x)] = c\dfrac{d}{dx}f(x)$

Some Important Differentiation

Following are differentiation of some functions.

1. $\dfrac{d}{dx}x^n = nx^{n-1}$ 　　2. $\dfrac{d}{dx}e^x = e^x$

3. $\dfrac{d}{dx}a^x = a^x \log a$ 　　4. $\dfrac{d}{dx}\log x = \dfrac{1}{x}$

Derivatives of Composite Functions

Derivative of a composite function can be found out by chain rule.

Chain Rule

Chain rule is applied when the given function is the function of function, i.e. a function is in the form of $fog(x)$ or $f[g(x)]$.

Let $y = f(u)$ and $u = f(x)$, then by using chain rule, we may write

$$\frac{dy}{dx} = \frac{dy}{du} \cdot \frac{du}{dx},$$

when $\dfrac{dy}{du}$ and $\dfrac{du}{dx}$ both exist.

Solved Examples

Example 1. Find the derivative of $x^{2/3}$ using first principle.

Sol. Let $\qquad f(x) = x^{2/3}$

$$f(x+h) = (x+h)^{2/3}$$

$\therefore \qquad \dfrac{d}{dx}f(x) = \lim_{h \to 0}\dfrac{f(x+h) - f(x)}{h}$

$$= \lim_{h \to 0}\left[\frac{(x+h)^{2/3} - x^{2/3}}{h}\right]$$

$$= \lim_{(x+h) \to x}\left[\frac{(x+h)^{2/3} - x^{2/3}}{(x+h) - x}\right]$$

$$= \frac{2}{3}(x)^{\frac{2}{3}-1} \qquad \left[\because \lim_{x \to a}\frac{x^x - a^n}{x - a} = n\,a^{n-1}\right]$$

$$= \frac{2}{3}x^{-1/3}$$

Example 2. Find the derivative of $f(x) = \dfrac{ax+b}{cx+d}$ using first principle.

Sol. Let $\qquad f(x) = \dfrac{ax+b}{cx+d}$

$$f(x+h) = \frac{a(x+h)+b}{c(x+h)+d}$$

$\therefore \, \dfrac{d}{dx}f(x) = \lim_{h \to 0}\dfrac{1}{h}[f(x+h) - f(x)]$

$$= \lim_{h \to 0}\frac{1}{h}\left[\frac{a(x+h)+b}{c(x+h)+d} - \frac{ax+b}{cx+d}\right]$$

$$= \lim_{h \to 0}\frac{1}{h}\left[\frac{ax+b+ah}{c(x+h)+d} - \frac{ax+b}{cx+d}\right]$$

$$= \lim_{h \to 0}\frac{1}{h}\left[\frac{(ax+ah+b)(cx+d) - (ax+b\{c(x+h)+d\}}{\{c(x+h)+d\}(cx+d)}\right]$$

$$= \lim_{h \to 0}\frac{1}{h}\left[\frac{(ax+ah+b)(cx+d) - (ax+b)(cx+ch+d)}{\{c(x+h)+d\}(cx+d)}\right]$$

$$= \lim_{h \to 0}\frac{1}{h}\left[\frac{\begin{array}{l}acx^2 + achx + bcx + adx + adh + bd\\ - \{acx^2 + achx + adx + bcx + bch + bd\}\end{array}}{\{c(x+h)+d\}(cx+d)}\right]$$

$$= \lim_{h \to 0}\frac{1}{h}\left[\frac{\begin{array}{l}acx^2 + achx + bcx + adx + adh + bd\\ - acx^2 - achx - adx - bcx - bch - bd\end{array}}{\{c(x+h)+d\}(cx+d)}\right]$$

$$= \lim_{h \to 0}\frac{1}{h}\left[\frac{adh - bch}{\{c(x+h)+d\}(cx+d)}\right]$$

$$= \lim_{h \to 0}\frac{ac - bd}{\{c(x+h)+d\}(cx+d)}$$

$$= \frac{ac - bd}{(cx+d)^2}$$

Example 3. Find the derivative of $x^4 + 3x^{5/3} + 10x + 7$.

Sol. Let $y = x^4 + 3x^{5/3} + 10x + 7$

On differentiating both sides, w.r.t. x, we get

$$\frac{dy}{dx} = \frac{d}{dx}(x^4 + 3x^{5/3} + 10x + 7)$$

$$= \frac{d}{dx}(x^4) + \frac{d}{dx}(3x^{5/3}) + \frac{d}{dx}(10x) + \frac{d}{dx}(7)$$

[using sum and difference rule]

$$= 4x^{4-1} + 3\left(\frac{5}{3}\right)x^{\frac{5}{3}-1} + 10x^{1-1} + 0$$

$$\left[\because \frac{d}{dx}x^n = nx^{n-1}; \frac{d}{dx}(cx^n) = cnx^{n-1}\right.$$

$$\left. \text{and } \frac{d}{dx}(\text{constant}) = 0\right]$$

$$= 4x^3 + 5x^{2/3} + 10$$

Example 4. If $f(x) = \dfrac{x^3 + 2x^2 + x + 4}{3x^2 + 2x + 5}$, then find the derivative of function.

Sol. Given, $f(x) = \dfrac{x^3 + 2x^2 + x + 4}{3x^2 + 2x + 5}$

$$f'(x) = \frac{dy}{dx}$$

$$= \frac{(3x^2 + 2x + 5)\dfrac{d}{dx}(x^3 + 2x^2 + x + 4) - (x^3 + 2x^2 + x + 4)\dfrac{d}{dx}(3x^2 + 2x + 5)}{(3x^2 + 2x + 5)^2}$$

[by using quotient rule of derivative]

$$= \frac{(3x^2 + 2x + 5)(3x^2 + 4x + 1) - (x^3 + 2x^2 + x + 4)(6x + 2)}{(3x^2 + 2x + 5)^2}$$

$$= \frac{\begin{aligned}&9x^4 + 6x^3 + 15x^2 + 12x^3 + 8x^2 + 20x + 3x^2 + 2x + 5\\ &- 6x^4 - 12x^3 - 6x^2 - 24x - 2x^3 - 4x^2 - 2x - 8\end{aligned}}{(3x^2 + 2x + 5)^2}$$

$$= \frac{3x^4 + 4x^3 + 16x^2 - 4x - 3}{(3x^2 + 2x + 5)^2}$$

Example 5. Find $\dfrac{dy}{dx}$ of $f(x) = \dfrac{1}{ax^2 + bx + c}$.

Sol. Let $y = \dfrac{1}{ax^2 + bx + c} = (ax^2 + bx + c)^{-1}$

$$\therefore \quad \frac{dy}{dx} = -(ax^2 + bx + c)^{-2}(2ax + b) \qquad \text{[by chain rule]}$$

$$= \frac{-(2ax + b)}{(ax^2 + bx + c)^2}$$

Example 6. If $x^y = e^{x-y}$, then prove that $\dfrac{dy}{dx} = \dfrac{\log x}{(1 + \log x)^2}$.

Sol. Given, $x^y = e^{x-y}$

On taking log both sides, we get

$$y \log_e x = (x - y)\log_e e$$

$$\Rightarrow \quad y \log_e x = x - y \qquad [\because \log_e e = 1]$$

$$\Rightarrow \quad y(1 + \log x) = x$$

$$\Rightarrow \quad y = \frac{x}{1 + \log x}$$

On differentiating both sides w.r.t. x, we get

$$\frac{dy}{dx} = \frac{(1 + \log x)\dfrac{d}{dx}(x) - x\dfrac{d}{dx}(1 + \log x)}{(1 + \log x)^2}$$

[by using quotient rule of derivative]

$$= \frac{1 + \log x - x \cdot \dfrac{1}{x}}{(1 + \log x)^2}$$

$$= \frac{1 + \log x - 1}{(1 + \log x)^2}$$

Hence, $\dfrac{dy}{dx} = \dfrac{\log x}{(1 + \log x)^2}$ **Hence proved.**

Example 7. Differentiate the following function with respect to x.

$$(\log x)^x + x^{\log x}$$

Sol. Let $y = (\log x)^x + x^{\log x}$

Also, let $u = (\log x)^x$ and $v = x^{\log x}$, then $y = u + v$

$$\Rightarrow \quad \frac{dy}{dx} = \frac{du}{dx} + \frac{dv}{dx} \qquad \dots\text{(i)}$$

Now, consider $u = (\log x)^x$

On taking log both sides, we get

$$\log u = \log(\log x)^x = x \log(\log x)$$

On differentiating both sides w.r.t. x, we get

$$\frac{1}{u}\frac{du}{dx} = x \cdot \frac{d}{dx}\log(\log x) + \log(\log x) \cdot \frac{d}{dx}(x)$$

$$= \frac{x}{\log x} \cdot \frac{1}{x} + \log(\log x)$$

$$\frac{du}{dx} = u\left[\frac{1}{\log x} + \log(\log x)\right]$$

$$\Rightarrow \quad \frac{du}{dx} = (\log x)^x\left[\frac{1}{\log x} + \log(\log x)\right] \qquad \dots\text{(ii)}$$

$$[\because u = (\log x)^x]$$

Since, $v = x^{\log x}$

On taking log both sides, we get

$$\log v = \log(x^{\log x})$$

$$= (\log x)(\log x) = (\log x)^2$$

On differentiating both sides w.r.t. x, we get

$$\frac{1}{v}\frac{dv}{dx} = 2\log x \cdot \frac{1}{x}$$

$$\Rightarrow \quad \frac{dv}{dx} = v\left[\frac{2\log x}{x}\right]$$

$$\Rightarrow \quad \frac{dv}{dx} = x^{\log x}\left[\frac{2\log x}{x}\right] \qquad [\because v = x^{\log x}] \dots\text{(iii)}$$

From Eqs. (i), (ii) and (iii), we get

$$\frac{dy}{dx} = (\log x)^x\left\{\frac{1}{\log x} + \log(\log x)\right\} + 2\left(\frac{\log x}{x}\right)x^{\log x}$$

Example 8. If $\log(\sqrt{1+x^2}-x)=y\sqrt{1+x^2}$, then show that $(1+x^2)\dfrac{dy}{dx}+xy+1=0$.

Sol. Given, $\log(\sqrt{1+x^2}-x)=y\sqrt{1+x^2}$ ...(i)

On differentiating both sides w.r.t. x, we get

$$\frac{1}{\sqrt{1+x^2}-x}\frac{d}{dx}[\sqrt{1+x^2}-x]$$

$$=y\frac{d}{dx}\sqrt{1+x^2}+\sqrt{1+x^2}\frac{dy}{dx}$$

[by using chain rule and product rule of derivative]

$$\Rightarrow \frac{1}{\sqrt{1+x^2}-x}\left[\frac{1}{2\sqrt{1+x^2}}\frac{d}{dx}(1+x^2)-1\right]$$

$$=\frac{y}{2\sqrt{1+x^2}}\frac{d}{dx}(1+x^2)+\sqrt{1+x^2}\frac{dy}{dx}$$

$$\Rightarrow \frac{1}{\sqrt{1+x^2}-x}\left[\frac{2x}{2\sqrt{1+x^2}}-1\right]$$

$$=y\times\frac{2x}{2\sqrt{1+x^2}}+\sqrt{1+x^2}\cdot\frac{dy}{dx}$$

$$\Rightarrow \frac{1}{\sqrt{1+x^2}-x}\left[\frac{x-\sqrt{1+x^2}}{\sqrt{1+x^2}}\right]$$

$$=\frac{xy}{\sqrt{1+x^2}}+\sqrt{1+x^2}\cdot\frac{dy}{dx}$$

$$\Rightarrow \frac{-1}{\sqrt{1+x^2}}=\frac{xy+(1+x^2)\dfrac{dy}{dx}}{\sqrt{1+x^2}}$$

$$\Rightarrow -1=xy+(1+x^2)\frac{dy}{dx}$$

$$\therefore \quad (1+x^2)\frac{dy}{dx}+xy+1=0 \qquad \textbf{Hence proved.}$$

Example 9. If $y=\log[x+\sqrt{x^2+a^2}]$, then show that $(x^2+a^2)\dfrac{d^2y}{dx^2}+x\dfrac{dy}{dx}=0$.

Sol. Given, $y=\log[x+\sqrt{x^2+a^2}]$

On differentiating both sides w.r.t. x, we get

$$\frac{dy}{dx}=\frac{1}{x+\sqrt{x^2+a^2}}\frac{d}{dx}\left(x+\sqrt{x^2+a^2}\right)$$

$$\left[\because \frac{d}{dx}(\log f(x))=\frac{1}{f(x)}\frac{d}{dx}f(x)\right]$$

$$\Rightarrow \frac{dy}{dx}=\frac{1}{x+\sqrt{x^2+a^2}}\left(1+\frac{2x}{2\sqrt{x^2+a^2}}\right)$$

$$\left[\because \frac{d}{dx}\left(\sqrt{x^2+a^2}\right)=\frac{1}{2\sqrt{x^2+a^2}}\times 2x\right]$$

$$\Rightarrow \frac{dy}{dx}=\frac{1}{x+\sqrt{x^2+a^2}}\left(\frac{\sqrt{x^2+a^2}+x}{\sqrt{x^2+a^2}}\right)$$

$$\Rightarrow \frac{dy}{dx}\left(\sqrt{x^2+a^2}\right)=1$$

Again, on differentiating both sides w.r.t. x, we get

$$\sqrt{x^2+a^2}\frac{d}{dx}\left(\frac{dy}{dx}\right)+\frac{dy}{dx}\cdot\frac{d}{dx}\left(\sqrt{x^2+a^2}\right)=\frac{d(1)}{dx}$$

[by using product rule of derivative]

$$\Rightarrow \frac{d^2y}{dx^2}\left(\sqrt{x^2+a^2}\right)+\frac{dy}{dx}\frac{1\cdot 2x}{2\sqrt{x^2+a^2}}=0 \qquad (1)$$

On multiplying both sides by $\sqrt{x^2+a^2}$, we get

$$\frac{d^2y}{dx^2}\left(\sqrt{x^2+a^2}\right)^2+\frac{dy}{dx}\times\frac{x\sqrt{x^2+a^2}}{\sqrt{x^2+a^2}}=0$$

$$\therefore \quad (x^2+a^2)\frac{d^2y}{dx^2}+x\frac{dy}{dx}=0 \qquad \textbf{Hence proved.}$$

Chapter Practice

Objective Questions

- **Multiple Choice Questions**

1. If $f(x) = 2x + 3$, then $f'(3)$ is equal to

(a) 1   (b) 2
(c) 3   (d) 0

2. $\dfrac{d}{dx}\left(\dfrac{1}{\log_e x}\right)$ is equal to

(a) x (b) $-\dfrac{1}{x^2}$ (c) $-x$ (d) $-\dfrac{1}{x}$

3. If $y = \log(1 + x^2)$, then $\dfrac{dy}{dx}$ is equal to

(a) $\dfrac{2}{1 + x^2}$ (b) $\dfrac{x}{1 + x^2}$

(c) $\dfrac{2x}{1 + x^2}$ (d) None of these

4. If $y = \sqrt{x} + \dfrac{1}{\sqrt{x}}$, then $2x\dfrac{dy}{dx}$ is equal to

(a) $\sqrt{x} + \dfrac{1}{\sqrt{x}}$ (b) $\sqrt{x} - \dfrac{1}{\sqrt{x}}$

(c) 0   (d) None of these

5. If $y = 3^{x^2 + 2x}$ and $\dfrac{dy}{dx} = ky(x + 1)$, then k is equal to

(a) $\log 9$ (b) $\log 3$
(c) $\log 27$ (d) None of these

6. If $y = \log_{10} 10 + \log_x x$, then $\dfrac{dy}{dx}$ is equal to

(a) 1   (b) $\dfrac{1}{x}$

(c) x (d) 0

7. If $f(x) = 1 + x + \dfrac{x^2}{2} + \dots + \dfrac{x^{100}}{100}$, then $f'(1)$ is equal to

(a) 0   (b) 50

(c) 100   (d) $\dfrac{1}{100}$

8. If $f(x) = \dfrac{x - 4}{2\sqrt{x}}$, then $f'(1)$ is equal to

(a) $\dfrac{5}{4}$ (b) $\dfrac{4}{5}$
(c) 1   (d) 0

9. If $f(x) = (ax^2 + b)^2$ and $f'(x) = g(x)(ax^2 + b)$, then $g(x)$ is equal to

(a) ax (b) $2ax$
(c) $3ax$ (d) $4ax$

10. If $f(x) = \log(3x + 2)$ and $f'(x) = \dfrac{\lambda}{3x + 2}$, then λ is a polynomial of degree

(a) 0   (b) 1
(c) 2   (d) 3

11. If $xy = 4$, then $x\left(\dfrac{dy}{dx} + y^2\right)$ is equal to

(a) y (b) $2y$
(c) $3y$ (d) $4y$

12. If $y = \sqrt{x^2 + x + 1}$, then $y\dfrac{dy}{dx}$ is equal to

(a) $2x + 1$ (b) $\dfrac{1}{2}(2x + 1)$

(c) $\dfrac{1}{4}(2x + 1)$ (d) None of these

13. If $f(x) = \dfrac{e^x + e^{-x}}{e^x - e^{-x}}$ and $f'(x) = \dfrac{k}{(e^x - e^{-x})^2}$, then k is equal to

(a) 2   (b) 4
(c) -2 (d) -4

14. If $y = \dfrac{1}{(x^2 + 3)^2}$, then $\dfrac{dy}{dx}$ is equal to

(a) $\dfrac{4x}{(x^2 + 3)^3}$

(b) $\dfrac{-4x}{(x^2 + 3)^3}$

(c) $\dfrac{2x}{(x^2 + 3)^3}$

(d) $\dfrac{-2x}{(x^2 + 3)^3}$

15. If $y = \left(\dfrac{x^a}{x^b}\right)^{a+b} \cdot \left(\dfrac{x^b}{x^c}\right)^{b+c} \cdot \left(\dfrac{x^c}{x^a}\right)^{c+a}$, then $\dfrac{dy}{dx}$ is equal to

(a) 0   (b) 1

(c) x (d) $-x$

• Case Based MCQs

16. Let $f(x)$ be a differentiable function.

Consider the curve $y = f(x)$.

Then, derivative of the function $y = f(x)$ at point $P(x_1, y_1)$ gives the slope of tangent at point $P(x_1,\ y_1)$. On the basis of above information, answer the following questions.

(i) If $y = \dfrac{x-1}{x+2}$, then $\dfrac{dy}{dx}$ is equal to

(a) $\dfrac{1}{(x+2)^2}$ (b) $\dfrac{2}{(x+2)^2}$

(c) $\dfrac{3}{(x+2)^2}$ (d) $\dfrac{4}{(x+2)^2}$

(ii) If $y = 2x^6 + x^4 - 1$, then slope of tangent at $x = 1$ is equal to

(a) 16   (b) 14

(c) 12   (d) 10

(iii) If $y = x^3 - x^2 + 3x + 1$, then value of $\dfrac{dy}{dx}$ at $x = 1$ is equal to

(a) 1   (b) 2

(c) 3   (d) 4

(iv) If $y = \dfrac{e^x}{x+1}$, then at $x = 0$, then value of $\dfrac{dy}{dx}$ is equal to

(a) $\dfrac{e^x}{(x+1)^2}$ (b) $\dfrac{xe^x}{(x+1)^2}$

(c) $\dfrac{xe^x}{(x+1)}$ (d) None of these

(v) If $y = \dfrac{1}{f(x)}$, and $\dfrac{dy}{dx} = \dfrac{k \cdot f'(x)}{[f(x)]^2}$, then k is equal to

(a) 1   (b) -1

(c) 2   (d) -2

PART 2
Subjective Questions

• Short Answer Type Questions

1. If $f(x) = x^2 + 1$, then find $f'(2)$ from first principle..

2. Find the derivative of $f(x) = \dfrac{1}{x}$ from first principle.

3. Find the derivative of $f(x) = ax + b$, where a and b are non-zero constants, by first principle.

4. Find the derivative of $(x-1)(x-2)$ from first principle.

5. Find the derivative of $\left(\dfrac{x+1}{x-1}\right)$ from the first principle.

6. Find the derivative of e^x, using first principle.

7. Find the derivative of a^x from first principle.

8. Find the derivative of e^{x^2} from first principle.

9. Find the derivative of $e^{\sqrt{x}}$ from first principle.

10. Find the derivative of the function $\log x$, by using first principle.

11. If $y = 1 + \dfrac{x}{1!} + \dfrac{x^2}{2!} + \dfrac{x^3}{3!} + \dots$, show that $\dfrac{dy}{dx} = y$.

12. If $y = (x-1)\log(x-1) - (x+1)\log(x+1)$, prove that $\dfrac{dy}{dx} = \log\left(\dfrac{x-1}{1+x}\right)$.

13. Find the differential coefficient of $(7x^5 + 9)(px^{7/2} + q)$.

14. If $f(x) = x^n + x^{n-1} + x^{n-2} + \dots + x^2 + x + 1$, then $f'(1) = 5050$. Find the value of n.

• Long Answer Type Questions

15. Find the derivative of $f(x) = 2x^2 + 3x - 5$ using first principle. Also, prove that $f'(0) + 3f'(-1) = 0$.

16. If $y = [x + \sqrt{x^2 + a^2}\,]^n$, then prove that

$$\frac{dy}{dx} = \frac{ny}{\sqrt{x^2 + a^2}}.$$

17. If $y = \dfrac{x}{x+5}$, then prove that $x\dfrac{dy}{dx} = y(1-y)$.

18. Differentiate $\dfrac{x^2 + 3x - 9}{x^2 - 9x + 3}$ w.r.t. x.

19. Find the derivative of $f(x) = x^n$, where n is positive integer, by first principle.

• Case Based Questions

20. $\dfrac{d}{dx}$ is an operator such that when it is applied on

$y = f(x)$, gives us $\dfrac{d}{dx}[f(x)] = \dfrac{dy}{dx}$. The operator $\dfrac{d}{dx}$ is called the differential operator.

Input

f(x)

Operator

$\dfrac{d}{dx}$

$\dfrac{d}{dx} f(x)$

Operator

On the basis of above information, answer the following questions.

(i) Find the derivative of $e^{\sqrt{x}}$.

(ii) Find the derivative of $x^2 e^x$.

(iii) Find the derivative of $\dfrac{x}{x+1}$.

(iv) Find the derivative of $\log(x^2 + 3x + 1)$.

SOLUTIONS

Objective Questions

1. (b) We have, $f(x) = 2x + 3$

$$\Rightarrow \quad f'(3) = \lim_{h \to 0} \frac{f(3+h) - f(3)}{h}$$

$$= \lim_{h \to 0} \frac{[2(3+h) + 3] - [2 \times 3 + 3]}{h}$$

$$= \lim_{h \to 0} \frac{9 + 2h - 9}{h}$$

$$= \lim_{h \to 0} 2$$

$$= 2$$

2. (d) Let $y = \dfrac{1}{\log_e x} = (\log_e x)^{-1} = -\log_e x$

$$\therefore \quad \frac{dy}{dx} = -\frac{1}{x}$$

3. (c) We have, $y = \log(1 + x^2)$

$$\Rightarrow \quad \frac{dy}{dx} = \frac{1}{1+x^2} \cdot (0 + 2x) = \frac{2x}{1+x^2}$$

4. (b) We have, $y = \sqrt{x} + \dfrac{1}{\sqrt{x}}$

$$\Rightarrow \quad \frac{dy}{dx} = \frac{1}{2\sqrt{x}} - \frac{1}{2x\sqrt{x}}$$

$$\Rightarrow \quad 2x\frac{dy}{dx} = 2x\left[\frac{1}{2\sqrt{x}} - \frac{1}{2x\sqrt{x}}\right]$$

$$= \sqrt{x} - \frac{1}{\sqrt{x}}$$

5. (a) We have, $y = 3^{x^2 + 2x}$

$$\Rightarrow \quad \frac{dy}{dx} = 3^{x^2 + 2x} \cdot \log 3 \cdot (2x + 2)$$

$$= 2\log 3 \cdot 3^{x^2 + 2x} \cdot (x + 1)$$

$$= 2\log 3 y(x + 1)$$

$$\therefore \quad k = 2\log 3 = \log 3^2 = \log 9$$

6. (d) We have, $y = \log_{10} 10 + \log_x x$

$$= 1 + 1$$

$$= 2$$

$$\therefore \quad \frac{dy}{dx} = 0$$

7. (c) We have, $f(x) = 1 + x + \dfrac{x^2}{2} + \ldots + \dfrac{x^{100}}{100}$

$$\therefore \quad f'(x) = 0 + 1 + \frac{2x}{2} + \ldots + \frac{100x^{99}}{100}$$

$$= 1 + x + \ldots + x^{99}$$

$$\therefore \quad f'(1) = 1 + 1 + \ldots + 1 = 100$$

8. (a) We have, $f(x) = \dfrac{x - 4}{2\sqrt{x}}$

$$\therefore \quad f'(x) = \frac{1 \cdot (2\sqrt{x}) - (x - 4) \cdot 2\dfrac{1}{2\sqrt{x}}}{4x}$$

$$= \frac{2x - x + 4}{4x\sqrt{x}}$$

$$= \frac{x + 4}{4x\sqrt{x}}$$

$$\therefore \quad f'(1) = \frac{1 + 4}{4(1)\sqrt{1}} = \frac{5}{4}$$

9. (d) We have, $f(x) = (ax^2 + b)^2$

$$\therefore \quad f'(x) = 2(ax^2 + b)(2ax + 0) = 4ax(ax^2 + b)$$

$$\therefore \quad g(x) = 4ax$$

10. (d) We have, $f(x) = \log(3x + 2)$

$\therefore \qquad f'(x) = \dfrac{1}{3x + 2} \cdot 3 = \dfrac{3}{3x + 2}$

$\therefore \qquad \lambda = 3,$

which is a constant polynomial of degree zero.

11. (c) We have, $\quad xy = 4$

$\therefore \qquad 1 \cdot y + x\dfrac{dy}{dx} = 0$

$\Rightarrow \qquad \dfrac{dy}{dx} = -\dfrac{y}{x}$

Now, $x\left(\dfrac{dy}{dx} + y^2\right) = x\left(-\dfrac{y}{x} + y^2\right)$

$\qquad\qquad = -y + xy^2$

$\qquad\qquad = -y + (xy) \cdot y$

$\qquad\qquad = -y + 4y \qquad\qquad [\because xy = 4]$

$\qquad\qquad = 3y$

12. (b) We have, $\quad y = \sqrt{x^2 + x + 1}$

$\therefore \qquad \dfrac{dy}{dx} = \dfrac{1}{2\sqrt{x^2 + x + 1}} \cdot (2x + 1 + 0)$

$\Rightarrow \sqrt{x^2 + x + 1} \cdot \dfrac{dy}{dx} = \dfrac{1}{2}(2x + 1)$

$\Rightarrow \qquad y\dfrac{dy}{dx} = \dfrac{1}{2}(2x + 1)$

13. (d) We have,

$$f(x) = \dfrac{e^x + e^{-x}}{e^x - e^{-x}}$$

$\therefore \quad f'(x) = \dfrac{(e^x - e^{-x})(e^x - e^{-x}) - (e^x + e^{-x})(e^x - (-e^{-x}))}{(e^x - e^{-x})^2}$

$\qquad = \dfrac{(e^x - e^{-x})^2 - (e^x + e^{-x})^2}{(e^x - e^{-x})^2}$

$\qquad = \dfrac{(e^{2x} + e^{-2x} - 2e^x \cdot e^{-x}) - (e^{2x} + e^{-2x} + 2e^x \cdot e^{-x})}{(e^x - e^{-x})^2}$

$\qquad = \dfrac{-4}{(e^x - e^{-x})^2}$

$\therefore \qquad k = -4$

14. (b) We have, $\quad y = \dfrac{1}{(x^2 + 3)^2} = (x^2 + 3)^{-2}$

$\therefore \qquad \dfrac{dy}{dx} = -2(x^2 + 3)^{-3}(2x)$

$\qquad\qquad = \dfrac{-4x}{(x^2 + 3)^3}$

15. (a) We have, $\quad y = \left(\dfrac{x^a}{x^b}\right)^{a+b} \cdot \left(\dfrac{x^b}{x^c}\right)^{b+c} \cdot \left(\dfrac{x^c}{x^a}\right)^{c+a}$

$\qquad = (x^{a-b})^{a+b} \cdot (x^{b-c})^{(b+c)} \cdot (x^{c-a})^{(c+a)}$

$\qquad = x^{a^2 - b^2 + b^2 - c^2 + c^2 - a^2}$

$\qquad = x^0 = 1$

$\therefore \qquad \dfrac{dy}{dx} = 0$

16. (i) (c) We have,

$$y = \dfrac{x - 1}{x + 2}$$

$\Rightarrow \quad \dfrac{dy}{dx} = \dfrac{(1 - 0)(x + 2) - (x - 1)(1 + 0)}{(x + 2)^2}$

$\qquad = \dfrac{x + 2 - x + 1}{(x + 2)^2} = \dfrac{3}{(x + 2)^2}$

(ii) (a) Slope of tangent $= \dfrac{dy}{dx}\Big|_{P(x_1, y_1)}$

$\qquad = \dfrac{d}{dx}(2x^6 + x^4 - 1)$

$\qquad = 12x^5 + 4x^3$

$\qquad = 12(1)^5 + 4(1)^3 \qquad [\because x = 1]$

$\qquad = 16$

(iii) (d) $y = x^3 - x^2 + 3x + 1$

$\therefore \dfrac{dy}{dx} = 3x^2 - 2x + 3$

So, at $x = 1$,

$\qquad \dfrac{dy}{dx} = 3(1)^2 - 2(1) + 3 = 4$

(iv) (b) $y = \dfrac{e^x}{x + 1}$

$\therefore \dfrac{dy}{dx} = \dfrac{(x + 1)\dfrac{d}{dx}e^x - e^x \cdot \dfrac{d}{dx}(x + 1)}{(x + 1)^2}$

$\qquad = \dfrac{(x + 1) \cdot e^x - e^x \cdot 1}{(x + 1)^2} = \dfrac{xe^x}{(x + 1)^2}$

(v) (b) $y = \dfrac{1}{f(x)} = [f(x)]^{-1}$

$\therefore \dfrac{dy}{dx} = -1 \cdot f[(x)]^{-1-1} \cdot f'(x)$

$\qquad = \dfrac{-f'(x)}{[f(x)]^2}$

$\therefore \qquad k = -1$

Subjective Questions

1. We have,

$$f(x) = x^2 + 1$$

$\therefore \qquad f'(2) = \lim_{h \to 0} \dfrac{f(2 + h) - f(2)}{h}$

$\qquad = \lim_{h \to 0} \dfrac{[(2 + h)^2 + 1] - [2^2 + 1]}{h}$

$\qquad = \lim_{h \to 0} \dfrac{(2 + h)^2 - 4}{h}$

$\qquad = \lim_{h \to 0} \dfrac{4 + h^2 + 4h - 4}{h}$

$\qquad = \lim_{h \to 0}(h + 4)$

$\qquad = 4$

2. We have, $f(x) = \dfrac{1}{x}$

By using first principle, $f'(x) = \lim\limits_{h \to 0} \dfrac{f(x+h) - f(x)}{h}$

$\therefore f'(x) = \lim\limits_{h \to 0} \dfrac{\dfrac{1}{x+h} - \dfrac{1}{x}}{h}$ $\qquad \left[\begin{array}{l} \because \quad f(x) = \dfrac{1}{x} \\ \therefore f(x+h) = \dfrac{1}{x+h} \end{array} \right]$

$= \lim\limits_{h \to 0} \dfrac{1}{h} \left[\dfrac{x - (x+h)}{x(x+h)} \right]$

$= \lim\limits_{h \to 0} \dfrac{1}{h} \left[\dfrac{-h}{x(x+h)} \right]$

$= \lim\limits_{h \to 0} \left[\dfrac{-1}{x(x+h)} \right] = \dfrac{-1}{x^2}$

3. We have, $f(x) = ax + b$

By definition of first principle, we have

$f'(x) = \lim\limits_{h \to 0} \dfrac{f(x+h) - f(x)}{h}$

$= \lim\limits_{h \to 0} \dfrac{a(x+h) + b - (ax+b)}{h}$

$= \lim\limits_{h \to 0} \dfrac{ah}{h} = a$

4. Let $f(x) = (x-1)(x-2) = x^2 - 3x + 2$

By first principle of derivative, we have

$f'(x) = \lim\limits_{h \to 0} \dfrac{f(x+h) - f(x)}{h}$

$= \lim\limits_{h \to 0} \dfrac{[(x+h)^2 - 3(x+h) + 2] - [x^2 - 3x + 2]}{h}$

$= \lim\limits_{h \to 0} \dfrac{[x^2 + h^2 + 2xh - 3x - 3h + 2] - [x^2 - 3x + 2]}{h}$

$= \lim\limits_{h \to 0} \dfrac{2hx + h^2 - 3h}{h}$

$= \lim\limits_{h \to 0} \dfrac{h(2x + h - 3)}{h} = 2x - 3$

5. Let $f(x) = \dfrac{x+1}{x-1}$

By first principle of derivative, we have

$f'(x) = \lim\limits_{h \to 0} \dfrac{f(x+h) - f(x)}{h}$

$= \lim\limits_{h \to 0} \dfrac{\left[\dfrac{(x+h)+1}{(x+h)-1} - \dfrac{x+1}{x-1} \right]}{h}$

$= \lim\limits_{h \to 0} \dfrac{(x+h+1)(x-1) - (x+1)(x+h-1)}{h(x+h-1)(x-1)}$

$= \lim\limits_{h \to 0} \dfrac{(x^2 - x + xh - h + x - 1) - (x^2 + xh - x + x + h - 1)}{h(x+h-1)(x-1)}$

$= \lim\limits_{h \to 0} \dfrac{-2h}{h(x+h-1)(x-1)}$

$= \lim\limits_{h \to 0} \dfrac{-2}{(x+h-1)(x-1)} = \dfrac{-2}{(x-1)^2}$

6. Let $f(x) = e^x$

By using first principle of derivative, we have

$f'(x) = \lim\limits_{h \to 0} \dfrac{f(x+h) - f(x)}{h}$

$= \lim\limits_{h \to 0} \dfrac{e^{x+h} - e^x}{h}$

$= \lim\limits_{h \to 0} \dfrac{e^x(e^h - 1)}{h}$

$= e^x \lim\limits_{h \to 0} \dfrac{(e^h - 1)}{h}$

$= \lim\limits_{h \to 0} \dfrac{\left[\left(1 + \dfrac{h}{1!} + \dfrac{h^2}{2!} + \dfrac{h^3}{3!} + \dots \infty \right) - 1 \right]}{h}$

$= \lim\limits_{h \to 0} \dfrac{h \left[1 + \dfrac{h}{2!} + \dfrac{h^2}{3!} + \dots \infty \right]}{h} = e^x \times 1 = e^x$

7. Let $f(x) = a^x$.

By using first principle of derivative, we have

$\therefore \qquad f'(x) = \lim\limits_{h \to 0} \dfrac{f(x+h) - f(x)}{h}$

$\Rightarrow \qquad f'(x) = \lim\limits_{h \to 0} \dfrac{a^{x+h} - a^x}{h} = \lim\limits_{h \to 0} \dfrac{a^x a^h - a^x}{h}$

$\Rightarrow \qquad f'(x) = a^x \lim\limits_{h \to 0} \left(\dfrac{a^h - 1}{h} \right) = a^x \log_e a$

$\qquad \left[\because \lim\limits_{x \to 0} \dfrac{a^x - 1}{x} = \log_e a \right]$

8. Let $f(x) = e^{x^2}$

By using first principle of derivative, we have

$f'(x) = \lim\limits_{h \to 0} \dfrac{f(x+h) - f(x)}{h}$

$= \lim\limits_{h \to 0} \dfrac{e^{(x+h)^2} - e^{x^2}}{h}$

$= \lim\limits_{h \to 0} \dfrac{e^{x^2 + h^2 + 2hx} - e^{x^2}}{h}$

$= \lim\limits_{h \to 0} e^{x^2} \left[\dfrac{e^{h(h+2x)} - 1}{h} \right] \times \dfrac{(h+2x)}{(h+2x)}$

$= e^{x^2} \lim\limits_{h \to 0} \left[\dfrac{e^{h(h+2x)} - 1}{h(h+2x)} \right] \times \lim\limits_{h \to 0}(h+2x)$

$= e^{x^2} \times 1 \times (0 + 2x)$

$= 2x \, e^{x^2}$ $\qquad \left[\because \lim\limits_{y \to 0} \dfrac{e^y - 1}{y} = 1 \right]$

9. Let $f(x) = e^{\sqrt{x}}$

By using first principle of derivative, we have

$f'(x) = \lim\limits_{h \to 0} \dfrac{f(x+h) - f(x)}{h}$

$= \lim\limits_{x \to 0} \dfrac{e^{\sqrt{x+h}} - e^{\sqrt{x}}}{h}$

$$= \lim_{h\to 0} \frac{e^{\sqrt{x}}(e^{\sqrt{x+h}-\sqrt{x}}-1)}{(x+h)-x}$$

$$= \lim_{h\to 0} \frac{e^{\sqrt{x}}(e^{\sqrt{x+h}-\sqrt{x}}-1)}{(\sqrt{x+h}-\sqrt{x})(\sqrt{x+h}+\sqrt{x})}$$

$$= e^{\sqrt{x}} \lim_{h\to 0} \frac{e^{\sqrt{x+h}-\sqrt{x}}-1}{(\sqrt{x+h}-\sqrt{x})} \times \lim_{h\to 0}\frac{1}{(\sqrt{x+h}+\sqrt{x})}$$

$$= e^{\sqrt{x}} \times 1 \times \frac{1}{2\sqrt{x}} = \frac{e^{\sqrt{x}}}{2\sqrt{x}} \qquad \left[\because \lim_{y\to 0}\frac{e^y-1}{y}=1\right]$$

10. Let $f(x)=\log x$

By using first principle of derivative, we have

$$f'(x) = \lim_{h\to 0}\frac{f(x+h)-f(x)}{h} = \lim_{h\to 0}\frac{\log(x+h)-\log x}{h}$$

$$= \lim_{h\to 0}\frac{\log\left(\dfrac{x+h}{x}\right)}{h} = \lim_{h\to 0}\frac{\log\left(1+\dfrac{h}{x}\right)}{\dfrac{h}{x}} \times \frac{1}{x}$$

$$= 1 \times \frac{1}{x} = \frac{1}{x} \qquad \left[\because \lim_{y\to 0}\log\left(\frac{1+y}{y}\right)=1\right]$$

11. We have, $y = 1 + \dfrac{x}{1!} + \dfrac{x^2}{2!} + \dfrac{x^3}{3!} + \ldots$

$$\frac{dy}{dx} = \frac{d}{dx}(1) + \frac{d}{dx}\left(\frac{x}{1!}\right) + \frac{d}{dx}\left(\frac{x^2}{2!}\right) + \frac{d}{dx}\left(\frac{x^3}{3!}\right) + \ldots$$

$$= \frac{d}{dx}(1) + \frac{1}{1!}\frac{d}{dx}(x) + \frac{1}{2!}\frac{d}{dx}(x)^2 + \frac{1}{3!}\frac{d}{dx}(x^3) + \ldots$$

$$= 0 + \frac{1}{1!}\cdot 1 + \frac{1}{2!}\cdot 2x + \frac{1}{3!}\cdot 3x^2 + \ldots$$

$$= 1 + x + \frac{x^2}{2!} + \ldots$$

$$= y$$

12. We have, $y = (x-1)\log(x-1) - (x+1)\log(x+1)$

$$\therefore \quad \frac{dy}{dx} = \frac{d}{dx}[(x-1)\log(x-1)] - \frac{d}{dx}[(x+1)\log(x+1)]$$

$$= \left[(x-1)\frac{d}{dx}\log(x-1) + \log(x-1)\cdot\frac{d}{dx}(x-1)\right]$$

$$\quad - \left[(x+1)\frac{d}{dx}\log(x+1) + \log(x+1)\frac{d}{dx}(x+1)\right]$$

$$= \left[\frac{x-1}{x-1} + \log(x-1)\cdot 1\right] - \left[\frac{x+1}{x+1} + \log(x+1)\cdot 1\right]$$

$$= 1 + \log(x-1) - 1 - \log(x+1)$$

$$= \log(x-1) - \log(x+1)$$

$$= \log\left(\frac{x-1}{x+1}\right)$$

13. Let $y = (7x^5 + 9)(px^{7/2} + q)$

On differentiating both sides w.r.t. x, we get

$$\frac{dy}{dx} = (7x^5 + 9)\frac{d}{dx}(px^{7/2} + q) + (px^{7/2} + q)\frac{d}{dx}(7x^5 + 9)$$

[using product rule]

$$= (7x^5 + 9)\left(p\cdot\frac{7}{2}x^{\frac{7}{2}-1} + 0\right) + (px^{7/2} + q)(7\cdot 5x^{5-1} + 0)$$

$$= \frac{7p}{2}x^{5/2}(7x^5 + 9) + 35x^4(px^{7/2} + q)$$

14. We have,

$$f(x) = x^n + x^{n-1} + x^{n-2} + \ldots + x^2 + x + 1$$

$$\therefore \quad f'(x) = nx^{n-1} + (n-1)x^{n-2} + (n-2)x^{n-3}$$
$$\qquad\qquad\qquad + \ldots + 2x + 1 + 0$$

$$= nx^{n-1} + (n-1)x^{n-2} + (n-2)x^{n-3} + \ldots + 2x + 1$$

$$\therefore \quad f'(1) = n(1)^{n-1} + (n-1)(1)^{n-2} + (n-2)(1)^{n-3}$$
$$\qquad\qquad\qquad + \ldots + 2(1) + 1$$

$$= n + (n-1) + (n-2) + \ldots + 2 + 1 = \frac{n(n+1)}{2}$$

Now, $\qquad f'(1) = 5050 \Rightarrow \dfrac{n(n+1)}{2} = 5050$

$$\Rightarrow \qquad n(n+1) = 2 \times 5050$$

$$\Rightarrow \qquad n(n+1) = 101 \times 100 \Rightarrow n = 100$$

15. We have, $f(x) = 2x^2 + 3x - 5$

$$\therefore \quad f'(x) = \lim_{h\to 0}\frac{f(x+h)-f(x)}{h}$$

$$= \lim_{h\to 0}\frac{[2(x+h)^2 + 3(x+h) - 5] - [2x^2 + 3x - 5]}{h}$$

$$= \lim_{h\to 0}\frac{2x^2 + 4hx + 2h^2 + 3x + 3h - 5 - 2x^2 - 3x + 5}{h}$$

$$= \lim_{h\to 0}\frac{4hx + 2h^2 + 3h}{h}$$

$$= \lim_{h\to 0}(4x + 2h + 3) = 4x + 3$$

Again, $f'(0) + 3f'(-1) = (4\times 0 + 3) + 3[4(-1) + 3]$
$$= 0 + 3 + 3(-4 + 3) = 3 - 3 = 0$$

16. We have, $y = \left[x + \sqrt{x^2 + a^2}\right]^n$

On differentiating both sides w.r.t. x, we get

$$\frac{dy}{dx} = n\left[x + \sqrt{x^2 + a^2}\right]^{n-1} \cdot \frac{d}{dx}\left[x + \sqrt{x^2 + a^2}\right]$$

[by chain rule of derivative]

$$= n\left[x + \sqrt{x^2 + a^2}\right]^{n-1}\left[1 + \frac{1}{2\sqrt{x^2 + a^2}}\frac{d}{dx}(x^2 + a^2)\right]$$

[by chain rule of derivative]

$$= n\left[x + \sqrt{x^2 + a^2}\right]^{n-1}\left[1 + \frac{1}{2\sqrt{x^2 + a^2}}\cdot 2x\right]$$

$$= n\left[x + \sqrt{x^2 + a^2}\right]^{n-1}\left[\frac{\sqrt{x^2 + a^2} + x}{\sqrt{x^2 + a^2}}\right]$$

$$= \frac{n\left[x + \sqrt{x^2 + a^2}\right]^n}{\sqrt{x^2 + a^2}}$$

$$\Rightarrow \frac{dy}{dx} = \frac{ny}{\sqrt{x^2 + a^2}} \qquad \left[\because y = (x + \sqrt{x^2 + a^2})^n\right]$$

Hence proved.

17. We have, $y = \dfrac{x}{x+5}$ ...(i)

On differentiating both sides of Eq. (i) w.r.t. x, we get

$$\frac{dy}{dx} = \frac{d}{dx}\left(\frac{x}{x+5}\right)$$

$$= \frac{(x+5)\dfrac{d}{dx}x - x\dfrac{d}{dx}(x+5)}{(x+5)^2}$$

$$\left[\because \frac{d}{dx}\left(\frac{u}{v}\right) = \frac{v\dfrac{du}{dx} - u\dfrac{dv}{dx}}{v^2}\right]$$

$$= \frac{(x+5)(1) - x(1+0)}{(x+5)^2} = \frac{x+5-x}{(x+5)^2}$$

$$\Rightarrow \quad \frac{dy}{dx} = \frac{5}{(x+5)^2}$$

Now, LHS $= x\dfrac{dy}{dx} = \dfrac{5x}{(x+5)^2}$ ...(ii)

and RHS $= y(1-y) = \dfrac{x}{x+5}\left(1 - \dfrac{x}{x+5}\right)$

$$= \frac{x}{x+5}\left(\frac{x+5-x}{x+5}\right) = \frac{5x}{(x+5)^2} \quad ...(iii)$$

From Eqs. (ii) and (iii), we get

$$x\frac{dy}{dx} = y(1-y) \qquad \textbf{Hence proved.}$$

18. Let $y = \dfrac{x^2 + 3x - 9}{x^2 - 9x + 3}$

On differentiating both sides w.r.t. x, we get

$$\frac{dy}{dx} = \frac{d}{dx}\left[\frac{x^2 + 3x - 9}{x^2 - 9x + 3}\right]$$

$$= \frac{\left\{(x^2 - 9x + 3)\left[\dfrac{d}{dx}(x^2 + 3x - 9)\right] - (x^2 + 3x - 9)\dfrac{d}{dx}(x^2 - 9x + 3)\right\}}{(x^2 - 9x + 3)^2}$$

[using quotient rule of derivative]

$$= \frac{\left[(x^2 - 9x + 3)(2x + 3 - 0) - (x^2 + 3x - 9) \times (2x - 9 + 0)\right]}{(x^2 - 9x + 3)^2}$$

$$= \frac{[(x^2 - 9x + 3)(2x + 3) - (x^2 + 3x - 9)(2x - 9)]}{(x^2 - 9x + 3)^2}$$

$$= \frac{\left[2x(x^2 - 9x + 3) + 3(x^2 - 9x + 3) - 2x(x^2 + 3x - 9) + 9(x^2 + 3x - 9)\right]}{(x^2 - 9x + 3)^2}$$

$$= \frac{\left[2x(x^2 - 9x + 3 - x^2 - 3x + 9) + (3x^2 - 27x + 9 + 9x^2 + 27x - 81)\right]}{(x^2 - 9x + 3)^2}$$

$$= \frac{2x(-12x + 12) + (12x^2 - 72)}{(x^2 - 9x + 3)^2}$$

$$= \frac{-24x^2 + 24x + 12x^2 - 72}{(x^2 - 9x + 3)^2}$$

$$= \frac{-12x^2 + 24x - 72}{(x^2 - 9x + 3)^2} = \frac{-12(x^2 - 2x + 6)}{(x^2 - 9x + 3)^2}$$

19. By definition of first principle, we have

$$f'(x) = \lim_{h\to 0}\frac{f(x+h) - f(x)}{h} = \lim_{h\to 0}\frac{(x+h)^n - x^n}{h} \quad ...(i)$$

By binomial theorem, we have

$$(x+h)^n = {}^nC_0 x^n + {}^nC_1 x^{n-1}h + {}^nC_2 x^{n-2}h^2 + ... + {}^nC_n h^n$$

$$\Rightarrow \quad (x+h)^n = x^n + nhx^{n-1} + \frac{n(n-1)}{2}h^2 x^{n-2} + ... + h^n$$

$$\Rightarrow (x+h)^n - x^n = nhx^{n-1} + \frac{n(n-1)}{2}h^2 x^{n-2} + ... + h^n$$

On putting this value in Eq. (i), we get

$$f'(x) = \lim_{h\to 0}\frac{nhx^{n-1} + \dfrac{n(n-1)}{2}h^2 x^{n-2} + ... + h^n}{h}$$

$$= \lim_{h\to 0}\frac{h\left(nx^{n-1} + \dfrac{n(n-1)}{2}hx^{n-2} + ... + h^{n-1}\right)}{h}$$

$$= \lim_{n\to 0}\left[nx^{n-1} + \frac{n(n-1)}{2}hx^{n-2} + ... + h^{n-1}\right] = nx^{n-1}$$

Hence, $f'(x)$ or $\dfrac{d}{dx}f(x) = nx^{n-1}$.

20. (i) Let $y = e^{\sqrt{x}}$

$$\therefore \frac{dy}{dx} = \frac{d}{dx}(e^{\sqrt{x}}) = e^{\sqrt{x}} \cdot \frac{d}{dx}(\sqrt{x})$$

$$= e^{\sqrt{x}} \cdot \frac{1}{2\sqrt{x}} = \frac{e^{\sqrt{x}}}{2\sqrt{x}}$$

(ii) Let $y = x^2 e^x$

$$\therefore \frac{dy}{dx} = e^x \cdot \frac{d}{dx}(x^2) + x^2\frac{d}{dx}(e^x) = e^x(2x) + x^2(e^x)$$

$$= 2xe^x + x^2 e^x = xe^x(2 + x)$$

(iii) Let $y = \dfrac{x}{x+1}$

$$\therefore \frac{dy}{dx} = \frac{(x+1)\cdot\dfrac{d}{dx}(x) - x\dfrac{d}{dx}(x+1)}{(x+1)^2}$$

$$= \frac{1.(x+1) - x(1+0)}{(x+1)^2} = \frac{x+1-x}{(x+1)^2} = \frac{1}{(x+1)^2}$$

(iv) Let $y = \log(x^2 + 3x + 1)$

$$\therefore \frac{dy}{dx} = \frac{d}{dx}\log(x^2 + 3x + 1)$$

$$= \frac{1}{x^2 + 3x + 1}\frac{d}{dx}(x^2 + 3x + 1) = \frac{2x + 3}{x^2 + 3x + 1}$$

Chapter Test

Multiple Choice Questions

1. If $y = e^{\sqrt{x}}$, then $2\sqrt{x}\,\dfrac{dy}{dx}$ is equal to

(a) y (b) $-y$

(c) $\dfrac{1}{y}$ (d) $-\dfrac{1}{y}$

2. If $y = \dfrac{x+1}{x+2}$, then $y'(0)$ is equal to

(a) $\dfrac{1}{2}$ (b) $\dfrac{1}{3}$

(c) $\dfrac{1}{4}$ (d) $\dfrac{1}{6}$

3. If $y = \sqrt{x^2 + a^2}$, then $y\,\dfrac{dy}{dx}$ is equal to

(a) 1 (b) -1

(c) x (d) $-x$

4. If $f(x) = x + \dfrac{1}{x}$, then $x^2\,\dfrac{dy}{dx} - xy$ is equal to

(a) 1 (b) -1

(c) 2 (d) -2

5. If $y = xe^x$, then $\dfrac{dy}{dx} - y$ is equal to

(a) 0 (b) 1

(c) e^x (d) $-e^x$

Case Based MCQs

6. The meaning of the term "Rate of change of y with respect to x" is that, if x increased by an additional unit the change in y is given by $\dfrac{dy}{dx}$.

So, we can say that the derivative of a function $y = f(x)$ is same as the rate of change of $f(x)$ with respect to x.

On the basis of above information, answer the following questions.

(i) If $f(x) = e^x + x^2 - 2$, then $f'(0)$ is equal to

(a) 0 (b) 1

(c) -1 (d) 2

(ii) If $f(x) = \dfrac{2-x}{x-2}$, then $f'(x)$ is equal to

(a) 0 (b) 1

(c) -1 (d) 2

(iii) If $f(x) = 2^{\log_e x}$, then $f'(x)$ is equal to

(a) $2^{\log_e x}\log 2$ (b) $2^{\log_e x}$

(c) $\log_e 2 \cdot x^{(\log_e 2 - 1)}$ (d) None of these

(iv) If $f(x) = \left(x + \dfrac{1}{x}\right)^2$, then $f'(x)$ is equal to

(a) $2x + \dfrac{2}{x^3}$ (b) $x - \dfrac{1}{x}$

(c) $x + \dfrac{1}{x}$ (d) $2x - \dfrac{2}{x^3}$

(v) If $f(x) = \dfrac{1+x}{1+\frac{1}{x}}$, then $f'(x)$ is equal to

(a) 0 (b) 1

(c) -1 (d) 2

Short Answer Type Questions

7. If $f(x) = x^2 - 2$, then find $f'(10)$.

8. Differentiate $f(x) = \sqrt{2x + 3}$, using first principle.

9. If $f(x) = (x^2 - 3x + 2)(x + 2)$, then find $f'(x)$.

10. Find the derivative of $\dfrac{(x-1)(x-2)}{(x-3)(x-4)}$.

11. If $f(x) = 1 - x + x^2 - x^3 + \ldots - x^{99} + x^{100}$, then find $f'(1)$.

Long Answer Type Questions

12. Differentiate $f(x) = \dfrac{2x+3}{3x+2}$, using first principle.

13. If $y = \log[x + 2 + \sqrt{x^2 + 4x + 1}]$, prove that $\sqrt{x^2 + 4x + 1}\,\dfrac{dy}{dx} - 1 = 0$.

Answers

1. (a)   **2.** (c)   **3.** (c)   **4.** (d)   **5.** (c)

6. (i) (b)   (ii) (a)   (iii) (c)   (iv) (d)   (v) (b)

7. 20   **8.** $\dfrac{1}{\sqrt{2x+3}}$ **9.** $3x^2 - 2x - 4$ **10.** $\dfrac{-4x^2 + 20x - 22}{(x-3)^2(x-4)^2}$

11. 50   **12.** $\dfrac{-5}{(3x+2)^2}$

For Detailed Solutions

Scan the code

CHAPTER 04

Probability

In this Chapter...

- Conditional Probability
- Multiplication Theorem on Probability
- Independent and Dependent Events
- Theorem of Total Probability
- Baye's Theorem

Quick Review of Probability

- An operation which can produce some well-defined outcomes is called an **experiment.**

- An experiment is called **random experiment**, if it satisfies the following two conditions

  (i) It has more than one possible outcomes.

  (ii) It is not possible to predict the outcome in advance.

- A possible result of a random experiment is called its **outcome.**

- The set of all possible outcomes of a random experiment is called its **sample space.** It is usually denoted by S. Each element of a sample space is called a sample point or an event point.

- When a random experiment is repeated under identical conditions and it does not give the same result each time but may result in anyone of the several possible outcomes, then each such action is called a **trial** and the outcomes are called **cases.** The number of times the experiment is repeated, is called the **number of trials.**

- A subset of the sample space associated with a random experiment is called an **event.**

- The empty set ϕ and the sample space S describe events (as S and ϕ are also subset of S). The empty set ϕ is called an **impossible event** and whole sample space S is called the **sure event.**

- If an event has only one sample point of a sample space, then it is called a **simple** or **elementary event.**

- If an event has more than one sample point, then it is called a **compound event.**

- The given events are said to be **equally likely**, if none of them is expected to occur in preference to the other.

- Two or more events are said to be **mutually exclusive**, if the happening of one excludes the happening of the other i.e. if no two of them can occur together. If A and B are mutually exclusive events, then $(A \cap B) = \phi$.

- A set of events are said to be **exhaustive**, if one of them necessarily occurs whenever the experiment is performed. Let $E_1, E_2, ..., E_n$ be subsets of sample space S. Then, events $E_1, E_2, ..., E_n$ are exhaustive events,

  if $E_1 \cup E_2 \cup ... \cup E_n = S$.

- Let A be an event in a sample space S, then **complement of A** is the set of all sample points, which are not in A and it is denoted by A' or $\overline{A}$. i.e. $A' = \{n : n \in S, n \notin A\}$

Probability of an Event

If there are n elementary equally likely events associated with a random experiment and m of them are favourable to an event A, then the **probability of happening or occurrence of A** is denoted by $P(A)$ and defined as

$$P(A) = \frac{m}{n} = \frac{\left[\begin{array}{c}\text{Number of elementary events} \\ \text{favourable to event } A\end{array}\right]}{\left[\begin{array}{c}\text{Total number of elementary} \\ \text{events to the experiment}\end{array}\right]}$$

Note

(i) $0 \le P(A) \le 1$

(ii) $P(A \cup A') = 1$

(iii) $P(A \cap A') = 0$

(iv) $P(A')' = P(A)$

(v) Probability of impossible event is zero.

(vi) Probability of sure event is 1.

(vii) Sometimes, we have to select r objects from n distinct objects, then we use the formula,

$$^nC_r = \frac{n!}{r!(n-r)!}, \quad 0 \le r \le n.$$

Important Laws on Probability

1. Addition Theorem of Probability

(i) For two events A and B,

$$P(A \cup B) = P(A) + P(B) - P(A \cap B)$$
$$= P(A-B) + P(B-A) + P(A \cap B)$$
$$= P(A) + P(B-A)$$
$$= P(B) + P(A-B)$$

If A and B are mutually exclusive events, then

$$P(A \cup B) = P(A) + P(B)$$

$$[\text{for mutually exclusive events, } P(A \cap B) = 0]$$

(ii) For three events A, B and C,

$$P(A \cup B \cup C) = P(A) + P(B) + P(C)$$
$$- P(A \cap B) - P(B \cap C)$$
$$- P(A \cap C) + P(A \cap B \cap C)$$

If A, B and C are mutually exclusive events, then

$$P(A \cup B \cup C) = P(A) + P(B) + P(C)$$

$$[\because \text{ for mutually exclusive events,}$$
$$P(A \cap B) = P(B \cap C) = P(C \cap A) = P(A \cap B \cap C) = 0]$$

(iii) If $A_1, A_2, A_3, \ldots, A_n$ are mutually exclusive events associated with a random experiment, then

$$P(A_1 \cup A_2 \cup A_3 \cup \ldots \cup A_n)$$
$$= P(A_1) + P(A_2) + P(A_3) + \ldots + P(A_n).$$

2. If A and B are two events associated with a random experiment, then

(i) $P(\overline{A} \cap B) = P(B) - P(A \cap B)$

(ii) $P(A \cap \overline{B}) = P(A) - P(A \cap B)$

(iii) $P[(A \cap \overline{B}) \cup (\overline{A} \cap B)] = P(A) + P(B) - 2P(A \cap B)$

(iv) $P(\overline{A} \cap \overline{B}) = 1 - P(A \cup B)$

(v) $P(\overline{A} \cup \overline{B}) = 1 - P(A \cap B)$

(vi) $P(A) = P(A \cap B) + P(A \cap \overline{B}) = P(A-B) + P(A \cap B)$

(vii) $P(B) = P(A \cap B) + P(B \cap \overline{A}) = P(B-A) + P(A \cap B)$

(viii) $P(\text{exactly one of } A, B \text{ occurs})$
$$= P(A) + P(B) - 2P(A \cap B)$$
$$= P(A \cup B) - P(A \cap B)$$

3. If A, B and C are three events, then

$P(\text{exactly one of } A, B, C \text{ occurs})$
$$= P(A) + P(B) + P(C) - 2P(A \cap B) - 2P(B \cap C)$$
$$- 2P(A \cap C) + 3P(A \cap B \cap C)$$

4. $P(\overline{A}) = 1 - P(A)$

5. If $A \subseteq B$, then

(i) $P(A) \le P(B)$

(ii) $P(B-A) = P(B) - P(A)$

Conditional Event

If A and B are events of a sample space S that associated with a random experiment and A occurs after the occurrence of B, then occurrence of event A under the condition that B has already occurred is called conditional event. It is denoted by A/B. Similarly, we define B/A.

Conditional Probability

If A and B are two events associated with the same sample space of a random experiment, then **conditional probability** of the event A given that B has occurred, i.e. $P(A/B)$ is given by

$$P\left(\frac{A}{B}\right) = \frac{P(A \cap B)}{P(B)}, \text{ provided } P(B) \ne 0$$

Probability of occurrence of event B, when A has already occurred i.e. $P(B/A)$ is given by

$$P\left(\frac{B}{A}\right) = \frac{P(B \cap A)}{P(A)}, \text{ provided } P(A) \ne 0$$

Properties of Conditional Probability

Let A and B be the events of a sample space S of an experiment, then

(i) The conditional probability of an event A given that B has occurred lies between 0 and 1,

i.e. $\qquad 0 \le P(A/B) \le 1.$

(ii) $P(S/A) = P(A/A) = 1$

(iii) If A and B are any two events of a sample space S and C is an event of S, such that $P(C) \ne 0$, then

$$P\{(A \cup B)/C\} = P(A/C) + P(B/C) - P\{(A \cap B)/C\}$$

In particular, if A and B are disjoint events, then

$$P\left(\frac{A \cup B}{C}\right) = P\left(\frac{A}{C}\right) + P\left(\frac{B}{C}\right)$$

(iv) The conditional property of an event A given that B has occurred lies between 0 and 1.

(v) $P(A'/B) = 1 - P(A/B)$, where A' is complement of A.

(vi) If A and B are mutually exclusive events, then

$$P(A/B) = 0 = P(B/A)$$

Multiplication Theorem

Let A and B be two events associated with a random experiment, then

$$P(A \cap B) = \begin{cases} P(A) \cdot P(B/A), \text{ where } P(A) \neq 0 \\ P(B) \cdot P(A/B), \text{ where } P(B) \neq 0 \end{cases}$$

Here, $A \cap B$ denotes the simultaneous occurrence of the events A and B. The event $A \cap B$ is also written as AB.

The above result is known as the **multiplication rule of probability.**

Extension of Multiplication Theorem

(i) If A, B and C are three events associated with a random experiment, then

$$P(A \cap B \cap C) = P(A) \cdot P\left(\frac{B}{A}\right) \cdot P\left(\frac{C}{A \cap B}\right)$$

(ii) If $A_1, A_2, \ldots, A_n$ are n events associated with a random experiment, then

$$P(A_1 \cap A_2 \cap \ldots \cap A_n) = P(A_1)P\left(\frac{A_2}{A_1}\right)$$
$$\ldots P\left(\frac{A_n}{A_1 \cap A_2 \cap \ldots \cap A_{n-1}}\right)$$

Independent Events

Two events A and B are said to be independent, if the occurrence or non-occurrence of one event does not affect the occurrence or non-occurrence of another event. Two events E and F are said to be **independent**, if

$$P\left(\frac{F}{E}\right) = P(F), \text{ provided } P(E) \neq 0$$

and $\qquad P\left(\frac{E}{F}\right) = P(E), \text{ provided } P(F) \neq 0.$

In other words, let E and F be two events associated with the same random experiment, then E and F are said to be **independent**, if $P(E \cap F) = P(E) \cdot P(F)$.

Some Important Results

1. Two events E and F are said to be dependent, if they are not independent,

   i.e. $\qquad P(E \cap F) \neq P(E) \cdot P(F)$

2. Two experiments are said to be independent, if for every pair of events E and F, where E is associated with the first experiment and F with the second experiment, the probability of the simultaneous occurrence of the events E and F is the product of $P(E)$ and $P(F)$ calculated separately on the basis of two experiments,

   i.e. $\qquad P(E \cap F) = P(E) \cdot P(F)$

3. **Difference between independent events and mutually exclusive events**

   - Term independent is defined in terms of probability of events whereas mutually exclusive is defined in terms of subset of sample space.
   - Mutually exclusive events never have an outcome common, but independent events may have common outcome. In other words, two independent events having non-zero probabilities of occurrence cannot be mutually exclusive and conversely i.e. two mutually exclusive events having non-zero probabilities of occurrence cannot be independent.

4. Three events A, B and C are said to be mutually independent, if

$$P(A \cap B) = P(A) \cdot P(B)$$
$$P(A \cap C) = P(A) \cdot P(C)$$
$$P(B \cap C) = P(B) \cdot P(C)$$
$$\text{and} \quad P(A \cap B \cap C) = P(A) \cdot P(B) \cdot P(C)$$

If atleast one of the above is not true for three given events, then events are not independent. i.e. dependent.

Properties of Independent Events

If A and B are independent events, then

(i) A and B' are also independent events.

(ii) A' and B are also independent events.

(iii) A' and B' are also independent events.

Dependent Events

Two events are said to be **dependent**, if the occurrence or non-occurrence of the one event in any trial affects the probability of the other subsequent trials. If the occurrence of one event affects the happening of the other events, then they are said to be **dependent events**.

Partition of a Sample Space

A set of mutually exclusive and exhaustive events $E_1, E_2, \ldots, E_n$ is said to represent a partition of the sample space S, if it satisfies the following conditions

(i) $E_i \cap E_j = \phi, i \neq j; i, j = 1, 2, \ldots, n$

(ii) $E_1 \cup E_2 \cup \ldots \cup E_n = S$

(iii) $P(E_i) > 0, \forall i = 1, 2, \ldots, n.$

In other words, the events $E_1, E_2, ..., E_n$ represent a partition of the sample space S, if they are pairwise disjoint, exhaustive and have non-zero probabilities.

> **Note** The partition of a sample space is not unique. There can be several partitions of the same sample space.

Theorem of Total Probability

Let $\{E_1, E_2, ..., E_n\}$ be a partition of the sample space S and suppose that each of the events $E_1, E_2, ..., E_n$ has non-zero probability of occurrence.

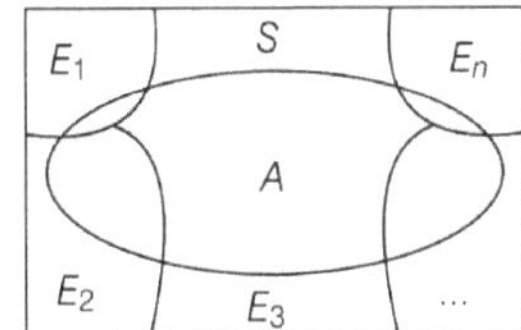

Let A be any event associated with S, then

$$P(A) = P(E_1) \cdot P(A/E_1) + P(E_2) \cdot P(A/E_2)$$
$$+ ... + P(E_n) \cdot P(A/E_n)$$
$$= \sum_{j=1}^{n} P(E_j) \cdot P(A/E_j)$$

Baye's Theorem

If $E_1, E_2, ..., E_n$ are non-empty events, which constitute a partition of sample space S, i.e. $E_1, E_2, ..., E_n$ are pairwise disjoint, $E_1 \cup E_2 \cup ... \cup E_n = S$ and $P(E_i) > 0$, $\forall i = 1, 2, 3, ..., n$.

Also, let A be any event of non-zero probability, then

$$P(E_i / A) = \frac{P(E_i) \cdot P(A/E_i)}{\sum_{j=1}^{n} P(E_j) \cdot P(A/E_j)}, \text{ for any } i = 1, 2, 3, ..., n$$

Or

Let $E_1, E_2, E_3, ..., E_n$ be n mutually exclusive and exhaustive events associated with a random experiment.

If A is an event, which occurs together with E_i's.

Then,

$$P(E_i / A) = \frac{P(E_i) \cdot P(A/E_i)}{\sum_{j=1}^{n} P(E_j) \cdot P(A/E_j)}$$

Here, events $E_1, E_2, ..., E_n$ are called **hypothesis**.

The probability $P(E_i)$ is called the **priori probability** of the hypothesis E_i and the conditional probability $P(E_i/A)$ is called a posteriori probability of the hypothesis E_i.

Baye's theorem is also called the formula for the probability of causes.

Solved Examples

Example 1. If $P(A) = \dfrac{6}{11}$, $P(B) = \dfrac{5}{11}$ and $P(A \cup B) = \dfrac{7}{11}$, then find

(i) $P(A \cap B)$ (ii) $P(A/B)$ (iii) $P(B/A)$.

Sol. Given, $P(A) = \dfrac{6}{11}$, $P(B) = \dfrac{5}{11}$ and $P(A \cup B) = \dfrac{7}{11}$

(i) $P(A \cup B) = P(A) + P(B) - P(A \cap B)$

$$\Rightarrow \quad \frac{7}{11} = \frac{6}{11} + \frac{5}{11} - P(A \cap B)$$

$$\therefore \ P(A \cap B) = \frac{6}{11} + \frac{5}{11} - \frac{7}{11} = \frac{4}{11}$$

(ii) $P\left(\dfrac{A}{B}\right) = \dfrac{P(A \cap B)}{P(B)} = \dfrac{4/11}{5/11} = \dfrac{4}{5}$ $\left[\because P(A \cap B) = \dfrac{4}{11}\right]$

(iii) $P\left(\dfrac{B}{A}\right) = \dfrac{P(A \cap B)}{P(A)} = \dfrac{4/11}{6/11} = \dfrac{4}{6} = \dfrac{2}{3}$

Example 2. In a college, 70% students pass in Physics, 75% pass in Mathematics and 10% students fail in both. One student is chosen at random. What is the probability that

(i) he passes in Physics and Mathematics?

(ii) he passes Mathematics given that he passes in Physics?

(iii) he passes in Physics given that he passes in Mathematics?

Sol. Given, $P(A) = $ Probability of students passed in Physics

$$= \frac{70}{100}$$

$P(B) = $ Probability of students passed in Mathematics

$$= \frac{75}{100}$$

$P(A' \cap B') = $ Probability of students fail in both $= \dfrac{10}{100}$

$\because \ P(A' \cap B') = P(A \cup B)' = 1 - P(A \cup B)$

$\Rightarrow P(A \cup B) = 1 - P(A' \cap B') = 1 - \dfrac{10}{100} = \dfrac{90}{100}$

(i) Probability of passing in Physics and Mathematics

$$= P(A \cap B) = P(A) + P(B) - P(A \cup B)$$

$$= \frac{70}{100} + \frac{75}{100} - \frac{90}{100} = \frac{55}{100} = \frac{11}{20}$$

(ii) P (he passes in Mathematics given that he passes in Physics), $P\left(\dfrac{B}{A}\right) = \dfrac{P(A \cap B)}{P(A)} = \dfrac{55/100}{70/100} = \dfrac{55}{70} = \dfrac{11}{14}$

(iii) P (he passes in Physics given that he passes in Mathematics) $P\left(\dfrac{A}{B}\right) = \dfrac{P(A \cap B)}{P(B)} = \dfrac{55/100}{75/100} = \dfrac{55}{75} = \dfrac{11}{15}$

Example 3. Given that, the two numbers appearing on throwing two dice are different. Find the probability of the events

(i) the sum of numbers on the dice is 4.

(ii) the sum of numbers on the dice is not 4.

Sol. Here, two dice are thrown, so number of outcomes in the sample space, $S = 6 \times 6 = 36$ (equally likely sample events) i.e. $n(S) = 36$.

Let E be the event of getting sum of the numbers on the dice is 4 and F be the event that numbers appearing on the two dice are different.

Then, $E = \{(1, 3), (2, 2), (3, 1)\} \Rightarrow n(E) = 3$

$$\text{and} \quad F = \begin{cases} (1, 2), (1, 3), (1, 4), (1, 5), (1, 6), \\ (2, 1), (2, 3), (2, 4), (2, 5), (2, 6), \\ (3, 1), (3, 2), (3, 4), (3, 5), (3, 6), \\ (4, 1), (4, 2), (4, 3), (4, 5), (4, 6), \\ (5, 1), (5, 2), (5, 3), (5, 4), (5, 6), \\ (6, 1), (6, 2), (6, 3), (6, 4), (6, 5) \end{cases}$$

$\Rightarrow n(F) = 30$

Here, $E \cap F = \{(1, 3), (3, 1)\} = 2$

$$\therefore \quad P(F) = \frac{\text{Number of favourable outcomes}}{\text{Total number of outcomes}}$$

$$= \frac{30}{36} = \frac{5}{6}$$

and $P(E \cap F) = \dfrac{2}{36} = \dfrac{1}{18}$

(i) The probability that the sum of numbers on the dice showing different number is 4,

$$P\left(\frac{E}{F}\right) = \frac{P(E \cap F)}{P(F)}$$

$$= \frac{\dfrac{1}{18}}{\dfrac{5}{6}} = \frac{1}{15}$$

(ii) The probability that the sum of numbers on the dice showing different numbers is not 4,

$$P\left(\frac{E'}{F}\right) = 1 - P\left(\frac{E}{F}\right)$$

$$= 1 - \frac{1}{15} = \frac{14}{15}$$

Example 4. Consider the experiment of tossing a coin. If the coin shows head, toss it again but if it shows tail, then throw a die. Find the conditional probability of the event that 'the die shows a number greater than 4' given that there is atleast one tail.

Sol. The outcomes of the experiment can be represented in the following tree diagram.

The sample space S of the experiment is given as

$S = \{(H, H), (H, T), (T, 1), (T, 2), (T, 3),$
$(T, 4), (T, 5), (T, 6)\}$

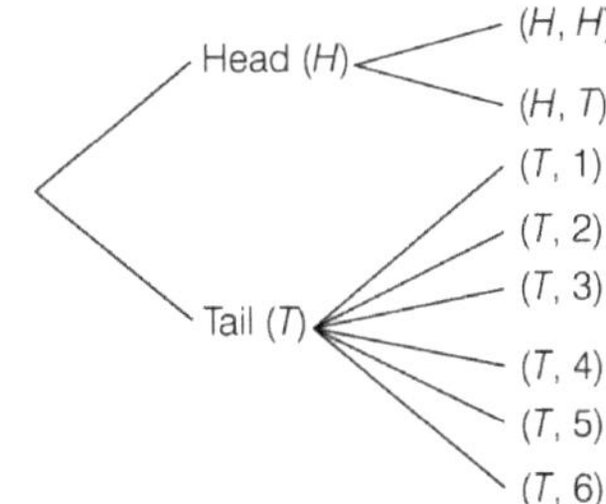

The probabilities of these elementary events are

$$P\{(H, H)\} = \frac{1}{2} \times \frac{1}{2} = \frac{1}{4}, \quad P\{(H, T)\} = \frac{1}{2} \times \frac{1}{2} = \frac{1}{4},$$

$$P\{(T, 1)\} = \frac{1}{2} \times \frac{1}{6} = \frac{1}{12}, \quad P\{(T, 2)\} = \frac{1}{2} \times \frac{1}{6} = \frac{1}{12},$$

$$P\{(T, 3)\} = \frac{1}{2} \times \frac{1}{6} = \frac{1}{12}, \quad P\{(T, 4)\} = \frac{1}{2} \times \frac{1}{6} = \frac{1}{12},$$

$$P\{(T, 5)\} = \frac{1}{2} \times \frac{1}{6} = \frac{1}{12} \text{ and } P\{(T, 6)\} = \frac{1}{2} \times \frac{1}{6} = \frac{1}{12}$$

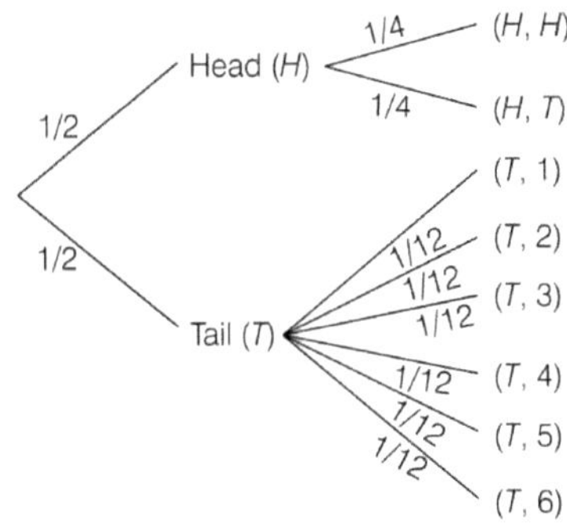

Consider the following events

A = the die shows a number greater than 4

and $\quad B$ = there is atleast one tail.

We have, $A = \{(T, 5), (T, 6)\}$,

$\quad B = \{(H, T), (T, 1), (T, 2), (T, 3), (T, 4), (T, 5), (T, 6)\}$

and $A \cap B = \{(T, 5), (T, 6)\}$

$\therefore \quad P(B) = P\{(H, T)\} + P\{(T, 1)\} + P\{(T, 2)\} + P\{(T, 3)\}$
$\qquad\qquad + P\{(T, 4)\} + P\{(T, 5)\} + P\{(T, 6)\}$

$$\Rightarrow \quad P(B) = \frac{1}{4} + \frac{1}{12} + \frac{1}{12} + \frac{1}{12} + \frac{1}{12} + \frac{1}{12} + \frac{1}{12} = \frac{3}{4}$$

and $P(A \cap B) = P\{(T, 5)\} + P\{(T, 6)\} = \frac{1}{12} + \frac{1}{12} = \frac{1}{6}$

$\therefore$ Required probability,

$$P\left(\frac{A}{B}\right) = \frac{P(A \cap B)}{P(B)} = \frac{1/6}{3/4} = \frac{4}{18} = \frac{2}{9}$$

Example 5. Find the probability of drawing a diamond card in each of the two consecutive draws from a well-shuffled pack of cards, if the card drawn is not replaced after the first draw.

Sol. Let A be the event of drawing a diamond card in the first draw and B be the event of drawing a diamond card in the second draw.

Then, $\qquad P(A) = \frac{13}{52} = \frac{1}{4}$

After drawing a diamond card in first draw, 51 cards are left out of which 12 cards are diamond cards.

$\therefore P(B / A)$ = Probability of drawing a diamond card in second draw when a diamond card has already been drawn in first draw

$$\Rightarrow \quad P\left(\frac{B}{A}\right) = \frac{12}{51} = \frac{4}{17}$$

Now, required probability,

$$P(A \cap B) = P(A) \cdot P\left(\frac{B}{A}\right) = \frac{1}{4} \times \frac{4}{17} = \frac{1}{17}$$

Example 6. A bag contains 19 tickets, numbered from 1 to 19. A ticket is drawn and then another ticket is drawn without replacement. Find the probability that both tickets will show even numbers.

Sol. Let A be the event of drawing an even numbered ticket in first draw and B be the event of drawing an even numbered ticket in the second draw. Then,

Required probability = $P(A \cap B) = P(A) \cdot P(B / A)$ ...(i)

Since, there are 19 tickets numbered 1 to 19 in the bag, out of which 9 are even numbered viz. 2, 4, 6, 8, 10, 12, 14, 16 and 18.

Therefore, $\quad P(A) = \frac{9}{19}$

Since, the ticket drawn in the first draw is not replaced, therefore second ticket drawn is from the remaining 18 tickets, out of which 8 are even numbered.

$$\therefore \qquad P\left(\frac{B}{A}\right) = \frac{8}{18} = \frac{4}{9}$$

Hence, required probability = $P(A \cap B)$
$$= P(A) \cdot P(B / A) \text{ [from Eq. (i)]}$$
$$= \frac{9}{19} \times \frac{4}{9} = \frac{4}{19}$$

Example 7. Three cards are drawn successively without replacement from a pack of 52 well-shuffled cards. What is the probability that first two cards are king and the third card drawn is an ace?

Sol. There are 52 cards in a pack.

$\therefore \qquad\qquad n(S) = 52$

Let A = event that the card drawn is king

and B = event that the card drawn is an ace.

Now, $P(A) = 4/52$

$P\left(\frac{A}{A}\right)$ = Probability of drawing second king when one king has already been drawn = $\frac{3}{51}$

$\qquad\qquad [\because \text{ remaining cards are } (52 - 1) = 51]$

$P(B / AA)$ = Probability of drawing third card to be an ace when two kings have already been drawn = $\frac{4}{50}$

Now, probability of getting first two cards are king and third card is an ace $= P(A \cap A \cap B)$

$$= P(A) \cdot P\left(\frac{A}{A}\right) \cdot P\left(\frac{B}{AA}\right)$$

[by multiplication theorem]

$$= \frac{4}{52} \times \frac{3}{51} \times \frac{4}{50} = \frac{2}{5525}$$

Example 8. A bag contains 5 white, 7 red and 8 black balls. If four balls are drawn one by one without replacement, then find the probability of getting all white balls.

Sol. Let A, B, C and D denote events of getting a white ball in first, second, third and fourth draw, respectively. Then, required probability $= P(A \cap B \cap C \cap D)$

$$= P(A)\, P(B/A)\, P(C/A \cap B)\, P(D/A \cap B \cap C) \quad …(i)$$

Now, $P(A) = $ Probability of drawing a white ball in first draw

$$= \frac{5}{20} = \frac{1}{4}$$

When a white ball is drawn in the first draw, there are 19 balls left in the bag, out of which 4 are white.

$$\therefore \qquad P(B/A) = \frac{4}{19}$$

Since, the ball drawn is not replaced, therefore after drawing a white ball in second draw, there are 18 balls left in the bag, out of which 3 are white.

$$\therefore \qquad P(C/A \cap B) = \frac{3}{18} = \frac{1}{6}$$

After drawing a white ball in third draw, there are 17 balls left in the bag, out of which 2 are white.

$$\therefore \qquad P(D/A \cap B \cap C) = \frac{2}{17}$$

Hence, required probability

$$= P(A \cap B \cap C \cap D)$$
$$= P(A) \cdot P(B/A)\, P(C/A \cap B)\, P(D/A \cap B \cap C)$$
$$= \frac{1}{4} \times \frac{4}{19} \times \frac{1}{6} \times \frac{2}{17} = \frac{1}{969}$$

Example 9. A problem is given to three students whose chances of solving it are $\frac{1}{4}, \frac{1}{5}$ and $\frac{1}{3}$, respectively.

Find the probability that the problem is solved.

Sol. Clearly, the problem will be solved, when atleast one of them solve the problem.

$\therefore$ Required probability $= P$

(at least one of them solved the problem)

$$= 1 - P(\text{none of them solved the problem})$$
$$= 1 - \left(1 - \frac{1}{4}\right)\left(1 - \frac{1}{5}\right)\left(1 - \frac{1}{3}\right)$$
$$= 1 - \frac{3}{4} \times \frac{4}{5} \times \frac{2}{3} = 1 - \frac{2}{5} = \frac{3}{5}$$

Example 10. Three persons A, B and C shoot to hit a target. If in trials A hits the target 4 times in

5 shots, B hits 3 times in 4 shots and C hits 2 times in 3 trials. Find the probability that

(i) exactly two persons hit the target.

(ii) atleast two persons hit the target.

(iii) None hit the target.

Sol. Given, $P(A) = \frac{4}{5}$, $P(B) = \frac{3}{4}$ and $P(C) = \frac{2}{3}$

Then, $P(\overline{A}) = 1 - \frac{4}{5} = \frac{1}{5}$,

$$P(\overline{B}) = 1 - \frac{3}{4} = \frac{1}{4},$$
$$P(\overline{C}) = 1 - \frac{2}{3} = \frac{1}{3}$$

(i) Probability that exactly two persons hit the target

$$= P(AB\overline{C}) + P(A\overline{B}C) + P(\overline{A}BC)$$
$$= P(A)\, P(B)\, P(\overline{C}) + P(A)\, P(\overline{B})\, P(C)$$
$$\qquad\qquad\qquad + P(\overline{A})\, P(B)\, P(C)$$

[since, A, B and C are independent events]

$$= \frac{4}{5} \times \frac{3}{4} \times \left(1 - \frac{2}{3}\right) + \frac{4}{5} \times \left(1 - \frac{3}{4}\right) \times \frac{2}{3}$$
$$\qquad\qquad + \left(1 - \frac{4}{5}\right) \times \frac{3}{4} \times \frac{2}{3}$$
$$= \frac{4}{5} \times \frac{3}{4} \times \frac{1}{3} + \frac{4}{5} \times \frac{1}{4} \times \frac{2}{3} + \frac{1}{5} \times \frac{3}{4} \times \frac{2}{3}$$
$$= \frac{1}{5} + \frac{2}{15} + \frac{1}{10} = \frac{6 + 4 + 3}{30} = \frac{13}{30} \quad …(i)$$

(ii) Probability that atleast two persons hit the target

$$= P(AB\overline{C}) + P(A\overline{B}C) + P(\overline{A}BC) + P(ABC)$$
$$= \frac{13}{30} + P(A)\, P(B)\, P(C) \qquad [\text{from Eq. (i)}]$$
$$= \frac{13}{30} + \frac{4}{5} \times \frac{3}{4} \times \frac{2}{3}$$
$$= \frac{13}{30} + \frac{2}{5} = \frac{13 + 12}{30} = \frac{25}{30} = \frac{5}{6}$$

(iii) The probability that none of them hit the target.

$$= P(\overline{A} \cap \overline{B} \cap \overline{C})$$
$$= P(\overline{A})\, P(\overline{B})\, P(\overline{C})$$
$$= \frac{1}{5} \times \frac{1}{4} \times \frac{1}{3} = \frac{1}{60}$$

Example 11. Two horses are considered for a race. The probability of selection of the first horse is $1/4$ and that of the second is $1/3$. What is the probability that

(i) both of them will be selected.

(ii) only one of them will be selected.

(iii) none of them will be selected.

Sol. Let $A :$ Selection of I Horse

$\qquad\quad B :$ Selection of II Horse $\qquad\qquad$ [given]

$$\therefore \quad P(A) = P(\text{I Horse selection}) = \frac{1}{4}$$

and $P(B) = P(\text{II Horse selection}) = \frac{1}{3}$

(i) P (both of them will be selected)

$$= P(AB) = P(A)\ P(B)$$

[since, A and B are independent events]

$$= \frac{1}{4} \times \frac{1}{3} = \frac{1}{12}$$

(ii) P (only one of them will be selected)

$$= P(A\overline{B}) + P(\overline{A}B)$$

$$= P(A)\ P(\overline{B}) + P(\overline{A})\ P(B)$$

[If A and B independent, then A and $\overline{B}$, $\overline{A}$ and B are independent]

$$= \frac{1}{4} \times \left(1 - \frac{1}{3}\right) + \left(1 - \frac{1}{4}\right) \times \frac{1}{3}$$

$$= \frac{1}{4} \times \frac{2}{3} + \frac{3}{4} \times \frac{1}{3} = \frac{1}{6} + \frac{1}{4} = \frac{2+3}{12} = \frac{5}{12}$$

(iii) P (None of them will be selected)

$$= P(\overline{AB}) = P(\overline{A})\ P(\overline{B})$$

$$= \left(1 - \frac{1}{4}\right)\left(1 - \frac{1}{3}\right) = \frac{3}{4} \times \frac{2}{3} = \frac{1}{2}$$

Example 12. There are two bags. One bag contains six green and three red balls. The second bag contains five green and four red balls. One ball is transferred from the first bag to the second bag. Then, one ball is drawn from the second bag. Find the probability that it is a red ball.

Sol. **Bag I** 6 green and 3 red balls

Bag II 5 green and 4 red balls

Case **I** When one green ball is transferred from bag I to bag II,

Then, its probability, $P_1 = \dfrac{6}{6+3} = \dfrac{6}{9} = \dfrac{2}{3}$

Now, bag II contains 6 green and 4 red balls.

Probability that a red ball drawn from bag II,

Then its probability, $P_2 = \dfrac{4}{6+4} = \dfrac{4}{10} = \dfrac{2}{5}$

Probability of both the events occurring together

$$= P_1 P_2 = \frac{2}{3} \times \frac{2}{5} = \frac{4}{15} \qquad \dots(i)$$

[multiplication theorem for independent events]

Case **II** When one red ball is transferred from bag I to bag II, $P_3 = \dfrac{3}{6+3} = \dfrac{3}{9} = \dfrac{1}{3}$

Now, bag II contains 5 green and 5 red balls.

Probability that a red ball is drawn from bag II,

$$P_4 = \frac{5}{5+5} = \frac{5}{10} = \frac{1}{2}$$

Probability of both the events occurring together

$$= P_3 P_4 = \frac{1}{3} \times \frac{1}{2} = \frac{1}{6} \qquad \dots(ii)$$

On adding Eqs. (i) and (ii), we get the required probability

$$P_1 P_2 + P_3 P_4 = \frac{4}{15} + \frac{1}{6} = \frac{8+5}{30} = \frac{13}{30}$$

Example 13. A committee of 4 persons has to be chosen from 8 boys and 6 girls, consisting of atleast one girl. Find the probability that the committee consists of more girls than boys.

Sol. Given, number of boys = 8

and number of girls = 6

We have to make a committee of 4 persons.

If the committee consists of more girls than boys, then

Number of ways this can be done

$$= {}^{8}C_0 \times {}^{6}C_4 + {}^{8}C_1 \times {}^{6}C_3$$

$$= 1 \times \frac{6!}{4!\ 2!} + 8 \times \frac{6!}{3!\ 3!}$$

$$= \frac{6 \times 5}{2} + \frac{8 \times 6 \times 5 \times 4}{3 \times 2}$$

$$= 15 + 160 = 175$$

$\therefore$ Total number of ways

$$= {}^{8}C_0 \times {}^{6}C_4 + {}^{8}C_1 \times {}^{6}C_3 + {}^{8}C_2 \times {}^{6}C_2 + {}^{8}C_3 \times {}^{6}C_1$$

$$= 15 + 8 \times 20 + 28 \times 15 + 56 \times 6$$

$$= 15 + 160 + 420 + 336 = 931$$

Hence, required probability $= \dfrac{175}{931} = 0.187$

Example 14. Bag A contains three red and four white balls and bag B contains two red and three white balls. If one ball is drawn from bag A and two balls from bag B, find the probability that

(i) one ball is red and two balls are white.

(ii) all the three balls are of the same colour.

Sol. **Bag A** : Three red balls and four white balls

Bag B : Two red balls and three white balls

(i) P (one red ball and two white balls)

$= P$ (1 white ball from bag A and 1 white and 1 red ball from bag B) + P (1 red ball from bag A and 2 white balls from Bag B)

$$= \frac{{}^{4}C_1}{{}^{7}C_1} \times \frac{{}^{2}C_1 \times {}^{3}C_1}{{}^{5}C_2} + \frac{{}^{3}C_1}{{}^{7}C_1} \times \frac{{}^{3}C_2}{{}^{5}C_2}$$

$$= \frac{4}{7} \times \frac{2 \times 3 \times 2}{5 \times 4} + \frac{3}{7} \times \frac{3 \times 2}{5 \times 4}$$

$$= \frac{12}{35} + \frac{9}{70} = \frac{24 + 9}{70} = \frac{33}{70}$$

(ii) P (all balls are of same colour)

$= P$ (all white balls) + P (all red balls)

$= P$ (1 white ball from bag A and 2 white balls from bag B) + P (1 red ball from bag A and 2 red balls from bag B).

$$= \frac{{}^{4}C_1}{{}^{7}C_1} \times \frac{{}^{3}C_2}{{}^{5}C_2} + \frac{{}^{3}C_1}{{}^{7}C_1} \times \frac{{}^{2}C_2}{{}^{5}C_2}$$

$$= \frac{4}{7} \times \frac{3}{5 \times 2} + \frac{3}{7} \times \frac{1 \times 2}{5 \times 4} = \frac{6}{35} + \frac{3}{70}$$

$$= \frac{12 + 3}{70} = \frac{15}{70} = \frac{3}{14}$$

Example 15. Bag A contains 1 white, 2 blue and 3 red balls. Bag B contains 3 white, 3 blue and 2 red balls. Bag C contains 2 white, 3 blue and 4 red balls. One bag is selected at random and then two balls are drawn from the selected bag. Find the probability that the balls drawn are white and red.

Sol. Let E_1 is event of selecting bag A.

E_2 is event of selecting bag B.

E_3 is event of selecting bag C.

E is event of drawing two balls which one of the three bags is selected randomly.

$\therefore P(E_1) = \dfrac{1}{3}$, $P(E_2) = \dfrac{1}{3}$ and $P(E_3) = \dfrac{1}{3}$

Now, $P(E / E_1) = $ Probability of drawing two balls, which are white and red, from bag A

$$= \dfrac{1 \times {}^3C_1}{{}^6C_2}$$

$[\because$ bag A contains 1 white 2 blue and 3 red balls$]$

$$= \dfrac{1 \times 3}{15} = \dfrac{1}{5}$$

$P(E / E_2) = $ Probability of drawing two balls, which are white and red, from bag B

$$= \dfrac{{}^3C_1 \times {}^2C_1}{{}^8C_2}$$

$[\because$ bag B contains 3 white, 3 blue and 2 red balls$]$

$$= \dfrac{3 \times 2}{28} = \dfrac{3}{14}$$

$P(E / E_3) = $ Probability of drawing two balls, which are white and red, from bag C

$$= \dfrac{{}^2C_1 \times {}^4C_1}{{}^9C_2}$$

$[\because$ bag C contains 2 white, 3 blue and 4 red balls$]$

$$= \dfrac{2 \times 4}{36} = \dfrac{2}{9}$$

Now, by using the law of total probability, we get

$$P(E) = P(E_1)P(E / E_1) + P(E_2)P(E / E_2) + P(E_3)P(E / E_3)$$

$$= \dfrac{1}{3} \times \dfrac{1}{5} + \dfrac{1}{3} \times \dfrac{3}{14} + \dfrac{1}{3} \times \dfrac{2}{9} = \dfrac{1}{15} + \dfrac{1}{14} + \dfrac{2}{27} = \dfrac{401}{1890}$$

Example 16. An urn contains 10 white and 3 black balls while another urn contains 3 white and 5 black balls. Two balls are drawn from the first urn and put into the second urn and then a ball is drawn from the second urn. Find the probability that the ball drawn from the second urn is a white ball.

Sol. Here, there are three cases:

Case I When the balls transferred from Urn I to Urn II are white.

Here, the probability of transferring two white balls from

$$\text{Urn I} = \dfrac{{}^{10}C_2}{{}^{13}C_2} = \dfrac{\dfrac{10 \times 9}{2 \times 1}}{\dfrac{13 \times 12}{2 \times 1}} = \dfrac{15}{26}$$

In Urn II, white balls $= 3 + 2 = 5$

$\therefore$ Probability of drawing a white ball from Urn II

$$= \dfrac{{}^5C_1}{{}^{10}C_1} = \dfrac{5}{10} = \dfrac{1}{2}$$

$\therefore$ Probability of these events occurring together

$$= \dfrac{15}{26} \times \dfrac{1}{2} = \dfrac{15}{52}.$$

Case II When one white and one black is transferred from Urn I to Urn II.

$\therefore$ The probability of transferring a white ball and a black ball from Urn I into Urn II $= \dfrac{{}^{10}C_1 \times {}^3C_1}{{}^{13}C_2}$

$$= \dfrac{10 \times 3}{\dfrac{13 \times 12}{2 \times 1}} = \dfrac{30}{13 \times 6} = \dfrac{5}{13}$$

Now, in Urn II, white balls $= 4$ and black balls $= 6$

$\therefore P$ (getting a white ball from Urn II) $= \dfrac{{}^4C_1}{{}^{10}C_1} = \dfrac{4}{10} = \dfrac{2}{5}$

$\therefore$ Probability of these events occurring together $= \dfrac{5}{13} \times \dfrac{2}{5}$

$$= \dfrac{2}{13}$$

Case III When two black balls are transferred from Urn I to Urn II.

$\therefore P$ (transferring 2 black balls from Urn I to Urn II)

$$= \dfrac{{}^3C_2}{{}^{13}C_2} = \dfrac{{}^3C_1}{{}^{13}C_2} = \dfrac{3}{\dfrac{13 \times 12}{2 \times 1}} = \dfrac{3}{13 \times 6} = \dfrac{1}{26}$$

Now, in Urn II, white balls $= 3$ and balls $= 5 + 2 = 7$.

$\therefore P$ (getting a white ball) $= \dfrac{{}^3C_1}{{}^{10}C_1} = \dfrac{3}{10}$

Now, probability of these events occurring together

$$= \dfrac{1}{26} \times \dfrac{3}{10} = \dfrac{3}{260}$$

Since, all the three cases are mutually exclusive. Thus, only one of them can happen at a time.

Hence, the required probability of drawing a white ball

$$= \dfrac{15}{52} + \dfrac{2}{13} + \dfrac{3}{260} = \dfrac{118}{260} = \dfrac{59}{130}$$

Example 17. In an automobile factory, certain parts are to be fixed into the chassis in a section before it moves into another section. On a given day, one of the three persons A, B and C carries out this task. A has 45% chance, B has 35% chance and C has 20% chance of doing the task. The probability that A, B and C will take more than the allotted time is $\dfrac{1}{6}$, $\dfrac{1}{10}$ and $\dfrac{1}{20}$, respectively. If it is found that the time taken is more than the allotted time, then what is the probability that A has done the task?

Sol. Let E_1, E_2, E_3 and A be the events defined as follows

$E_1 = A$ has done the task

$E_2 = B$ has done the task

$E_3 = C$ has done the task and

$A =$ Person takes more than the allotted time.

$\therefore \quad P(E_1) = \dfrac{45}{100} = \dfrac{9}{20}, P(E_2) = \dfrac{35}{100} = \dfrac{7}{20}$

$P(E_3) = \dfrac{20}{100} = \dfrac{4}{20}, P(A/E_1) = \dfrac{1}{6}$

$P(A/E_2) = \dfrac{1}{10}$ and $P(A/E_3) = \dfrac{1}{20}$

By Baye's theorem, we have

$$P\left(\dfrac{E_1}{A}\right) = \dfrac{P(E_1)\,P(A/E_1)}{\left[\begin{array}{c} P(E_1)\,P(A/E_1) + P(E_2)\,P(A/E_2) \\ + P(E_3)\,P(A/E_3) \end{array}\right]}$$

$$= \dfrac{\dfrac{9}{20} \times \dfrac{1}{6}}{\dfrac{9}{20} \times \dfrac{1}{6} + \dfrac{7}{20} \times \dfrac{1}{10} + \dfrac{4}{20} \times \dfrac{1}{20}}$$

$$= \dfrac{0.075}{0.075 + 0.035 + 0.01} = 0.625$$

Example 18. A fair die is rolled. If face 1 turns up, a ball is drawn from Bag A. If face 2 or 3 turns up, a ball is drawn from Bag B. If face 4 or 5 or 6 turns up, a ball is drawn from Bag C. Bag A contains 3 red and 2 white balls, Bag B contains 3 red and 4 white balls and Bag C contains 4 red and 5 white balls. The die is rolled, a Bag is picked up and a ball is drawn. If the drawn ball is red, what is the probability that it is drawn from Bag B?

Sol. Let us define the following events.

E_1 : Bag A is chosen.

E_2 : Bag B is chosen.

E_3 : Bag C is chosen.

Then, $P(E_1) = \dfrac{1}{6}$

$P(E_2) = \dfrac{2}{6} = \dfrac{1}{3}; \ P(E_3) = \dfrac{3}{6} = \dfrac{1}{2}$

Also, let event E : The drawn ball is red.

Then, $P(E/E_1) = \dfrac{3}{5}$

$P(E/E_2) = \dfrac{3}{7}; \ P(E/E_3) = \dfrac{4}{9}$

Now, required probability

$$P(E_2/E) = \dfrac{P(E/E_2)P(E_2)}{P(E/E_2)P(E_2) + P(E/E_1)P(E_1) + P(E/E_3)P(E_3)}$$

$$P(E_2/E) = \dfrac{\dfrac{3}{7} \times \dfrac{1}{3}}{\dfrac{3}{7} \times \dfrac{1}{3} + \dfrac{3}{5} \times \dfrac{1}{6} + \dfrac{4}{9} \times \dfrac{1}{2}}$$

$$= \dfrac{\dfrac{1}{7}}{\dfrac{1}{7} + \dfrac{1}{10} + \dfrac{2}{9}} = \dfrac{\dfrac{1}{7}}{\dfrac{90 + 63 + 2 \times 70}{630}}$$

$$= \dfrac{1}{7} \times \dfrac{630}{293} = \dfrac{90}{293}$$

Example 19. Box I contains two white and three black balls. Box II contains four white and one black balls and box III contains three white and four black balls. A die having three red, two yellow and one green face, is thrown to select the box, if red face turns up, we pick up box I, if a yellow face turns up we pick up box II, otherwise, we pick up box III. Then, we draw a ball from the selected box. If the ball drawn is white, what is the probability that the dice had turned up with a red face?

Sol. Let B and W denote for black and white balls.

Given, Bag I $= \{2\,W, 3B\}$

Bag II $= \{4W, 1B\}$

and Bag III $= \{3W, 4B\}$

Let $E_1 = A$ die have red face.

$E_2 = A$ die have yellow face.

and $E_3 = A$ die have green face.

Total number of face is a die is six.

Then, $P(E_1) = \dfrac{3}{6} = \dfrac{1}{2},$

$P(E_2) = \dfrac{2}{6} = \dfrac{1}{3}$

and $P(E_3) = \dfrac{1}{6}$

Let $E =$ Event of drawing a white ball

Now, $P\left(\dfrac{E}{E_1}\right) = \dfrac{1}{2} \times \dfrac{2}{5} = \dfrac{1}{5}; P\left(\dfrac{E}{E_2}\right) = \dfrac{1}{3} \times \dfrac{4}{5} = \dfrac{4}{15}$

and $P(E_3) = \dfrac{1}{6} \times \dfrac{3}{7} = \dfrac{1}{14}$

$\therefore$ The probability that the white ball is selected when a die turn up red face.

$$P\left(\dfrac{E_1}{E}\right) = \dfrac{P(E_1)P\left(\dfrac{E}{E_1}\right)}{P(E_1)P\left(\dfrac{E}{E_1}\right) + P(E_2)P\left(\dfrac{E}{E_2}\right) + P(E_3)P\left(\dfrac{E}{E_3}\right)}$$

[by using Baye's theorem]

$$= \dfrac{\dfrac{1}{2} \times \dfrac{1}{5}}{\dfrac{1}{2} \times \dfrac{1}{5} + \dfrac{1}{3} \times \dfrac{4}{15} + \dfrac{1}{6} \times \dfrac{1}{14}} = \dfrac{\dfrac{1}{10}}{\dfrac{1}{10} + \dfrac{4}{45} + \dfrac{1}{84}}$$

$$= \dfrac{\dfrac{1}{10}}{\dfrac{378 + 336 + 45}{3780}}$$

$$= \dfrac{3780}{10 \times 759} = \dfrac{378}{759} = \dfrac{126}{253}$$

Chapter Practice

Objective Questions

- **Multiple Choice Questions**

1. A coin is tossed twice. Then, the probability that atleast one tail occurs is

(a) $\dfrac{1}{4}$ (b) $\dfrac{1}{2}$

(c) $\dfrac{1}{3}$ (d) $\dfrac{3}{4}$

2. Let S be a sample space containing outcomes ω_1, $\omega_2, \omega_3, \ldots, \omega_n$ i.e., $S = \{\omega_1, \omega_2, \ldots, \omega_n\}$.

Then, which of the following is true?

I. $0 \le P(\omega_i) \le 1$ for each $\omega_i \in S$

II. $P(\omega_1) + P(\omega_{2)} + \ldots + P(\omega_n) = 1$

III. For any event A, $P(A) = \Sigma P(\omega_i), \omega_i \in A$

(a) Only I   (b) Only II

(c) Only III   (d) All of these

3. Three dice are thrown together. The probability of getting a total of at least 6 is

(a) $\dfrac{101}{108}$ (b) $\dfrac{103}{108}$

(c) $\dfrac{105}{108}$ (d) $\dfrac{107}{108}$

4. If A, B and C are three mutually exclusive and exhaustive events of an experiment such that $4P(A) = 2P(B) = P(C)$, then $P(A)$ is equal to ...K... .

Here, K refers to

(a) $\dfrac{1}{7}$ (b) $\dfrac{2}{7}$ (c) $\dfrac{5}{7}$ (d) $\dfrac{6}{7}$

5. In an essay competition, the odds in favour of competitors P, Q, R and S are $1:2$, $1:3$, $1:4$ and $1:5$ respectively. Then, the probability that one of them wins the competition, is

(a) $\dfrac{112}{120}$ (b) $\dfrac{113}{120}$ (c) $\dfrac{114}{120}$ (d) $\dfrac{115}{120}$

6. A card is drawn from a well-shuffled deck of cards. The probability of getting a queen of club or king of heart is

(a) $\dfrac{1}{52}$ (b) $\dfrac{1}{26}$

(c) $\dfrac{1}{13}$ (d) $\dfrac{1}{56}$

7. If A and B are two events such that $P(A) = 0.42$, $P(B) = 0.48$ and $P(A \cap B) = 0.16$, then $P(A \cup B)$ is equal to

(a) 0.11   (b) 0.54

(c) 0.52   (d) 0.74

8. Probability that a truck stopped at a roadblock will have faulty brakes and badly worn tires, are 0.23 and 0.24, respectively. Also, the probability is 0.38 that a truck stopped at the roadblock will have faulty brakes or badly worn tires. Then, the probability that a truck stopped at this roadblock will have faulty breaks as well as badly worn tires, is ...K... . Here, K refers to

(a) 0.04   (b) 0.07

(c) 0.06   (d) 0.09

9. If A and B are mutually exclusive events, then

(a) $P(A) \le P(\overline{B})$ (b) $P(A) \ge P(\overline{B})$

(c) $P(A) < P(\overline{B})$ (d) None of these

10. If $P(B) = \dfrac{3}{4}$, $P(A \cap B \cap \overline{C}) = \dfrac{1}{3}$ and $P(\overline{A} \cap B \cap \overline{C}) = \dfrac{1}{3}$, then $P(B \cap C)$ equals

(a) $\dfrac{1}{12}$ (b) $\dfrac{1}{6}$

(c) $\dfrac{1}{15}$ (d) $\dfrac{1}{9}$

11. If $2P(A) = P(B) = \dfrac{5}{13}$ and $P(A/B) = \dfrac{2}{5}$, then $P(A \cup B)$ is equal to

(a) $\dfrac{11}{26}$ (b) $\dfrac{13}{25}$

(c) $\dfrac{11}{24}$ (d) $\dfrac{11}{21}$

12. If $P(A) = \dfrac{1}{2}$, $P(B) = 0$, then $P\left(\dfrac{A}{B}\right)$ is

(a) zero   (b) $\dfrac{1}{2}$

(c) not defined   (d) 1

13. If A and B are two events and $A \neq \phi$, $B \neq \phi$, then

(a) $P(A / B) = P(A) \cdot P(B)$ (b) $P(A / B) = \dfrac{P(A \cap B)}{P(B)}$

(c) $P(A / B) \cdot P(B / A) = 1$ (d) $P(A / B) = P(A) / P(B)$

14. A card is drawn from an ordinary pack of 52 cards and a gambler bets that, it is a spade or an ace. The odds against his winning this bet is

(a) $4 : 9$ (b) $9 : 4$ (c) $3 : 8$ (d) $8 : 3$

15. If $P(A) = \dfrac{3}{10}$, $P(B) = \dfrac{2}{5}$ and $P(A \cup B) = \dfrac{3}{5}$, then

$P(B/A) + P(A/B)$ equals to

(a) $\dfrac{1}{4}$ (b) $\dfrac{1}{3}$

(c) $\dfrac{5}{12}$ (d) $\dfrac{7}{12}$

16. Bag I contains 3 black and 2 white balls, bag II contains 2 black and 4 white balls. A bag and a ball is selected at random. The probability of selecting a black ball is

(a) $\dfrac{4}{15}$ (b) $\dfrac{7}{15}$

(c) $\dfrac{8}{15}$ (d) None of these

17. Of cigarette smoking population 70% are men and 30% are women, 10% of these men and 20% of these women smoke Wills. The probability that a person seen smoking a Wills to be men is

(a) $\dfrac{1}{5}$ (b) $\dfrac{7}{13}$

(c) $\dfrac{5}{13}$ (d) $\dfrac{7}{10}$

18. An observed event B can occur after one of the three events A_1, A_2, A_3. If
$P(A_1) = P(A_2) = 0.4$, $P(A_3) = 0.2$
and $P(B/A_1) = 0.25$, $P(B/A_2) = 0.4$
$P(B/A_3) = 0.125$, what is the probability of A_1 after observing B?

(a) $\dfrac{1}{3}$ (b) $\dfrac{6}{19}$

(c) $\dfrac{20}{57}$ (d) $\dfrac{2}{5}$

19. An insurance company insured 2000 scooter drivers, 4000 car drivers and 6000 truck drivers. The probabilities of an accident involving a scooter driver, car driver and a truck driver are 0.01, 0.03 and 0.15, respectively. One of the insured persons meets with an accident. The probability that the person is a scooter driver, is

(a) $\dfrac{1}{52}$ (b) $\dfrac{3}{52}$

(c) $\dfrac{15}{52}$ (d) $\dfrac{19}{52}$

20. Suppose a girl throws a die. If she gets 1 or 2, she tosses a coin three times and notes the number of tails. If she gets 3, 4, 5 or 6, she tosses a coin once and notes whether a 'head' or 'tail' is obtained. If she obtained exactly one 'tail', what is the probability that she threw 3, 4, 5 or 6 with the die?

(a) $\dfrac{5}{11}$ (b) $\dfrac{6}{11}$

(c) $\dfrac{7}{11}$ (d) $\dfrac{8}{11}$

• Case Based MCQs

21. Four friends Daksh, Yash, Sourabh, and Raju playing cards, Daksh, shuffling cards and told to Raju choose any four cards.

Based on the above information, answer the following questions.

(i) What is the probability that Raju getting all face card.

(a) $\dfrac{^{12}C_4}{^{52}C_4}$ (b) $\dfrac{^{16}C_4}{^{52}C_4}$

(c) $\dfrac{(^{12}C_2)^2}{^{52}C_4}$ (d) None of these

(ii) What is the probability that Raju getting two red cards and two black card.

(a) $\dfrac{(^{13}C_2)^2}{^{52}C_4}$ (b) $\dfrac{^{26}C_4}{^{52}C_4}$

(c) $\dfrac{(^{26}C_2)^2}{^{52}C_4}$ (d) $\dfrac{(^{26}C_4)^2}{^{52}C_4}$

(iii) What is the probability that Raju getting one card from each suit.

(a) $\dfrac{^{13}C_4}{^{52}C_4}$ (b) $\dfrac{(13)^4}{^{52}C_4}$

(c) $\dfrac{(^{13}C_4)^2}{^{52}C_4}$ (d) None of these

(iv) What is the probability that Raju getting all king cards.

(a) $\dfrac{1}{^{52}C_4}$

(b) $\dfrac{2}{^{52}C_4}$

(c) $\dfrac{4}{^{52}C_4}$

(d) $\dfrac{6}{^{52}C_4}$

(v) What is the probability that Raju getting two king and two Jack cards.

(a) $\dfrac{^4C_2}{^{52}C_4}$

(b) $\dfrac{36}{^{52}C_4}$

(c) $\dfrac{6}{^{52}C_4}$

(d) None of these

22. On her vacation, Veena visits four cities. Delhi, Lucknow, Agra, Meerut. In a random order.

Based on the above information, answer the following questions.

(i) What is the probability that she visits Delhi before Lucknow.

(a) $\dfrac{1}{2}$

(b) $\dfrac{1}{3}$

(c) $\dfrac{1}{6}$

(d) $\dfrac{1}{12}$

(ii) What is the probability she visit Delhi before Lucknow and Lucknow before Agra.

(a) $\dfrac{1}{2}$

(b) $\dfrac{1}{4}$

(c) $\dfrac{1}{6}$

(d) $\dfrac{1}{12}$

(iii) What is the probability she visits Delhi first and Lucknow last.

(a) $\dfrac{1}{6}$

(b) $\dfrac{1}{4}$

(c) $\dfrac{1}{2}$

(d) $\dfrac{1}{12}$

(iv) What is the probability she visits Delhi either first or second.

(a) $\dfrac{1}{3}$

(b) $\dfrac{2}{3}$

(c) $\dfrac{1}{2}$

(d) $\dfrac{1}{6}$

(v) What is the probability she visits Delhi just before Lucknow.

(a) $\dfrac{1}{4}$

(b) $\dfrac{1}{6}$

(c) $\dfrac{2}{3}$

(d) $\dfrac{1}{12}$

PART 2
Subjective Questions

• Short Answer Type Questions

1. The probability that atleast one of the two events A and B occurs is 0.6. If A and B occur simultaneously with probability 0.3, then evaluate $P(\overline{A}) + P(\overline{B})$.

2. If A and B are events such that $P(A) = \dfrac{1}{2}$, $P(B) = \dfrac{1}{3}$ and $P(A \cap B) = \dfrac{1}{4}$, then find

(i) $P\left(\dfrac{A}{B}\right)$

(ii) $P\left(\dfrac{B}{A}\right)$.

3. Three events A, B and C have probabilities $\dfrac{2}{5}, \dfrac{1}{3}$ and $\dfrac{1}{2}$, respectively. If $P(A \cap C) = \dfrac{1}{5}$ and $P(B \cap C) = \dfrac{1}{4}$, then find the values of $P(C / B)$ and $P(A' \cap C')$.

4. If a leap year is selected at random, then what is the chance that it will contain 53 Tuesday?

5. If $P(B) = \dfrac{3}{5}$, $P(A /B) = \dfrac{1}{2}$ and $P(A \cup B) = \dfrac{4}{5}$, then find $P(A \cup B)' + P(A' \cup B)$.

6. A fair die is rolled. Consider the following events $A = \{2, 4, 6\}$, $B = \{4, 5\}$ and $C = \{3, 4, 5, 6\}$

Find

(i) $P(A \cup B / C)$

(ii) $P(A \cap B / C)$

7. An instructor has a question bank consisting of 300 easy true/false questions, 200 difficult true/false questions, 500 easy multiple choice questions and 400 difficult multiple choice questions. If a question is selected at random from the question bank, then what is the probability that it will be an easy question, given that it is a multiple choice questions?

8. In a hostel, 60% of the students read Hindi newspaper, 40% read English newspaper and 20% read both Hindi and English newspapers. A student is selected at random,

  (i) find the probability that he/she reads neither Hindi nor English newspaper.

  (ii) if he/she reads Hindi newspaper, then find the probability that he/she reads English newspaper.

  (iii) if he/she reads English newspaper, then find the probability he/she reads Hindi newspaper.

9. Two cards are drawn at random and without replacement from a pack of 52 playing cards. Find the probability that both the cards are black.

10. A fair coin and an unbiased die are tossed. Let A be the event 'head appears on the coin' and B be the event '3 on the die'. Check whether A and B are independent events or not.

11. Prove that if E and F are independent events, then the events E and F' are also independent.

12. A die marked 1, 2, 3 in red and 4, 5, 6 in green is tossed. Let A be the event, 'number is odd' and B be the event, 'number is green'. Are A and B independent?

13. In a race, the probabilities of A and B winning the race are $\dfrac{1}{3}$ and $\dfrac{1}{6}$ respectively. Find the probability of neither of them winning the race.

14. Kamal and Monica appear for an interview for two vacancies. The probability of Kamal's selection is $1/3$ and that of Monica's selection is $1/5$. Find the probability that only one of them will be selected.

15. The probability of A, B and C solving a problem are $\dfrac{1}{3}, \dfrac{2}{7}$ and $\dfrac{3}{8}$, respectively. If all try and solve the problem simultaneously, find the probability that only one of them will solve it.

16. Akhil and Vijay appear for an interview for two vacancies. The probability of Akhil's selection is $\dfrac{1}{4}$ and Vijay's selection is $\dfrac{2}{3}$. Find the probability that only one of them will be selected.

17. There are 3 urns A, B and C. Urn A contains 4 red balls and 3 black balls. Urn B contains 5 red balls and 4 black balls. Urn C contains 4 red balls and 4 black balls. One ball is drawn from each of these urns. What is the probability that the 3 balls drawn consist of 2 red balls and 1 black ball?

18. A candidate is selected for interview of management trainees in 3 companies. For the first company, there are 12 candidates, for the second, there are 15 candidates and for the third, there are 10 candidates. Find the probability that he is selected by atleast one of the companies.

19. If A and B are two independent events, then prove that the probability of occurrence of atleast one of A and B is given by $1 - P(A') \cdot P(B')$.

20. Probability of solving specific problem independently by A and B are 1/2 and 1/3, respectively. If both try to solve the problem independently, then find the probability that

  (i) the problem is solved.

  (ii) exactly one of them solves the problem.

21. Bag A contains 5 white and 4 black balls, any bag B contains 7 white and 6 black balls. One ball is drawn from the bag A and without noticing its colour, is put in the bag B. If the ball is drawn from bag B, then find the probability that it is black in colour.

22. A word consists of 9 different alphabets, in which there are 4 consonants and 5 vowels. Three alphabets are chosen at random. What is the probability that more than one vowel will be selected?

23. An urn contains 2 white and 2 black balls. A ball is drawn at random. If it is white, it is not replaced into the urn. Otherwise, it is replaced with another ball of the same colour. The process is repeated. Find the probability that the third ball drawn is black.

24. A bag contains 4 white and 5 black balls. Another bag contains 9 white and 7 black balls. A ball is transferred from the first bag to the second bag and then a ball is drawn at random from the second bag. Find the probability that the ball drawn is white.

25. For A, B and C the chances of being selected as the manager of a firm are $4 : 1 : 2$, respectively. The probabilities for them to introduce a radical change in the marketing strategy are 0.3, 0.8 and 0.5, respectively. If a change takes place, then find the probability that it is due to the appointment of B.

• Long Answer Type Questions

26. Two dice are thrown together and the total score is noted. The events E, F and G are 'a total of 4', 'a total of 9 or more' and 'a total divisible by 5', respectively. Calculate $P(E)$, $P(F)$ and $P(G)$ and decide which pairs of events, if any are independent?

27. If A and B are two independent events such that $P(\bar{A} \cap B) = \dfrac{2}{15}$ and $P(A \cap \bar{B}) = \dfrac{1}{6}$, then find $P(A)$ and $P(B)$.

28. A bag contains 5 white and 4 black balls and another bag contains 7 white and 9 black balls. A ball is drawn from the first bag and two balls drawn from the second bag. What is the probability of drawing one white and two black balls?

29. Bag I contains 3 red and 4 black balls and bag II contains 4 red and 5 black balls. One ball is transferred from bag I to bag II and then ball is drawn from bag II. The ball so drawn is found to be red in colour. Find the probability that the transferred ball is black.

30. Bag A contains 2 white, 1 black and 3 red balls, bag B contains 3 white, 2 black and 4 red balls and bag C contains 4 white, 3 black and 2 red balls. One bag is chosen at random and 2 balls are drawn at random from that bag. If the randomly drawn balls happen to be red and black, then what is the probability that both balls come from bag B?

31. A shopkeeper sells three types of flower seeds A_1, A_2 and A_3. They are sold as a mixture, where the proportions are $4 : 4 : 2$, respectively. The germination rates of the three types of seeds are 45%, 60% and 35%. Calculate the probability

(i) Of a randomly chosen seed to germinate.

(ii) That it will not germinate given that the seed is of type A_3.

(iii) That it is of the type A_2 given that a randomly chosen seed does not germinate.

32. In a class of 75 students, 15 are above average, 45 are average and the rest below average achievers. The probability that an above average achieving student fail is 0.005, that an average achieving student fails is 0.05 and the probability of a below average achieving student failing is 0.15. If a student is known to have passed, then what is the probability that he is a below average achiever?

33. A laboratory blood test is 99% effective in detecting a certain disease,when it is infact present. However, the test also yields a false positive result for 0.5% of the healthy person tested (i.e. if a healthy person is tested, then with probability 0.005, the test will imply he has the disease). If 0.1% of the population actually has the disease, then what is the probability that a person has disease, given that his test result is positive?

34. By examining the chest X-ray, the probability that TB is detected when a person is actually suffering is 0.99. The probability of an healthy person diagnosed to have TB is 0.001. In a certain city, 1 in 1000 people suffers from TB. A person is selected at random and is diagnosed to have TB. What is the probability that he actually has TB?

35. Suppose a girl throws a die. If she gets a 5 or 6, she tosses a coin three times and notes the number of heads. If she gets 1, 2, 3 or 4, she tosses a coin once and notes whether a head or tail is obtained. If she obtained exactly one head, then what is the probability that she threw 1, 2, 3 or 4 with the die?

36. A factory has three machines A, B and C producing 1500, 2500 and 3000 bulbs per day, respectively. Machine A produces 1.5% defective bulbs, machine B produces 2% defective bulbs and machine C produces 2.5% defective bulbs. At the end of the day, a bulb is drawn at random and is found to be defective. What is the probability that the defective bulb has been produced by machine B?

37. A manufacturing firm produces steel pipes in three plants A, B and C with daily production of 500, 1000 and 2000 units, respectively. The fractions of defective steel pipes output produced by the plants A, B and C are respectively 0.005, 0.008 and 0.010. If a pipe is selected from a day's total production and found to be defective, then find out the probability that it came from the first plant.

• Case Based Questions

38. Two students Anil and Vijay appeared in an examination. The probability that Anil will qualify the examination is 0.05 and that Vijay will qualify is 0.10. The probability that both will qualify is 0.02.

Based on the above information, answer the following questions.

(i) Find the probability that Vijay will not qualify the exam.

(ii) Find the probability that atleast one of them will qualify the exam.

(iii) Find the probability that atleast one of them will not qualify the exam.

(iv) Find the probability that both Anil and Vijay will not qualify the exam.

(v) Find the probability that only one of them will qualify the exam.

SOLUTIONS

Objective Questions

1. (*d*) The sample space is $S = \{HH, HT, TH, TT\}$

Let E be the event of getting atleast one tail

$$E = \{HT, TH, TT\}$$

$\therefore$ Required probability P

$$= \frac{\text{Number of favourable outcomes}}{\text{Total number of outcomes}}$$

$$= \frac{n(E)}{n(S)} = \frac{3}{4}$$

2. (*d*) Let S be a sample space containing outcomes $\omega_1, \omega_2, \ldots \omega_n$, i.e. $S = \{\omega_1, \omega_2, \ldots \omega_n\}$

It follows from the axiomatic definition of probability that

(i) $0 \leq P(\omega_i) \leq 1$ for each $\omega_i \in S$

(ii) $P(\omega_1) + P(\omega_2) + \ldots + P(\omega_n) = 1$

(iii) For any event A, $P(A) = \Sigma\, P(\omega_i)$, $\omega_i \in A$.

3. (*b*) The total number of elementary events $= 6 \times 6 \times 6 = 216$

Let A be the event of getting a total of at least 6.

Then, $\overline{A}$ denotes the event of getting a total of less than 6 i.e. 3, 4, 5.

$$\therefore \quad \overline{A} = \{(1, 1, 1), (1, 1, 2), (1, 2, 1), (2, 1, 1), (1, 1, 3),$$
$$(1, 3, 1), (3, 1, 1), (1, 2, 2), (2, 1, 2), (2, 2, 1)\}$$

So, $n(\overline{A}) = 10$

$$\therefore \ P(\overline{A}) = \frac{10}{216}$$

$$\therefore \ P(A) = 1 - P(\overline{A}) = 1 - \frac{10}{216} = \frac{103}{108}$$

4. (*a*) Let $4P(A) = 2P(B) = P(C) = p$, which gives $P(A) = \dfrac{p}{4}$,

$P(B) = \dfrac{p}{2}$ and $P(C) = p$

Now, since A, B, C are mutually exclusive and exhaustive events, we have

$$P(A) + P(B) + P(C) = 1$$

$$\Rightarrow \qquad\qquad\qquad\qquad p = \frac{4}{7}$$

Hence, $\qquad\qquad\qquad P(A) = \dfrac{p}{4} = \dfrac{1}{7}$

5. (*c*) Let A, B, C and D be the events that the competitors P, Q, R and S respectively win the competition.

Then, $P(A) = \dfrac{1}{3}$, $P(B) = \dfrac{1}{4}$, $P(C) = \dfrac{1}{5}$ and $P(D) = \dfrac{1}{6}$

Since, only one competitors can win the competition.

Therefore, A, B, C, D are mutually exclusive events.

$\therefore$ Required probability $= P(A \cup B \cup C \cup D)$

$$= P(A) + P(B) + P(C) + P(D)$$

$$= \frac{1}{3} + \frac{1}{4} + \frac{1}{5} + \frac{1}{6} = \frac{114}{120}$$

6. (*b*) Here, $n\ (S) = 52$, $n(E_1) = 1$, $n(E_2) = 1$, $n(E_1 \cap E_2) = \phi$

$$\therefore \ P(E_1 \cup E_2) = P(E_1) + P(E_2) - P(E_1 \cap E_2)$$

$$= \frac{1}{52} + \frac{1}{52} - 0 = \frac{1}{26}$$

7. (*d*) Given, $P(A) = 0.42$, $P(B) = 0.48$ and $P(A \cap B) = 0.16$

$$\therefore \qquad P(A \cup B) = P(A) + P(B) - P(A \cap B)$$

$$= 0.42 + 0.48 - 0.16$$

$$= 0.90 - 0.16 = 0.74$$

8. (*d*) Let B be the event that a truck stopped at the roadblock will have faulty brakes and T be the event that it will have badly worn tires.

We have, $P(B) = 0.23$, $P(T) = 0.24$ and $P(B \cup T) = 0.38$

and $\quad P(B \cup T) = P(B) + P(T) - P(B \cap T)$

So, $\qquad 0.38 = 0.23 + 0.24 - P(B \cap T)$

$$\Rightarrow \quad P(B \cap T) = 0.09$$

9. (*a*) Given that, A and B are two mutually exclusive events.

Then, $\qquad P(A \cup B) = P(A) + P(B) \qquad [\because (A \cap B) = \phi]$

$$P(A) + P(B) \leq 1$$

$$P(A) + 1 - P(\overline{B}) \leq 1$$

$$P(A) \leq P(\overline{B})$$

10. (*a*) We have, $\qquad P(\overline{A} \cap B \cap \overline{C}) = \dfrac{1}{3}$

$$\Rightarrow \qquad\qquad P((B \cap \overline{C}) \cap \overline{A}) = \frac{1}{3}$$

$$\Rightarrow \quad P(B \cap \overline{C}) - P((B \cap \overline{C}) \cap A) = \frac{1}{3}$$

$$[\because P(X \cap \overline{Y}) = P(X) - P(X \cap Y)]$$

$$\Rightarrow \qquad P(B \cap \overline{C}) - P(A \cap B \cap \overline{C}) = \frac{1}{3}$$

$$\Rightarrow \qquad\qquad P(B \cap \overline{C}) - \frac{1}{3} = \frac{1}{3}$$

$$\Rightarrow \qquad\qquad\qquad P(B \cap \overline{C}) = \frac{2}{3}$$

$$\Rightarrow \qquad\qquad P(B) - P(B \cap C) = \frac{2}{3}$$

Now, $P(B \cap C) = P(B) - \dfrac{2}{3} = \dfrac{3}{4} - \dfrac{2}{3} = \dfrac{1}{12}$

11. (*a*) Given, $2P(A) = P(B) = \dfrac{5}{13} \Rightarrow P(A) = \dfrac{5}{26}$ and $P(B) = \dfrac{5}{13}$

Now, $\qquad P\left(\dfrac{A}{B}\right) = \dfrac{P(A \cap B)}{P(B)}$

$$\Rightarrow \qquad\qquad \frac{2}{5} = \frac{P(A \cap B)}{\dfrac{5}{13}}$$

$$\Rightarrow \qquad P(A \cap B) = \frac{2}{5} \times \frac{5}{13} = \frac{2}{13}$$

Again, $P(A \cup B) = P(A) + P(B) - P(A \cap B)$

$$= \frac{5}{26} + \frac{5}{13} - \frac{2}{13} = \frac{5 + 10 - 4}{26} = \frac{11}{26}$$

12. (*c*) It is given that $P(A) = \dfrac{1}{2}$ and $P(B) = 0$

$$P\left(\frac{A}{B}\right) = \frac{P(A \cap B)}{P(B)} = \frac{P(A \cap B)}{0} = \infty$$

Therefore, $P\left(\dfrac{A}{B}\right)$ is not defined.

13. (*b*) If $A \neq \phi$ and $B \neq \phi$, then

$$P(A/B) = \frac{P(A \cap B)}{P(B)}$$

14. (*b*) Let A be the event of getting a spade or an ace from a pack of 52 cards.

Then, total number of possible outcomes $= {}^{52}C_1 = 52$

Since, there are 13 spade cards including an ace of spade and three aces other than an ace of spade.

$\therefore$ Number of favourable outcomes $= {}^{16}C_1 = 16$

$$\therefore \qquad P(A) = \frac{16}{52} = \frac{4}{13}$$

Hence, odds against A are $P(\overline{A}) : P(A) = \frac{9}{13} : \frac{4}{13}$

$$= 9 : 4$$

15. (*d*) Here, $P(A) = \frac{3}{10}$, $P(B) \frac{2}{5}$ and $P(A \cup B) = \frac{3}{5}$

$$P(B/A) + P(A/B) = \frac{P(B \cap A)}{P(A)} + \frac{P(A \cap B)}{P(B)}$$

$$= \frac{P(A) + P(B) - P(A \cup B)}{P(A)} + \frac{P(A) + P(B) - P(A \cup B)}{P(B)}$$

$$= \frac{\frac{3}{10} + \frac{2}{5} - \frac{3}{5}}{\frac{3}{10}} + \frac{\frac{3}{10} + \frac{2}{5} - \frac{3}{5}}{\frac{2}{5}}$$

$$= \frac{\frac{1}{10}}{\frac{3}{10}} + \frac{\frac{1}{10}}{\frac{2}{5}} = \frac{1}{3} + \frac{1}{4} = \frac{7}{12}$$

16. (*b*) Let E_1 = Bag I is selected

$\qquad\quad E_2$ = Bag II is selected

and $\qquad A$ = Black ball is drawn

Then, $P(E_1) = P(E_2) = \frac{1}{2}$, $P\left(\frac{A}{E_1}\right) = \frac{3}{5}$, $P\left(\frac{A}{E_2}\right) = \frac{2}{6}$

$$\because \qquad P(A) = P(E_1) \times P\left(\frac{A}{E_1}\right) + P(E_2) \times P\left(\frac{A}{E_2}\right)$$

$$= \frac{1}{2} \times \frac{3}{5} + \frac{1}{2} \times \frac{2}{6}$$

$$= \frac{3}{10} + \frac{1}{6} = \frac{9+5}{30} = \frac{14}{30} = \frac{7}{15}$$

17. (*b*) Let E_1 and E_2 denote the cigarette smoking population of men and women, respectively.

Given, $P(E_1) = 0.7$, $P(E_2) = 0.3$

$$P\left(\frac{A}{E_1}\right) = 0.1, P\left(\frac{A}{E_2}\right) = 0.2$$

Using Baye's theorem,

$$P(E_1/A) = \frac{P(E_1)P(A/E_1)}{P(E_1) \times P(A/E_1) + P(E_2)P(A/E_2)}$$

$$= \frac{0.7 \times 0.1}{0.7 \times 0.1 + 0.3 \times 0.2}$$

$$= \frac{0.07}{0.07 + 0.06} = \frac{0.07}{0.13} = \frac{7}{13}$$

18. (*c*) Required probability $= P(A_1/B)$

$$= \frac{P(A_1)P(B/A_1)}{P(A_1)P(B/A_1) + P(A_2)P(B/A_2) + P(A_3)P(B/A_3)}$$

$$= \frac{0.4 \times 0.25}{0.4 \times 0.25 + 0.4 \times 0.4 + 0.2 \times 0.125}$$

$$= \frac{0.1}{0.1 + 0.16 + 0.025} = \frac{0.1}{0.285} = \frac{20}{57}$$

19. (*a*) Let $P(A) = P(\text{scooter}) = \frac{2000}{12000} = \frac{1}{6}$

$$P(B) = P(\text{car}) = \frac{4000}{12000} = \frac{1}{3}$$

and $\qquad P(C) = P(\text{truck}) = \frac{6000}{12000} = \frac{1}{2}$

Let E = Event that person meets with accident.

Then, $P\left(\frac{E}{A}\right) = \frac{1}{100}$, $P\left(\frac{E}{B}\right) = \frac{3}{100}$, $P\left(\frac{E}{C}\right) = \frac{15}{100}$

$\therefore$ Required probability

$$P(A/E) = \frac{P(A) \cdot P\left(\dfrac{E}{A}\right)}{P(A) \cdot P\left(\dfrac{E}{A}\right) + P(B) \cdot P\left(\dfrac{E}{B}\right) + P(C) \cdot P\left(\dfrac{E}{C}\right)}$$

$$= \frac{\dfrac{1}{6} \times \dfrac{1}{100}}{\dfrac{1}{6} \times \dfrac{1}{100} + \dfrac{1}{3} \times \dfrac{3}{100} + \dfrac{1}{2} \times \dfrac{15}{100}} = \frac{\dfrac{1}{6}}{\dfrac{1}{6} + 1 + \dfrac{15}{2}}$$

$$= \frac{\dfrac{1}{6}}{\dfrac{1 + 6 + 45}{6}} = \frac{1}{52}$$

20. (*d*) Let E_1 be the event that the girl gets 1 or 2.

E_2 be the event that the girl gets 3, 4, 5 or 6.

and A be the event that the girl gets exactly a 'tail'.

Then, $\qquad P(E_1) = \frac{2}{6} = \frac{1}{3}$

and $\qquad P(E_2) = \frac{4}{6} = \frac{2}{3}$

$P\left(\dfrac{A}{E_1}\right) = P$ (getting exactly one tail when a coin is tossed three times) $= \dfrac{3}{8}$

$P\left(\dfrac{A}{E_2}\right) = P$ (getting exactly a tail when a coin is tossed once)

$$= \frac{1}{2}$$

Now, required probability

$$P\left(\frac{E_2}{A}\right) = \frac{P(E_2) \cdot P\left(\dfrac{A}{E_2}\right)}{P(E_1) \cdot P\left(\dfrac{A}{E_1}\right) + P(E_2) \cdot P\left(\dfrac{A}{E_2}\right)}$$

$$= \frac{\dfrac{2}{3} \cdot \dfrac{1}{2}}{\dfrac{1}{3} \cdot \dfrac{3}{8} + \dfrac{2}{3} \cdot \dfrac{1}{2}} = \frac{\dfrac{1}{3}}{\dfrac{1}{8} + \dfrac{1}{3}} = \frac{8}{11}$$

21. Total number of possible outcomes $= {}^{52}C_4$

  (i) (a) We know that, there are 12 face cards

    $\therefore$ Number of favourable outcomes $= {}^{12}C_4$

    $\therefore$ Required probability $= \dfrac{{}^{12}C_4}{{}^{52}C_4}$

  (ii) (c) We know that there are 26 red and 26 black cards

    $\therefore$ Number of favourable outcomes $= {}^{26}C_2 \times {}^{26}C_2$

    $\therefore$ Required probability $= \dfrac{\left({}^{26}C_2\right)^2}{{}^{52}C_4}$

  (iii) (b) There are 4 suits each having 13 cards

    $\therefore$ Number of favourable outcomes $= \left({}^{13}C_1\right)^4$

    $\therefore$ Required probability $= \dfrac{(13)^4}{{}^{52}C_4}$

  (iv) (a) There are 4 king

    $\therefore$ Number of favourable outcomes $= {}^4C_4 = 1$

    Required probability $= \dfrac{1}{{}^{52}C_4}$

  (v) (b) In playing cards there are 4 kings and 4 Jack cards.

    $\therefore$ Number of favourable outcomes $= \left({}^4C_2 \times {}^4C_2\right)$

$$= 6 \times 6 = 36$$

    Required probability $= \dfrac{36}{{}^{52}C_4}$

22. Let the Veena visits four cities Delhi, Lucknow, Agra, Meerut A, B, C and D respectively. Number of way's in which Veena can visit four cities A, B, C and D is $4!$ i.e. 24.

$\therefore\ \ n(S) = 24$

Clearly, sample space for this experiment is

$$S = \begin{cases} ABCD, ABDC, ACBD, ACDB, ADBC, ADCB, \\ BACD, BADC, BCAD, BCDA, BDAC, BDCA, \\ CABD, CADB, CBAD, CBDA, CDAB, CDBA, \\ DABC, DACB, DCAB, DCBA, DBAC, DBCA \end{cases}$$

  (i) (a) Let E_1 be the event that Veena visits A before B. Then,

$$E_1 = \begin{cases} ABCD, ABDC, ACBD, ACDB, ADBC, ADCB, \\ CABD, CADB, CDAB, DABC, DACB, DCAB \end{cases}$$

$\Rightarrow\quad\quad n(E_1) = 12$

$\therefore$ P(she visits A before B) $= P(E_1) = \dfrac{n(E_1)}{n(S)}$

$$= \dfrac{12}{24} = \dfrac{1}{2}$$

  (ii) (c) Let E_2 be the event that she visits A before B and B before C. Then, $E_2 = \{ABCD, ABDC, ADBC, DABC\}$

$\Rightarrow\quad\quad n(E_2) = 4$

$\therefore$ P (she visits A before B and B before C) $= P(E_2)$

$$= \dfrac{n(E_2)}{n(S)}$$

$$= \dfrac{4}{24} = \dfrac{1}{6}$$

  (iii) (d) Let E_3 be the event that she visits A first and B last.

    Then, $E_3 = \{ACDB, ADCB\}$

$$n(E_3) = 2$$

    $\therefore$ P (she visits A first and B last) $= P(E_3)$

$$= \dfrac{n(E_3)}{n(S)} = \dfrac{2}{24} = \dfrac{1}{12}$$

  (iv) (c) Let E_4 be the event that she visits A either first or second. Then,

$$E_4 = \begin{cases} ABCD, ABDC, ACBD, ACDB, ADBC, ADCB, \\ BACD, BADC, CABD, CADB, DABC, DACB \end{cases}$$

$\Rightarrow\quad\quad n(E_4) = 12$

    Hence, P (she visits A either first or second)

$$= P(E_4) = \dfrac{n(E_4)}{n(S)} = \dfrac{12}{24} = \dfrac{1}{2}$$

  (v) (a) Let E_5 be the event that she visits A just before B. Then,

$$E_5 = \{ABCD, ABDC, CABD, CDAB, DABC, DCAB\}$$

$\Rightarrow n(E_5) = 6$

    Hence, P (she visits A just before B)

$$= P(E_5) = \dfrac{n(E_5)}{n(S)} = \dfrac{6}{24} = \dfrac{1}{4}$$

Subjective Questions

1. We know that, $A \cup B$ denotes the occurrence of atleast one of A and B and $A \cap B$ denotes the occurrence of both A and B, simultaneously.

Then, $P(A \cup B) = 0.6$ and $P(A \cap B) = 0.3$

$\because\ P(A \cup B) = P(A) + P(B) - P(A \cap B)$

$\therefore\quad\quad 0.6 = P(A) + P(B) - 0.3 \Rightarrow P(A) + P(B) = 0.9$

$\Rightarrow\ \{[1 - P(\overline{A})] + [1 - P(\overline{B})]\} = 0.9$

$$[\because\ P(A) = 1 - P(\overline{A}) \text{ and } P(B) = 1 - P(\overline{B})]$$

$\Rightarrow\quad\quad P(\overline{A}) + P(\overline{B}) = 2 - 0.9 = 1.1$

2. Given, $P(A) = \dfrac{1}{2},\ P(B) = \dfrac{1}{3}$ and $P(A \cap B) = \dfrac{1}{4}$

  (i) $P\left(\dfrac{A}{B}\right) = \dfrac{P(A \cap B)}{P(B)} = \dfrac{1/4}{1/3} = \dfrac{3}{4}$

  (ii) $P\left(\dfrac{B}{A}\right) = \dfrac{P(A \cap B)}{P(A)} = \dfrac{1/4}{1/2} = \dfrac{2}{4} = \dfrac{1}{2}$

Thus, the required value of $P(A/B)$ and $P(B/A)$ are $\dfrac{3}{4}$ and $\dfrac{1}{2}$, respectively.

3. Given, $P(A) = \dfrac{2}{5},\ P(B) = \dfrac{1}{3},\ P(C) = \dfrac{1}{2},\ P(A \cap C) = \dfrac{1}{5}$

and $P(B \cap C) = \dfrac{1}{4}$

$\therefore\quad\quad P\left(\dfrac{C}{B}\right) = \dfrac{P(B \cap C)}{P(B)} = \dfrac{1/4}{1/3} = \dfrac{3}{4}$

and $P(A' \cap C') = 1 - P(A \cup C)$

$$= 1 - [P(A) + P(C) - P(A \cap C)]$$

$$= 1 - \left(\dfrac{2}{5} + \dfrac{1}{2} - \dfrac{1}{5}\right) = 1 - \left(\dfrac{4 + 5 - 2}{10}\right)$$

$$= 1 - \dfrac{7}{10} = \dfrac{3}{10}$$

4. In a leap year, there are 366 days, i.e. 52 weeks and 2 days extra.

There are 52 tuesday and 2 days extra.

For the remaining two days, there are following 7 cases

  (i) Sunday and Monday

  (ii) Monday and Tuesday

  (iii) Tuesday and Wednesday

  (iv) Wednesday and Thursday

  (v) Thursday and Friday

  (vi) Friday and Saturday

  (vii) Saturday and Sunday

Out of these seven possibilities, only two are favourable to the events "53 tuesday".

$\therefore$ Total number of cases = 7 and favourable cases = 2

Hence, required probability is $\dfrac{2}{7}$.

5. Here, $P(B) = \dfrac{3}{5}$, $P(A/B) = \dfrac{1}{2}$ and $P(A \cup B) = \dfrac{4}{5}$

Since, $P(A/B) = \dfrac{P(A \cap B)}{P(B)}$

$\Rightarrow \quad P(A \cap B) = P(A/B) \cdot P(B)$

$$= \dfrac{1}{2} \times \dfrac{3}{5} = \dfrac{3}{10}$$

Also, $P(A \cup B) = P(A) + P(B) - P(A \cap B)$

$\Rightarrow \quad P(A) = \dfrac{4}{5} - \dfrac{3}{5} + \dfrac{3}{10} = \dfrac{1}{2}$

$\therefore \quad P(A \cup B)' = 1 - P(A \cup B) = 1 - \dfrac{4}{5} = \dfrac{1}{5}$

and $P(A' \cup B) = P(A') + P(B) - P(A' \cap B)$

$$= P(A') + P(B) - P(B) + P(A \cap B)$$

$$= P(A') + P(A \cap B) = \dfrac{1}{2} + \dfrac{3}{10} = \dfrac{4}{5}$$

$\Rightarrow P(A \cup B)' + P(A' \cup B) = \dfrac{1}{5} + \dfrac{4}{5} = \dfrac{5}{5} = 1$

6. Given events are $A = \{2, 4, 6\}$, $B = \{4, 5\}$ and $C = \{3, 4, 5, 6\}$

Sample space, $S = \{1, 2, 3, 4, 5, 6\}$

Now, $\quad A \cup B = \{2, 4, 5, 6\}$, $A \cap B = \{4\}$

$\quad (A \cup B) \cap C = \{2, 4, 5, 6\} \cap \{3, 4, 5, 6\} = \{4, 5, 6\}$

and $\quad A \cap B \cap C = \{4\} \cap \{3, 4, 5, 6\} = \{4\}$

$\therefore \quad n(S) = 6$, $n[((A \cup B) \cap C)] = 3$, $n(A \cap B \cap C) = 1$

and $n(C) = 4$

  (i) $P\left(\dfrac{A \cup B}{C}\right) = \dfrac{P((A \cup B) \cap C)}{P(C)}$

$$= \dfrac{n((A \cup B) \cap C)/n(S)}{n(C)/n(S)}$$

$$= \dfrac{3/6}{4/6} = \dfrac{3}{4}$$

  (ii) $P\left(\dfrac{A \cap B}{C}\right) = \dfrac{P(A \cap B \cap C)}{P(C)}$

$$= \dfrac{n(A \cap B \cap C)/n(S)}{n(C)/n(S)}$$

$$= \dfrac{1/6}{4/6} = \dfrac{1}{4}$$

7. Total number of questions,

$$n(S) = 300 + 200 + 500 + 400 = 1400$$

Let E be the event that question is easy and F be the event that question is a multiple choice.

Then, $\quad n(E) = 500 + 300 = 800$

$\therefore \quad P(E) = \dfrac{\text{Number of easy questions}}{\text{Total number of questions}}$

$$= \dfrac{n(E)}{n(S)} = \dfrac{800}{1400} = \dfrac{4}{7}$$

Also, $\quad n(F) = 500 + 400 = 900$

$\therefore \quad P(F) = \dfrac{\text{Number of multiple choice questions}}{\text{Total number of questions}}$

$$= \dfrac{n(F)}{n(S)} = \dfrac{900}{1400} = \dfrac{9}{14}$$

and $P(E \cap F)$

$$= \dfrac{\text{Total number of easy multiple choice questions}}{\text{Total number of questions}}$$

$$= \dfrac{500}{1400} = \dfrac{5}{14}$$

$\therefore \quad P\left(\dfrac{E}{F}\right) = \dfrac{P(E \cap F)}{P(F)} = \dfrac{5/14}{9/14} = \dfrac{5}{9}$

8. Let H = student reading Hindi newspaper

and E = student reading English newspaper

Let $n(S) = 100$, then $n(H) = 60$,

$\quad n(E) = 40$ and $n(H \cap E) = 20$

$\therefore \quad P(H) = \dfrac{n(H)}{n(S)} = \dfrac{60}{100} = \dfrac{3}{5}$

$$P(E) = \dfrac{n(E)}{n(S)} = \dfrac{40}{100} = \dfrac{2}{5}$$

and $\quad P(H \cap E) = \dfrac{n(H \cap E)}{n(S)} = \dfrac{20}{100} = \dfrac{1}{5}$

  (i) Required probability = P(student reads neither Hindi nor English newspaper)

$$= P(H' \cap E') = P(H \cup E)'$$

$$= 1 - P(H \cup E)$$

$$= 1 - [P(H) + P(E) - P(H \cap E)]$$

$$= 1 - \left[\dfrac{3}{5} + \dfrac{2}{5} - \dfrac{1}{5}\right] = 1 - \dfrac{4}{5} = \dfrac{1}{5}$$

  (ii) Required probability

$= P$(student reads English newspaper, if he/she reads Hindi newspaper)

$\therefore \quad P\left(\dfrac{E}{H}\right) = \dfrac{P(E \cap H)}{P(H)} = \dfrac{1/5}{3/5} = \dfrac{1}{3}$

  (iii) Required probability

$= P$(student reads Hindi newspaper when it is given that he/she reads English newspaper)

$\therefore \quad P\left(\dfrac{H}{E}\right) = \dfrac{P(H \cap E)}{P(E)} = \dfrac{1/5}{2/5} = \dfrac{1}{2}$

9. There are 26 black cards in a pack of 52 cards.

Required probability $= P(E \text{ and } F) = P(E) \cdot P\left(\dfrac{F}{E}\right)$

where, E : First card drawn is black

and F : Second card drawn is black.

$$P(E) = \frac{\text{Number of favourable outcomes}}{\text{Total number of outcomes}} = \frac{26}{52} = \frac{1}{2}$$

$$P\left(\frac{F}{E}\right) = \frac{25}{51} \qquad \text{[after drawing 1 black card, there will be 25 black cards left]}$$

∴ Required probability,

$$P(E \cap F) = P(E) \cdot P\left(\frac{F}{E}\right) = \frac{1}{2} \times \frac{25}{51} = \frac{25}{102}$$

10. If a fair coin and an unbiased die are tossed, then the sample space S is given by

$$S = \begin{Bmatrix} (H, 1), (H, 2), (H, 3), (H, 4), (H, 5), (H, 6), \\ (T, 1), (T, 2), (T, 3), (T, 4), (T, 5), (T, 6) \end{Bmatrix}$$

$\Rightarrow \quad n(S) = 12$

Also, A : Head appears on the coin and B : 3 appears on die.

$\Rightarrow \quad A$ = Event having head on coin

$\quad = \{(H, 1), (H, 2), (H, 3), (H, 4), (H, 5), (H, 6)\}$

$\quad B$ = Event having 3 on die

$\quad = \{(H, 3), (T, 3)\}\, ; A \cap B = \{(H, 3)\}$

∴ $n(A) = 6, n(B) = 2, n(A \cap B) = 1$

Hence, $P(A) = \dfrac{n(A)}{n(S)} = \dfrac{6}{12} = \dfrac{1}{2}, P(B) = \dfrac{n(B)}{n(S)} = \dfrac{2}{12} = \dfrac{1}{6}$

and $\quad P(A \cap B) = \dfrac{n(A \cap B)}{n(S)} = \dfrac{1}{12}$

Now, $\quad P(A) \times P(B) = \dfrac{1}{2} \times \dfrac{1}{6} = \dfrac{1}{12} = P(A \cap B)$

Hence, A and B are independent events.

11. Given, E and F are independent events, therefore

$\Rightarrow \qquad P(E \cap F) = P(E)\, P(F) \qquad \qquad \text{...(i)}$

Now, we have

$\quad P(E \cap F') + P(E \cap F) = P(E)$

$\Rightarrow \qquad P(E \cap F') = P(E) - P(E \cap F)$

$\Rightarrow \qquad P(E \cap F') = P(E) - P(E)\,P(F)$

$\qquad \qquad \qquad \qquad \qquad \qquad \text{[using Eq. (i)]}$

$\Rightarrow \qquad P(E \cap F') = P(E)[1 - P(F)]$

$\Rightarrow \qquad P(E \cap F') = P(E)\,P(F')$

∴ E and F' are also independent events.   **Hence proved.**

12. When a die is thrown, then sample space,

$$S = \{1, 2, 3, 4, 5, 6\} \Rightarrow n(S) = 6$$

Also, A : Number is odd and B : Number is green

∴ $\qquad A = \{1, 3, 5\}, B = \{4, 5, 6\}$ and $A \cap B = \{5\}$

$\Rightarrow \quad n(A) = 3, n(B) = 3, n(A \cap B) = 1$

Now, $P(A) = \dfrac{n(A)}{n(S)} = \dfrac{3}{6} = \dfrac{1}{2},$

$\quad P(B) = \dfrac{n(B)}{n(S)} = \dfrac{3}{6} = \dfrac{1}{2},$

$\quad P(A \cap B) = \dfrac{n(A \cap B)}{n(S)} = \dfrac{1}{6}$

and $P(A) \times P(B) = \dfrac{1}{2} \times \dfrac{1}{2} = \dfrac{1}{4} \neq \dfrac{1}{6} = P(A \cap B)$

∴ $\qquad P(A \cap B) \neq P(A) \times P(B)$

Thus, A and B are not independent events.

13. Given, $P(A) = \dfrac{1}{3}, P(B) = \dfrac{1}{6}$

∴ $\qquad P(A') = 1 - \dfrac{1}{3} = \dfrac{2}{3}$ and $P(B') = 1 - \dfrac{1}{6} = \dfrac{5}{6}$

Thus, required probability $= P(A') \times P(B') = \dfrac{2}{3} \times \dfrac{5}{6} = \dfrac{5}{9}$

14. Let E_1 = Kamal's selection after appearing for an interview and E_2 = Monica's selection after appearing for an interview

Then, $P(E_1) = \dfrac{1}{3}$ and $P(E_2) = \dfrac{1}{5}$ \qquad [given]

P (either Kamal's or Monica's selection)

$= P(E_1 \overline{E_2}) + P(\overline{E_1}\, E_2) = P(E_1)\, P(\overline{E_2}) + P(\overline{E_1})\, P(E_2)$

$\qquad \qquad$ [since, E_1 and E_2 are independent events]

$= \dfrac{1}{3} \times \left(1 - \dfrac{1}{5}\right) + \left(1 - \dfrac{1}{3}\right) \times \dfrac{1}{5}$

$= \dfrac{1}{3} \times \dfrac{4}{5} + \dfrac{2}{3} \times \dfrac{1}{5} = \dfrac{4}{15} + \dfrac{2}{15} = \dfrac{6}{15} = \dfrac{2}{5}$

15. Let A : Problem is solved by A

$\quad B$: Problem is solved by B

$\quad C$: Problem is solved by C

Given, $P(A) = \dfrac{1}{3}, P(B) = \dfrac{2}{7}$ and $P(C) = \dfrac{3}{8}$

P (only one of A, B and C solve the problem)

$= P(\overline{A}B\overline{C}) + P(\overline{A}\overline{B}C) + P(A\overline{B}\overline{C})$

$= P(\overline{A})P(\overline{B})P(C) + P(\overline{A})P(B)P(\overline{C}) + P(A)P(\overline{B})P(\overline{C})$

$\qquad$ [since, A, B and C are independent events]

$= \left(1 - \dfrac{1}{3}\right)\left(1 - \dfrac{2}{7}\right) \times \dfrac{3}{8} + \left(1 - \dfrac{1}{3}\right) \times \dfrac{2}{7}$

$\qquad \qquad \times \left(1 - \dfrac{3}{8}\right) + \dfrac{1}{3} \times \left(1 - \dfrac{2}{7}\right)\left(1 - \dfrac{3}{8}\right)$

$= \dfrac{2}{3} \times \dfrac{5}{7} \times \dfrac{3}{8} + \dfrac{2}{3} \times \dfrac{2}{7} \times \dfrac{5}{8} + \dfrac{1}{3} \times \dfrac{5}{7} \times \dfrac{5}{8}$

$= \dfrac{1}{3 \times 7 \times 8}(30 + 20 + 25)$

$= \dfrac{75}{3 \times 7 \times 8} = \dfrac{25}{56}$

16. Given, probability of Akhil's selection; $P(A) = \dfrac{1}{4}$

Probability of Vijay's selection; $P(B) = \dfrac{2}{3}$

Probability that only one of them will be selected for an interview $= P$ (A selected and B is not salected for an interview) $+ P(B$ selected and A is not selected for an interview)

$= P(A) \times P(\overline{B}) + P(B) \times P(\overline{A})$

$= \dfrac{1}{4} \times \left(1 - \dfrac{2}{3}\right) + \dfrac{2}{3} \times \left(1 - \dfrac{1}{4}\right)$

$= \dfrac{1}{4} \times \dfrac{1}{3} + \dfrac{2}{3} \times \dfrac{3}{4} = \dfrac{1}{12} + \dfrac{6}{12} = \dfrac{7}{12}$

17. Urn A : 4 red balls and 3 black balls

Urn B : 5 red balls and 4 black balls

Urn C : 4 red balls and 4 black balls

Three balls are drawn in such a way that 2 are red balls and 1 is black ball.

$\therefore$ Required probability

$$= P(R_A R_B B_C) + P(R_A B_B R_C) + P(B_A R_B R_C)$$

$$= \frac{4}{7} \times \frac{5}{9} \times \frac{4}{8} + \frac{4}{7} \times \frac{4}{9} \times \frac{4}{8} + \frac{4}{7} \times \frac{3}{9} \times \frac{5}{8}$$

$$= \frac{4}{8}\left(\frac{20}{63} + \frac{16}{63} + \frac{15}{63}\right) = \frac{1}{2} \times \frac{51}{63} = \frac{17}{42}$$

18. Let C_1, C_2 and C_3 be the companies,

$P(C_1) =$ Probability of selection in $C_1 = \dfrac{1}{12}$

$P(C_2) =$ Probability of selection in $C_2 = \dfrac{1}{15}$

$P(C_3) =$ Probability of selection in $C_3 = \dfrac{1}{10}$

Probability of no selection in all,

$$P(\overline{C_1}\overline{C_2}\overline{C_3}) = P(\overline{C_1})\,P(\overline{C_2})\,P(\overline{C_3})$$

$$[C_1,\ C_2 \text{ and } C_3 \text{are in dependents}]$$

$$= \left(1 - \frac{1}{12}\right) \times \left(1 - \frac{1}{15}\right) \times \left(1 - \frac{1}{10}\right)$$

$$= \frac{11}{12} \times \frac{14}{15} \times \frac{9}{10} = \frac{231}{300}$$

Probability of selection in atleast one of the companies

$$= 1 - \text{Probability of no selection in all}$$

$$= 1 - \frac{231}{300} = 1 - 0.77 = 0.23$$

19. Required probability $= P(A \cup B)$

$$= P(A) + P(B) - P(A) \cdot P(B)$$
$$= P(A)\,[1 - P(B)] + 1 - P(B')$$
$$= P(A)P(B') - P(B') + 1$$
$$= 1 - P(B')\,[1 - P(A)]$$
$$= 1 - P(A')P(B') \qquad \textbf{Hence proved.}$$

20. We have, $\ P(A) = \dfrac{1}{2}$ and $P(B) = \dfrac{1}{3}$

$\therefore \qquad P(\overline{A}) = 1 - P(A) = 1 - \dfrac{1}{2} = \dfrac{1}{2}$

and $\qquad P(\overline{B}) = 1 - P(B) = 1 - \dfrac{1}{3} = \dfrac{2}{3}$

(i) P(problem is solved)

$$= P(\text{atleast one of them will solve the problem})$$
$$= 1 - P(\text{none of them solve the problem})$$
$$= 1 - P(\overline{A}) \cdot P(\overline{B})$$

$$[\because A \text{ and } B \text{ are independent events, then}$$
$$\overline{A} \text{ and } \overline{B} \text{ are also independent events}]$$

$$= 1 - \frac{1}{2} \times \frac{2}{3} = 1 - \frac{1}{3} = \frac{2}{3}$$

(ii) P (exactly one of them solves the problem)

$$= P(A \cap \overline{B}) + P(\overline{A} \cap B)$$
$$= P(A) \cdot P(\overline{B}) + P(\overline{A}) \cdot P(B)$$

$$[\because A \text{ and } B \text{ are independent events, then } A, \overline{B}$$
$$\text{and } \overline{A}, B \text{ are also independent events}]$$

$$= \frac{1}{2} \times \frac{2}{3} + \frac{1}{2} \times \frac{1}{3} = \frac{3}{6} = \frac{1}{2}$$

21. Given, Bag A : 5 white and 4 black balls

Bag B : 7 white and 6 black balls

Case I When 1 white ball is transferred from bag A to bag B. Then, its probability,

$$P_1 = \frac{5}{5+4} = \frac{5}{9}$$

Now, bag B contains 8 white and 6 black balls. Then, the probability of drawing a ball from bag B black in colour,

$$P_2 = \frac{6}{8+6} = \frac{6}{14} = \frac{3}{7}$$

Thus, the probability of both occurring together $= P_1 P_2$

$$= \frac{5}{9} \times \frac{3}{7} = \frac{15}{63} \qquad \ldots(i)$$

$$[\text{multiplication theorem for independent events}]$$

Case II When 1 black ball is transferred from bag A to bag B. Then, its probability,

$$P_3 = \frac{4}{5+4} = \frac{4}{9}$$

Now, the bag B contains 7 white and 7 black balls. Then, the probability of drawing a ball from bag B black in colour,

$$P_4 = \frac{7}{7+7} = \frac{7}{14} = \frac{1}{2}$$

Thus, the probability of both occurring together

$$= P_3 P_4 = \frac{4}{9} \times \frac{1}{2} = \frac{2}{9} \qquad \ldots(ii)$$

On adding Eqs. (i) and (ii) we get the required probability

$$= \frac{15}{63} + \frac{2}{9} = \frac{15+14}{63} = \frac{29}{63}$$

22. In a given word consists of 9 different alphabets, there are 4 consonants and 5 vowels. Three alphabets are chosen at random.

$\therefore$ Probability that more than one vowel will be selected

$$= P (\text{two vowels and one consonants}) + P (\text{three vowels})$$

$$= \frac{{}^5C_2 \times {}^4C_1}{{}^9C_3} + \frac{{}^5C_3}{{}^9C_3}$$

$$= \frac{1}{{}^9C_3}\left(\frac{5 \times 4 \times 4}{2 \times 1} + \frac{5 \times 4 \times 3}{3 \times 2 \times 1}\right)$$

$$= \frac{3 \times 2 \times 1}{9 \times 8 \times 7}(40 + 10)$$

$$= \frac{1}{84} \times 50 = \frac{25}{42}$$

23. Let E_{wb} denote the event that the first ball drawn has colour w and second ball drawn has colour b.

Let B denote the event that the third ball drawn is black.

Now, $\quad P(E_{ww}) = \dfrac{2}{4} \times \dfrac{1}{3} = \dfrac{1}{6}, \quad P(E_{wb}) = \dfrac{2}{4} \times \dfrac{2}{3} = \dfrac{1}{3}$

$$P(E_{bw}) = \frac{2}{4} \times \frac{2}{5} = \frac{1}{5}, \quad P(E_{bb}) = \frac{2}{4} \times \frac{3}{5} = \frac{3}{10}$$

Also, $P(B/E_{ww}) = \dfrac{2}{2} = 1, \ P(B/E_{wb}) = \dfrac{3}{4}$

$$P(B/E_{bw}) = \frac{3}{4}, \ P(B/E_{bb}) = \frac{4}{6} = \frac{2}{3}$$

Now, by total probability,

$$P(B) = P(E_{ww})P(B/E_{ww}) + P(E_{wb})$$
$$P(B/E_{wb}) + P(E_{bw}) \, P\, P(B/E_{bw})$$
$$+ P(E_{bb}) \, P\, P(B/E_{bb})$$

$$= \frac{1}{6} \times 1 + \frac{1}{3} \times \frac{3}{4} + \frac{1}{5} \times \frac{3}{4} + \frac{3}{10} \times \frac{2}{3}$$

$$= \frac{1}{6} + \frac{1}{4} + \frac{3}{20} + \frac{1}{5} = \frac{23}{30}$$

24. Given first bag contains

$$W_1 = \{4 \text{ white balls}\}, \ B_1 = \{5 \text{ black balls}\},$$

and second bag contains

$$W_2 = \{9 \text{ white balls}\} \text{ and } B_2 = \{7 \text{ black balls}\}$$

Let E_1 be the event that ball transferred from the first bag is white and E_2 be the event that the ball transferred from the first bag is black.

Also, E is the event that the ball drawn from the second bag is white.

$$\therefore \quad P\left(\frac{E}{E_1}\right) = \frac{10}{17} \text{ and } P\left(\frac{E}{E_2}\right) = \frac{9}{17}$$

[if we transferred one white ball from bag I to bag II, then the second bag contains $(9 + 1)$, i.e. 10 white balls. Similarly, if we transferred one black ball from bag I to bag II, then the second bag contains $(7 + 1)$, i.e. 8 black balls]

$$P(E_1) = \frac{4}{9} \text{ and } P(E_2) = \frac{5}{9}$$

$\therefore$ Required probability,

$$P(E) = P(E_1) \cdot P\left(\frac{E}{E_1}\right) + P(E_2) \cdot P\left(\frac{E}{E_2}\right)$$

$$= \frac{4}{9} \times \frac{10}{17} + \frac{5}{9} \times \frac{9}{17}$$

$$= \frac{40 + 45}{153} = \frac{85}{153} = \frac{5}{9}$$

25. Let E_1, E_2 and E_3 be the events of chances of A, B and C being selecting as the managers, respectively and S be the event for selected person as the manager of a firm.

Since, the ratio of chances between A, B and C is $4 : 1 : 2$.

So, the total chances $= 7$

Therefore, $P(E_1) = \dfrac{4}{7}$, $P(E_2) = \dfrac{1}{7}$ and $P(E_3) = \dfrac{2}{7}$

Also given, the probability for them introduce a radical change in market strategy,

$$P\left(\frac{S}{E_1}\right) = 0.3, \ P\left(\frac{S}{E_2}\right) = 0.8, \ P\left(\frac{S}{E_3}\right) = 0.5$$

By using Baye's theorem,

$$P\left(\frac{E_2}{S}\right) = \frac{P(E_2) \cdot P\left(\dfrac{S}{E_2}\right)}{P(E_1) \cdot P\left(\dfrac{S}{E_1}\right) + P(E_2) \cdot P\left(\dfrac{S}{E_2}\right) + P(E_3) \cdot P\left(\dfrac{S}{E_3}\right)}$$

$$= \frac{\dfrac{1}{7} \times 0.8}{\dfrac{4}{7} \times 0.3 + \dfrac{1}{7} \times 0.8 + \dfrac{2}{7} \times 0.5}$$

$$= \frac{\dfrac{0.8}{7}}{\dfrac{1.2}{7} + \dfrac{0.8}{7} + \dfrac{1}{7}} = \frac{\dfrac{8}{70}}{\dfrac{12}{70} + \dfrac{8}{70} + \dfrac{1}{7}}$$

$$= \frac{\dfrac{8}{70}}{\dfrac{12 + 8 + 10}{70}} = \frac{8}{70} \times \frac{70}{30} = \frac{8}{30} = \frac{4}{15}$$

26. Two dice are thrown together, so number of outcomes in the sample space is 36

$$\Rightarrow \quad n(S) = 36$$
$$E = \text{Total of } 4 = \{(2, 2), (3, 1), (1, 3)\}$$
$$\Rightarrow \quad n(E) = 3$$
$$F = \text{Total of 9 or more}$$
$$= \begin{Bmatrix} (3, 6), (6, 3), (4, 5), (5, 4), (4, 6), \\ (6, 4), (5, 5), (5, 6), (6, 5), (6, 6) \end{Bmatrix}$$
$$\Rightarrow \quad n(F) = 10$$

and $\quad G = $ Total divisible by 5
$$= \{(1, 4), (4, 1), (2, 3), (3, 2), (4, 6), (6, 4), (5, 5)\}$$
$$\Rightarrow \quad n(G) = 7$$

Here, $(E \cap F) = \phi$ and $(E \cap G) = \phi$

Also, $(F \cap G) = \{(4, 6), (6, 4), (5, 5)\}$
$$\Rightarrow \quad n(F \cap G) = 3 \text{ and } (E \cap F \cap G) = \phi$$

$$\therefore \quad P(E) = \frac{n(E)}{n(S)} = \frac{3}{36} = \frac{1}{12}$$

$$P(F) = \frac{n(F)}{n(S)} = \frac{10}{36} = \frac{5}{18},$$

and $\quad P(G) = \dfrac{n(G)}{n(S)} = \dfrac{7}{36}$

$$P(F \cap G) = \frac{3}{36} = \frac{1}{12}$$

and $\ P(F) \cdot P(G) = \dfrac{5}{18} \times \dfrac{7}{36} = \dfrac{35}{648}$

Here, we see that $P(F \cap G) \neq P(F) \cdot P(G)$

[since only F and G have common events, so only F and G are used here]

Hence, there is no pair which is independent.

27. Given, A and B are two independent events with
$$P(\overline{A} \cap B) = \frac{2}{15} \text{ and } P(A \cap \overline{B}) = \frac{1}{6}.$$

We know that if A and B are independent events, then $\overline{A}, B$ and $A, \overline{B}$ are independent events.

Now, $\ P(\overline{A} \cap B) = \dfrac{2}{15} \Rightarrow P(B) \cdot P(\overline{A}) = \dfrac{2}{15}$

$$\Rightarrow \quad P(B) \cdot [1 - P(A)] = \frac{2}{15}$$

$$\Rightarrow \quad P(B) - P(A) \cdot P(B) = \frac{2}{15} \qquad \text{...(i)}$$

and $\qquad P(A \cap \overline{B}) = \dfrac{1}{6} \Rightarrow P(A) \cdot P(\overline{B}) = \dfrac{1}{6}$

$$\Rightarrow \quad P(A) \cdot [1 - P(B)] = \frac{1}{6}$$

$$\Rightarrow \quad P(A) - P(A)P(B) = \frac{1}{6} \qquad \text{...(ii)}$$

On subtracting Eq. (i) from Eq. (ii), we get

$$P(A) - P(B) = \frac{1}{6} - \frac{2}{15} = \frac{5-4}{30} = \frac{1}{30}$$

$$\Rightarrow \qquad P(A) = \frac{1}{30} + P(B) \qquad \qquad \ldots(iii)$$

Now, substituting the value of $P(A)$ in Eq. (i), we get

$$P(B) - \left[\frac{1}{30} + P(B)\right] \cdot P(B) = \frac{2}{15}$$

Let $P(B) = x$, then

$$x - \left(\frac{1}{30} + x\right)x = \frac{2}{15}$$

$$\Rightarrow \qquad 30x - (1 + 30x)x = 4$$

$$\Rightarrow \qquad 30x - x - 30x^2 = 4$$

$$\Rightarrow \qquad 30x^2 - 29x + 4 = 0$$

$$\Rightarrow \qquad (6x - 1)(5x - 4) = 0$$

$$\Rightarrow \qquad x = \frac{1}{6} \text{ or } \frac{4}{5}$$

$$\Rightarrow \qquad P(B) = \frac{1}{6} \text{ or } \frac{4}{5} \qquad [\because x = P(B)]$$

Now, if $P(B) = \dfrac{1}{6}$, then $P(A) = \dfrac{1}{5}$ [from Eq. (iii)]

and if $P(B) = \dfrac{4}{5}$, then $P(A) = \dfrac{5}{6}$

28. Given, Bag I : 5 white and 4 black balls

        Bag II : 7 white and 9 black balls

Case I 1 black ball from 1st bag, 1 black and 1 white balls from 2nd bag.

$$P(A) = \frac{^4C_1}{^9C_1} \times \left(\frac{^7C_1 \times {}^9C_1}{^{16}C_2}\right)$$

$$= \frac{4 \times 7 \times 9 \times 2}{9 \times 16 \times 15} = \frac{7}{15 \times 2} = \frac{7}{30}$$

Case II 1 white ball from 1st bag, 2 black balls from 2nd bag.

$$P(B) = \frac{^5C_1}{^9C_1} \times \left(\frac{^9C_2}{^{16}C_2}\right) = \frac{5 \times 9 \times 8 \times 2}{2 \times 9 \times 16 \times 15} = \frac{1}{6}$$

$\therefore$ Required probability $= P(A) + P(B)$

$$= \frac{7}{30} + \frac{1}{6} = \frac{12}{30} = \frac{2}{5}$$

29. Let E_1 = Red ball is transferred from bag I to bag II.

and E_2 = Black ball is transferred from bag I to bag II.

So, E_1 and E_2 are mutually exclusive and exhaustive events.

$$\therefore \qquad P(E_1) = \frac{3}{3+4} = \frac{3}{7}$$

and $\qquad P(E_2) = \dfrac{4}{3+4} = \dfrac{4}{7}$

Let E be the event that the ball drawn is red.

Then, $\qquad P\left(\dfrac{E}{E_1}\right) = \dfrac{4+1}{(4+1)+5} = \dfrac{5}{10} = \dfrac{1}{2}$

and $\qquad P\left(\dfrac{E}{E_2}\right) = \dfrac{4}{4+(5+1)} = \dfrac{4}{10} = \dfrac{2}{5}$

$\therefore$ Required probability,

$$P\left(\frac{E_2}{E}\right) = \frac{P\left(\dfrac{E}{E_2}\right) \cdot P(E_2)}{P\left(\dfrac{E}{E_1}\right) \cdot P(E_1) + P\left(\dfrac{E}{E_2}\right) \cdot P(E_2)}$$

$$= \frac{\dfrac{2}{5} \times \dfrac{4}{7}}{\dfrac{1}{2} \times \dfrac{3}{7} + \dfrac{2}{5} \times \dfrac{4}{7}} \qquad \text{[by using Baye's theorem]}$$

$$= \frac{\dfrac{8}{35}}{\dfrac{3}{14} + \dfrac{8}{35}} = \frac{\dfrac{8}{35}}{\dfrac{105 + 112}{14 \times 35}} = \frac{8 \times 14}{217} = \frac{16}{31}$$

Hence, the probability that the transferred ball is black is $\dfrac{16}{31}$.

30. Let E_1, E_2 and E_3 be the events for chosen bags A, B and C, respectively.

So, $P(E_1) = P(E_2) = P(E_3) = \dfrac{1}{3}$

Bag A contains 2 white, 1 black and 3 red balls.

Bag B contains 3 white, 2 black and 4 red balls.

Bag C contains 4 white, 3 black and 2 red balls.

If A be the event of choosing two balls, i.e. one red and one black

$$\therefore \qquad P\left(\frac{A}{E_1}\right) = \frac{^3C_1 \, {}^1C_1}{^6C_2} = \frac{3 \times 1}{\dfrac{6 \times 5}{2 \times 1}} = \frac{1}{5}$$

$$P\left(\frac{A}{E_2}\right) = \frac{^4C_1 \times {}^2C_1}{^9C_2} = \frac{4 \times 2}{\dfrac{9 \times 8}{2 \times 1}} = \frac{2}{9}$$

$$P\left(\frac{A}{E_3}\right) = \frac{^2C_1 \times {}^3C_1}{^9C_2} = \frac{2 \times 3}{\dfrac{9 \times 8}{2 \times 1}} = \frac{1}{6}$$

Probability that both balls drawn from the bag B, having red and black balls

$$P\left(\frac{E_2}{A}\right) = \frac{P(E_2) P\left(\dfrac{A}{E_2}\right)}{P(E_1) P\left(\dfrac{A}{E_1}\right) + P(E_2) P\left(\dfrac{A}{E_2}\right) + P(E_3) P\left(\dfrac{A}{E_3}\right)}$$

$$= \frac{\dfrac{1}{3} \times \dfrac{2}{9}}{\dfrac{1}{3} \times \dfrac{1}{5} + \dfrac{1}{3} \times \dfrac{2}{9} + \dfrac{1}{3} \times \dfrac{1}{6}}$$

$$= \frac{\dfrac{1}{3} \times \dfrac{2}{9}}{\dfrac{1}{3}\left(\dfrac{1}{5} + \dfrac{2}{9} + \dfrac{1}{6}\right)} = \frac{2/9}{\dfrac{1}{5} + \dfrac{2}{9} + \dfrac{1}{6}}$$

$$= \frac{2/9}{\dfrac{18 + 20 + 15}{90}} = \frac{2/9}{53/90}$$

$$= \frac{2}{9} \times \frac{90}{53} = \frac{2}{53} \times 10 = \frac{20}{53}$$

31. We have, $A_1 : A_2 : A_3 = 4 : 4 : 2$

$\therefore \quad P(A_1) = \dfrac{4}{10}, \ P(A_2) = \dfrac{4}{10}$ and $P(A_3) = \dfrac{2}{10}$

where A_1, A_2 and A_3 denote the event of choosing flower seeds A_1, A_2 and A_3 respectively.

Let E be the event that a seed germinates and $\overline{E}$ be the event that a seed does not germinate.

Then, $P\left(\dfrac{E}{A_1}\right) = \dfrac{45}{100}, \ P\left(\dfrac{E}{A_2}\right) = \dfrac{60}{100}, \ P\left(\dfrac{E}{A_3}\right) = \dfrac{35}{100}$

and $\quad P\left(\dfrac{\overline{E}}{A_1}\right) = \dfrac{55}{100}, \ P\left(\dfrac{\overline{E}}{A_2}\right) = \dfrac{40}{100}, \ P\left(\dfrac{\overline{E}}{A_3}\right) = \dfrac{65}{100}$

  (i) Probability that a randomly chosen seed to germinate,

$$P(E) = P(A_1) \cdot \left(\dfrac{E}{A_1}\right) + P(A_2) \cdot P\left(\dfrac{E}{A_2}\right) + P(A_3) \cdot P\left(\dfrac{E}{A_3}\right)$$

$$= \dfrac{4}{10} \times \dfrac{45}{100} + \dfrac{4}{10} \times \dfrac{60}{100} + \dfrac{2}{10} \times \dfrac{35}{100}$$

$$= \dfrac{180}{1000} + \dfrac{240}{1000} + \dfrac{70}{1000} = \dfrac{490}{1000} = 0.49$$

  (ii) $P\left(\dfrac{\overline{E}}{A_3}\right) = 1 - P\left(\dfrac{E}{A_3}\right) = 1 - \dfrac{35}{100} = \dfrac{65}{100}$

  (iii) $P\left(\dfrac{A_2}{\overline{E}}\right) = \dfrac{P(A_2) \cdot P\left(\dfrac{\overline{E}}{A_2}\right)}{P(A_1) \cdot P\left(\dfrac{\overline{E}}{A_1}\right) + P(A_2) \cdot P\left(\dfrac{\overline{E}}{A_2}\right) + P(A_3) \cdot P\left(\dfrac{\overline{E}}{A_3}\right)}$

$$= \dfrac{\dfrac{4}{10} \times \dfrac{40}{100}}{\dfrac{4}{10} \times \dfrac{55}{100} + \dfrac{4}{10} \times \dfrac{40}{100} + \dfrac{2}{10} \times \dfrac{65}{100}}$$

$$= \dfrac{\dfrac{160}{1000}}{\dfrac{220}{1000} + \dfrac{160}{1000} + \dfrac{130}{1000}} = \dfrac{\dfrac{160}{1000}}{\dfrac{510}{1000}} = \dfrac{16}{51}$$

$$= 0.313725 = 0.314$$

32. Let E_1, E_2 and E_3 be the events of achievers for above average, average and below average respectively.

The total number of students $= 75$

Let A be the event of passed student.

So, $\quad P(E_1) = \dfrac{15}{75} = \dfrac{1}{5}$ and $P(E_2) = \dfrac{45}{75} = \dfrac{3}{5}$

$$P(E_3) = \dfrac{75 - (15 + 45)}{75} = \dfrac{15}{75} = \dfrac{1}{5}$$

Also, $P\left(\dfrac{A}{E_1}\right) = 1 - 0.005 = 1 - \dfrac{5}{1000} = \dfrac{995}{1000} = \dfrac{199}{200}$

$$P\left(\dfrac{A}{E_2}\right) = 1 - 0.05 = 1 - \dfrac{5}{100} = \dfrac{95}{100} = \dfrac{19}{20}$$

$$P\left(\dfrac{A}{E_3}\right) = 1 - 0.15 = 1 - \dfrac{15}{100} = \dfrac{85}{100} = \dfrac{17}{20}$$

The probability of below average achievers students who have passed

$$P\left(\dfrac{E_3}{A}\right) = \dfrac{P(E_3) \cdot P(A/E_3)}{P(E_1) \cdot P(A/E_1) + P(E_2) \cdot P(A/E_2) + P(E_3) \cdot P(A/E_3)}$$

$$= \dfrac{\dfrac{1}{5} \times \dfrac{17}{20}}{\dfrac{1}{5} \times \dfrac{199}{200} + \dfrac{3}{5} \times \dfrac{19}{20} + \dfrac{1}{5} \times \dfrac{17}{20}}$$

[by using Baye's theorem]

$$= \dfrac{\dfrac{17}{100}}{\dfrac{199}{1000} + \dfrac{57}{100} + \dfrac{17}{100}}$$

$$= \dfrac{17/100}{\dfrac{199 + 570 + 170}{1000}} = \dfrac{17}{100} \times \dfrac{1000}{939} = \dfrac{170}{939}$$

33. Let $E_1 = $ Event that the person has disease and $E_2 = $ Event that the person is healthy.

Then, E_1 and E_2 are mutually exclusive and exhaustive events.

$\therefore \quad P(E_1) = 0.1\% = \dfrac{0.1}{100} = 0.001$

and $\quad P(E_2) = 1 - 0.001 = 0.999$

Let $E :$ Event that test is positive.

$P\left(\dfrac{E}{E_1}\right) = P$ (result is positive, given that person has disease)

$$= 99\% = \dfrac{99}{100} = 0.99$$

$P\left(\dfrac{E}{E_2}\right) = P$ (result is positive, given that person does not have disease)

$$= 0.5\% = \dfrac{0.5}{100} = 0.005$$

Probability that a person has disease, given that test result is positive, is given by

$$P\left(\dfrac{E_1}{E}\right) = \dfrac{P(E_1) \cdot P\left(\dfrac{E}{E_1}\right)}{P(E_1) \cdot P\left(\dfrac{E}{E_1}\right) + P(E_2) \cdot P\left(\dfrac{E}{E_2}\right)}$$

[by Baye's theorem]

$$= \dfrac{0.001 \times 0.99}{0.001 \times 0.99 + 0.999 \times 0.005}$$

$$= \dfrac{0.00099}{0.00099 + 0.004995}$$

$$= \dfrac{0.00099}{0.005985} = \dfrac{990}{5985} = \dfrac{110}{665} = \dfrac{22}{133}$$

Hence, the required probability is $\dfrac{22}{133}$.

34. Let E_1 be the event that person is suffering from TB and E_2 be the event that person is not suffering from TB. Let E be the event that the doctor diagnoses that person has TB.

Then, $P(E_1) = \dfrac{1}{1000}$

$$P(E_2) = 1 - \dfrac{1}{1000} = \dfrac{999}{1000}$$

$P\left(\dfrac{E}{E_1}\right) = P$ (TB is detected when a person is actually Suffering)

$$= 0.99 = \dfrac{990}{1000}$$

and $P\left(\dfrac{E}{E_2}\right) = P$ (TB is detected when a person is not actually suffering)

$$= 0.001 = \dfrac{1}{1000}$$

P (A selected person has actually TB), is given by

$$P\left(\dfrac{E_1}{E}\right) = \dfrac{P(E_1) \cdot P\left(\dfrac{E}{E_1}\right)}{\left[P(E_1) \cdot P\left(\dfrac{E}{E_1}\right) + P(E_2) \cdot P\left(\dfrac{E}{E_2}\right)\right]}$$

$$\text{[by Baye's theorem]}$$

$$= \dfrac{\left(\dfrac{1}{1000}\right)\left(\dfrac{990}{1000}\right)}{\left(\dfrac{1}{1000}\right)\left(\dfrac{990}{1000}\right) + \left(\dfrac{999}{1000}\right)\left(\dfrac{1}{1000}\right)}$$

$$= \dfrac{\dfrac{990}{1000000}}{\left(\dfrac{990 + 999}{1000000}\right)}$$

$$= \dfrac{990}{1989} = \dfrac{110}{221}$$

Hence, the probability that a selected person has actually TB is $\dfrac{110}{221}$.

35. Let $E_1 =$ Event that 5 or 6 is shown on die

and $E_2 =$ Event that 1, 2, 3 or 4 is shown on die.

Here, $n(E_1) = 2$ and $n(E_2) = 4$

Also, $n(S) = 6$

$$\therefore \quad P(E_1) = \dfrac{2}{6} = \dfrac{1}{3}$$

and $P(E_2) = \dfrac{4}{6} = \dfrac{2}{3}$

Let $E =$ The event that exactly one head show up.

$$\therefore P\left(\dfrac{E}{E_1}\right) = P \text{ (exactly one head show up when}$$

$$\text{coin is tossed thrice)}$$

$$= P\{HTT, THT, TTH\} = \dfrac{3}{8}$$

$$[\because \text{ total number of outcomes} = 2^3 = 8]$$

$$P\left(\dfrac{E}{E_2}\right) = P \text{ (head shows up when coin is tossed once)} = \dfrac{1}{2}$$

The probability that the girl threw 1, 2, 3 or 4 with the die, if she obtained exactly one head, is given by

$$P\left(\dfrac{E_2}{E}\right) = \dfrac{P(E_2) \cdot P\left(\dfrac{E}{E_2}\right)}{P(E_1) \cdot P\left(\dfrac{E}{E_1}\right) + P(E_2) \cdot P\left(\dfrac{E}{E_2}\right)}$$

$$\text{[by Baye's theorem]}$$

$$= \dfrac{\dfrac{2}{3} \times \dfrac{1}{2}}{\dfrac{1}{3} \times \dfrac{3}{8} + \dfrac{2}{3} \times \dfrac{1}{2}} = \dfrac{\dfrac{1}{3}}{\dfrac{1}{8} + \dfrac{1}{3}} = \dfrac{8}{8+3} = \dfrac{8}{11}$$

36. Given, factory A production per day $= 1500$

The factory B production per day $= 2500$

The factory C production per day $= 3000$

The total production of factories A, B and C

$$= 1500 + 2500 + 3000 = 7000$$

Let $E_1 =$ Event of selecting a bulb produced by A,

$E_2 =$ Event of selecting a bulb produced by B,

and $E_3 =$ Event of selecting a bulb produced by C.

Let S be the event of selecting a defective bulb.

$$P(S/E_1) = 1.5\% = \dfrac{1.5}{100},$$

$$P(S/E_2) = 2\% = \dfrac{2}{100}$$

and $\quad P(S/E_3) = 2.5\% = \dfrac{2.5}{100}$

Also, $\qquad P(E_1) = \dfrac{1500}{7000} = \dfrac{3}{14},$

$$P(E_2) = \dfrac{2500}{7000} = \dfrac{5}{14}$$

and $\qquad P(E_3) = \dfrac{3000}{7000} = \dfrac{3}{7}$

$\therefore$ The probability that the selecting bulb produced by B is defective,

$$P(E_2/S) = \dfrac{P(E_2) \cdot P(S/E_2)}{P(E_1) \cdot P(S/E_1) + P(E_2) \cdot P(S/E_2) + P(E_3) \cdot P(S/E_3)}$$

$$\text{[by using Baye's theorem]}$$

$$= \dfrac{\dfrac{5}{14} \times \dfrac{2}{100}}{\dfrac{3}{14} \times \dfrac{1.5}{100} + \dfrac{5}{14} \times \dfrac{2}{100} + \dfrac{3}{7} \times \dfrac{2.5}{100}}$$

$$= \dfrac{\dfrac{5}{14} \times \dfrac{2}{100}}{\dfrac{1}{100}\left(\dfrac{3}{14} \times 1.5 + \dfrac{5}{14} \times 2 + \dfrac{3}{7} \times 2.5\right)}$$

$$= \dfrac{\dfrac{5}{14} \times 2}{\dfrac{3}{14} \times 1.5 + \dfrac{5}{14} \times 2 + \dfrac{3}{7} \times 2.5}$$

$$= \dfrac{\dfrac{10}{14}}{\dfrac{4.5}{14} + \dfrac{10}{14} + \dfrac{7.5}{7}} = \dfrac{\dfrac{10}{14}}{\dfrac{4.5 + 10 + 15}{14}}$$

$$= \dfrac{\dfrac{10}{14}}{\dfrac{29.5}{14}} = \dfrac{10}{14} \times \dfrac{14}{29.5} = \dfrac{10}{29.5}$$

$$= \dfrac{\dfrac{100}{100}}{295} = \dfrac{20}{59}$$

37. Given, per day production from plant $A = 500$ units,

per day production from plant $B = 1000$ units

and per day production from plant $C = 2000$ units

Let the events be

E_1 = Selecting the pipe from (plant) A

E_2 = Selecting the pipe from (plant) B

E_3 = Selecting the pipe from (plant) C.

Let D be the event of selecting defective pipe.

Now, $P(E_1) = \dfrac{500}{500 + 1000 + 2000}$

$= \dfrac{500}{3500} = \dfrac{1}{7}$

$P(E_2) = \dfrac{1000}{3500} = \dfrac{2}{7}$

and $P(E_3) = \dfrac{2000}{3500} = \dfrac{4}{7}$

Now, the probability that defective pipe produce from plant A, $P(D/E_1) = 0.005$

The probability that defective pipe produce from plant B, $P(D/E_2) = 0.008$

The probability that the defective pipe produce from plant C, $P(D/E_3) = 0.010$

$\therefore$ The probability that the selecting pipe produce from plant A is defective is

$$P(E_1/D) = \dfrac{P(E_1) \cdot P(D/E_1)}{P(E_1) \cdot P(D/E_1) + P(E_2) \cdot P(D/E_2) + P(E_3) \cdot P(D/E_3)}$$

[by using Baye's theorem]

$$= \dfrac{\dfrac{1}{7} \times 0.005}{\dfrac{1}{7} \times 0.005 + \dfrac{2}{7} \times 0.008 + \dfrac{4}{7} \times 0.010}$$

$$= \dfrac{\dfrac{1}{7} \times 0.005}{\dfrac{1}{7}(0.005 + 2 \times 0.008 + 4 \times 0.010)}$$

$$= \dfrac{0.005}{0.005 + 0.016 + 0.04} = \dfrac{0.005}{0.061} = \dfrac{5}{61}$$

38. Let E_1 and E_2 denotes the events that Anil and Vijay will respectively qualify the exam.

(i) The probability that Vijay will not qualify the exam
$$= 1 - P(E_2) = 1 - 0.10 = 0.9$$

(ii) $P(E_1 \cup E_2) = P(E_1) + P(E_2) - P(E_1 \cap E_2)$
$$= 0.05 + 0.10 - 0.02 = 0.13$$

(iii) Probability of atleast one of them does not qualify
$$= P(E'_1 \cup E'_2) = P((E_1 \cap E_2)')$$
$$= 1 - P(E_1 \cap E_2) = 1 - 0.02 = 0.98$$

(iv) Probability that both Anil and Vijay will not qualify the exam $= P(E'_1 \cap E'_2) = P((E_1 \cup E_2)')$
$$= 1 - P(E_1 \cup E_2) = 1 - 0.13 = 0.87$$

(v) Probability that only one of them will qualify the exam
$$= P((E_1 - E_2) \cup (E_2 - E_1))$$
$$= P(E_1 - E_2) + P(E_2 - E_1)$$
$$= P(E_1 \cup E_2) - P(E_1 \cap E_2) = 0.13 - 0.02 = 0.11$$

Chapter Test

Multiple Choice Questions

1. If there are 4 addressed envelopes and 4 letters. Then, the chance that all the letters are not mailed through proper envelope is

(a) $\dfrac{1}{24}$ (b) 1 (c) $\dfrac{23}{24}$ (d) $\dfrac{9}{2}$

2. Two events A and B have probability 0.25 and 0.50. The probability that both occur simultaneously is 0.14. Then, probability that neither A nor B occur is

(a) 0.75 (b) 0.61

(c) 0.39 (d) None of these

3. If $P(A) = \dfrac{4}{5}$ and $P(A \cap B) = \dfrac{7}{10}$, then $P(B/A)$ is equal to

(a) $\dfrac{1}{10}$ (b) $\dfrac{1}{8}$ (c) $\dfrac{7}{8}$ (d) $\dfrac{17}{20}$

4. If $P(A) = 0.4$, $P(B) = 0.8$ and $P(B/A) = 0.6$, then $P(A \cup B)$ is equal to

(a) 0.24 (b) 0.3 (c) 0.48 (d) 0.96

5. If A and B are two events such that $P(B) = \dfrac{3}{5}$, $P(A/B) = \dfrac{1}{2}$ and $P(A \cup B) = \dfrac{4}{5}$, then $P(A)$ equals to

(a) $\dfrac{3}{10}$ (b) $\dfrac{1}{5}$ (c) $\dfrac{1}{2}$ (d) $\dfrac{3}{5}$

6. Two cards are drawn at random and without replacement from a pack of 52 playing cards. The probability that both the cards are black, is

(a) $\dfrac{25}{102}$ (b) $\dfrac{27}{51}$

(c) $\dfrac{25}{52}$ (d) None of these

Case Based MCQs

7. In a play zone, Ravi is playing crane game. It has 8 blue balls, 10 red balls, 5 yellow balls and 12 green balls. If Ravi draws two balls one after the other without replacement.

On the basis of above information, answer the following questions.

(i) What is the probability that the first ball is green and the second ball is blue?

(a) $\dfrac{47}{595}$ (b) $\dfrac{48}{595}$ (c) $\dfrac{46}{595}$ (d) $\dfrac{45}{595}$

(ii) What is the probability that the first ball is red and the second ball is yellow?

(a) $\dfrac{5}{119}$ (b) $\dfrac{8}{119}$

(c) $\dfrac{24}{119}$ (d) None of these

(iii) What is the probability that both the balls are green?

(a) $\dfrac{48}{595}$ (b) $\dfrac{24}{595}$ (c) $\dfrac{66}{595}$ (d) $\dfrac{64}{595}$

(iv) What is the probability that the first ball is green and the second ball is not yellow?

(a) $\dfrac{104}{595}$ (b) $\dfrac{176}{595}$

(c) $\dfrac{174}{595}$ (d) None of these

(v) What is the probability that both the balls are not blue?

(a) $\dfrac{351}{595}$ (b) $\dfrac{317}{595}$ (c) $\dfrac{326}{595}$ (d) $\dfrac{253}{595}$

Short Answer Type Questions

8. Assume that each born child is equally likely to be a boy or a girl. If a family has two children, then what is the conditional probability that both are girls? Given that

(i) the youngest is a girl?

(ii) atleast one is a girl?

9. Evaluate $P(A \cup B)$, if $2P(A) = P(B) = \dfrac{5}{13}$ and $P(A/B) = \dfrac{2}{5}$.

10. A couple has 2 children. Find the probability that both are boys, if it is known that

(i) one of them is a boy.

(ii) the older child is a boy.

11. Let bag A contains 4 black and 6 red balls and bag B contains 7 black and 3 red balls. A die is thrown. If 1 or 2 appears on it, then bag A is chosen, otherwise bag B. If two balls are drawn at random (without replacement) from the selected bag, then find the probability of one of them being red and another black.

12. If A and B are independent events such that $P(A) = \dfrac{1}{5}$, $P(A \cup B) = \dfrac{7}{10}$, then what is $P(\bar{B})$ equal to?

Long Answer Type Questions

13. There are three identical boxes I, II and III, each containing two coins. In box I, both coins are gold coins, in box II, both are silver coins and in box III, there is one gold and one silver coin. A person chooses a box at random and take out a coin. If the coin is of gold, then what is the probability that the other coin in box is also of gold?

14. In a class, 5% of boys and 10% of girls have an IQ of more than 150. In the class, 60% are boys and rest are girls. If a student is selected at random and found to have an IQ of more than 150, then find the probability that the student is a boy.

Answers

1. (c)   2. (c)   3. (c)   4. (d)   5. (c)   6. (a)

7. (i) (b) (ii) (a) (iii) (c) (iv) (c) (v) (a)

8. (i) $\dfrac{1}{2}$ (ii) $\dfrac{1}{3}$ 9. $\dfrac{11}{26}$ 10. (i) $\dfrac{1}{3}$ (ii) $\dfrac{1}{2}$ 11. $\dfrac{22}{45}$ 12. $\dfrac{3}{8}$ 13. $\dfrac{2}{3}$ 14. $\dfrac{3}{7}$

For Detailed Solutions

Scan the code

CHAPTER 05

Annuities

In this Chapter...

- Types of Annuities
- Taxation
- Goods and Service Tax (GST)

An **annuity** is a sequence of equal payments made at equal intervals of time with compound interest on these payments.

There are some related terms to annuities given below

- **Payment Period** The time period between successive payments is called payment period or payment interval. It may be weekly, monthly, quarterly, annually etc., or any fixed period of time.
- **Duration of the Annuity** The time from the beginning of the first interval to the end of the last interval is called the term or duration of the annuity.
- **Periodic Payment** The size of each payment of an annuity is called the periodic payment of the annuity. The person who receives the payment is called annuitant.
- **Instalment** The payment of each single annuity is called an instalment.

Types of Annuities

Annuities are of three types

(i) **Certain annuities** the number of payments is fixed i.e. the payments begin and end on fixed dates.

(ii) A **contingent annuity** is one where the term depends upon some event whose occurrence is not fixed.

(iii) A **perpetual annuity** or **perpetuity** is an annuity whose term does not end i.e. it extends till infinity.

Annuities are further classified in three categories on the basis of payment dates

(i) **Ordinary Annuity or Immediate Annuity** An ordinary annuity or immediate annuity is an annuity, where payments are made at the end of each payment period i.e. first payment is made at the end of the first payment interval and so on.

(ii) **Annuity Due** An annuity due is an annuity, where payments are made at the beginning of each period.

(iii) **Deferred Annuity** If the payments start after a specified number of periods, we get a deferred annuity.

In deferred annuity a first payment is postponed for a certain number of payment periods.

Future Value (A)

The amount or future value of an annuity is the total amount due at the end of the term of the annuity.

The future value of an annuity is

Case I In case of annuity due

$$A = \frac{a}{i}(1 + i)[(1 + i)^n - 1]$$

Case II In case of immediate annuity

$$A = \frac{a}{i}[(1 + i)^n - 1]$$

[for deferred annuity use same formula]

where, A = Future value, a = Monthly instalment,

i = Interest rate, n = Time

Present Value/Worth

The present value or the present worth of a given annuity is the sum of the present values of its different instalments.

Present value of an annuity $= \text{Amount} \times (1 + i)^{-n}$

Present Value in Different Cones

In case of an **ordinary annuity,** the present value (P) is

$$P = \frac{a}{i}[1 - (1 + i)^{-n}]$$

where, $a =$ Monthly instalment, $i =$ Interest rate, $n =$ Time

In case of an **annuity due** the present value (P) is

$$P = \frac{a}{i}(1 + i)[1 - (1 + i)^{-n}]$$

where, $a =$ Monthly instalment, $i =$ Interest rate, $n =$ Time

The present value (P) for **perpetual annuity** is

$$P = \frac{a}{i}$$

where, $a =$ Monthly instalment, $i =$ Interest rate

Taxation

The Central (or State) Government provides various types of facilities to public, such as construction and maintenance of roads, schools, hospitals, etc.

In order to provide above facilities, the government needs money which is collected by imposing different types of taxes on people and organisations such as, income tax, goods and service tax etc.

The taxation can be classified in two main categories

(i) **Direct tax** The tax which is imposed directly on a tax payer is called direct tax.

e.g. Income tax, wealth tax, corporate tax etc.

(ii) **Indirect tax** The tax which is collected by one entity in the supply chain and paid to be government.

e.g. Sales tax, service tax, value added tax (VAT) etc.

Goods and Services Tax (GST)

It is an indirect tax levied by Central Government. In this tax there are so many tax merged such as Excise Duty, Custom Duty, Service Tax, Value Added Tax, Entertainment Tax and Lottery Tax etc. The purpose of GST is to make a one nation and one tax.

There are various terms related to GST, which are as follow

(i) **Manufacturer** The person who produce goods for sale, is called manufacturer.

(ii) **Dealer** The person, who purchases goods for resale, is known as a dealer (trader).

(iii) **Turnover** The total amount received from sale of goods (excluding tax) by a dealer during any fixed period, is called turnover.

(iv) **Intra State Sales** Suppose a person do a business and they sales their goods (items) and provide their services in the same state (or union territory), then it is said to be Intra state sales.

(v) **Inter State Sales** Suppose a person do a business and they sales their goods (items) and provide their services outside the state (or union territory), then it is said to be Inter state sales.

(vi) **Input GST** The tax paid by a dealer on his/her purchase of goods and providing services, is called Input GST.

(vii) **Output GST** The tax charged by a dealer on his/her sales of goods and providing services is called output GST.

Different Types of Taxes Used in GST

In this system, there are three taxes applicable, which are given below

(i) **State (or Union Territory) Goods and Service Tax** (SGST or UTGST) This tax is collected by the State (or union territory) Government on an intra-state sale.

e.g. Suppose any goods is manufacturing in Uttar Pradesh and sales this goods also in Uttar Pradesh, then tax on this transaction is said to be SGST.

(ii) **Central Goods and Services Tax (CGST)** This tax is collected by the Central Government on an intra state sale.

Both SGST (or UTGST) and CGST are levied on intra state (i.e. same state) sales of goods and services. In intra-state sales, GST is equally divided between Central and State Governments.

e.g. Suppose a dealer of Tamil Nadu sells some goods at the rate of ₹ 4000 to the consumer in the same state (i.e. Tamil Nadu). Suppose GST is charged at the rate of 18% on that goods, the GST will comprises of CGST at the rate 9% and SGST at the rate of 9%. Therefore, the seller will collect the CGST amount of ₹ 360 (i.e. 9% of ₹ 4000) and this amount goes to the account of Central Government and seller will also collect the SGST amount of ₹ 360 (i.e. 9% of ₹ 4000) which will go the account of State Government of Tamil Nadu.

Hence, the dealer collects the 18% GST amount on ₹ 4000 (i.e. ₹ 720), which will equally (i.e. 360 each) distribute in State (i.e. Tamil Nadu) and Central Government.

(iii) **Integrated Goods and Services Tax** (IGST) It is levied on inter state sales of goods and services outside the state. This tax is also levied on import of goods and services from one country to another country.

This tax is collected only by the Central Government for inter state sale.

e.g. Suppose a dealer from Gujarat sells goods worth of ₹ 8000 to a another dealer of Rajasthan. Suppose rate of GST is 12% on the goods, then the seller will collect 12% of ₹ 8000 (i.e. 960) under as IGST and the whole amount of IGST will go the Central Government.

Rate Structure for GST

Generally, structure of goods and services are divided into 5 slabs, which are given below

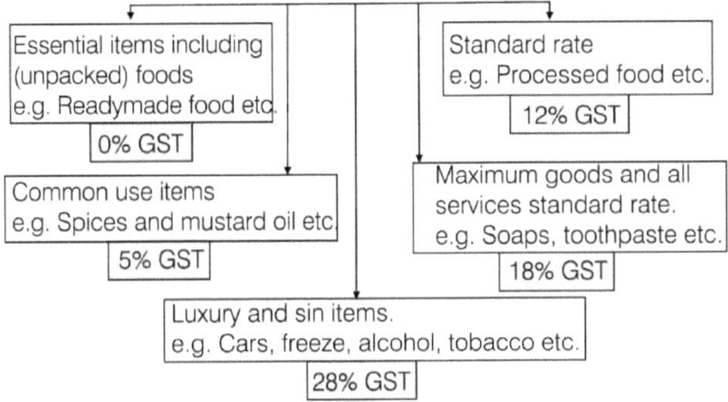

Note *Rates of GST given here are according to the latest information, these rates may be changed by the Government.*

Input and Output GST Credit

When any supply of services or goods is supplied to a taxable person, then GST is charged, which is known as input tax, it is changed against of the output GST (i.e. GST collected) as follows

	Input GST credit	Output GST
(i)	CGST credit	First CGST, then IGST
(ii)	SGST/UTGST credit	First SGST/UTGST, then IGST
(iii)	IGST credit	First IGST, second CGST, then SGST/UTGST

Both Central Government and State Government distribute the set off input GST against off output GST. While saling and purchasing of goods and services in each deal, dealer has to pay net GST (output GST − input GST).

Objectives and Advantages of GST

Some of the objectives and advantages are given below

(i) The important advantage is that to reduce the multiplicity of taxes and make a unified common national market.

(ii) Through GST, the tax system becomes more transparent, regular and predictable.

(iii) **Ease of doing business** It means their are some administrative rule set up between the Central Government and State Government, so that their is no interruption of doing business.

(iv) **Reduce Tax Evasion** Some of the persons are evading tax. So reduce tax evasion, use GST. In this procedure each tax payer registered under GST to make a GST return file electronically for each transaction (either purchase or sale) and this file should match with the input GST credit against the output GST and lastly paid net GST.

Utility Bill

A utility bill is a detailed invoice, issued and paid once a month for utilities such as electric, natural gas, water and waste, on a typical utility bill, we can see basic information such as account number, invoice number, date of issue, service address and service period.

Tariff Rate

A tariff is a tax imposed by a government on goods and services imported from other countries. It consists two parts

(i) Fixed charge   (ii) Variable charge

Surcharge

A surcharge is an additional charge, tax or payment that a company adds to the already existent cost of a good or service.

e.g. a customer may see a regulatory recovery fee on a cable bill.

Service Charge

The service charges are a type of fee collected to pay for services associated with the purchase of the primary product or service.

Electricity Bill

Electricity bill is determined by three elements

(i) Number of units consumed

(ii) Tariff category of the consumer

(iii) Fixed charges, surcharges and energy tax.

Water Bills

Water bill is determined by main three elements.

(i) Connection fee

(ii) Water tax

(iii) Water charge

Solved Examples

Example 1. Find the amount of an ordinary annuity of ₹ 600 payable at the end of each year for 8 yr at 8% per year compounded annually.
(given, $(1.08)^8 = 1.8509$)

Sol. Given, $R = ₹ 600$, $n = 8$ yr and $i = \dfrac{8}{100} = 0.08$

We know that, $A = R\left[\dfrac{(1+i)^n - 1}{i}\right]$

$\Rightarrow \qquad A = 600\left[\dfrac{(1+0.08)^8 - 1}{0.08}\right]$

$= 600\left[\dfrac{(1.08)^8 - 1}{0.08}\right]$

$= \dfrac{600}{0.08}(1.8509 - 1)$

$= \dfrac{600}{0.08} \times 0.8509$

$= ₹ 6381.98$

Example 2. Find the present value of a regular annuity of ₹ 2000 payable for 5 yr at 10% per annum compounded annually. (given, $(1.10)^{-5} = 0.6209$)

Sol. Given, $R = ₹ 2000$, $i = \dfrac{10}{100} = 0.10$ and $n = 5$ yr

We know that,

$$P = R\left[\dfrac{1 - (1+i)^{-n}}{i}\right]$$

$= 2000\left[\dfrac{1 - (1+0.10)^{-5}}{0.10}\right]$

$= \dfrac{2000}{0.10}[1 - (1.10)^{-5}]$

$= 20000(1 - 0.6209)$

$= 20000 \times 0.3790$

$= ₹ 7581.57$

Example 3. Rohan deposited in a bank ₹ 12000 at the end of each year for 8 yr. If compound interest at 12% per annum is reckoned, what would be the sum standing to his credit at the end of period.
(given, $(1.12)^8 = 2.4759$)

Sol. Given, $R = ₹ 12000$, $n = 8$ yr and $i = \dfrac{12}{100} = 0.12$

$\therefore \qquad A = R\left[\dfrac{(1+i)^n - 1}{i}\right]$

$= 12000\left[\dfrac{(1+0.12)^8 - 1}{0.12}\right]$

$= 12000\left[\dfrac{(1.12)^8 - 1}{0.12}\right]$

$= 12000\left(\dfrac{2.4759 - 1}{0.12}\right)$

$= 12000\left(\dfrac{1.4759}{0.12}\right)$

$= ₹ 147590$

Example 4. A retailer buys a luxury wrist watch from a manufacturer at the listed price of ₹ 50000. He marks the price of watch 25% above the listed price and sells it to a customer at 15% discount on the market price. If the sales are intra-state and rate of GST is 18%, then the amount paid by the customer to the retailer.

Sol. Market price of watch $= 50000 \times \dfrac{125}{100}$

$= ₹ 62500$

Discount $= 15\%$ of market price

$= 15\%$ of ₹ 62500

$= \dfrac{15}{100} \times 62500$

$= ₹ 9375$

$\therefore$ Selling price of watch $= ₹ (62500 - 9375)$

$= ₹ 53125$

As the sales are intra-state and the rate of GST is 18%

$\therefore$ GST paid by the customer $= \dfrac{18}{100} \times 53125$

$= ₹ 9562.5$

Amount paid by the customer $= ₹ (53125 + 9562.5)$

$= ₹ 62687.5$

Example 5. A shopkeeper buys an article whose printed price is ₹ 5000 from wholesaler at a discount of 20% and sells it to a consumer at the printed price. If the sales are intra-state and the rate of GST is 12%, then the amount of tax (under GST) paid by the shopkeeper to the state government.

Sol. Amount of discount $= 20\%$ of ₹ 5000

$= \dfrac{20}{100} \times 5000$

$= ₹ 1000$

$\therefore$ The price of the article which the shopkeeper paid to the wholesaler $= ₹\,(5000 - 1000) = ₹\,4000$

Amount of GST paid by the shopkeeper to the wholesaler

$CGST = 6\%$ of $₹4000$

$$= \frac{6}{100} \times 4000$$

$$= ₹\,240$$

$SGST = 6\%$ of $₹4000 = ₹\,240$

Amount of GST collected by the shopkeeper (or paid by consumer)

$CGST = 6\%$ of $₹\,5000$

$$= \frac{6}{100} \times 5000$$

$$= ₹\,300$$

$SGST = 6\%$ of 5000

$$= \frac{6}{100} \times 5000$$

$$= ₹\,300$$

Amount of tax (under GST) paid by the shopkeeper to the state government $=$ Output SGST $-$ input SGST

$$= ₹\,(300 - ₹\,240)$$

$$= ₹\,60$$

Example 6. Vinod Verma from Delhi consumed $25\ \text{m}^3$ of water in one month. Calculate his water bill for that month.

Tariff plan is given below

Monthly Consumption (in m^3)	Water charges per m^3 (in ₹)
upto 20	₹ 5.0
20-30	₹ 12.0
30-50	₹ 15
50 > 0	₹ 25

Meter rent $= ₹\,45$ and sewerage charge is 20% of water charges.

Sol. Given, Vinod Verma consumed $25\ \text{m}^3$ of water in one month.

$\therefore$ Water charge $= ₹\,(20 \times 5 + 5 \times 12)$

$$= ₹\,160$$

Sewerage charge $=$ 20% of water charge

$$= 20\% \text{ of } ₹\,160$$

$$= \frac{20}{100} \times 160$$

$$= ₹\,32$$

$\therefore$ Total water bill $=$ Water charges $+$ Sewerage charges $+$ Meter rent

$$= ₹\,(160 + 32 + 45)$$

$$= ₹\,237$$

Chapter Practice

Objective Questions

• Multiple Choice Questions

1. The sum of all payments made and the compound interest earned on these payments at the end of the term is called
(a) future value
(b) present value
(c) net present value
(d) annuity

2. The difference between the sum of present values of all cash inflows and the sum of present values of all cash outflows is
(a) principal value
(b) payment period
(c) net present value
(d) periodic payment

3. If a bank pays 6% interest per annum compounded half-yearly. Then, the equal amount should be deposited at the end of each half-year for $2\frac{1}{2}$ yr to get an amount of ₹ 3000 at the end of 30 months is (given, $(1.03)^5 = 1.159$)
(a) ₹ 504.02
(b) ₹ 414.40
(c) ₹ 565.06
(d) ₹ 706.5

4. The amount of regular annuity of ₹ 4000 payable at the end of each year for 3 yr at 5% per annum compounded annually is (given, $(1.05)^3 = 1.1576$)
(a) ₹ 12610.4
(b) ₹ 16850.3
(c) ₹ 144320.5
(d) ₹ 15430.6

5. The amount of regular annuity of ₹ 6000 payable at the end of each year for 11 yr at 8% per annum compounded annually is
(a) ₹ 560.92
(b) ₹ 726.35
(c) ₹ 819.50
(d) ₹ 936.50

6. The least number of years for which an annuity of ₹ 1500 per annum must run in order that its amount just exceeds ₹ 30000 at 9% compounded annually is
(a) 15
(b) 20
(c) 12
(d) 16

7. The amount of an annuity consisting of payments of ₹ 500 made at the end of every 3 months for 4 yr at the rate of 6% compounded quarterly, is
(a) ₹ 9268.52
(b) ₹ 8866.66
(c) ₹ 6985.6
(d) ₹ 7650.82

8. An annuity consists of 24 quarterly instalments of ₹ 800 each, the first being made at the end of 4 yr. The amount of this annuity, if money is worth 10% per annum compounded quarterly, is
(a) ₹ 25792
(b) ₹ 21684
(c) ₹ 32450
(d) ₹ 35640

9. The present value of a regular annuity of ₹ 1200 payable for 4 yr at 10% per annum compounded annually,is
(a) ₹ 10243.2
(b) ₹ 11520.4
(c) ₹ 15002.6
(d) ₹ 139952.6

10. A bank pays 8% interest per annum compounded half-yearly. What equal amount should be deposited at the end of each half-year for $1\frac{1}{2}$ yr to get an amount of ₹ 2000 at the end of 18 months?
(a) ₹ 890
(b) ₹ 640
(c) ₹ 470
(d) ₹ 960

11. When does liability to pay GST aries in case of supply of goods?
(a) On raising of invoice
(b) At the time of supply of goods
(c) On receipt of payment
(d) Earliest of any of above

12. The time limit to pay the value of supply with taxes.
(a) 4 months
(b) 3 months
(c) 10 months
(d) 180 days

13. Taxes that are levied on any intra-state purchase rate are
(a) SGST
(b) IGST
(c) CGST and SGST
(d) None of these

14. The maximum rate of CGST is
(a) 20%
(b) 17%
(c) 24%
(d) 14%

15. The number of structure in India's GST model is?
   (a) 5   (b) 6   (c) 4   (d) 3

16. The deduction of maximum amount is allowed under section 80C is
   (a) ₹ 1.5 Lakh   (b) ₹ 1.2 Lakh
   (c) ₹ 1.9 Lakh   (d) ₹ 1.4 Lakh

17. The total income of an individual earned from different sources in a financial year is
   (a) net income   (b) gross income
   (c) final income   (d) actual income

• Case Based MCQs

18. The printed price of an item is ₹ 50000. The manufacturer allows a discount of 20% to a dealer Tarun. The dealer Tarun sells the item to another dealer Sachin at a discount of 5% on the marked price. The dealer Sachin sells is to a consumer at 2% above the printed price. Suppose all the sales are intra-state and the rate of GST is 12%.

Based on the above information, answer the following questions.

(i) The dealer Tarun pays the price of the item inclusive tax (under GST) is
   (a) ₹ 44800   (b) ₹ 41520
   (c) ₹ 36500   (d) ₹ 40000

(ii) The dealer Sachin pays the price of an item inclusive tax (under GST) is
   (a) ₹ 44530   (b) ₹ 53200
   (c) ₹ 60380   (d) ₹ 65000

(iii) How much the consumer pays the amount for an item?
   (a) ₹ 57120   (b) ₹ 61430
   (c) ₹ 64520   (d) ₹ 50120

(iv) The amount of tax (under GST) paid by dealer Tarun to the Central Government is
   (a) ₹ 320   (b) ₹ 630   (c) ₹ 450   (d) ₹ 525

(v) The amount of tax (under GST) paid by dealer Sachin to the State Government is
   (a) ₹ 280   (b) ₹ 260   (c) ₹ 260   (d) ₹ 210

PART 2
Subjective Questions

• Short Answer Type Questions

1. What is Annuity?

2. What is Deferred Annuity?

3. What is GST?

4. Write some objectives and advantages of GST.

5. What is Integrated Goods and Service Tax (IGST)?

6. What is a utility bill?

7. Find the present value of a regular annuity of ₹ 1000 payable for 3 yr at 12% per annum compounded annually.

8. A person deposits in a bank ₹ 5000 at the end of each year, for 10 yr. If compound interest at 10% per annum is reckoned, what would be the sum standing to his credit at the end of the period (given, $(1.1)^{10} = 2.594$)

9. A man wants to have ₹ 15000 in his account after 10 yr. He deposits, annual payments in account that pays 4% rate of interest compounded annually. How much should he deposited each year? (given, $(1.04)^{10} = 1.479$)

10. Mr. Sharma goes to a shop and buy a Jacket having cost ₹ 1180 (list price). The rate of GST 18%. He tells the shopkeeper to reduce the price such an extent that he has to pay ₹ 1180 inclusive of GST. Find the reduction needed in the price of the jacket.

11. A retailer buys a TV from a manufacturer of ₹ 30000. He marks the price of the TV 25% above his cost price and sells it to a consumer at 10% discount on the marked price. Find the selling price of the TV by the retailer.

12. The price of a bicycle is ₹ 3136 inclusive of tax (under GST) at the rate of 12% on its listed price. A buyer asks for a discount on the listed price, so that after charging GST, the selling price becomes equal to the listed price. Find the amount of discount which the seller has to allow for the deal.

13. A shopkeeper buys an item whose printed price is ₹ 3000 from a wholesaler at a discount of 15% and sells it to a consumer at the printed price. If the sales are intra state and the rate of GST is 12%, find the price of the item inclusive of GST at which the shopkeeper bought it.

14. Sachin from UP consumed 20 m^3 of water in one month. Calculate his water bill for that month. Tariff plan is given below

Monthly consumption (in m^3)	Water charges per m^3 (in ₹)
upto 15	₹ 4.0
15 − 25	₹ 10
25 − 50	₹ 18
> 50	₹ 25

Meter rent = ₹ 42 and sewerage charge is 25% of water charges.

15. Ram Prakash goes to a shop to buy a coat which costs ₹ 1003 (list price). The rate of GST is 18%. He tells the shopkeeper to reduce the price to such an extent that he has to pay ₹ 1003, inclusive of GST. Find the reduction needed in the price of the coat.

16. A shopkeeper buys an article whose printed price is ₹ 5000 from a wholesaler at a discount of 15% and sells it to a consumer at the printed price. If the sales are intra-state and the rate of GST is 12%, then find the price of the article inclusive of GST at which the shopkeeper bought it.

17. A shopkeeper in Rajasthan buys an article at the printed price of ₹ 30000 from a wholesaler in Delhi. The shopkeeper sells the article to a consumer in Rajasthan at a profit of 20% on the basic cost price. If the rate of GST is 18%, then find the price of the article inclusive of tax (under GST) at which the shopkeeper bought it.

18. A retailer buys a TV set for ₹ 40000 from a wholesaler at a discount of 20% on the printed price and sells it to a consumer at the printed price. If the sales are intra-state and the rate of GST is 12%. Find the price at which the consumer bought the TV set.

19. A manufacturer sells a refrigerator to a dealer for ₹ 50000. The dealer sells it to a customer at a profit of ₹ 5000. If the sales are intra-state and the rate of GST is 12%, then find the amount of input GST for the dealer.

• Long Answer Type Questions

20. A machine costs ₹ 98000 and its effective life is estimated to 12 yr. If the scrap value is ₹ 3000 only, what should be retained out of profits at the end of each year to accumulate at compound interest at 5% per annum for depreciation, so that a new machine can be purchased at the same price after 12 yr. [given, $\log 1.05 = 0.0212$ and $\log 1.797 = 0.2544$]

21. Find the present value of a sequence of annual payments of ₹ 10000 each, the first being made at the end of 5th year and the last being made at the end of 12th year, if money is worth 6%.

22. The price of a motorcycle is ₹ 44880 including tax (under GST) at the rate of 18% on its listed price. A buyer asks for a discount on the listed price so that

after charging GST, the selling price of motorcycle becomes equal to the listed price. Find the discount amount in which the seller has to allow for the deal.

23. A shopkeeper has marked ₹ 7840 as the price of an article including 12% GST on the listed price. A buyer asks for discount on the listed price, so that after charging GST, the selling price becomes equal to the listed price. Find the amount, discount the shopkeeper has to offer for the deal.

24. Manufacturer Suresh sells a television to a dealer Anil for ₹ 20000. The dealer Anil sells it to a consumer at a profit of ₹ 2000. If the sales are intra-state and the rate of GST is 12%, find

(i) the amount of tax (under GST) paid by the dealer Anil to the Central Government.

(ii) the amount of tax (under GST) received by the State Government.

(iii) the amount that the consumer pays for the television.

25. A consumer in East Delhi consumes 540 units of electricity in a month. He has the connection of 4 kW. Calculate the electricity bill of consumer for that month, if the surcharges is ₹ 0.50 per unit for that month.

• Case Based Questions

26. A shopkeeper who lives in Rajasthan buys an article at the printed price of ₹ 35000 from a wholesaler who lives in Gujarat. The shopkeeper sells the article to a consumer in Rajasthan at a profit of 22% on the basic cost price.

If the rate of GST is 12%, answer the following questions.

(i) Find the price of an article inclusive tax (under GST) in which the shopkeeper bought it.

(ii) Find, how much the amount of tax (under GST) paid by the shopkeeper to Governments?

(iii) Find the amount of tax (under GST) received by Gujarat Government.

(iv) Find the amount of tax (under GST) received by Central Government.

(v) Find the amount which the consumer pays for the article.

SOLUTIONS

Objective Questions

1. (*a*) Clearly, the sum of all payments made and the compound interest earned on these payments at the end of the term is called present value.

2. (*c*) The sum of present value of all cash inflows

     − The sum of present values of all cash outflows

     = Net present value

3. (*c*) We have, $A = ₹\, 3000,$

$$i = \frac{6}{2 \times 100} = 0.03 \text{ and } n = 5$$

$\therefore \qquad A = R\left[\dfrac{(1+i)^n - 1}{i}\right]$

$\Rightarrow \quad 3000 = R\left[\dfrac{(1+0.03)^5 - 1}{0.03}\right]$

$\Rightarrow \quad 3000 = R\left[\dfrac{(1.03)^5 - 1}{0.03}\right]$

$\Rightarrow \quad 3000 = R\left[\dfrac{1.159 - 1}{0.03}\right]$

$\Rightarrow \quad 3000 = R\left[\dfrac{0.159}{0.03}\right]$

$\Rightarrow \quad 3000 = R(5.3091)$

$\Rightarrow \quad R = \dfrac{3000}{5.3091} = ₹\, 565.06$

4. (*a*) We have, $R = ₹\, 4000,\ i = \dfrac{5}{100} = 0.05$ and $n = 3$

We know that,

$$A = R\left[\dfrac{(1+i)^n - 1}{i}\right]$$

$= 4000\left[\dfrac{(1+0.05)^3 - 1}{0.05}\right]$

$= 4000\left[\dfrac{(1.05)^3 - 1}{0.05}\right]$

$= 4000\left(\dfrac{1.1576 - 1}{0.05}\right)$

$= 4000\left(\dfrac{0.1576}{0.05}\right)$

$= 4000(3.1525) = ₹\, 12610.4$

5. (*b*) We have, $R = ₹\, 6000,\ i = \dfrac{8}{100} = 0.08$ and $n = 11$

$\therefore$ We know that,

Required amount, $A = R\left[\dfrac{(1+i)^n - 1}{i}\right]$

$= 6000\left[\dfrac{(1+0.08)^{11} - 1}{11}\right]$

$= 6000\left(\dfrac{1.33}{11}\right)$

$= 6000 \times 0.12 = ₹\, 726.35$

6. (*c*) Given, $R = 1500,\ A = 30000$ and $i = \dfrac{9}{100} = 0.09$

$\therefore \qquad A = R\left(\dfrac{(1+i)^n - 1}{i}\right)$

$\Rightarrow \quad 30000 = 1500\left(\dfrac{(1+0.09)^n - 1}{0.09}\right)$

$\Rightarrow \quad (1.09)^n - 1 = 20 \times 0.09$

$\Rightarrow \quad (1.09)^n = 1.8 + 1 = 2.8$

$\Rightarrow \quad n\log(1.09) = \log(2.8)$

$\Rightarrow \quad n = \dfrac{\log(2.8)}{\log(1.09)} = \dfrac{0.4472}{0.0374} = 11.957 = 12$

Hence, the least number of years is 12.

7. (*b*) Given, $R = ₹\, 500,\ n = 4 \times 4 = 16$

and $\qquad i = \dfrac{6}{4 \times 100} = 0.015$

We know that,

$$A = R\left[\dfrac{(1+i)^n - 1}{i}\right]$$

$= 500\left[\dfrac{(1+0.015)^n - 1}{0.015}\right]$

$= 500\left[\dfrac{(1.015)^{16} - 1}{0.015}\right] \qquad \ldots(\text{i})$

Let $\qquad x = (1.015)^{16}$

$\Rightarrow \quad \log x = 16\log(1.015)$

$\qquad\qquad = 16 \times 0.0064 = 0.1024$

$\Rightarrow \quad x = \text{antilog}\,(0.1024)$

$\Rightarrow \quad x = 1.266$

Putting the value of x in (i), we get

$$A = 500\left[\dfrac{1.266 - 1}{0.015}\right]$$

$\Rightarrow \quad A = \dfrac{500 \times 0.266}{0.015} = ₹\, 8866.66$

8. (*a*) We have, $R = ₹\, 800,\ i = \dfrac{10}{4 \times 100} = 0.025$ and $n = 24$

$\therefore$ Amount of annuity,

$$A = R\left[\dfrac{(1+i)^n - 1}{i}\right]$$

$= 800\left[\dfrac{(1+0.025)^n - 1}{0.025}\right]$

$\Rightarrow \quad A = 800\left[\dfrac{(1.025)^{24} - 1}{0.025}\right] \qquad \ldots(\text{i})$

Let $\qquad x = (1.025)^{24}$

$\Rightarrow \quad \log x = 24\log(1.025)$

$\qquad\qquad = 24 \times 0.0107 = 0.2568$

$\Rightarrow \quad x = \text{antilog}\,(0.2568) = 1.806$

On putting value of x in (i), we get

$$A = 800\left[\frac{1.806 - 1}{0.025}\right]$$

$$\Rightarrow \quad A = 800\left(\frac{0.806}{0.025}\right) = ₹\,25792$$

9. (a) Given, $R = ₹\,1200$, $i = \dfrac{10}{100} = 0.10$ and $n = 4$

We know that,

$$P = R\left[\frac{1 - (1 + i)^{-n}}{i}\right]$$

$$\Rightarrow \quad P = 1200\left[\frac{1 - (1 + 0.10)^{-4}}{0.10}\right]$$

$$\Rightarrow \quad P = \frac{1200}{0.10}[1 - (1.10)^{-4}] \qquad \ldots(i)$$

Let $\quad x = (1.10)^{-4}$

$$\Rightarrow \quad \log x = -4\log(1.10)$$

$$= -4 \times 0.0414$$

$$= -0.1656$$

$$\Rightarrow \quad x = \text{antilog}(-0.1656)$$

$$= \text{antilog}(1.1656)$$

$$\Rightarrow \quad x = 0.1464$$

On putting the value of x in Eq. (i), we get

$$P = \frac{1200}{0.10}(1 - 0.1464)$$

$$= \frac{1200}{0.10} \times 0.8536 = ₹\,10243.2$$

10. (b) Given, $A = ₹\,2000$, $i = \dfrac{8}{2 \times 100} = 0.04$ and $n = 3$

We know that,

$$A = R\left[\frac{(1 + i)^{n} - 1}{i}\right]$$

$$\Rightarrow \quad 2000 = R\left[\frac{(1 + 0.04)^{3} - 1}{0.04}\right]$$

$$\Rightarrow \quad 2000 \times 0.04 = R\,[(1 + 0.04)^{3} - 1]$$

$$\Rightarrow \quad 80 = R\,[(1.04)^{3} - 1] \qquad \ldots(i)$$

Let $\quad x = (1.04)^{3}$

$$\Rightarrow \quad \log x = 3\log(1.04)$$

$$= 3 \times 0.017$$

$$= 0.0510$$

$$\Rightarrow \quad x = \text{antilog}(0.0510)$$

$$= 1.125$$

On putting value of x in Eq. (i), we get

$$80 = R\,[1.125 - 1] = R\,(0.125)$$

$$\Rightarrow \quad R = \frac{80}{0.125} = 640$$

Therefore, ₹ 640 should be deposited at the end of each half-year.

11. (d) Earliest of any of above

12. (d) Clearly, the time limit to pay the value of supply with taxes is 180 days.

13. (c) Both CGST and SGST are levied on intra-state (i.e. same state) sales of goods and services. In intra-state sales, GST is equally divided between central and state governments.

14. (a) The maximum rate of CGST is 20%.

15. (c) The GST was carefully crafted to keep both the burden of the common man and inflation rates in mind.

The 4-tier tax structure contains four separate rates : a zero rate, a lower rate, a standard rate, and a higher rate.

16. (a) A person can claim a deduction of upto ₹ 1.5 lakh under section 80 C.

17. (b) The total income of an individual earned from different sources in a financial year is called gross income.

18. Here, sales are intra-state and rate of GST is 12%, so GST comprises of CGST at 6% and SGST at 6%.

(i) (a) Also given, the printed price of an item is ₹ 50000.

Since, the manufacturer sells the item to the dealer Tarun at 20% discount.

Therefore, the selling price of an item by manufacturer to the dealer Tarun

$$= ₹\left(1 - \frac{20}{100}\right) \times 50000$$

$$= \left(1 - \frac{1}{5}\right) \times 50000 = \frac{4}{5} \times 50000$$

$$= ₹\,40000$$

$\therefore$ Manufacturer collect the GST amount from dealer Tarun (or dealer Tarun pays to the manufacturer),

$$\text{CGST} = 6\% \text{ of } ₹\,40000 = \frac{6}{100} \times 40000 = ₹\,2400$$

and $\text{SGST} = 6\%$ of $₹\,40000 = \dfrac{6}{100} \times 40000 = ₹\,2400$

$\therefore$ Dealer Tarun pays the price of the item inclusive tax (under GST) = Cost price of an item for dealer Tarun + Dealer Tarun pays GST (i.e. CGST and SGST)

$$= ₹\,(40000 + 2400 + 2400) = ₹\,44800$$

(ii) (b) Since, dealer Tarun sells the item to dealer Sachin at a discount of 5% on the marked price.

Therefore, the selling price of an item by dealer Tarun to dealer Sachin

$$= ₹\left(1 - \frac{5}{100}\right) \times 50000 = \left(1 - \frac{1}{20}\right) \times 50000$$

$$= \frac{19}{20} \times 50000 = ₹\,47500$$

$\therefore$ GST amount collected by dealer Tarun from dealer Sachin (or dealer Sachin pays to dealer Tarun),

$$\text{CGST} = 6\% \text{ of } ₹\,47500$$

$$= \frac{6}{100} \times 47500$$

$$= ₹\,2850$$

and $\text{SGST} = 6\%$ of $₹\,47500$

$$= \frac{6}{100} \times 47500$$

$$= ₹\,2850$$

$\therefore$ Dealer Sachin pays the price of an item inclusive tax (under GST) = Cost price of an item for dealer Sachin + Dealer Sachin pays GST (i.e. CGST and SGST)

$$= ₹(47500 + 2850 + 2850) = ₹53200$$

(iii) (a) Since, the dealer Sachin sells the item to the consumer at 2% above the printed price. Therefore, the selling price of an item by dealer Sachin to a consumer

$$= ₹\left(1 + \frac{2}{100}\right) \times 50000 = \left(1 + \frac{1}{50}\right) \times 50000$$

$$= \frac{51}{50} \times 50000 = ₹51000$$

$\therefore$ Dealer Sachin collects the GST amount from consumer (or consumer pays the dealer Sachin)

$$\text{CGST} = 6\% \text{ of } ₹51000 = \frac{6}{100} \times 51000 = ₹3060$$

$$\text{and SGST} = 6\% \text{ of } ₹51000 = \frac{6}{100} \times 51000 = ₹3060$$

$\therefore$ Consumer pays the amount for an item

= Cost price of an item for consumer + Consumer pays GST (i.e. SGST and CGST)

$$= ₹(51000 + 3060 + 3060) = ₹57120$$

(iv) (c) $\because$ Dealer Tarun has input CGST = ₹2400

and Tarun dealer has output CGST = ₹2850

$\therefore$ Amount of tax (under GST) paid by dealer Tarun to the Central Government.

$$= \text{Output CGST} - \text{Input CGST}$$
$$= ₹(2850 - 2400)$$
$$= ₹450$$

(v) (d) $\because$ Dealer Sachin has input SGST = ₹2850

and dealer Sachin has output SGST = ₹3060

$\therefore$ Amount of tax (under GST) paid by dealer Sachin to the State Government

$$= \text{Output SGST} - \text{Input SGST}$$
$$= ₹(3060 - 2850) = ₹210$$

Subjective Questions

1. An annuity is a sequence of equal payments made at equal intervals of time.

2. An annuity in which first payment is postponed for a period of time.

3. It is an indirect tax levied by Central Government. In this tax there are so many tax merged such as Excise Duty, Custom Duty, Service Tax, Value Added Tax, Entertainment Tax and Lottery Tax etc. The purpose of GST is to make a one nation and one tax.

4. Some of the objectives and advantages are given below

(i) The important advantage is that to reduce the multiplicity of taxes and make a unified common national market.

(ii) Through GST, the tax system becomes more transparent, regular and predictable.

(iii) **Ease of doing business** It means their are some administrative rule set up between the Central Government and State Government, so that their is no interruption of doing business.

(iv) **Reduce Tax Evasion** Some of the persons are evading tax. So reduce tax evasion, use GST. In this procedure each tax payer registered under GST to make a GST return file electronically for each transaction (either purchase or sale) and this file should match with the input GST credit against the output GST and lastly paid net GST.

5. It is levied on inter state sales of goods and services outside the state. This tax is also levied on import of goods and services from one country to another country.

This tax is collected only by the Central Government for inter state sale.

e.g. Suppose a dealer from Gujarat sells goods worth of ₹8000 to a another dealer of Rajasthan. Suppose rate of GST is 12% on the goods, then the seller will collect 12% of ₹8000 (i.e. 960) under as IGST and the whole amount of IGST will go the Central Government.

6. A utility bill is a detailed invoice, issued and paid once a month for utilities such as electric, natural gas, water and waste on a typical utility bill, we can see basic information such as account number, invoice number, date of issue, service address and service period.

7. We have, $R = ₹1000$, $i = \frac{12}{100} = 0.12$ and $n = 3$

Since, $\qquad P = R\left[\dfrac{1 - (1 + i)^{-n}}{i}\right]$

$$= \frac{1000}{0.12}[1 - (1 + 0.12)^{-3}]$$

$$= \frac{1000}{0.12}(1 - (1.12)^{-3})$$

Let $\qquad x = (1.12)^{-3}$

$\Rightarrow \qquad \log x = -3\log 1.12$

$$= -3 \times 0.0492$$
$$= -0.1476$$

$\Rightarrow \qquad x = \text{antilog}(-0.1476)$

$$= 0.7119$$

$\therefore \qquad P = \dfrac{1000}{0.12}(1 - 0.7119)$

$$= \frac{1000}{0.12} \times 0.2881$$

$$= ₹2400.83$$

$\therefore$ Hence, present value of the annuity = ₹2400.83

8. Given, $R = ₹5000$, $n = 10$ and $i = \dfrac{10}{100} = 0.1$

$\therefore \qquad A = R\left[\dfrac{(1 + i)^n - 1}{i}\right]$

$$= 5000\left[\frac{(1 + 0.1)^{10} - 1}{0.1}\right]$$

$$= \frac{5000}{0.1}\{(1.1)^{10} - 1\}$$

$$= 50000(2.594 - 1)$$

$$= 50000 \times 1.594$$

$$= ₹79700$$

9. Given, $A = ₹\, 15000$, $n = 10$ and $i = \dfrac{4}{100} = 0.04$

We know that,

$$A = R\left[\frac{(1+i)^n - 1}{i}\right]$$

$$\Rightarrow \quad 15000 = R\left[\frac{(1 + 0.04)^{10} - 1}{i}\right]$$

$$\Rightarrow \quad 15000 \times 0.04 = R\,\{(1.04)^{10} - 1\}$$

$$\Rightarrow \quad R = \frac{15000 \times 0.04}{(1.04)^{10} - 1}$$

$$= \frac{600}{(1.479 - 1)}$$

$$= \frac{600}{0.479}$$

$$= ₹\, 1252.61$$

10. Let the reduced price of jacket be $₹\, x$.

Then, amount of GST on $₹\, x = 18\%$ of $₹\, x = ₹\left(\dfrac{18}{100} \times x\right)$

$\therefore$ Mr. Sharma pays the amount for jacket

$$= ₹\left(x + \frac{18}{100}x\right) = ₹\left(1 + \frac{18}{100}\right)x$$

$$= ₹\left(1 + \frac{9}{50}\right)x = ₹\left(\frac{59}{50}\right)x$$

According to the given condition,

$$\frac{59}{50}x = 1180$$

$$\Rightarrow \quad x = \frac{1180 \times 50}{59} = ₹\, 1000$$

$\therefore$ Reduced price of the jacket $= ₹\, 1000$

Thus, the reduction needed in the price of jacket

$$= ₹\,(1180 - 1000) = ₹\, 180$$

11. The market price of the TV $= ₹\left(1 + \dfrac{25}{100}\right) \times 30000$

$$= ₹\left(\frac{125}{100}\right) \times 30000$$

$$= ₹\, 37500$$

Since, the retailer sells the TV to a consumer at 10% discount on the market price.

$\therefore$ SP of the TV to a consumer by the retailer

$$= \left(1 - \frac{10}{100}\right) \times 37500$$

$$= \frac{90}{100} \times 37500$$

$$= ₹\, 33750$$

12. Let the listed price of the bicycle be $₹\, P$.

Amount of GST on $₹\, P = 12\%$ of $₹\, P$

$$= \frac{12}{100} \times P$$

$$= ₹\, \frac{3}{25}P$$

$\therefore$ According to the question,

$$₹\left(P + \frac{3}{25}P\right) = ₹\, 3136$$

$$\Rightarrow \quad \frac{28}{25}P = 3136$$

$$\Rightarrow \quad P = \frac{3136 \times 25}{28} = ₹\, 2800$$

Now, let amount of discount be $₹\, x$.

$\therefore$ Reduced price of the bicycle $= ₹\,(2800 - x)$

Amount of GST on $₹\,(2800 - x) = 12\%$ of $₹\,(2800 - x)$

$$= \frac{3}{25}(2800 - x)$$

Now, new SP of the bicycle including GST

$$= (2800 - x) + \frac{3}{25}(2800 - x) = ₹\, 2800$$

$$\Rightarrow \quad \frac{28}{25}(2800 - x) = 2800$$

$$\Rightarrow \quad 2800 - x = 100 \times 25$$

$$\Rightarrow \quad x = 2800 - 2500 = 300$$

$\therefore$ Amount of discount $= ₹\, 300$

13. We have sales are intra-state and the rate of GST is 12%, so GST comprises of CGST at 6% and SGST at 6%.

Also, given printed price of an item $= ₹\, 3000$

and rate of discount $= 15\%$

$\therefore$ Amount of discount $= 15\%$ of $₹\, 3000$

$$= \frac{15}{100} \times 3000$$

$$= ₹\, 450$$

$\therefore$ Shopkeeper paid the amount to the wholesaler

$$= ₹\,(3000 - 450) = ₹\, 2550$$

$\therefore$ Shopkeeper paid the amount of GST to the wholesaler,

$$\text{CGST} = 6\% \text{ of } ₹\, 2550$$

$$= \frac{6}{100} \times 2550 = ₹\, 153$$

and $\text{SGST} = 6\%$ of $₹\, 2550 = \dfrac{6}{100} \times 2550 = ₹\, 153$

$\therefore$ Price of an item inclusive GST at which the shopkeeper bought it $= ₹\,(2550 + 153 + 153)$

$$= ₹\, 2856$$

14. Given, Sachin consumed 20 m^3 of water in one month.

$\therefore$ Water charge $= ₹\,(15 \times 4.0) + ₹\,(5 \times 10)$

$$= ₹\,(60 + 50)$$

$$= ₹\, 110$$

Sewerage charge $= 25\%$ of water charge

$$= 25\% \text{ of } ₹\, 110$$

$$= \frac{25}{100} \times 110$$

$$= ₹\, 27.5$$

Total water bill $=$ Water charges $+$ Sewerage charges
$+$ Meter rent

$$= 110 + 275 + 42$$

$$= ₹\, 179.5$$

15. Let the reduced price of the coat be ₹ x.

Amount of GST on ₹ x = 18% of ₹ x

$$= ₹ \frac{18}{100} x$$

∴ The amount to be paid by Ram Prakash for the coat

$$= x + \frac{18}{100} x$$

$$= ₹ \frac{59}{50} x$$

According to the question,

$$\frac{59}{50} x = 1003$$

$$\Rightarrow \qquad x = \frac{1003 \times 50}{59}$$

$$= 17 \times 50$$

$$= 850$$

∴ The reduced price of the coat = ₹ 850

Thus, the reduction needed in the price of coat

$$= ₹(1001 - 850)$$

$$= ₹ 151$$

16. We have, printed price = ₹ 5000

Rate of discount = 15%

Amount of discount = 15% of ₹ 5000

$$= \frac{15}{100} \times 5000$$

$$= ₹ 750$$

The price of the article, which the shopkeeper paid to the wholesaler = ₹ (5000 − 750) = ₹ 4250

Amount of GST paid by the shopkeeper to the wholesaler

$$\text{CGST} = 6\% \text{ of } ₹ 4250$$

$$= \frac{6}{100} \times 4250$$

$$= ₹ 255$$

and $\qquad \text{SGST} = 6\% \text{ of } ₹ 4250$

$$= \frac{6}{100} \times 4250$$

$$= ₹ 255$$

∴ The price of the article inclusive of GST at which the shopkeeper bought = ₹ (4250 + 255 + 255)

$$= ₹ (4250 + 510)$$

$$= ₹ 4760$$

17. IGST collected by wholesaler from shopkeeper

$$= 18\% \text{ of } ₹ 30000$$

$$= \frac{18}{100} \times 30000$$

$$= ₹ 5400$$

∴ The price of the article inclusive of tax (under GST) at which the shopkeeper bought is ₹ 30000+ IGST paid by shopkeeper to wholesaler = ₹ (30000 + 5400)

$$= ₹ 35400$$

18. SGST paid by the consumer to the retailer

$$= 6\% \text{ of } ₹ 40000$$

$$= \frac{6}{100} \times 40000 = ₹ 2400$$

CGST paid by the consumer to the retailer

$$= 6\% \text{ of } ₹ 40000$$

$$= \frac{6}{100} \times 40000 = ₹ 2400$$

GST paid by the consumer to the retailer = SGST + CGST

$$= ₹ (2400 + 2400)$$

$$= ₹ 4800$$

Price at which the consumer bought the TV set

$$= \text{SP} + \text{GST}$$

$$= ₹ (40000 + 4800)$$

$$= ₹ 44800$$

19. CGST paid by the dealer = 6% of ₹ 50000

$$= \frac{6}{100} \times 50000$$

$$= ₹ 3000$$

SGST paid by the dealer = 6% of ₹ 50000

$$= \frac{6}{100} \times 50000 = ₹ 3000$$

Total GST paid by the dealer = CGST + SGST

$$= ₹ (3000 + 3000)$$

$$= ₹ 6000$$

∴ Input GST for the dealer is ₹ 6000.

20. Given,

Total cost of Machine = ₹ 98000

Amount realised from scrap = ₹ 3000

∴ Remaining amount = ₹ (98000 − 3000)

$$= ₹ 95000$$

$$n = 12 \text{ and } i = \frac{5}{100} = 0.05$$

$$\therefore \qquad A = R \left\{ \frac{(1 + i)^n - 1}{i} \right\}$$

$$\Rightarrow \qquad 95000 = R \left\{ \frac{(1 + 0.05)^{12} - 1}{0.05} \right\}$$

$$\Rightarrow \qquad 95000 = R \left\{ \frac{(1.05)^{12} - 1}{0.05} \right\}$$

Let $\qquad x = (1.05)^{12}$

$$\Rightarrow \qquad \log x = 12 \log 1.05$$

$$= 12 \times 0.0212$$

$$= 0.2544$$

$$\Rightarrow \qquad x = 1.797$$

$$\Rightarrow \qquad 95000 = R \left(\frac{1.797 - 1}{0.05} \right)$$

$$\Rightarrow \qquad R = \frac{95000 \times 0.05}{0.797}$$

$$\Rightarrow \qquad R = 5959.84$$

Thus, ₹ 5959.84 should be retain out.

21. We have a defferred annuity of 8 terms, i.e. $n = 8$
and defferred for 4 terms i.e. $m = 4$
$$R = ₹\,10000 \text{ and } i = \frac{6}{100} = 0.06$$
Now, we know that
$$P = \frac{R}{i}\left[\frac{1}{(1+i)^m} - \frac{1}{(1+i)^{m+n}}\right]$$
$$= \frac{10000}{0.06}\left[\frac{1}{(1+0.06)^4} - \frac{1}{(1+0.06)^{4+8}}\right]$$
$$= \frac{10000}{0.06}[(1.06)^{-4} - (1.06)^{-12}] \qquad …(i)$$
Let $\quad x = (1.06)^{-4}$ and $y = (1.06)^{-12}$
Now, $\quad \log x = -4\log(1.06)$
$\Rightarrow \quad \log x = -4 \times 0.0253$
$\Rightarrow \quad \log x = -0.1012$
$\Rightarrow \quad x = \text{antilog}(-0.1012) \Rightarrow x = 0.7921$
Find, $\quad \log y = -12\log(1.06)$
$\Rightarrow \quad \log y = -12 \times 0.0253$
$\Rightarrow \quad \log y = -0.3036$
$\Rightarrow \quad y = \text{antilog}(-0.3036)$
$\Rightarrow \quad y = 0.4971$
Now, putting value of x and y in Eq. (i), we get
$$P = \frac{10000}{0.06}[0.7921 - 0.4971] = \frac{10000}{0.06} \times 0.295$$
$$= ₹\,49166.67$$

22. Let the listed price of motorcycle be ₹ x and the discount be ₹ y.
Amount of GST on ₹ $x = 18\%$ of ₹ x
$$= ₹\left(\frac{18}{100} \times x\right) = ₹\left(\frac{9}{50}x\right)$$
Selling price of the motorcycle including tax
$$= ₹\left(x + \frac{9}{50}x\right) = ₹\left(\frac{59}{50}x\right)$$
According to the given condition,
$$\frac{59}{50}x = ₹\,44880$$
$\Rightarrow \qquad x = \dfrac{44880 \times 50}{59} = ₹\,38034$
∴ List price of the motorcycle $= ₹\,38034$
Now, the reduced price of the motorcycle $= ₹\,(38034 - y)$
Amount of GST on ₹ $(38034 - y) = 18\%$ of ₹ $(38034 - y)$
$$= \frac{18}{100} \times (38034 - y)$$
$$= \frac{9}{50}(38034 - y)$$
∴ New SP of the motor cycle including GST
$$= (38034 - y) + \frac{9}{50}(38034 - y)$$
$$= \left(1 + \frac{9}{50}\right)(38034 - y)$$
$$= \frac{59}{50}(38034 - y)$$

According to the given condition,
Selling price of motorcycle including GST
$$= \text{Listed price of motorcycle}$$
$∴ \qquad \dfrac{59}{50}(38034 - y) = 38033$
$\Rightarrow \qquad 2244006 - 59y = 1901650$
$\Rightarrow \qquad 59y = 342356$
$\Rightarrow \qquad y = 5803$
Hence, the amount of discount is ₹ 5803.

23. Let the listed price of the article be ₹ P.
Since, GST on listed price $= 12\%$
∴ Amount of GST on ₹$P = 12\%$ of ₹ P
$$= \frac{12}{100} \times P = ₹\,\frac{3P}{25}$$
∴ Selling price of the article including GST $= ₹\left(P + \dfrac{3P}{25}\right)$
$$= ₹\,\frac{28P}{25}$$
According to the question,
$$\frac{28P}{25} = 7840$$
$\Rightarrow \qquad P = ₹\,7000$
Let amount of discount be ₹ x.
Then, price of the article $= ₹\,(7000 - x)$.
∴ GST on the reduced price $= ₹\,\dfrac{12}{100}(7000 - x)$
$$= ₹\,\frac{3}{25}(7000 - x)$$
∴ SP of the article $= ₹\,(7000 - x) + ₹\,\dfrac{3}{25}(7000 - x)$
$$= ₹\left[\frac{28}{25}(7000 - x)\right]$$
$∴ \qquad \dfrac{28}{25}(7000 - x) = 7000$
$\Rightarrow \qquad 7000 - x = 7000 \times \dfrac{25}{28} = 6250$
$\Rightarrow \qquad x = 7000 - 6250$
$\Rightarrow \qquad x = 750$
∴ Amount of discount $= ₹\,750$

24. We have sales are intra-state and the rate of GST is 12%, so GST comprises of CGST at 6% and SGST at 6%.
Also, given manufacturer Suresh sells the television to dealer Anil for ₹ 20000.

The GST amount collected by manufacturer Suresh from dealer Anil are
$$CGST = 6\% \text{ of } ₹\,20000 = \frac{6}{100} \times 20000 = ₹\,1200$$
and $SGST = 6\%$ of ₹ $20000 = \dfrac{6}{100} \times 20000 = ₹\,1200$

∴ Amount of input GST for dealer Anil,
input CGST $= ₹\,1200$, input SGST $= ₹\,1200$

Thus, manufacturer Suresh will pay ₹ 1200 for CGST and ₹ 1200 for SGST.

As the dealer Anil sells the television to a consumer at a profit of ₹ 2000, the selling price of television by dealer Anil (or cost price of television for the consumer)
$$= ₹ (20000 + 2000) = ₹ 22000$$
The amount of GST collected by dealer Anil (or paid by consumer)
$$CGST = 6\% \text{ of } ₹ 22000 = \frac{6}{100} \times ₹ 22000 = ₹1320$$
$$\text{and } SGST = 6\% \text{ of } ₹ 22000 = \frac{6}{100} \times ₹ 22000 = ₹ 1320$$
∴ Amount of output GST for dealer Anil,
$$\text{Output } CGST = ₹ 1320$$
$$\text{Output } SGST = ₹ 1320$$

(i) Amount of tax (under GST) paid by dealer Anil to the Central Government
$$= \text{CGST paid by dealer Anil to the Central Government}$$
$$= \text{Output CGST – Input CGST}$$
$$= ₹ (1320 - 1200) = ₹ 120$$

(ii) Amount of SGST paid by dealer Anil
$$= \text{Output SGST – Input SGST}$$
$$= ₹ (1320 - 1200) = ₹ 120$$

(iii) Amount that the customer pays for the television
$$= \text{Cost price of television for customer}$$
$$+ \text{ CGST paid by consumer}$$
$$+ \text{ SGST paid by consumer}$$
$$= ₹ (22000 + 1320 + 1320) = ₹ 24640$$

25. Given, Number of units consumed $= 540$ units

Connection load $= 4\,kW$

∴ Energy charges

Units	Price	Amount
0-200	₹ 3.5	₹ 700
201-400	₹ 5.0	₹ 1000
400-540	₹ 7.0	₹ 980
	Total	**₹ 2680**

Fixed Charges $= ₹(50 \times 4) = ₹ 200$

Surcharges $= ₹ (0.40 \times 540) = ₹ 216$

Energy tax $= 5\%$ of (Energy charges + fixed charges)
$$= 5\% \text{ of } (2680 + 200)$$
$$= \frac{5}{100} \times 2880$$
$$= ₹ 144$$

Electricity bill $= ₹ (2680 + 200 + 216 + 144)$
$$= ₹ 3240$$

26. Given, shopkeeper buys an article from wholesaler
$$= ₹ 35000$$
and rate of GST $= 12\%$

Here, transaction is one state to another state, so IGST is levied on sale.

∴ Wholesaler collects the IGST amount from shopkeeper
$$= 12\% \text{ of } ₹ 35000$$

$$= \frac{12}{100} \times 35000 = ₹ 4200$$

(i) Price of an article inclusive tax (under GST) in which the shopkeeper bought
$$= \text{CP of article for shopkeeper}$$
$$+ \text{ Shopkeeper pays GST amount}$$
$$= ₹ 35000 + \text{Shopkeeper pays the IGST}$$
$$\text{amount to the wholesaler}$$
$$= ₹ (35000 + 4200) = ₹ 39200$$

(ii) Since, the wholesaler will pay IGST amount ₹ 4200 to the Central government.

∴ Shopkeeper has input IGST amount $= ₹ 4200$

As the shopkeeper sells the article to a consumer at a profit of 22% on the basic cost price, therefore the selling price of the article by the shopkeeper
$$= \left(1 + \frac{22}{100}\right) \times 35000$$
$$= \frac{122}{100} \times 35000 = ₹ 42700$$

Since, the shopkeeper sells the article to a consumer in Rajasthan, so this sale is intra state. Therefore, GST comprises of CGST at 6% and SGST at 6%.

∴ Shopkeeper collects the GST amount from consumer,
$$CGST = 6\% \text{ of } ₹ 42700 = \frac{6}{100} \times 42700 = ₹ 2562$$
$$\text{and } SGST = 6\% \text{ of } ₹ 42700 = \frac{6}{100} \times 42700 = ₹ 2562$$

Amount of output GST for the shopkeeper,
$$CGST = ₹ 2562 \text{ and } SGST = ₹ 2562$$

Amount of tax (under GST) paid by the shopkeeper to the Central Government;

First set off ₹ 4200 input IGST against ₹ 2562 output CGST.

Then, set off the balance ₹ (4200 - 2562)

i.e. ₹ 1638 input IGST against output SGST.

∴ SGST paid by the shopkeeper to the State Government (Rajasthan)
$$= \text{Output SGST – Balance of Input IGST}$$
$$= ₹ (2562 - 1638) = ₹ 924$$

∴ Net tax (under GST) paid by shopkeeper to the Central Government = No tax paid to the Central Government.

∴ Tax paid to Rajasthan Government $= ₹ 924$

(iii) Amount of tax (under GST) received by Gujarat Government is nil.

(iv) Amount of tax (under GST) received by the Central Government = IGST received from wholesaler
$$+ \text{ CGST received from shopkeeper}$$
$$= ₹ (4200 + \text{Nil}) = ₹ 4200$$

(v) Amount which the consumer pays for the article
$$= \text{Cost price of article to consumer}$$
$$+ \text{ Consumer pays GST (i.e. CGST and SGST)}$$
$$= ₹ (42700 + 2562 + 2562)$$
$$= ₹ 47824$$

Chapter Test

Multiple Choice Questions

1. The amount of an ordinary annuity of ₹ 1500 at the end of each year for 3 yr at 10% per year compounded annually, is
   (a) ₹ 5132   (b) ₹ 4965   (c) ₹ 3743   (d) ₹ 6354

2. A shopkeeper buys an article whose printed price is ₹ 5000 from a wholesaler at a discount of 20% and sells it to a consumer at the printed price. If the sales are intra-state and rate of GST is 12%.The price of the article inclusive of GST at which the shopkeeper bought it, is
   (a) ₹ 4480   (b) ₹ 3000   (c) ₹ 5000   (d) ₹ 5200

3. The printed price of a carpet is ₹ 3400. A wholesaler in UP buys the carpet from a manufacturer in Bihar at a discount of 12% on the printed price. The wholesaler sells the carpet to a retailer in Delhi at 32% above the market price. If the rate of GST on the carpet is 5%, the price inclusive of tax (under GST) at which the retailer bought the carpet.
   (a) ₹ 4910.6   (b) ₹ 5264.6   (c) ₹ 4712.4   (d) ₹ 6943.00

4. Which of the following tax was abolished by GST?
   (a) Wealth Tax   (b) Service Tax
   (c) Corporation Tax   (d) Income Tax

Case Based MCQs

5. A project requires an initial investment of ₹ 250000 and is expected to generate the following net cash inflows year-1 : ₹ 98000, year-2 : ₹ 120000, year-3 : ₹ 150000. The discount rate is 12% per annum.

Based on the above information, answer the following questions.

 (i) The present value of cash inflow expected to generate at the end of year-1 is
   (a) ₹ 87500   (b) ₹ 76100   (c) ₹ 82540   (d) ₹ 92640

 (ii) The present value of cash inflow expected to generate at the end of second year is [given, $(1.12)^{-2} = 0.7973$]
   (a) ₹ 90106   (b) ₹ 94350   (c) ₹ 95676   (d) ₹ 97520

 (iii) The present value of cash inflow expected to generate at end of third year is [given, $(1.12)^{-3} = 0.7119$]
   (a) ₹ 100524   (b) ₹ 106785
   (c) ₹ 110321   (d) ₹ 995432

 (iv) The net present value of the investment is
   (a) ₹ 289961   (b) ₹ 150672
   (c) ₹ 310514   (d) ₹ 413539

 (v) The difference between the net present value and the present value of cash outflow is
   (a) ₹ 56429   (b) ₹ 42516
   (c) ₹ 35628   (d) ₹ 39961

Short Answer Type Questions

6. If a person wants to accumulate ₹ 42000 by making equal payments at the end of each quarter for the next 5 yr, what will be the size of these investments, if money is worth 6% converted quarterly?
(given, $(1.015)^{20} = 1.343$)

7. Veena is allotted a LIG flat for which she has to make an immediate payment of ₹ 300000 and 12 semi-annual instalments of ₹ 10000 each, the first being paid at the end of 4 yr. Find the cash price of the flat, if money is worth 16% per annum computed semi-annually.

8. Prashant goes to a shop to buy a bag which cost ₹ 1298 (list price). The rate of GST is 18%. He tells the shopkeeper to reduce the price so such an extent that he has to pays ₹ 1200, inclusive of GST. Find the reduction needed in price of the bag.

9. What is standard deduction?

10. The following table shows the water tariff in Delhi

Monthly consumption (in kL)	Service Charge (in ₹)	Volumetric charge per kL (in ₹)
upto 20	₹ 146.41	₹ 5.27
20-30	₹ 219.62	₹ 26.36
> 30	₹ 292.82	₹ 43.93

Plus sewer maintenance charge 60% of volumetric charge

Rahul lives in Delhi. He consumed 24 kL of water in October. Determine his water bill for this month.

Long Answer Type Questions

11. The price of a tape recorder is ₹ 1561. A person purchases it by paying ₹ 300 in cash and the balance is to be paid with due interest in 3 half-yearly equal instalments. If the dealer charges interest at the rate of 10% per annum compounded half-yearly, then find the value of each instalment.

12. How much should a company set aside at the end of each year, if it has to buy a machine expected to cost ₹ 100000 at the end of 4 yr and the rate of interest is 5% per annum compounded annually?

13. The printed price of a panasonic air conditioner (PAC) is ₹ 35000. The wholesaler allows a discount of 14% to a dealer. The dealer sells the air conditioner to a consumer at a discount of 6% on the marked price. If the sales are intra state and rate of GST is 18%, then find how much

 (i) the dealer pays the amount of tax (under GST) to the Central and State Governments?

 (ii) Central and State Governments receive the amount of tax (under GST)?

 (iii) the consumer pays the total amount (inclusive of tax) for the panasonic AC?

Answers

1. (b)   *2.* (a)   *3.* (c)   *4.* (b)   *5.* (i) (a) (ii) (c) (iii) (b) (iv) (a) (v) (d)

6. ₹ 1816.60   *7.* ₹ 343972   *8.* ₹ 198   *10.* ₹ 556.964

11. ₹462.92   *12.* ₹ 23201.85   *13.* (i) ₹ 252 (ii) ₹ 2961 (iii) ₹ 38822

CHAPTER 06

Interest and Present Value

In this Chapter...

- Interest
- Simple Interest
- Compound Interest
- Present Value

Interest

When a person borrows some amount of money from another person or organisation (bank), then the person borrowing money (borrower) pays some extra money during repayment that extra money during repayment is called interest.

e.g. If A takes ₹ 50 from B and after using ₹ 50, A returns ₹ 55 to B, then A pays $(55 - 50)$

i.e. ₹ 5 as interest.

Let us consider following definitions before proceeding chapter.

- **Principal (P)** Principal is the money borrowed or deposited for a certain time.
- **Amount (A)** The sum of principal and interest in called amount.

    Amount = Principal + Simple Interest

- **Rate of Interest (r)** It is the rate at which the interest charged on principal. It is always specified is percentage terms.
- **Time (t)** The period, for which the money is borrowed or deposited, is called time.

Simple Interest (SI)

If the interest is calculated on the original principal for any length of time, then it is called simple interest.

$$\text{Simple Interest} = \frac{\text{Principal} \times \text{Rate} \times \text{Time}}{100}$$

or
$$\text{SI} = \frac{P \times r \times t}{100}$$

Basic Formulae Related to Simple Interest

$$P = \frac{100 \times A}{100 + rt} \quad \text{and} \quad \text{SI} = \frac{A \times r \times t}{100 + rt}$$

Here, SI = Simple Interest, P = Principal, r = Rate of interest, t = Time and A = Amount

Compound Interest

As we know that when we borrow some money from bank or any person, then we have to pay some extra money at the time of repaying. This extra money is known as interest, if interest accrued on principal, it is known as simple interest.

Sometimes, it happens that we repay the borrow money some late. After the completion of specific period, interest occured on principal as well as interest due to the principal. Then, it is known as compound interest.

Compound interest = Amount − Principal

Basic Formulae Related to Compound Interest

Let principal = P, rate = $r\%$ per annum and time = n yr

(i) If interest is compounded annually, then

$$\text{Amount} = P\left(1 + \frac{r}{100}\right)^n$$

Compound interest = Amount − Principal

$$\text{Compound interest} = P\left[\left(1 + \frac{r}{100}\right)^n - 1\right]$$

(ii) If interest is compounded half-yearly, then

$$r = \frac{r}{2} \text{ and } n = 2n$$

$$\text{Amount} = P\left(1 + \frac{r}{2 \times 100}\right)^{2n}$$

(iii) If interest is compounded quarterly, then

$$r = \frac{r}{4} \text{ and } n = 4n$$

$$\text{Amount} = P\left(1 + \frac{r}{4 \times 100}\right)^{4n}$$

(iv) If interest in compounded annually but time is in fraction (suppose time $= n\dfrac{a}{b}$ yr), then

$$\text{Amount} = P\left(1 + \frac{r}{100}\right)^{n} \times \left(1 + \frac{(a/b)r}{100}\right)$$

(v) If rates of interest are r_1%, r_2% and r_3% for 1st, 2nd and 3rd yr respectively, then

$$\text{Amount} = P\left(1 + \frac{r_1}{100}\right)\left(1 + \frac{r_2}{100}\right)\left(1 + \frac{r_3}{100}\right)$$

Effective Rate of Interest

Effective interest rate is the true interest rate that a company or an individual earns or pay over a given period of time as a result of compounding.

$$\text{Effective rate of interest } (r_e) = \left(1 + \frac{r}{m}\right)^{m} - 1$$

where, r = nominal rate of interest

m = conversion period in a year

Present Value

If money is worth i per period, then the present value of amount S due n periods.

Hence, is that principal which, invested now at the rate i per period will amount to S in n period.

The present value P of an amount S due n period.

Hence, at the rate i per period is given by $P = S(1 + i)^{-n}$.

Solved Examples

Example 1. A sum at simple interest of 15% per annum amounts to ₹ 4550 in 5 yr. Find the sum.

Sol. Let sum = ₹ P, $r = 15\%$ and $t = 5$ yr

Then,

$$SI = \frac{P \times r \times t}{100}$$

$$= \frac{P \times 15 \times 5}{100}$$

$$= \frac{3P}{4}$$

$\therefore$ Amount $= ₹\left(P + \frac{3P}{4}\right) = ₹\,\frac{7P}{4}$

According to question,

$$\frac{7P}{4} = 4550$$

$$\Rightarrow \qquad P = \frac{4 \times 4550}{7}$$

$$= ₹\,2600$$

Example 2. Find the compound interest on ₹ 12000 at 20% per annum for 9 months compounded quarterly.

Sol. Given that, $P = ₹\,12000$,

$$n = 9 \text{ months} = \frac{3}{4} \text{ yr}$$

and $\qquad r = 20\%$ per annum

$\therefore$ Amount $= P\left(1 + \dfrac{r}{4 \times 100}\right)^{4n}$

$$= 12000\left(1 + \frac{20}{400}\right)^{3/4 \times 4}$$

$$= 12000\left(1 + \frac{5}{100}\right)^{3}$$

$$= 12000 \times \frac{21}{20} \times \frac{21}{20} \times \frac{21}{20}$$

$$= ₹\,13891.5$$

$\therefore \qquad CI = ₹\,(13891.5 - 12000)$

$$= ₹\,1891.5$$

Example 3. Find the amount to which ₹ 10000 will accumulate at the effective rate of 4% for 8 yr 6% for 6 yr and 10% for 4 yr. (given, $(1.04)^8 = 1.3685$, $(1.06)^6 = 1.4185$ and $(1.10)^4 = 1.4641$)

Sol. Let S be the required sum,

Since, the effective rate is the actual rate compounded annually.

Here, $P = 10000$, $r_1 = 4\%$, $r_2 = 6\%$, $r_3 = 10\%$, $n_1 = 8$, $n_2 = 6$ and $n_3 = 4$

$\therefore S = 10000\left(1 + \dfrac{4}{100}\right)^8\left(1 + \dfrac{6}{100}\right)^6\left(1 + \dfrac{10}{100}\right)^4$

$$= 10000(1 + 0.04)^8(1 + 0.06)^6(1 + 0.10)^4$$

$$= 10000\,(1.04)^8\,(1.06)^6(1.10)^4$$

$$= 10000(1.3685)(1.4185)(1.4641)$$

$$= ₹\,28421.36$$

Example 4. If the nominal rate 5.5% compounded monthly, find the corresponding effective rate. (given, $(1.0045833)^{12} = 1.05640$)

Sol. Given, nominal rate, $r = 5.5\%$

Number of conversions in a year, $p = 12$

Let r_e be the effective rate of interest.

Then, $\quad r_e = \left(1 + \dfrac{r}{100p}\right)^{12} - 1$

$$= \left(1 + \frac{5.5}{100 \times 12}\right)^{12} - 1$$

$$= (1 + 0.0045833)^{12} - 1$$

$$= (1.0045833)^{12} - 1$$

$$= 1.05640 - 1 = 0.05640$$

$\therefore$ Effective rate of interest $= (0.05640 \times 100)\% = 5.64\%$

Example 5. Money invested in a mutual fund double in 4 yr. What is the rate of interest?

Sol. Let P is the initial amount and $r\%$ be the annual rate of interest.

Then, $\qquad 2P = P\left(1 + \dfrac{r}{100}\right)^4$

$\Rightarrow \qquad \left(1 + \dfrac{r}{100}\right)^4 = 2$

Taking log on both sides, we get

$$4\log\left(1 + \frac{r}{100}\right) = \log 2$$

$\Rightarrow \quad \log\left(1 + \dfrac{r}{100}\right) = \dfrac{0.3010}{4}$

$\Rightarrow \quad \log\left(1 + \dfrac{r}{100}\right) = 0.0752$

$\Rightarrow \quad \left(1 + \dfrac{r}{100}\right) = \text{antilog}\,(0.0752) = 1.187$

$\Rightarrow \qquad \dfrac{r}{100} = 1.187 - 1$

$\Rightarrow \qquad \dfrac{r}{100} = 0.187$

$\Rightarrow \qquad r = 18.7\%$

Chapter Practice

Objective Questions

• Multiple Choice Questions

1. At what rate percent per annum simple interest will a sum of money triple itself in 25 yr?
(a) 9.5 %　　　　　　　　(b) 8 %
(c) 10 %　　　　　　　　(d) 8.5 %

2. A man invested $\frac{1}{3}$ rd of the sum of 7%, $\frac{1}{4}$ th at 8% and remaining at 10% for one year. If the annual interest is ₹ 408, then the investment is
(a) ₹ 7200　　　　　　　(b) ₹ 4800
(c) ₹ 5000　　　　　　　(d) ₹ 8400

3. ₹ 800 amounts to ₹ 920 in 3 yr at simple interest. If the interest is increased by 3% it would amount to
(a) ₹ 992　　　　　　　　(b) ₹ 1056
(c) ₹ 1112　　　　　　　(d) ₹ 1182

4. In a certain time, a sum becomes 4 times at the rate of 5% per annum. At what rate of simple interest, the same sum becomes 8 times in the same duration?
(a) $12\frac{2}{3}\%$　　　　　　(b) $11\frac{3}{5}\%$
(c) $11\frac{2}{3}\%$　　　　　　(d) $12\frac{3}{5}\%$

5. The sum which amounts to ₹ 364.80 in 8 yr at 3.5% simple interest per annum is
(a) ₹ 285　　　　　　　　(b) ₹ 280
(c) ₹ 270　　　　　　　　(d) ₹ 275

6. In 4 yr, ₹ 6000 amounts to ₹ 8000. In what time at the same rate, will ₹ 525 amount to ₹ 700?
(a) 2 yr　　　　　　　　(b) 3 yr
(c) 4 yr　　　　　　　　(d) 5 yr

7. The effective rate of return, which is equivalent to a declared rate of 6% compounded semi-annually is
(a) 6.5%　　　　　　　　(b) 6.05%
(c) 6.09%　　　　　　　(d) 6.9%

8. The declared rate of return compounded semi-annually which is equivalent to 8.16%, effective rate of return, is
(a) 8.05%　　　　　　　(b) 8%
(c) 8.1%　　　　　　　　(d) None of these

9. A sum amounts to ₹ 1352 in 2 yr at 4% compound interest. The sum is
(a) ₹ 1250　　　　　　　(b) ₹ 1200
(c) ₹ 1300　　　　　　　(d) ₹ 1260

10. What amount will be received on a sum of ₹ 1750 in $2\frac{1}{2}$ yr. If the interest is compounded at the rate of 8% per annum?
(a) ₹ 2125　　　　　　　(b) ₹ 2122.85
(c) ₹ 2100　　　　　　　(d) ₹ 2200

11. Simple interest on a sum at $12\frac{1}{2}\%$ per annum for 2 yr is ₹ 256. What is the compound interest on the same sum at the same rate and for the same time period?
(a) ₹ 272　　(b) ₹ 282　　(c) ₹ 292　　(d) ₹ 312

12. The difference between compound interest and simple interest for 2 yr on the sum of ₹ 1250 at 4% per annum is
(a) ₹ 3　　(b) ₹ 4　　(c) ₹ 2　　(d) ₹ 8

13. If the difference between the compound interest and simple interest on a certain sum for 2 yr at 8% per annum is ₹ 32, then the sum is
(a) ₹ 5000　　　　　　　(b) ₹ 5500
(c) ₹ 6000　　　　　　　(d) ₹ 5250

14. A sum amounts to ₹ 2916 in 2 yr and ₹ 3149.28 in 3 yr at compound interest. The sum is
(a) ₹ 1500　　　　　　　(b) ₹ 2500
(c) ₹ 2000　　　　　　　(d) ₹ 3000

15. A sum of ₹ 400 amounts to ₹ 441 in 2 yr. What will be the amount if the rate of interest is increased by 5%?
(a) ₹ 484　　　　　　　　(b) ₹ 560
(c) ₹ 512　　　　　　　　(d) ₹ 600

16. At what rate percent compounded annually, a certain sum amounts to 27 times of itself in 3 yr?
(a) 100%   (b) 150%   (c) 75%   (d) 200%

17. A sum of money is put at compound interest for two years at 20% per annum. It would fetch ₹ 482 more, if the interest was payable half-yearly than if it was payable yearly. Then, the sum is
(a) ₹ 20000   (b) ₹ 25000
(c) ₹ 40000   (d) ₹ 30000

18. The present value of ₹ 25000 due 10 yr, hence when interest of 8% is compounded annually, is
[given, $(1.08)^{-10} = 0.4632$]
(a) ₹ 11500   (b) ₹ 11680
(c) ₹ 11580   (d) ₹ 11780

19. The present value of ₹ 60000 due 20 yr hence when interest of 5% is compounded semi-annually is
[given, $(1.025)^{-40} = 0.3724$]
(a) ₹ 22344   (b) ₹ 22000
(c) ₹ 22444   (d) ₹ 22544

20. Aayushi shall receive ₹ 20000 after 4 yr. The present value of this future receipt, if the rate of interest is 8% per annum is
[given, $(1.08)^{-4} = 0.7350$]
(a) ₹ 15000   (b) ₹ 15700
(c) ₹ 14700   (d) ₹ 14000

PART 2
Subjective Questions

• Short Answer Type Questions

1. Raju lent ₹ 4000 to Sagar for 2 yr and ₹ 1000 to Manoj for 4 yr at SI and received from both ₹ 600 as collective interest. Find the rate of interest.

2. A sum of money invested at 20% per annum simple interest amounts to ₹ 650 in $1\frac{1}{2}$ yr. What will it amount to in 2 yr at 12% per annum simple interest?

3. A sum of money invested at a certain rate of simple interest, double itself in 10 yr. In how much time will it become three times of itself at the same rate?

4. Aman and Ajay borrowed ₹ 2500 and ₹ 3000 respectively at the same rate of simple interest for $2\frac{1}{2}$ yr. If Ajay paid ₹ 175 more interest than Aman. Find the rate of interest per annum.

5. The simple interest on a certain sum for 4 yr at 9% per annum is ₹ 216 less than simple interest on the same sum for 3 yr at 18% per annum. Find sum.

6. What will be ratio of simple interest earned by certain amount at the same rate of interest for 12 yr and for 18 yr?

7. Find the compound interest on ₹ 8000 at 5% per annum for 2 yr.

8. In what time will ₹ 64000 amount to ₹ 68921 at 5% per annum compounded semi-annually?

9. A sum of money doubles itself at compound interest in 15 yr. In how many years will it becomes 8 times?

10. At what annual rate of interest, compounded annually, will money double in 8 yr?

11. A sum of money lent at compound interest for 2 yr at 20% per annum would fetch ₹ 964 more, if the interest was payable half-yearly than if it was payable annually, what is the sum?

12. The compound interest on a sum of money for 2 yr is ₹ 410 and the simple interest on the same sum for the same time period and at the same rate is ₹ 400. Find the rate of interest.

13. Money invested in Kisan Vikas Patra doubles in 6 yr. What is the rate of interest?

14. How much will ₹ 25000 amounts to in 2 yr at compound interest, if the rates for the successive years are 4% and 5% respectively?

15. The difference between the compound interest and simple interest on a certain sum of money at 10% per annum for 2 yr is ₹ 500. Find the sum when the interest is compounded semi-annually.
(given, $(1.05)^4 = 1.2155$)

16. An investment of ₹ 25000 earns interest at 9%, compounded annually. What will be the value of investment at the end of 7 yr?

17. Which gives better yield, 7.8% compounded semi-annually or 8% effective?
(given, $(1.039)^2 = 1.0795$)

18. How many years will it take for money to double at the effective rate of 6%?

19. Find the amount to which ₹ 12000 will accumulate at the effective rate of 3% for 10 yr, 4% for 4 yr and 5% for 2 yr. (given, $(1.03)^{10} = 1.3439$, $(1.04)^4 = 1.1698$ and $(1.05)^2 = 1.1025$)

20. Find the present value of ₹ 30000 due 20 yr, hence when the interest is 6% compounded annually.
[given, $(1.06)^{-20} = 0.3118$]

21. Find the present value of ₹ 40000 due 20 yr, hence at the rate of 8% compounded semi-annually.
[given, $(1.04)^{-40} = 0.2082$]

22. How much money should Sanjiv deposit with the bank, so that he receives ₹ 25000 after 4 yr and another
₹ 50000 after 6 yr from the date of deposit, if the rate of interest is 8% per annum.
(given, $(1.08)^{-4} = 0.7350$ and $(1.08)^{-6} = 0.6302$)

• Long Answer Type Questions

23. A man borrowed ₹ 5000 for 4 yr under the following terms: 4% simple interest for the first $2\dfrac{1}{2}$ yr, 4% compound

interest for the rest of the period on the amount due after $2\dfrac{1}{2}$ yr, the interest being compounded semi-annually.

How much should be pay to settle the account? (given, $(1.02)^3 = 1.0612$)

24. Divide ₹ 15500 into two parts such that if one part be lent out at 15% per annum and the other at 24% per
annum the total income is ₹ 3000.

25. The simple interest on a certain sum for 2 yr is ₹ 5000 and compound interest is ₹ 5500 compounded annually.
Find the sum and rate of interest.

SOLUTIONS

Objective Questions

1. (b) Let the principal be ₹ P.

∴ Amount in 25 yr = ₹ $3P$

Rate of interest per annum $= r\%$

Time $= 25$ yr

$A = P + P \times r \times t$

∴ $\quad 3P = P[1 + r(25)] \Rightarrow 3 = 1 + 25r \Rightarrow r = \dfrac{2}{25}$

∴ Rate of interest $= \left(\dfrac{2}{25} \times 100\right)\% = 8\%$

2. (b) Let the investment be ₹ P.

∴Total interest in one year is ₹ 408.

∴7% of ₹ $\dfrac{P}{3}$ + 8% ₹ $\dfrac{P}{4}$ + 10% of ₹ $\left(P - \left(\dfrac{P}{3} + \dfrac{P}{4}\right)\right) = 408$

$\Rightarrow \qquad \dfrac{7P}{300} + \dfrac{8P}{400} + \dfrac{50P}{1200} = 408$

$\Rightarrow \qquad 28P + 24P + 50P = 408 \times 1200$

$\Rightarrow \qquad 102P = 408 \times 1200$

$\Rightarrow \qquad P = \dfrac{408 \times 1200}{102} = 4 \times 1200 = ₹ 4800$

3. (a) Here, $P = ₹ 800, S = ₹ 920$ and $t = 3$ yr

Simple interest $= S - P = 920 - 800 = ₹ 120$

$\qquad I = P \times r \times t \Rightarrow 120 = 800 \times r \times 3$

$\Rightarrow \qquad r = \dfrac{120}{800 \times 3} = 0.05$

Rate of interest $= (0.05 \times 100)\% = 5\%$

Now, rate of interest increased by 3%.

∴ $r = 8\%$

$\qquad I = 800 \times \dfrac{8}{100} \times 3 = ₹ 192$

∴ $S = P + I = ₹(800 + 192) = ₹ 992$

4. (c) Let the sum be ₹ P.

Then, for $R = 5\%$

$\qquad SI = 4P - P = 3P$

$\Rightarrow \qquad 3P = \dfrac{P \times 5 \times t}{100} \Rightarrow t = 60$ yr

Again, for another rate (R),

$\qquad SI = 8P - P = 7P$

$\Rightarrow \qquad 7P = \dfrac{P \times R \times 60}{100}$

$\Rightarrow \qquad R = \dfrac{35}{3}\%$

$\qquad = 11\dfrac{2}{3}\%$

5. (a) Given, $t = 8$ yr, $r = 3.5\%$ and $S = ₹ 364.80$

Let principal be ₹P.

Since, $\qquad S = P\left(1 + \dfrac{rt}{100}\right)$

$\Rightarrow \qquad 364.80 = P\left(1 + \dfrac{3.5 \times 8}{100}\right)$

$\Rightarrow \qquad \dfrac{36480}{100} = P\dfrac{(128)}{100}$

$\Rightarrow \qquad P = \dfrac{36480}{128} = ₹ 285$

6. (c) Here, $P = ₹ 6000, S = ₹ 8000$ and $t = 4$ yr

∴ $\qquad S = P\left(1 + \dfrac{rt}{100}\right)$

$\Rightarrow \qquad 8000 = 6000\left(1 + \dfrac{4r}{100}\right)$

$\Rightarrow \qquad \dfrac{4}{3} - 1 = \dfrac{4r}{100} \Rightarrow r = \dfrac{25}{3}\%$

Now, again

Here, $P = ₹\, 525$, $S = ₹\, 700$ and $r = \dfrac{25}{3}\%$

$$\Rightarrow \qquad S = P\left(1 + \dfrac{rt}{100}\right)$$

$$\Rightarrow \qquad 700 = 525\left(1 + \dfrac{25t}{300}\right)$$

$$\Rightarrow \qquad \dfrac{700}{525} = 1 + \dfrac{t}{12}$$

$$\Rightarrow \qquad \dfrac{t}{12} = \dfrac{700}{525} - 1 = \dfrac{700 - 525}{525} = \dfrac{175}{525}$$

$$\Rightarrow \qquad t = \dfrac{175 \times 12}{525} = 4 \text{ yr}$$

7. (c) Given, $r = 6\%$ per annum and $m = 2$

So, $\qquad r_e = \left(1 + \dfrac{r}{m}\right)^m - 1$

$$\Rightarrow \qquad r_e = \left(1 + \dfrac{6}{200}\right)^2 - 1$$

$$\Rightarrow \qquad r_e = (1.03)^2 - 1 = 1.0609 - 1 = 0.0609$$

Hence, the effective rate is $(0.0609 \times 100)\% = 6.09\%$

8. (b) Here, $r_e = 8.16\% \Rightarrow r_e = 0.0816$ and $m = 2$

$$\therefore \qquad r_e = \left(1 + \dfrac{r}{m}\right)^m - 1$$

$$\Rightarrow \qquad 0.0816 = \left(1 + \dfrac{r}{2}\right)^2 - 1$$

$$\Rightarrow \qquad \left(1 + \dfrac{r}{2}\right)^2 = 1 + 0.0816 = 1.0816$$

$$\Rightarrow \qquad 1 + \dfrac{r}{2} = 1.04$$

$$\Rightarrow \qquad \dfrac{r}{2} = 0.04$$

$$\Rightarrow \qquad r = 0.08$$

$\therefore$ Declared rate of interest $= (0.08 \times 100)\% = 8\%$

9. (a) Given, $A = ₹\, 1352$, $r = 4\%$ and $n = 2$

We know that, $A = P\left(1 + \dfrac{r}{100}\right)^n$

$$\Rightarrow \qquad 1352 = P\left(1 + \dfrac{4}{100}\right)^2$$

$$\Rightarrow \qquad 1352 = P(1.04)^2$$

$$\Rightarrow \qquad P = \dfrac{1352}{(1.04)^2} = ₹\, 1250$$

10. (b) Here, $P = ₹\, 1750$, $r = 8\%$ and $n = 2\dfrac{1}{2}$ yr

$$\therefore \qquad A = P\left(1 + \dfrac{r}{100}\right)^n$$

$$\Rightarrow \qquad A = 1750\left(1 + \dfrac{8}{100}\right)^2\left(1 + \dfrac{8}{100}\right)^{1/2}$$

$$\Rightarrow \qquad A = 1750\left(\dfrac{27}{25}\right)^2\left(1 + \dfrac{8}{200}\right)$$

$$[\because (1 + x)^n = 1 + nx]$$

$$\Rightarrow \qquad A = 1750 \times \dfrac{729}{625} \times \dfrac{208}{200} = ₹\, 2122.85$$

11. (a) Let Principal $= ₹\, P$, $SI = ₹\, 256$, $r = \dfrac{25}{2}\%$ and $t = 2$ yr

$$\therefore \qquad P = \dfrac{SI}{rt} = \dfrac{256 \times 100}{\dfrac{25}{2} \times 2} = ₹\, 1024$$

Principal $= ₹\, 1024$, $r = \dfrac{25}{2}\%$ and $n = 2$

$$CI = P\left[\left(1 + \dfrac{r}{100}\right)^2 - 1\right]$$

$$= 1024\left[\left(1 + \dfrac{25}{200}\right)^2 - 1\right]$$

$$= 1024\left[\left(\dfrac{9}{8}\right)^2 - 1\right]$$

$$= 1024\left(\dfrac{81 - 64}{64}\right)$$

$$= 1024 \times \dfrac{17}{64} = 16 \times 17 = 272$$

$\therefore$ Compound interest $= ₹\, 272$

12. (c) Here, $P = ₹\, 1250$, $r = 4\%$ and $n = 2$ yr

$$\therefore \qquad CI = P\left[\left(1 + \dfrac{r}{100}\right)^n - 1\right]$$

$$= 1250\left[\left(1 + \dfrac{4}{100}\right)^2 - 1\right]$$

$$= 1250\left[\left(\dfrac{26}{25}\right)^2 - 1\right] = 1250\left(\dfrac{676 - 625}{625}\right)$$

$$= 1250 \times \dfrac{51}{625} = ₹\, 102$$

$$SI = \dfrac{P \times r \times t}{100} = \dfrac{1250 \times 4 \times 2}{100} = ₹\, 100$$

$\therefore$ Difference $= ₹(102 - 100) = ₹\, 2$

13. (a) Here, $CI - SI = ₹\, 32$, $r = 8\%$ and $n = 2$ yr

$$CI - SI = P\left(1 + \dfrac{r}{100}\right)^2 - P - \dfrac{P \times r \times t}{100}$$

$$\Rightarrow \qquad 32 = P\left[\left(1 + \dfrac{8}{100}\right)^2 - 1 - \dfrac{8 \times 2}{100}\right]$$

$$\Rightarrow \qquad 32 = P\left[\left(\dfrac{27}{25}\right)^2 - 1 - \dfrac{4}{25}\right] = P\left(\dfrac{729}{625} - \dfrac{29}{25}\right)$$

$$\Rightarrow \qquad 32 = P\left(\dfrac{729 - 725}{625}\right) = \dfrac{4}{625}P$$

$$\Rightarrow \qquad P = \dfrac{625 \times 32}{4} = 625 \times 8 = ₹\, 5000$$

14. (b) Let the required amount be ₹P.

According to question,

$$2916 = P\left(1 + \frac{r}{100}\right)^2 \qquad \text{...(i)}$$

and

$$3149.28 = P\left(1 + \frac{r}{100}\right)^3 \qquad \text{...(ii)}$$

On dividing Eq. (ii) by Eq. (i), we get

$$1 + \frac{r}{100} = \frac{3149.28}{2916}$$

$$\Rightarrow \quad \frac{r}{100} = \frac{3149.28}{2916} - 1$$

$$= \frac{3149.28 - 2916}{2916}$$

$$\Rightarrow \quad \frac{r}{100} = \frac{233.28}{2916} = 0.08$$

$$\Rightarrow \quad r = 0.08 \times 100 = 8\%$$

From Eq. (i),

$$2916 = P\left(1 + \frac{8}{100}\right)^2$$

$$\Rightarrow \quad P = \frac{2916 \times 100 \times 100}{108 \times 108} = ₹\, 2500$$

15. (a) Here, $A = ₹\,441$, $P = ₹\,400$ and $n = 2$

$$\therefore \quad A = P\left(1 + \frac{r}{100}\right)^n$$

$$\Rightarrow \quad 441 = 400\left(1 + \frac{r}{100}\right)^2$$

$$\Rightarrow \quad \left(1 + \frac{r}{100}\right)^2 = \frac{441}{400}$$

$$\Rightarrow \quad 1 + \frac{r}{100} = \sqrt{\frac{441}{400}} = \frac{21}{20}$$

$$\Rightarrow \quad \frac{r}{100} = \frac{21}{20} - 1 = \frac{1}{20}$$

$$\Rightarrow \quad r = 5\%$$

Now, new rate is $(5 + 5)\% = 10\%$

$$\therefore \quad A = 400\left(1 + \frac{10}{100}\right)^2$$

$$= 400\left(\frac{11}{10}\right)^2 = 400 \times \frac{121}{100}$$

$$\Rightarrow \quad A = ₹\,484$$

16. (d) Let sum $= ₹\,P$, $n = 3$ and $A = 27P$

$$\therefore \quad A = P\left(1 + \frac{r}{100}\right)^n$$

$$\Rightarrow \quad 27P = P\left(1 + \frac{r}{100}\right)^3$$

$$\Rightarrow \quad \left(1 + \frac{r}{100}\right)^3 = 27$$

$$\Rightarrow \quad 1 + \frac{r}{100} = 3$$

$$\Rightarrow \quad \frac{r}{100} = 2$$

$$\Rightarrow \quad r = 200$$

Hence, rate of interest is 200%.

17. (a) Let the sum be ₹P.

When the interest is compounded half-yearly

$$n = 4 \text{ and } r = \frac{20}{2} = 10\%$$

$$\Rightarrow \quad A_1 = P\left(1 + \frac{20}{200}\right)^4 = P(1.10)^4$$

$$\left[\because A = P\left(1 + \frac{r}{100}\right)^n\right]$$

When the interest is compounded annually.

$$n = 2 \text{ and } r = 20\%$$

$$\Rightarrow \quad A_2 = P\left(1 + \frac{20}{100}\right)^2 = P(1.20)^2$$

It is given that,

$$A_1 - A_2 = 482$$

$$\Rightarrow \quad P(1.10)^4 - P(1.2)^2 = 482$$

$$\Rightarrow P[(1.10)^2 + (1.2)][(1.10)^2 - 1.2] = 482$$

$$\Rightarrow \quad P[1.21 + 1.20][1.21 - 1.2] = 482$$

$$\Rightarrow \quad P(2.41)(0.01) = 482$$

$$\Rightarrow \quad P = \frac{482}{2.41 \times 0.01}$$

$$\Rightarrow \quad P = ₹\,20000$$

18. (c) Here, $S = ₹\,25000$, $r = 8\% = 0.08$ and $n = 10$

We know that,

$$P = S(1 + r)^{-n}$$

$$= 25000(1 + 0.08)^{-10}$$

$$= 25000(1.08)^{-10} = 25000 \times 0.4632$$

$$= 11580$$

$$\therefore \text{ Present value} = ₹\,11580$$

19. (a) Here, $S = ₹\,60000$, $r = \frac{5}{2}\%$ (semi-annually)

and $\quad n = 20 \times 2 = 40$

$$\therefore \quad P = S(1 + r)^{-n}$$

$$= 60000\left(1 + \frac{5}{200}\right)^{-40}$$

$$= 60000(1.025)^{-40} = 60000 \times 0.3724$$

$$= 22344$$

$$\therefore \text{Present value} = ₹\,22344$$

20. (c) Let P be the present value of the sum, $S = ₹\,20000$

$r = 8\% = 0.08$ and $n = 4$

$$\therefore \quad P = S(1 + r)^{-n}$$

$$= 20000(1 + 0.08)^{-4}$$

$$= 20000(1.08)^{-4}$$

$$= 20000 \times 0.7350 = 14700$$

$$\therefore \text{ Present value} = ₹\,14700$$

Subjective Questions

1. Principal for Raju = ₹ 4000 and $t = 2$ yr

Let r be the rate of interest.

$\therefore$ Simple interest paid by Raju $= \dfrac{4000 \times r \times 2}{100} = 80r$

In second case,

$$P = ₹\,1000 \text{ and } t = 4$$

$\Rightarrow \qquad \text{SI} = \dfrac{1000 \times r \times 4}{100} = 40r \qquad \left[\because \text{SI} = \dfrac{P \times r \times t}{100}\right]$

According to the question,

$$80r + 40r = 600$$

$\Rightarrow \qquad\qquad 120r = 600$

$\Rightarrow \qquad\qquad r = \dfrac{600}{120} = 5$

Hence, rate of interest is 5 %.

2. Let P be the sum of money

We have, Principal $= P$, $r = 20\%$, $t = \dfrac{3}{2}$ yr and $A = ₹\,650$

$\therefore \qquad A = P(1 + rt) = P\left(1 + \dfrac{20 \times 3}{100 \times 2}\right)$

$\Rightarrow \qquad 650 = P\left(1 + \dfrac{3}{10}\right) = \dfrac{13P}{10}$

$\Rightarrow \qquad P = \left(\dfrac{10 \times 650}{13}\right) = ₹\,500$

This sum of money is invested for 2 yr at 12% per annum. Let S be the amount after 2 yr.

Then, $A = P(1 + rt)$

$= 500\left(1 + \dfrac{12}{100} \times 2\right) = 500\left(1 + \dfrac{6}{25}\right)$

$= 500 \times \dfrac{31}{25} = 620$

Hence, amount after 2 yr is ₹ 620.

3. Let the principal $= ₹P$, rate of interest $= r\%$, $t = 10$ yr and $A = 2P$

$\therefore \qquad A = P(1 + rt)$

$\Rightarrow \qquad 2P = P\left(1 + \dfrac{10r}{100}\right)$

$\Rightarrow \qquad 2 = 1 + \dfrac{r}{10}$

$\Rightarrow \qquad r = 10\%$

Same amount will be tripled at 10%.

Here, $P = P$, $A = 3P$, $r = 10\%$ and $t = ?$

$\therefore \qquad 3P = P\left(1 + \dfrac{10t}{100}\right)$

$\Rightarrow \qquad 3 = 1 + \dfrac{t}{10}$

$\Rightarrow \qquad 2 = \dfrac{t}{10}$

$\Rightarrow \qquad t = 20$

$\therefore$ The sum will become three times in 20 yr.

4. Let the rate of interest be $r\%$.

Let I_1 and I_2 be the interest paid by Aman and Ajay respectively.

Then, $I_1 = 2500 \times r \times \dfrac{5}{2}$ and $I_2 = 3000 \times r \times \dfrac{5}{2}$

Given, $I_2 - I_1 = 175$

$\therefore \quad 3000 \times r \times \dfrac{5}{2} - 2500 \times r \times \dfrac{5}{2} = 175$

$\Rightarrow \qquad \dfrac{5r}{2}(3000 - 2500) = 175$

$\Rightarrow \qquad r = \dfrac{175 \times 2}{5 \times 500} = \dfrac{175}{1250} = \dfrac{14}{100}$

Hence, rate of interest is $\left(\dfrac{14}{100} \times 100\right)\% = 14\%$

5. Let the principal be ₹ P.

Simple interest $= I_1$, $r = 9\%$ and $t = 4$ yr

$\because \qquad I_1 = \dfrac{P \times 9 \times 4}{100} = ₹\,\dfrac{36}{100}P$

Let the simple interest be I_2, $r = 18\%$ and $t = 3$ yr

$$I_2 = P\left(\dfrac{18 \times 3}{100}\right) = ₹\,\dfrac{54P}{100}$$

Given, $I_2 - I_1 = 216$

$\therefore \qquad \dfrac{54P - 36P}{100} = 216$

$\Rightarrow \qquad 18P = 21600$

$\Rightarrow \qquad P = \dfrac{21600}{18} = 1200$

Hence, the principal is ₹ 1200.

6. Let the principal be P.

Rate of interest $= r\%$

$$I_1 = \dfrac{P \times r \times 12}{100} = \dfrac{12Pr}{100}$$

$$I_2 = \dfrac{P \times r \times 18}{100} = \dfrac{18Pr}{100}$$

$$\dfrac{I_1}{I_2} = \dfrac{\dfrac{12Pr}{100}}{\dfrac{18Pr}{100}} = \dfrac{2}{3}$$

$\therefore$ Hence, ratio is $2 : 3$.

7. Given, $P = ₹\,8000$, $r = 5\%$ and $n = 2$ yr

$\therefore \qquad \text{CI} = P\left[\left(1 + \dfrac{r}{100}\right)^n - 1\right]$

$\Rightarrow \qquad \text{CI} = 8000\left[\left(1 + \dfrac{5}{100}\right)^2 - 1\right]$

$= 8000\left[\left(\dfrac{21}{20}\right)^2 - 1\right] = 8000\left(\dfrac{441}{400} - 1\right)$

$= 8000\left(\dfrac{441 - 400}{400}\right) = 8000 \times \dfrac{41}{400}$

$= 20 \times 41 = 820$

$\therefore$ Compound Interest $= ₹\,820$

8. Given, amount $= ₹\, 68921$

Principal $= ₹\, 64000$

Rate of interest $= 5\%$ (semi-annually)

$\therefore \qquad r = \dfrac{5}{2}\%$

Time period $(n) = 2n$

$\therefore \qquad A = P\left(1 + \dfrac{r}{100}\right)^{n}$

$\therefore \qquad 68921 = 64000\left(1 + \dfrac{5}{200}\right)^{2n}$

$\Rightarrow \qquad \left(1 + \dfrac{1}{40}\right)^{2n} = \dfrac{68921}{64000}$

$\Rightarrow \qquad \left(\dfrac{41}{40}\right)^{2n} = \left(\dfrac{41}{40}\right)^{3}$

$\Rightarrow \qquad 2n = 3$

$\Rightarrow \qquad n = \dfrac{3}{2} = 1\dfrac{1}{2}$

Hence, time is $1\dfrac{1}{2}$ yr.

9. Let the sum of money be $₹P$ invested at the rate of $r\%$ per annum.

It is given that money becomes double in 15 yr.

$\therefore \qquad A = 2P$ and $n = 15$ yr

$\Rightarrow \qquad A = P(1 + r)^{n}$

$\Rightarrow \qquad 2P = P(1 + r)^{15}$

$\Rightarrow \qquad 2 = (1 + r)^{15} \qquad \ldots(i)$

Let money becomes 8 times of itself in x yr.

$\therefore \qquad 8P = P(1 + r)^{x}$

$\Rightarrow \qquad 8 = (1 + r)^{x}$

$\Rightarrow \qquad (2)^{3} = (1 + r)^{x} \qquad \ldots(ii)$

From Eqs. (i) and (ii), we get

$\qquad (1 + r)^{45} = (1 + r)^{x}$

$\Rightarrow \qquad x = 45$

Hence, the money will become 8 times in 45 yr.

10. Let principal $= ₹P$, $n = 8$ and $A = 2P$

$\therefore \qquad A = P(1 + r)^{n}$

$\Rightarrow \qquad 2P = P(1 + r)^{8}$

$\Rightarrow \qquad 2 = (1 + r)^{8}$

Taking log on both sides, we get

$\qquad \log 2 = 8\log(1 + r)$

$\Rightarrow \qquad 0.3010 = 8\log(1 + r)$

$\Rightarrow \qquad \log(1 + r) = \dfrac{0.3010}{8} = 0.03765$

$\Rightarrow \qquad 1 + r = \text{antilog}\,(0.03765)$

$\qquad\qquad\qquad = 1.0904$

$\Rightarrow \qquad r = 1.0904 - 1$

$\qquad\qquad\quad = 0.0904$

Hence, rate of interest is $(0.0904 \times 100)\% = 9.04\%$

11. Let the principal be $₹\, P$.

Then, compound interest when compounded half-yearly

$\therefore \quad CI = P\left[\left(1 + \dfrac{20}{200}\right)^{4} - 1\right]$

$\qquad = P\left[\left(\dfrac{11}{10}\right)^{4} - 1\right] = P\left[\dfrac{14641}{10000} - 1\right] = ₹\,\dfrac{4641P}{10000}$

Compound interest when compounded annually

$CI = P\left[\left(1 + \dfrac{20}{100}\right)^{2} - 1\right] = P\left[\left(\dfrac{6}{5}\right)^{2} - 1\right]$

$\qquad = P\left(\dfrac{36}{25} - 1\right) = ₹\,\dfrac{11P}{25}$

According to the question,

$\qquad \dfrac{4641P}{10000} - \dfrac{11P}{25} = 964$

$\Rightarrow \qquad \left(\dfrac{4641 - 4400}{10000}\right)P = 964$

$\Rightarrow \qquad \dfrac{241}{10000}P = 964$

$\Rightarrow \qquad P = \dfrac{964 \times 10000}{241}$

$\qquad\qquad\quad = 40000$

$\therefore$ Principal $= ₹\, 40000$

12. We have, SI for 2 yr $= ₹\, 400$

Let principal $= P$ and $t = 2$ yr

$\therefore \qquad SI = \dfrac{P \times r \times t}{100} \Rightarrow 400 = \dfrac{2Pr}{100} \qquad \ldots(i)$

$\Rightarrow \qquad CI = P\left(\left(1 + \dfrac{r}{100}\right)^{2} - 1\right)$

$\Rightarrow \qquad 410 = P\left[\left(1 + \dfrac{r}{100}\right)^{2} - 1\right] \qquad \ldots(ii)$

Subtract Eq. (i) from Eq. (ii), we get

$410 - 400 = P\left(\left(1 + \dfrac{r}{100}\right)^{2} - 1 - \dfrac{2r}{100}\right)$

$10 = P\left(1 + \dfrac{r^{2}}{10000} + \dfrac{2r}{100} - \dfrac{2r}{100} - 1\right) = \dfrac{Pr^{2}}{10000}$

$\therefore \qquad Pr^{2} = 100000 \qquad \ldots(iii)$

From Eqs. (i) and (iii), we get

$\qquad\qquad r = 5$

$\therefore$ Rate of interest $= 5\%$

13. Let the principal $= ₹P$

Rate of interest $= r\%$

Now, principal becomes double in 6 yr.

$\therefore \qquad A = 2P$

$\Rightarrow \qquad A = P\left(1 + \dfrac{r}{100}\right)^{n}$

$\Rightarrow \qquad 2P = P\left(1 + \dfrac{r}{100}\right)^{6}$

$\Rightarrow \qquad 2 = \left(1 + \dfrac{r}{100}\right)^6$

$\Rightarrow \qquad \log 2 = 6\log\left(1 + \dfrac{r}{100}\right)$

$\Rightarrow \quad 6\log\left(1 + \dfrac{r}{100}\right) = 0.3010 \qquad [\because \log 2 = 0.3010]$

$\Rightarrow \quad \log\left(1 + \dfrac{r}{100}\right) = \dfrac{0.3010}{6} = 0.0502$

$\Rightarrow \quad 1 + \dfrac{r}{100} = \text{Antilog}\ (0.0502) = 1.123$

$\Rightarrow \quad \dfrac{r}{100} = 1.123 - 1 = 0.123 \Rightarrow r = 12.3$

Hence, rate of interest is 12.3%.

14. Given, $P = ₹\ 25000, n = 2$

Rate for successive years is 4% and 5%.

$\therefore \qquad A = P\left(1 + \dfrac{r_1}{100}\right)\left(1 + \dfrac{r_2}{100}\right)$

$\qquad = 25000\left(1 + \dfrac{4}{100}\right)\left(1 + \dfrac{5}{100}\right)$

$\qquad = 25000\left(\dfrac{26}{25}\right)\left(\dfrac{21}{20}\right)$

$\qquad = 27300$

$\therefore$ Amount $= ₹\ 27300$

15. Let the principal $= ₹\ P$

Rate of interest $= 10\%$

Time period $= 2$ yr

For compound interest,

Here, compounded semi-annually.

$\therefore \quad r = \dfrac{10}{2} = 5\%$ and $n = 2 \times 2 = 4$

$\therefore \quad \text{CI} = P\left[\left(1 + \dfrac{5}{100}\right)^4 - 1\right] \qquad \left[\because \text{CI} = P\left[\left(1 + \dfrac{r}{100}\right)^n - 1\right]\right]$

$\Rightarrow \ \text{CI} = P[(1.05)^4 - 1] = P(1.2155 - 1) = 0.2155P$

For simple interest,

$\qquad \text{SI} = \dfrac{P \times 10 \times 2}{100} = 0.2P \qquad \left[\because \text{SI} = \dfrac{P \times r \times t}{100}\right]$

Given, $\text{CI} - \text{SI} = 500$

$\therefore \quad 0.2155P - 0.2P = 500$

$\Rightarrow \qquad 0.0155P = 500$

$\Rightarrow \qquad P = \dfrac{500}{0.0155} = 32258$

Hence, principal are $₹\ 32258$.

16. Given, $P = ₹\ 25000\ r = 9\%$ compounded annually

and $n = 7$

$\therefore \qquad A = P\left(1 + \dfrac{r}{100}\right)^n \Rightarrow A = 25000\left(1 + \dfrac{9}{100}\right)^7$

$\qquad = 25000\,(1.09)^7$

$\qquad = 25000(1.8280) \qquad [\because (1.09)^7 = 1.8280]$

$\qquad = 45700$

The value of investment after 7 yr is $₹\ 45700$.

17. The effective rate corresponding to 7.8% compounded semi-annually is

We know that, $\quad r_e = \left(1 + \dfrac{r}{m}\right)^m - 1$

$\qquad r_e = \left(1 + \dfrac{0.078}{2}\right)^2 - 1$

$\qquad \left[\because r = \dfrac{7.8}{100} = 0.078 \text{ and } m = 2\right]$

$\Rightarrow \qquad r_e = (1 + 0.039)^2 - 1$

$\Rightarrow \qquad r_e = (1.039)^2 - 1 = 1.0795 - 1 = 0.0795$

So, the effective rate $= 0.0795 \times 100 = 7.95\%$ per annum

Clearly, 8% effective gives better yield.

18. Let the principal be $₹P$.

$A = 2P, r = 6\%$ compounded annually.

Time period $= n$ yr

$\therefore \qquad A = P\left(1 + \dfrac{r}{100}\right)^n$

$\Rightarrow \qquad 2P = P\left(1 + \dfrac{6}{100}\right)^n$

$\Rightarrow \qquad 2 = \left(1 + \dfrac{6}{100}\right)^n$

$\Rightarrow \qquad \log 2 = n\log(1.06)$

$\Rightarrow \qquad n = \dfrac{\log 2}{\log 1.06} = \dfrac{0.3010}{0.0253} = 11.89$

$\therefore$ Time $= 11.89$ yr

19. The effective rate is the actual rate compounded annually.

Here, $P = 12000, r_1 = 3\%, r_2 = 4\%, r_3 = 5\%,$

$n_1 = 10, n_2 = 4$ and $n_3 = 2$

$\qquad A = P\left(1 + \dfrac{r_1}{100}\right)^{n_1}\left(1 + \dfrac{r_2}{100}\right)^{n_2}\left(1 + \dfrac{r_3}{100}\right)^{n_3}$

$\Rightarrow \quad A = 12000\left(1 + \dfrac{3}{100}\right)^{10}\left(1 + \dfrac{4}{100}\right)^4\left(1 + \dfrac{5}{100}\right)^2$

$\Rightarrow \qquad A = 12000\,(1.03)^{10}(1.04)^4(1.05)^2$

$\Rightarrow \qquad A = 12000\,(1.3439)(1.1698)(1.1025)$

$\Rightarrow \qquad A = 12000 \times 1.7332 = 20798$

Hence, the amount is $₹\ 20798$.

20. Given, $S = ₹\ 30000, r = 6\% = 0.06, n = 20$ yr

We know, $P = S(1 + r)^{-n}$

$\qquad = 30000(1 + 0.06)^{-20} = 30000(1.06)^{-20}$

$\qquad = 30000(0.3118) = 9354$

Hence, present value is $₹\ 9354$.

21. Given, $S = ₹\ 40000, r = 8\%$ compounded semi-annually

$\therefore \qquad r = \dfrac{8}{2}\% = 0.04$

$\Rightarrow \qquad n = 20 \times 2 = 40$

$\therefore \qquad P = S(1 + r)^{-n}$

$\qquad = 40000(1 + 0.04)^{-40} = 40000(1.04)^{-40}$

$\qquad = 40000 \times 0.2082 = 8328$

Hence, present value are $₹\ 8328$.

22. Let P_1 be the present value of $S_1 = 25000$ due after 4 yr and P_2 be the present value of $S_2 = 50000$ due after 6 yr.

Then, $P_1 = S_1(1 + r)^{-4}$ and $P_2 = S_2(1 + r)^{-6}$

$\Rightarrow \quad P_1 = 25000(1 + 0.08)^{-4}$ and $P_2 = 50000(1 + 0.08)^{-6}$

$\Rightarrow \quad P_1 = 25000(1.08)^{-4}$ and $P_2 = 50000(1.08)^{-6}$

$\Rightarrow \quad P_1 = 25000(0.7350)$ and $P_2 = 50000(0.6302)$

$\Rightarrow \quad P_1 = 18375$ and $P_2 = 31525$

$\therefore P_1 + P_2 = 18375 + 31525 = 49900$

Hence, Sanjiv should deposit ₹ 49900.

23. Given, principal ₹ 5000, $r = 4\%$ and $t = \dfrac{5}{2}$ yr

$$\therefore \mathrm{SI} = \frac{P \times r \times t}{100} = \frac{5000 \times 4 \times 5}{100 \times 2} = ₹\ 500$$

Amount $= P + \mathrm{SI} = 5000 + 500 = 5500$

$\therefore$ Amount $= ₹\ 5500$

Now, ₹ 5500 is principal amount for compound interest

$\therefore\ P = ₹\ 5500,\ r = \dfrac{4}{2}\% = 2\%$ (semi-annually)

and $n = 2 \times \left(4 - \dfrac{5}{2}\right) = 3$ yr

$$\therefore \qquad A = P\left(1 + \frac{r}{100}\right)^{n}$$

$$= 5500\left(1 + \frac{2}{100}\right)^{3}$$

$$= 5500(1.02)^{3}$$

$$= 5500 \times 1.0612 = 5836.60$$

Total amount paid $= ₹\ 5836.60$

24. Let one part be ₹ x.

Then, the other part is ₹ $(15500 - x)$.

For the first part, we have

$$P = x,\ r = \frac{15}{100}\ \text{and}\ t = 1\ \text{yr}$$

$$\therefore\ I_1 = \mathrm{SI} = P \times r \times t = \frac{x \times 15 \times 1}{100} = \frac{3x}{20}$$

For the second part, we have

$$P = (15500 - x),\ r = \frac{24}{100} = \frac{6}{25}\ \text{and}\ t = 1\ \text{yr}$$

$$\therefore\ I_2 = \mathrm{SI} = P \times r \times t = \frac{(15500 - x) \times 6 \times 1}{25}$$

$$= \frac{1}{25}(93000 - 6x)$$

It is given that total annual interest is ₹ 3000.

$$\therefore \qquad I_1 + I_2 = 3000$$

$$\Rightarrow \quad \frac{3x}{20} + \frac{93000 - 6x}{25} = 3000$$

$$\Rightarrow \quad 15x + 372000 - 24x = 300000$$

$$\Rightarrow \qquad 9x = 72000$$

$$\Rightarrow \qquad x = 8000$$

Hence, two part are ₹ 8000 and ₹$(15500 - 8000) = ₹\ 7500$

25. Let the sum $= ₹\ P$ and rate of interest $= r\%$

Given, $\mathrm{SI} = ₹\ 5000$ and $t = 2$ yr

$$\therefore \qquad \mathrm{SI} = \frac{P \times r \times t}{100}$$

$$\Rightarrow \qquad 5000 = \frac{Pr \times 2}{100}$$

$$\Rightarrow \qquad Pr = 250000 \Rightarrow P = \frac{250000}{r}$$

Also, given $\mathrm{CI} = 5500$ and $n = 2$

$$\therefore \qquad \mathrm{CI} = P\left[\left(1 + \frac{r}{100}\right)^{2} - 1\right]$$

$$\Rightarrow \quad 5500 = P\left(1 + \frac{r^2}{10000} + \frac{2r}{100} - 1\right)$$

$$\Rightarrow \quad 5500 = P\left(\frac{r^2 + 200r}{10000}\right)$$

$$\Rightarrow \quad 5500 = \frac{250000}{r}\left(\frac{r^2 + 200r}{10000}\right) \quad \left[\because P = \frac{250000}{r}\right]$$

$$\Rightarrow \quad 5500r = 25(r^2 + 200r)$$

$$\Rightarrow \quad 5500r = 25r^2 + 5000r$$

$$\Rightarrow \quad 5500r - 5000r = 25r^2$$

$$\Rightarrow \qquad 500 = 25r$$

$$\Rightarrow \qquad r = \frac{500}{25} = 20\%$$

$$\Rightarrow \qquad P = \frac{250000}{r} = \frac{250000}{20} = 12500$$

$\therefore$ Rate of interest $= 20\%$ per annum

Sum of money $= ₹\ 12500$

Chapter Test

Multiple Choice Questions

1. The compound interest on ₹ 50000 at 5% per annum is ₹ 5125. The time period is
  (a) $1\frac{1}{2}$ yr (b) 2 yr
  (c) $2\frac{1}{2}$ yr (d) 3 yr

2. If the simple interest on a sum of money for 2 yr at 6% per annum is ₹ 120, then the compound interest on the same sum at the same rate for the same time is
  (a) ₹ 123.50 (b) ₹ 123.60
  (c) ₹ 123.80 (d) ₹ 123.90

3. The effective rate of return, which is equivalent to a declared rate of 10% compounded semi-annually is
  (a) 10.20% (b) 10.10%
  (c) 10.15% (d) 10.25%

4. The difference between compound and simple interest on an amount of ₹ 10000 for 2 yr is ₹ 64. The rate of interest per annum is
  (a) 5% (b) 6%
  (c) 8% (d) 10%

5. A sum of money lent out at simple interest amounts to ₹ 2200 in one year and to ₹ 2800 in 4 yr is
  (a) ₹ 2000 (b) ₹ 2100
  (c) ₹ 1800 (d) None of these

6. The declared rate of return compounded semi-annually which is equivalent to 12.36%, effective rate of return is
  (a) 11% (b) 12%
  (c) 12.25% (d) 12.20%

7. A sum invested under compound interest double itself in 10 yr. In how many years will it becomes 8 times of the initial sum.
  (a) 15 yr (b) 20 yr
  (c) 25 yr (d) 30 yr

8. The present value of ₹ 15000 due 15 yr, hence when the interest of 8% is compounded semi-annually is
  [given, $(1.04)^{-30} = 0.3083$]
  (a) ₹ 4000 (b) ₹ 5000
  (c) ₹ 4625 (d) ₹ 4825

Case Based MCQs

9. The effective rate of return is the rate of interest on an investment when compounding occurs more than once.

The formula for the effective rate of return is

Effective rate of return $(r_e) = \left(1 + \dfrac{r}{m}\right)^m - 1$

Where, r = annual rate of return

m = number of compounding in a year

Based on above information, answer the following questions.

(i) The effective rate of return, which is equivalent to declared rate of 6% compounded semi-annually is
  (a) 6.05% (b) 6.07% (c) 6.08% (d) 6.09%

(ii) The declared rate of return compounded semi-annually which is equivalent to 10.25%, effective rate of return is
  (a) 10.10% (b) 10% (c) 9.8% (d) 10.20%

(iii) The effective rate of return, which is equivalent to declared rate of 8% compounded quarterly is
  [given, $(1.02)^4 = 1.0824$]
  (a) 8.24% (b) 8.5% (c) 8.75% (d) 8.40%

(iv) The amount will ₹ 12000 accumulate in 12 yr, if invested at an effective rate of 5% is
  [given, $(1.05)^{12} = 1.7958)$]
  (a) ₹ 21550 (b) ₹ 21000
  (c) ₹ 24000 (d) ₹ 22560

(v) How many years will it take for money to double at the effective rate of 8%? (given, $\log(1.08) = 0.0334$)
  (a) 9 yr (b) 10 yr (c) 11 yr (d) 12 yr

Short Answer Type Questions

10. Divide ₹ 43500 in two parts so that the simple interest on the first when deposited for one year at 9% per annum and that on the second when deposited for two years at 10% per annum in a bank are the same.

11. In what time will ₹ 10800 amount to ₹ 18000 at 5% compounded quarterly. (given, $\log(1.0125) = 0.0053$)

12. On a certain sum of money, the difference between the compound interest for a year, payable half-yearly, and the simple interest for a year is ₹ 180. Find the sum lent out, if the rate of interest in both the cases is 10%.

13. Find the amount and the compound interest on ₹ 2000 in 2 yr, if the rate is 4% for the first year and 3% for the second year.

14. Ashwani invested ₹ 6000 in a company at compound interest compounded semi-annually. He receives ₹ 7986 after $1\frac{1}{2}$ yr from the company. Find the rate of interest per annum.

Long Answer Type Questions

15. The simple interest on a certain sum for 2 yr is ₹ 1200 and compound interest is ₹ 1290. Find the sum and rate of interest.

16. A sum of money is deposited in a bank at compound interest compounded semi-annually. The amount at the end of 4 yr is ₹ 10948.55 and the amount became ₹ 14983.85 at the end of 8 yr. Find the money deposited and the rate of interest.

Answers

1. (b) **2.** (b) **3.** (d) **4.** (c) **5.** (a) **6.** (b) **7.** (d) **8.** (c)

9. (i) (d) (ii) (b) (iii) (a) (iv) (a) (v) (a)

10. ₹ 30000 and ₹ 13500 **11.** 10.46 yr **12.** ₹ 72000 **13.** ₹ 142.40

14. 20% **15.** ₹ 4000 **16.** ₹ 8000

For Detailed Solutions

Scan the code

CHAPTER 07

Straight Lines

In this Chapter...

- Slope of a Straight Line
- Distance of a Point from a Line
- Application of the Straight Line in Demand Curve

Slope of a Straight Line

A **straight line** is a curve, such that all the points on the line segment joining any two points of it lies on it.

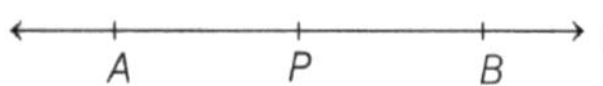

Angle of Inclination of a Line

An angle 'θ' made by the line with positive X-axis in anti-clockwise direction is called angle of inclination of a line.

Thus, $$0° \leq \theta \leq 180°$$

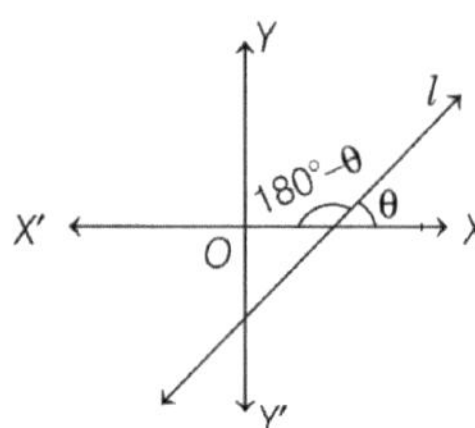

(i) When $\theta = 0°$, then line is parallel to X-axis (horizontal line).

(ii) When $\theta = 90°$, then line is perpendicular to X-axis i.e. parallel to Y-axis (vertical line).

Slope or Gradient of a Line

If θ is the angle of inclination of a line l, then $\tan \theta$ is called the slope or gradient of the line l and it is denoted by m.

i.e. $$m = \tan \theta$$

For $$0° \leq \theta \leq 180°$$

The slope of a line is the tangent of the angle made by the line in the anti-clockwise direction with the positive X-axis.

i.e. $$m = \tan \theta$$

Slope of a Line Joining Two Points

Let $A(x_1, y_1)$ and $B(x_2, y_2)$ be two given points and θ be the inclination of the line AB,

so that $$m = \tan \theta.$$

$$m = \tan \theta = \frac{y_2 - y_1}{x_2 - x_1}$$

or $$\frac{y_1 - y_2}{x_1 - x_2}$$

This relation is true in both the cases, whether θ is an acute angle or an obtuse angle.

Angle between Two Lines

Let l_1 and l_2 be two lines and their inclination are α_1 and α_2, respectively. Then, their slopes are $m_1 = \tan\alpha_1$ and $m_2 = \tan\alpha_2$.

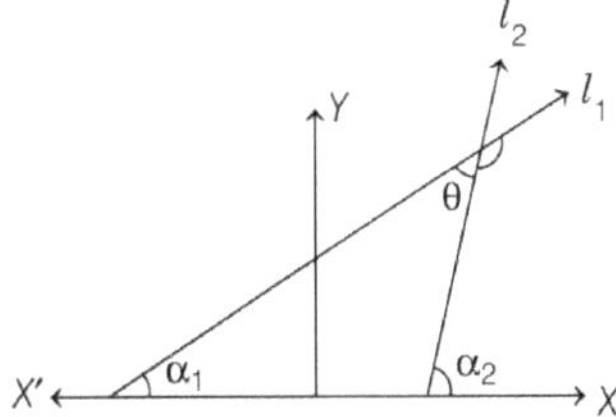

Let θ be the angle between l_1 and l_2, then.

$$\tan\theta = \pm\frac{m_2 - m_1}{1 + m_1 m_2}$$

For acute angle, we take $\tan\theta = \left|\dfrac{m_2 - m_1}{1 + m_1 m_2}\right|$

(i) If $m_1 = m_2$, then two lines are parallel.

(ii) If $m_1 m_2 = -1$, then two lines are perpendicular.

Equation of Line Parallel to X-axis (or Equation of horizontal line)

If straight line parallel to X-axis at a distance a from it, then the equation of line parallel to X-axis (i.e. equation of horizontal line) is either

$$y = a \text{ or } y = -a$$

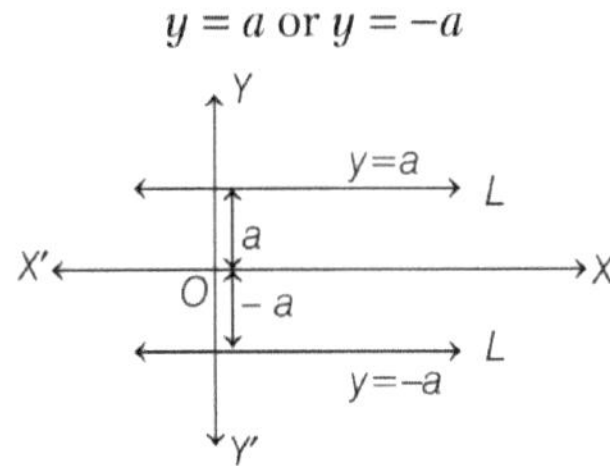

Equation of Line Parallel to Y-axis (or Equation of Vertical Line)

If straight line parallel to Y-axis at a distance b from it, then the equation of line parallel to Y-axis (i.e. equation of vertical line) is either

$$x = b \text{ or } x = -b$$

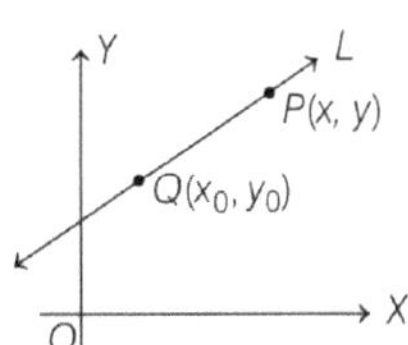

Note

(i) Equation of X-axis is y = 0. (ii) Equation of Y-axis is x = 0.

Point Slope Form

The equation of the straight line having slope m and passes through the point $Q(x_0, y_0)$ is

$$y - y_0 = m(x - x_0)$$

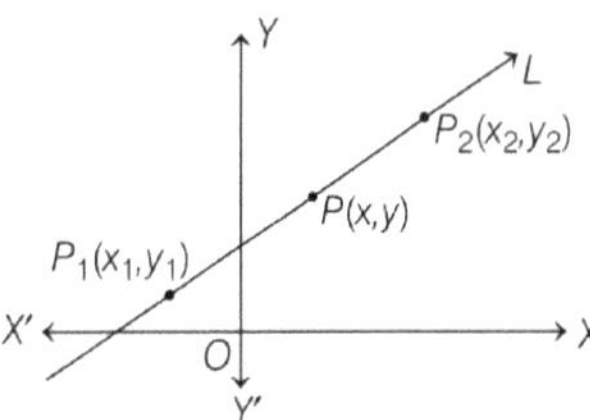

Two Points Form

The equation of a line passing through the points (x_1, y_1) and $(x_2, y_2,)$ is given by

$$y - y_1 = \frac{y_2 - y_1}{x_2 - x_1}(x - x_1)$$

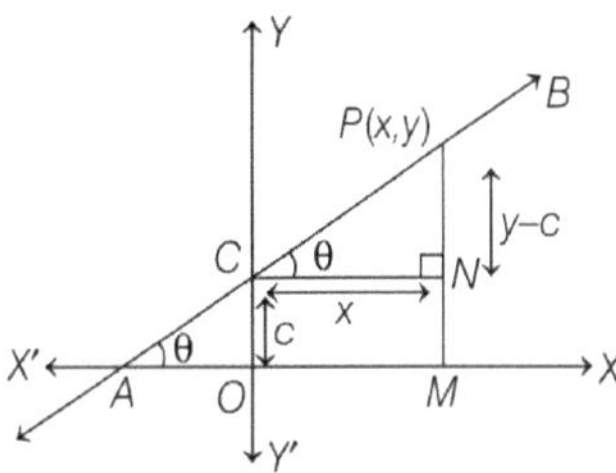

Slope Intercept Form

Suppose a line L with slope m cuts the Y-axis at a distance c from the origin (distance c is called the y-intercept of the line).

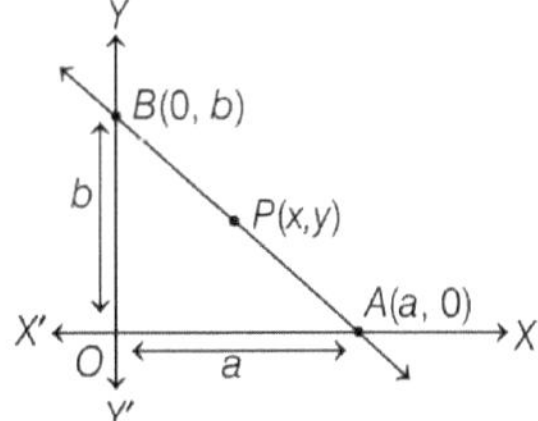

Then, equation of the line L is $y = mx + c$.

Intercept Form

The equation of a line which cuts-off intercepts a and b on the X-axis and Y-axis respectively, is

$$\frac{x}{a} + \frac{y}{b} = 1$$

Distance of a Point from a Line

The distance of a point from a line is the **length of perpendicular** drawn from the point to the line. Let $L: Ax + By + C = 0$ be a line, whose perpendicular distance from the point $P(x_1, y_1)$ is d.

Then, $\quad d = \dfrac{|Ax_1 + By_1 + C|}{\sqrt{A^2 + B^2}}$

Distance Between Two Parallel Lines

If two lines are parallel, then they have the same distance between them throughout.

The distance between two parallel lines $y = mx + c_1$ and $y = mx + c_2$ is given by

$$d = \dfrac{|c_1 - c_2|}{\sqrt{1 + m^2}}$$

Application of the Straight Line in Demand Curve

Demand curve, in economics, a graphic representation of the relationship between product price and the quantity of the product demanded.

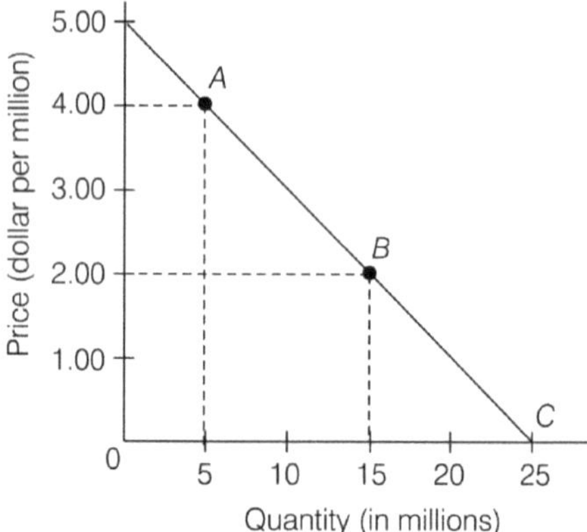

On a linear demand curve, elasticity decrease as the price falls and the quantity demanded increase.

Solved Examples

Example 1. Find the slope of line passing through given points $P_1(-2, -5)$ and $P_2(-3, 4)$.

Sol. Given, $P_1(-2, -5)$ and $P_2(-3, 4)$

$$\therefore \quad m = \frac{y_2 - y_1}{x_2 - x_1}$$

$$= \frac{-3 + 2}{4 + 5} = -\frac{1}{9}$$

$$\therefore \text{ Slope } (m) = -\frac{1}{9}$$

Example 2. Find the equation of lines passing through the point $(1, 2)$ and making angle $30°$ with Y-axis.

Sol. Given that, angle with Y-axis $= 30°$

and $\qquad$ angle with X-axis $= 60°$

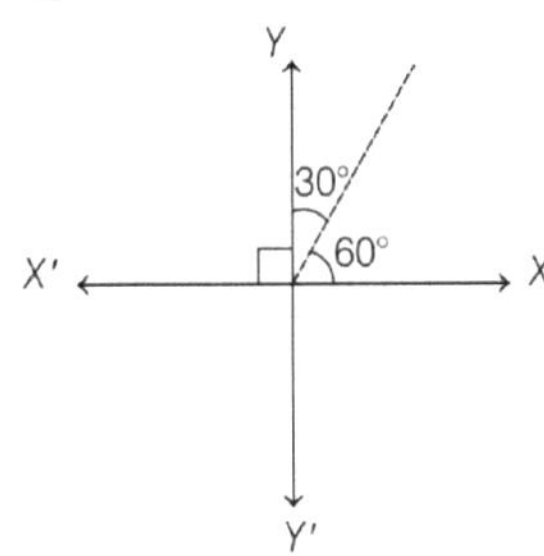

$\therefore$ Slope of the line, $m = \tan 60° = \sqrt{3}$

So, the equation of a line passing through the point $(1, 2)$ and having slope $\sqrt{3}$, is

$$y - 2 = \sqrt{3}(x - 1)$$

$$\Rightarrow \qquad y - 2 = \sqrt{3}x - \sqrt{3}$$

$$\Rightarrow \qquad y - \sqrt{3}x - 2 + \sqrt{3} = 0$$

Example 3. Find the slope of line passing through the points $A(1, -2)$ and $B(3, 4)$. Also, find the equation of line.

Sol. We know that, slope $= \dfrac{y_2 - y_1}{x_2 - x_1}$

Slope, $m = \dfrac{4 + 2}{3 - 1} = \dfrac{6}{2} = 3$

$$m = 3$$

Equation of line passing through given points when slope is given

$$(y - y_1) = m(x - x_1)$$

$$\Rightarrow \qquad y - (-2) = m(x - 1)$$

$$\Rightarrow \qquad y + 2 = 3(x - 1)$$

$$\Rightarrow \qquad y + 2 = 3x - 3$$

$$\Rightarrow \qquad y - 3x = -3 - 2$$

$$\Rightarrow \qquad -3x + y = -5$$

$$\Rightarrow \qquad 3x - y = 5$$

Example 4. Find the equation of the straight line which passes through the point $(1 - 2)$ and cuts off equal intercepts from axes.

Sol. Let the intercepts along the X and Y-axes are a and a respectively.

$\therefore$ Equation of the line is

$$\frac{x}{a} + \frac{y}{a} = 1 \qquad \qquad \text{...(i)}$$

Since, the point $(1, -2)$ lies on the line.

$$\therefore \qquad \frac{1}{a} - \frac{2}{a} = 1$$

$$\Rightarrow \qquad \frac{1 - 2}{a} = 1$$

$$\Rightarrow \qquad a = -1$$

On putting $a = -1$ in Eq. (i), we get

$$\frac{x}{-1} + \frac{y}{-1} = 1$$

$$\Rightarrow \qquad x + y = -1$$

$$\Rightarrow \qquad x + y + 1 = 0$$

Example 5. Find the angle between the lines $y = (2 - \sqrt{3})(x + 5)$ and $y = (2 + \sqrt{3})(x - 7)$.

Sol. Given lines, $y = (2 - \sqrt{3})(x + 5)$ $\qquad$ ...(i)

Slope of this line,

$$m_1 = (2 - \sqrt{3})$$

and $\qquad y = (2 + \sqrt{3})(x - 7)$ $\qquad$ ...(ii)

Slope of this line, $m_2 = (2 + \sqrt{3})$

Let θ be the angle between lines (i) and (ii), then

$$\tan \theta = \left| \frac{m_1 - m_2}{1 + m_1 m_2} \right|$$

$$\Rightarrow \qquad \tan \theta = \left| \frac{(2 - \sqrt{3}) - (2 + \sqrt{3})}{1 + (2 - \sqrt{3})(2 + \sqrt{3})} \right|$$

$$\Rightarrow \qquad \tan \theta = \left| \frac{-2\sqrt{3}}{1 + 4 - 3} \right|$$

$$\Rightarrow \qquad \tan \theta = \sqrt{3}$$

$$\Rightarrow \qquad \tan \theta = \tan \pi/3$$

$$\therefore \qquad \theta = \pi/3 = 60°$$

For obtuse angle $= \pi - \dfrac{\pi}{3}$

$$= \frac{2\pi}{3}$$

$$= 120°$$

Hence, the angle between the lines are $60°$ or $120°$.

Example 6. Show that the tangent of an angle between the lines $\dfrac{x}{a} + \dfrac{y}{b} = 1$ and $\dfrac{x}{a} - \dfrac{y}{b} = 1$ is $\dfrac{2ab}{a^2 - b^2}$.

Sol. Given, equation of lines are

$$\frac{x}{a} + \frac{y}{b} = 1 \qquad \ldots(i)$$

$\therefore$ Slope, $m_1 = -\dfrac{b}{a}$

and

$$\frac{x}{a} - \frac{y}{b} = 1 \qquad \ldots(ii)$$

$\therefore$ Slope, $m_2 = \dfrac{b}{a}$

Let θ be the angle between the given lines, then

$$\tan\theta = \left| \frac{m_1 - m_2}{1 + m_1 m_2} \right|$$

$$\Rightarrow \quad \tan\theta = \left| \frac{-\dfrac{b}{a} - \dfrac{b}{a}}{1 + \left(-\dfrac{b}{a}\right)\left(-\dfrac{b}{a}\right)} \right|$$

$$\Rightarrow \quad \tan\theta = \left| \frac{\dfrac{-2b}{a}}{\dfrac{a^2 - b^2}{a^2}} \right|$$

$$\Rightarrow \quad \tan\theta = \frac{2ab}{a^2 - b^2} \qquad \textbf{Hence proved.}$$

Example 7. A variable line passes through a fixed point P. The algebraic sum of the perpendiculars drawn from the points $(2, 0)$, $(0, 2)$ and $(1, 1)$ on the line is zero. Find the coordinates of the point P.

Sol. Let slope of the line be m and the coordinates of fixed point P are (x_1, y_1).

$\therefore$ Equation of line is $y - y_1 = m(x - x_1)$ $\qquad \ldots(i)$

Since, the given points are $A(2, 0)$, $B(0, 2)$ and $C(1, 1)$.

Now, perpendicular distance from A, is

$$\frac{0 - y_1 - m(2 - x_1)}{\sqrt{1 + m^2}}$$

Perpendicular distance from B, is

$$\frac{2 - y_1 - m(0 - x_1)}{\sqrt{1 + m^2}}$$

Perpendicular distance from C, is

$$\frac{1 - y_1 - m(1 - x_1)}{\sqrt{1 + m^2}}$$

Now, $\dfrac{-y_1 - 2m + mx_1 + 2 - y_1 + mx_1 + 1 - y_1 - m + mx_1}{\sqrt{1 + m^2}} = 0$

$\Rightarrow \qquad -3y_1 - 3m + 3mx_1 + 3 = 0$

$\Rightarrow \qquad -y_1 - m + mx_1 + 1 = 0$

Since, $(1, 1)$ lies on this line. So, the point P is $(1, 1)$.

Example 8. If p is the length of perpendicular from the origin on the line $\dfrac{x}{a} + \dfrac{y}{b} = 1$ and a^2, p^2 and b^2 are in AP, the show that $a^4 + b^4 = 0$.

Sol. Given, equation of line are

$$\frac{x}{a} + \frac{y}{b} = 1 \qquad \ldots(i)$$

Perpendicular length from the origin on the line (i) is given by p

i.e.

$$p = \frac{1}{\sqrt{\dfrac{1}{a^2} + \dfrac{1}{b^2}}}$$

$$= \frac{ab}{\sqrt{a^2 + b^2}}$$

$\therefore$

$$p^2 = \frac{a^2 b^2}{a^2 + b^2}$$

Given that, a^2, p^2 and b^2 are in AP.

$\therefore \qquad 2p^2 = a^2 + b^2$

$\Rightarrow \qquad \dfrac{2a^2 b^2}{a^2 + b^2} = a^2 + b^2$

$\Rightarrow \qquad 2a^2 b^2 = (a^2 + b^2)^2$

$\Rightarrow \qquad 2a^2 + b^2 = a^4 + b^4 + 2a^2 b^2$

$\Rightarrow \qquad a^4 + b^4 = 0$

Chapter Practice

Objective Questions

• Multiple Choice Questions

1. The distance between the points $(6, -4)$ and $(3, 0)$ is

(a) 7 units   (b) 25 units

(c) $\sqrt[3]{25}$ units   (d) 5 units

2. If θ is the inclination of a line l, then the slope or gradient of the line l is

(a) $\sin \theta$ (b) $\cos \theta$

(c) $\tan \theta$ (d) $\cot \theta$

3. The slope of a line is denoted by m. Thus,

(a) $m = \tan \theta$ (b) $m = \tan \theta, \theta \neq 90°$

(c) $m = \tan \theta, \theta \neq 0°$ (d) None of these

4. If the slope of the line joining the points $A(x, 2)$ and $B(6, -8)$ is $-5/4$, then the value of x is

(a) 3   (b) 2

(c) -1 (d) -2

5. The acute angle (θ) between lines L_1 and L_2 with slopes m_1 and m_2 respectively is given by

(a) $\tan \theta = \dfrac{m_1 - m_2}{1 + m_1 m_2}$, as $1 + m_1 m_2 \neq 0$

(b) $\tan \theta = \dfrac{m_2 - m_1}{1 + m_1 m_2}$, as $1 + m_1 m_2 \neq 0$

(c) $\tan \theta = \left| \dfrac{m_2 - m_1}{1 - m_1 m_2} \right|$, as $1 + m_1 m_2 \neq 0$

(d) None of the above

6. The lines whose slopes are $\sqrt{3}$ and $\dfrac{1}{\sqrt{3}}$, then the angle between the lines is

(a) 30°   (b) 60°

(c) 45°   (d) None of these

7. The angle between the X-axis and the line joining the points $(4, -2)$ and $(5, -3)$ is

(a) 45°   (b) 135°

(c) 90°   (d) 180°

8. The equation of X-axis is

(a) $x = 0$ (b) $y = 0$

(c) $x + y = 0$ (d) $x - y = 0$

9. The equation of the line through $(-2, 3)$ with slope -4 is

(a) $x + 4y - 10 = 0$ (b) $4x + y + 5 = 0$

(c) $x + y - 1 = 0$ (d) $3x + 4y - 6 = 0$

10. The equation of line passing through $(0, 2)$ and $(3, -3)$, is

(a) $5x + 3y - 6 = 0$ (b) $5x - 3y + 6 = 0$

(c) $3x + 5y - 6 = 0$ (d) $3x - 5y + 6 = 0$

11. Let the line L passes through two given points $P_1(x_1, y_1)$ and $P_2(x_2, y_2)$. Let $P(x, y)$ be general point on L. Then, the equation of the line passing through the points (x_1, y_1) and (x_2, y_2) is given by

(a) $y - y_1 = \dfrac{y_2 - y_1}{x_2 - x_1}(x_1 - x)$ (b) $y + y_1 = \dfrac{y_1 - y_2}{x_1 - x_2}(x + x_1)$

(c) $y - y_1 = \dfrac{y_2 - y_1}{x_2 - x_1}(x - x_1)$ (d) $y - y_1 = \dfrac{y_2 + y_1}{x_2 + x_1}(x - x_1)$

12. The equation of the line which have slope -2 and cuts-off an intercept -6 on X-axis, is

(a) $2x - y + 12 = 0$ (b) $2x + y + 12 = 0$

(c) $-2x + y + 12 = 0$ (d) $2x + y - 12 = 0$

13. A line passes through (x_1, y_1) and (h, k). If slope of the line is m, then

(a) $y_1 - k = m(h - x_1)$ (b) $k - y_1 = m(h - x_1)$

(c) $h - x_1 = m(y_1 - k)$ (d) $h - x_1 = m(k - y_1)$

14. The line which have slope $\dfrac{1}{2}$ and cuts-off an intercept -5 on Y-axis, then the equation of the line is

(a) $x - 2y - 10 = 0$ (b) $x + 2y - 10 = 0$

(c) $2x + y - 10 = 0$ (d) $x + 2y + 10 = 0$

15. A line cutting off intercept -3 from the Y-axis and the tangent at angle to the X-axis is $\dfrac{3}{5}$, then the equation is

(a) $5y + 3x - 15 = 0$ (b) $3x - 5y + 15 = 0$

(c) $5x - 3y + 15 = 0$ (d) $5y - 3x + 15 = 0$

16. If $lx + ly + p = 0$ and $lx + ly - r = 0$ are two parallel lines, then distance between them is equal to $\left|\dfrac{m}{n}\right|$, where m and n respectively are

(a) $p - r, \sqrt{2}l$
(b) $r - p, \sqrt{2}l$
(c) $p + r, \sqrt{2}l$
(d) $p + r, \sqrt{2}l$

17. The distance between the parallel lines $3x - 4y + 7 = 0$ and $3x - 4y + 5 = 0$, is

(a) $\dfrac{3}{7}$ unit
(b) $\dfrac{7}{5}$ units
(c) $\dfrac{2}{5}$ unit
(d) $\dfrac{3}{5}$ unit

18. The distance between two parallel lines $15x + 8y - 34 = 0$ and $15x + 8y + 31 = 0$ is

(a) $\dfrac{65}{17}$ units
(b) $\dfrac{3}{17}$ unit
(c) $\dfrac{2}{17}$ unit
(d) $\dfrac{60}{17}$ units

19. In case of straight line demand curve meeting two axes, the price elasticity of demand at the point where the curve meets Y-axis would be

(a) zero
(b) greater than one
(c) less than one
(d) infinity

20. If the price elasticity of demand is zero, then shape of the curve will be

(a) horizontal
(b) vertical
(c) slopping downward
(d) None of these

• Case Based MCQs

21. Four friends Rishabh, Shubham, Vikram and Rajkumar are sitting on vertices of a rectangle, whose coordinates are given.

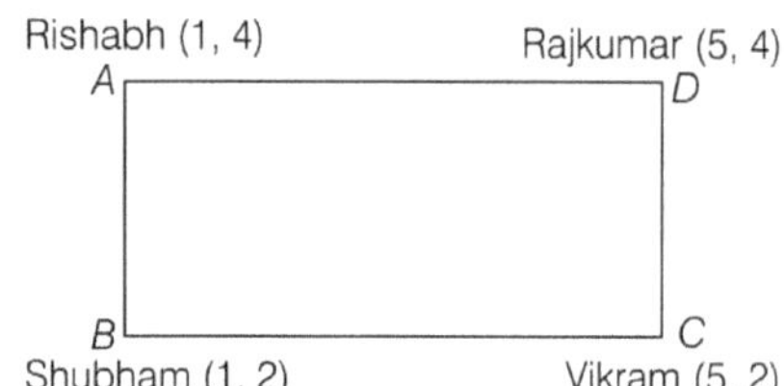

Based on the above information, answer the following questions.

(i) The equation formed by Shubham and Rajkumar is
(a) $x + 2y + 3 = 0$
(b) $x - 2y - 3 = 0$
(c) $x - 2y + 3 = 0$
(d) None of these

(ii) The equation formed by Rishabh and Vikram is
(a) $x + 2y + 9 = 0$
(b) $x + 2y - 9 = 0$
(c) $x - 2y - 9 = 0$
(d) None of these

(iii) The intersection point of above two equations is
(a) (1, 1)
(b) (2, 2)
(c) (3, 3)
(d) (4, 4)

(iv) Slope of equation of line formed by Rishabh and Rajkumar is
(a) zero
(b) 1
(c) 2
(d) 3

(v) Pair for the same slope is
(a) Rishabh-Rajkumar and Shubham-Vikram
(b) Rishabh-Rajkumar and Rajkumar-Vikram
(c) Rishabh-Rajkumar and Rishabh-Shubham
(d) None of the above

22. Population vs Year graph given below.

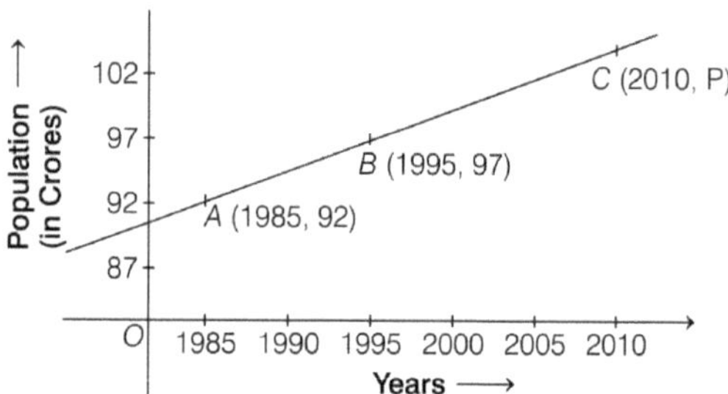

Based on the above information, answer the following questions.

(i) The slope of line AB is
(a) 2
(b) 1
(c) $\dfrac{1}{2}$
(d) $\dfrac{1}{3}$

(ii) The equation of line AB is
(a) $x + 2y = 1791$
(b) $x - 2y = 1801$
(c) $x - 2y = 1791$
(d) $x + 2y = 1801$

(iii) The population in year 2010 is (in crores)
(a) 104.5
(b) 119.5
(c) 109.5
(d) None of the above

(iv) The equation of line perpendicular to line AB and passing through (1995, 97) is
(a) $2x - y = 4087$
(b) $2x + y = 4087$
(c) $2x + y = 1801$
(d) None of the above

(v) In which year the population becomes 110 cr is
(a) 2020
(b) 2019
(c) 2021
(d) 2022

PART 2
Subjective Questions

• Short Answer Type Questions

1. Find the slope of a line, which makes an angle of $30°$ with the positive direction of Y-axis measured anti-clockwise.

2. What is the value of y, so that the line through $(3, y)$ and $(2, 7)$ is parallel to the line through $(-1, 4)$ and $(0, 6)$?

3. A ray of light coming from the point $(1, 2)$ is reflected at a point A on the X-axis and then passes through the point $(5, 3)$. Find the coordinates of the point A.

4. Two lines passing through the point $(2, 3)$ make an angle of $45°$. If the slope of one of the lines is 2, then find the slope of the other line.

5. If three points $(h, 0), (a, b)$ and $(0, k)$ lie on a line, show that $\dfrac{a}{h} + \dfrac{b}{k} = 1$.

6. Consider the following population and year graph (in figure).

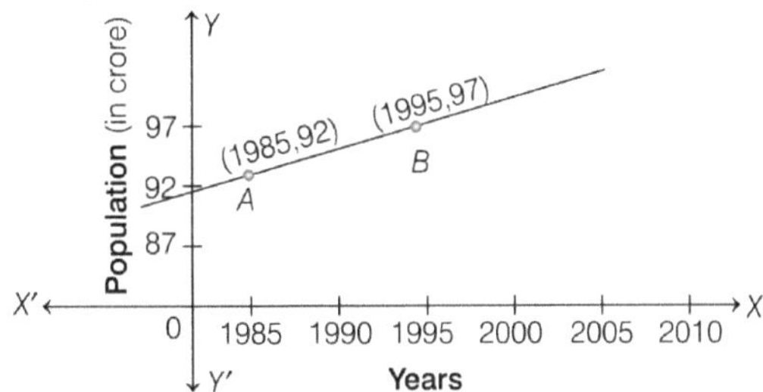

Find the slope of the line AB and using it, find what will be the population in the year 2010?

7. Find the equation of a line passing through the point $(-4, 3)$ with slope $-1/2$.

8. Find the equation of the line passing through the point of intersection of $2x + y = 5$ and $x + 3y + 8 = 0$ and parallel to the line $3x + 4y = 7$.

9. Find the equation of line joining the points $(1, 1)$ and $(2, 3)$.

10. Find the slope of a line perpendicular to the line, which passes through $(0, 8)$ and $(-5, 2)$.

11. Find the equation of the line passing through the point $(5, 2)$ and perpendicular to the line joining the points $(2, 3)$ and $(3, -1)$.

12. Find the equation of the lines which cuts-off intercepts on the axes whose sum and product are 1 and -6, respectively.

13. Find the equation of the line through the intersection of the lines $2x + 3y - 4 = 0$ and $x - 5y = 7$ that has its x-intercept equal to -4.

14. Find the tangent of angle between the lines, whose intercepts on the axes are $(a, -b)$ and $(b, -a)$, respectively.

15. Find the equation of the lines which passes through the point $(3, 4)$ and cuts off intercepts from the coordinate axes such that their sum is 14.

16. Find the value of m for which the lines $mx + (2m + 3)y + m + 6 = 0$ and $(2m + 1)x + (m - 1)y + m - 9 = 0$ intersect at a point on Y-axis.

17. Find the points on the line $x + y = 4$ which lie at a unit distance from the line $4x + 3y = 10$.

18. Find the values of k for which the length of perpendicular from the point $(4, 1)$ on the line $3x - 4y + k = 0$ is 2 units.

19. Find the points on the Y-axis, whose perpendicular distance from the line $4x - 3y - 12 = 0$ is 3.

20. Find the equation of the line, where length of the perpendicular segment from the origin to the line is 4 and the inclination of the perpendicular segment with the positive direction of X-axis is $45°$.

21. Find the coordinates of a point on the line $x + y + 3 = 0$, whose distance from the line $x + 2y + 2 = 0$ is $\sqrt{5}$.

22. Find the distance of the point $(2, 5)$ from the line $3x + y + 4 = 0$ measured parallel to the line $3x - 4y + 8 = 0$.

23. Find the ratio in which the line $3x + 4y + 2 = 0$ divides the distance between the lines $3x + 4y + 5 = 0$ and $3x + 4y - 5 = 0$.

24. If the equation of the base of an equilateral triangle is $x + y - 6 = 0$, and the opposite vertex is the point $(-1, -1)$, then find the area of the triangle.

25. If the equation of the base of an equilateral triangle is $x + y = 2$ and the vertex is $(2, -1)$, then find the length of the side of the triangle.

26. Find the distance of the point of intersection of the lines $2x - 3y + 5 = 0$ and $3x + 4y = 0$ from the line $5x - 2y = 0$.

27. The distance between the lines $3x + 4y = 9$ and $6x + 8y = 15$.

28. Prove that the line $12x - 5y - 3 = 0$ is mid-parallel to the lines $12x - 5y + 7 = 0$ and $12x - 5y - 13 = 0$.

• Long Answer Type Questions

29. Two lines passing through the point $(2, 3)$ intersect each other at an angle of $60°$. If slope of one line is 2, then find the equation of the other line.

30. Find the equation of the lines which passes through the point $(3, -2)$ and are inclined at $60°$ to the line $\sqrt{3}x + y = 1$.

31. Find the equation of the line through the point $(3, 2)$ and making an angle of $45°$ with the line $x - 2y = 3$.

32. Find the equation of one of the sides of an isosceles right-angled triangle whose hypotenuse is given by $3x + 4y = 4$ and the opposite vertex of the hypotenuse is $(2, 2)$.

33. Find the coordinates of the foot of perpendiculars from the point $(2, 3)$ on the line $y = 3x + 4$.

34. Find the image of the point $(3, 8)$ with respect to the line $x + 3y = 7$, assuming the line to be a plane mirror.

35. In the triangle with vertices $P(2, 3), Q(4, -1)$ and $R(-1, 2)$. Find the equation and length of altitude from the vertex P.

36. Find the equation of a straight line with a positive slope, which passes through the point $(-5, 0)$ and is at a perpendicular distance of 3 units from the origin.

37. Find the equations of the lines through the point of intersection of the lines $x - y + 1 = 0$ and $2x - 3y + 5 = 0$ and whose distance from the point $(3, 2)$ is $\dfrac{7}{5}$ units.

38. Find the equation of the line midway between the parallel lines $9x + 6y - 7 = 0$ and $3x + 2y + 6 = 0$.

39. Find the equations of the lines passing through the point $(1, 0)$ and at a distance $\dfrac{\sqrt{3}}{2}$ unit from the origin.

40. Find the point equidistant from the lines $4x + 3y + 10 = 0, 5x - 12y + 26 = 0$ and $7x + 24y - 50 = 0$.

• Case Based Questions

41. Assuming a straight line L is perpendicular to the line $5x - y = 1$ and the area of the triangle formed by the line L and the coordinate axes is 5 sq units.

Based on the above information, answer the following questions.

(i) Find the slope of line L.

(ii) Find the coordinate of the point A and B. If line L intersect X-axis at A and Y-axis at B.

(iii) Find the perpendicular distance between a line $5x - y = 1$ with origin.

(iv) If a line $10x - 2y - 7 = 0$ is parallel to a line $5x - y = 1$, then find the distance between them.

(v) Find the equation of the line L.

42. A straight line M is parallel to the line $3x - 2y = 1$ and the point $(2, 5)$ between the equal distance from the parallel line.

Based on the above information, answer the following questions.

(i) Find the equation of straight line mid the passes through the point $(1, 2)$.

(ii) Find the perpendicular distance between the point $(2, 5)$ and $3x - 2y = 1$.

(iii) Find the distance between the parallel lines.

SOLUTIONS

Objective Questions

1. (d) The distance between the points $(6, -4)$ and $(3, 0)$
$$= \sqrt{(6-3)^2 + (-4-0)^2}$$
$$= \sqrt{(3)^2 + (-4)^2} = \sqrt{9+16} = \sqrt{25} = 5 \text{ units}$$

2. (c) If θ is the inclination of a line l, then $\tan\theta$ is called the slope or gradient of the line l.

3. (b) The slope of a line is denoted by m.
Thus, $m = \tan\theta, \theta \neq 90°$.

4. (d) Given, slope of line $= -\dfrac{5}{4}$

and line passes through the point $A(x, 2)$ and $B(6, -8)$.

$\Rightarrow \qquad \dfrac{-8-2}{6-x} = \dfrac{-5}{4} \qquad \left[\because \text{Slope, } m = \dfrac{y_2 - y_1}{x_2 - x_1}\right]$

$\Rightarrow \qquad -10 \times 4 = -5(6-x)$

$\Rightarrow \qquad -40 = -30 + 5x$

$\Rightarrow \qquad -40 + 30 = 5x$

$\therefore \qquad x = \dfrac{-10}{5} = -2$

5. (b) The acute angle θ between lines L_1 and L_2, with slopes m_1 and m_2 respectively, is given by
$$\tan\theta = \left|\dfrac{m_2 - m_1}{1 + m_1 m_2}\right|, \text{ as } 1 + m_1 m_2 \neq 0$$

6. (a) Let θ be the angle between the given lines.

Let $m_1 = \sqrt{3}$ and $m_2 = \dfrac{1}{\sqrt{3}}$

We know that,
$$\tan\theta = \left|\dfrac{m_1 - m_2}{1 + m_1 . m_2}\right| = \left|\dfrac{\sqrt{3} - \dfrac{1}{\sqrt{3}}}{1 + \sqrt{3} \cdot \dfrac{1}{\sqrt{3}}}\right|$$

$\Rightarrow \qquad \tan\theta = \left(\dfrac{3-1}{\sqrt{3}}\right) \times \dfrac{1}{2} = \dfrac{1}{\sqrt{3}}$

$\Rightarrow \qquad \tan\theta = \tan 30°$

$\therefore \qquad \theta = 30°$

7. (b) Given, $(x_1, y_1) = (4, -2)$ and $(x_2, y_2) = (5, -3)$

Slope of line, $m = \dfrac{y_2 - y_1}{x_2 - x_1} = \dfrac{-3+2}{5-4}$

$\Rightarrow \qquad \tan\theta = \dfrac{-1}{1}$

$\Rightarrow \qquad \tan\theta = -1$

$\Rightarrow \qquad \tan\theta = -\tan 45° \qquad [\because 1 = \tan 45°]$

$\Rightarrow \qquad \tan\theta = \tan(180° - 45°)$

$\qquad\qquad\qquad [\because \tan(180° - \theta) = -\tan\theta]$

$\Rightarrow \qquad \tan\theta = \tan 135°$

$\Rightarrow \qquad \theta = 135°$

8. (b) Any point on X-axis is always in the form of $(x, 0)$.

y-coordinate is always zero on X-axis. So, equation of X-axis is $y = 0$.

9. (b) Using formula,
$$y - y_1 = m(x - x_1)$$
[where, $m = $ slope and (x_1, y_1) are the coordinate of point from which line passes through]

$\Rightarrow \qquad y - 3 = -4(x + 2)$

$\Rightarrow \qquad y - 3 = -4x - 8$

$\Rightarrow \qquad 4x + y + 5 = 0$

10. (a) We have, $(x_1, y_1) = (0, 2)$

$$(x_2, y_2) = (3, -3)$$

We know that, equation of line is
$$(y - y_1) = \dfrac{y_2 - y_1}{x_2 - x_1}(x - x_1)$$

$\Rightarrow \qquad (y - 2) = \dfrac{-3-2}{3-0}(x - 0)$

$\Rightarrow \qquad (y - 2) = -\dfrac{5}{3}(x)$

$\Rightarrow \qquad -5x = 3y - 6$

$\Rightarrow \qquad 5x + 3y - 6 = 0$

11. (c) We have, points are $P_1(x_1, y_1)$ and $P_2(x_2, y_2)$.

Slope of the line, $m = \dfrac{y_2 - y_1}{x_2 - x_1}$

By two points form, we get
$$(y - y_1) = \dfrac{y_2 - y_1}{x_2 - x_1}(x - x_1)$$

12. (b) Given, slope $(m) = -2$

and intercept on X-axis is -6

$\therefore \qquad y = -2(x + 6)$

$\Rightarrow \qquad y = -2x - 12 \Rightarrow 2x + y + 12 = 0$

13. (b) We know that, $m = \dfrac{y_2 - y_1}{x_2 - x_1}$

$\therefore \qquad m = \dfrac{k - y_1}{h - x_1}$

$\Rightarrow \qquad k - y_1 = m(h - x_1)$

14. (a) Given, $m = $ Slope of the line $= \dfrac{1}{2}$

Here, $c = $ Intercept of the line on Y-axis $= -5$

Hence, required equation of the line is
$$y = \dfrac{1}{2}x - 5 \qquad\qquad [\because y = mx + c]$$

$\Rightarrow \qquad x - 2y - 10 = 0$

15. (d) Slope of a line, $m = \tan\theta = \dfrac{3}{5}$

Since, the lines cut-off intercept -3 on Y-axis, then the line is passing through the point $(0, -3)$.

So, the equation of line is
$$y - y_1 = m(x - x_1)$$

$\Rightarrow \qquad y - (-3) = \dfrac{3}{5}(x - 0) \Rightarrow y + 3 = \dfrac{3}{5}x$

$\Rightarrow \qquad 5y + 15 = 3x \Rightarrow 5y - 3x + 15 = 0$

16. (*d*) Given, lines $lx + ly + p = 0$ and $lx + ly - r = 0$ are parallel.

$\therefore$ Distance between two parallel lines $= \left| \dfrac{p - (-r)}{\sqrt{(l)^2 + (l)^2}} \right|$

$$\left[\because \text{distance between two parallel lines} = \dfrac{c_1 - c_2}{\sqrt{a^2 + b^2}} \right]$$

$$= \left| \dfrac{p + r}{\sqrt{2l^2}} \right| = \left| \dfrac{p + r}{\sqrt{2}\, l} \right| \text{ units}$$

17. (*c*) Here, $A = 3, B = -4, C_1 = 7,$ and $C_2 = 5$.

Therefore, the required distance is

$$d = \dfrac{|7 - 5|}{\sqrt{3^2 + (-4)^2}} = \dfrac{2}{5} \text{ unit} \qquad \left[\because d = \dfrac{|C_1 - C_2|}{\sqrt{A^2 + B^2}} \right]$$

18. (*a*) Required distance,

$$d = \left| \dfrac{C_1 - C_2}{\sqrt{A^2 + B^2}} \right| = \left| \dfrac{-34 - 31}{\sqrt{15^2 + 8^2}} \right| = \dfrac{65}{17} \text{ units}$$

19. (*d*) Straight line demand curve meeting two axes, the price elasticity of demand at the point where the curve meets Y-axis would be infinity.

20. (*b*) If the price elasticity of demand is zero, the shape of the curve will be vertical.

21. (i) (*c*) We have the positions,

Shubham B (1, 2) and Rajkumar D (5, 4)

$$\text{Slope, } m_1 = \dfrac{4 - 2}{5 - 1} = \dfrac{2}{4} = \dfrac{1}{2} \qquad \left[\because \text{Slope, } m = \dfrac{y_2 - y_1}{x_2 - x_1} \right]$$

Taking point $(1, 2) = (x_1, y_1)$ and $m_1 = \dfrac{1}{2}$

Equation of line joining points B and D is

$$(y - y_1) = m_1(x - x_1) \Rightarrow (y - 2) = \dfrac{1}{2}(x - 1)$$

$\Rightarrow \quad 2y - 4 = x - 1 \Rightarrow x - 2y + 3 = 0$

(ii) (*b*) We have the positions,

Rishabh A (1, 4) and Vikram C (5, 2)

$$\text{Slope, } m_2 = \dfrac{2 - 4}{5 - 1} = \dfrac{-2}{4} = -\dfrac{1}{2}$$

Taking point $(x_1, y_1) = (1, 4)$ and $m_2 = -\dfrac{1}{2}$

Equation of line joining points A and C is

$$(y - y_1) = m_2(x - x_1)$$
$$(y - 4) = -\dfrac{1}{2}(x - 1)$$

$\Rightarrow \quad 2y - 8 = -x + 1$

$\Rightarrow \quad x + 2y - 9 = 0$

(iii) (*c*) We have, $x - 2y + 3 = 0$ ...(i)

and $\qquad x + 2y - 9 = 0$ ...(ii)

On adding Eqs. (i) and (ii), we get

$$2x - 6 = 0$$

$\Rightarrow \qquad x = 3$

$\therefore \qquad 3 + 2y - 9 = 0$ [From Eq. (ii)]

$\Rightarrow \qquad 2y = 6 \Rightarrow y = 3$

Hence, point of intersection is (3, 3).

(iv) (*a*) We have positions,

Rishabh A (1, 4) and Rajkumar D (5, 4)

$$\text{Slope } AD = \dfrac{4 - 4}{5 - 1} = 0$$

Hence, slope is zero.

(v) (*a*) The line formed by Rishabh-Rajkumar is opposite and parallel to the line formed by Shubham and Vikram. Hence, first pair have same slope.

22. (i) (*c*) Slope of line $AB = \dfrac{y_2 - y_1}{x_2 - x_1} = \dfrac{97 - 92}{1995 - 1985}$

$$= \dfrac{5}{10} = \dfrac{1}{2}$$

(ii) (*b*) Equation of line AB is

$$y - y_1 = m(x - x_1)$$

$\therefore \qquad y - 92 = \dfrac{1}{2}(x - 1985)$

$$2y - 184 = x - 1985$$

$$x - 2y = 1801$$

(iii) (*a*) Let the population in year 2010 is P.

Since, A, B, C are collinear

$\therefore \qquad$ Slope of $AB =$ Slope of BC

$$\dfrac{97 - 92}{1995 - 1985} = \dfrac{P - 97}{2010 - 1995}$$

$\Rightarrow \qquad \dfrac{1}{2} = \dfrac{P - 97}{15}$

$\Rightarrow \qquad 7.5 = P - 97$

$\Rightarrow \qquad P = 97 + 7.5 = 104.5 \text{ cr}$

(iv) (*b*) $\because$ Slope of $AB = \dfrac{1}{2}$

Slope of line perpendicular to $AB = \dfrac{-1}{\frac{1}{2}} = -2$

$\therefore$ Equation of line perpendicular to AB passing through (1995, 97) is

$$y - 97 = -2(x - 1995)$$

$\Rightarrow \qquad y - 97 = -2x + 3990$

$\Rightarrow \qquad 2x + y = 4087$

(v) (*c*) Equation of line AB is

$$x - 2y = 1801$$

Putting $y = 110$, we get

$\therefore \qquad x = 1801 + 220 \Rightarrow x = 2021$

$\therefore$ Population becomes 110 cr in 2021.

Subjective Questions

1. Given, $\angle YPQ = 30°$

To find $\angle PAX = ?$

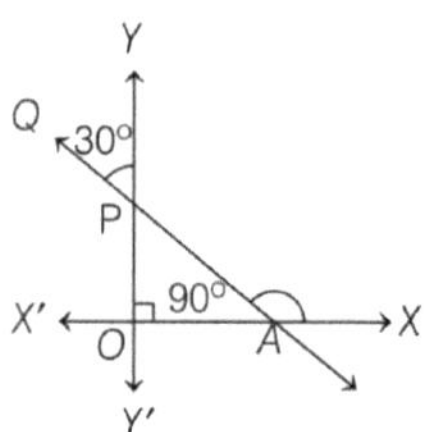

Here, $\angle YPQ = \angle OPA$ [vertically opposite angle]

$\because$ $\angle OPA + \angle POA + \angle PAO = 180°$

[$\because$ sum of all angles of a triangle is 180°]

$\therefore$ $30° + 90° + \angle PAO = 180°$

$\Rightarrow$ $\angle PAO = 180° - 120° = 60°$

$\Rightarrow$ $\angle PAX = 180° - 60° = 120°$

[by linear pair axiom]

$\therefore$ Slope of line $AQ = m = \tan 120°$ [$\because m = \tan \theta$]

$= \tan(180° - 60°)$

[$\because \tan(180° - \theta) = -\tan\theta$]

$= -\tan 60° = -\sqrt{3}$

2. Let $P(3, y)$, $Q(2, 7)$, $R(-1, 4)$ and $S(0, 6)$ be the given points.

Then, $m_1 =$ slope of the line $PQ = \dfrac{7-y}{2-3} = y - 7$

$m_2 =$ slope of the line $RS = \dfrac{6-4}{0-(-1)} = 2$

Since, PQ and RS are parallel,

therefore $m_1 = m_2$

$\Rightarrow$ $y - 7 = 2$

$\Rightarrow$ $y = 9$

3. Let the coordinates of point A be $(x, 0)$. From the figure, the slope of the reflected ray is given by

$$\tan\theta = \dfrac{3}{5-x} \qquad \ldots(i)$$

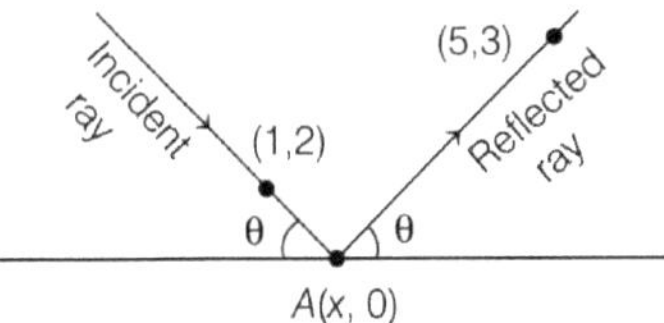

Again, the slope of the incident ray is given by

$$\tan(\pi - \theta) = \dfrac{-2}{x-1} \qquad \left[\because m = \dfrac{y_2 - y_1}{x_2 - x_1}\right]$$

$\Rightarrow$ $-\tan\theta = \dfrac{-2}{x-1}$ [$\because \tan(\pi - \theta) = -\tan\theta$]

$\Rightarrow$ $\tan\theta = \dfrac{2}{x-1}$ $\ldots(ii)$

From Eqs. (i) and (ii), we get

$$\dfrac{3}{5-x} = \dfrac{2}{x-1}$$

$\Rightarrow$ $3x - 3 = 10 - 2x \Rightarrow x = \dfrac{13}{5}$

Therefore, the required coordinates of the point A are $\left(\dfrac{13}{5}, 0\right)$.

4. Let the slope of two lines be m_1 and m_2 and $m_1 = 2$.

Angle between two lines is $\dfrac{\pi}{4}$, where

$$\tan\left(\dfrac{\pi}{4}\right) = \left|\dfrac{m_1 - m_2}{1 + m_1 m_2}\right| \Rightarrow 1 = \left|\dfrac{2 - m_2}{1 + 2m_2}\right|$$

$\Rightarrow$ $\dfrac{2 - m_2}{1 + 2m_2} = 1$ or -1

$\Rightarrow$ $2 - m_2 = 1 + 2m_2$ or $2 - m_2 = -1 - 2m_2$

$\Rightarrow$ $3m_2 = 1$ or $m_2 = -3$

$\Rightarrow$ $m_2 = \dfrac{1}{3}$ or -3

Thus, the slope of other line is $\dfrac{1}{3}$ or -3.

5. Let the given points be $A(h, 0)$, $B(a, b)$ and $C(0, k)$.

If A, B and C are collinear, then

Slope of $AB =$ Slope of $BC =$ Slope of CA

$\Rightarrow$ $\dfrac{b-0}{a-h} = \dfrac{k-b}{0-a} = \dfrac{0-k}{h-0}$

On taking first two terms, we get

$$\dfrac{b}{a-h} = \dfrac{k-b}{-a}$$

$\Rightarrow$ $-ab = (a-h)(k-b)$

$\Rightarrow$ $-ab = ak - ab - hk + bh$

$\Rightarrow$ $ak + bh = hk$

Dividing each term by hk, we get

$$\dfrac{ak}{hk} + \dfrac{bh}{hk} = \dfrac{hk}{hk}$$

$\Rightarrow$ $\dfrac{a}{h} + \dfrac{b}{k} = 1$ **Hence proved.**

6. Let the population in the year 2010 will be k crore. Then, $C(2010, k)$ be on the year population graph.

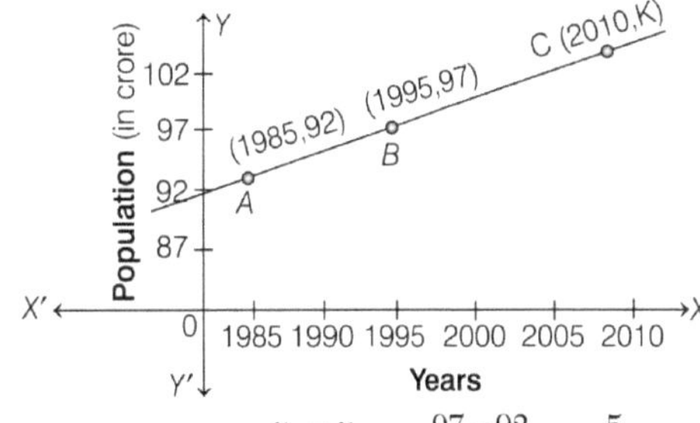

Now, slope of $AB = \dfrac{y_2 - y_1}{x_2 - x_1} = \dfrac{97 - 92}{1995 - 1985} = \dfrac{5}{10}$

[$\because x_1 = 1985$, $x_2 = 1995$, $y_1 = 92$ and $y_2 = 97$]

$\therefore$ Slope of $AB = \dfrac{1}{2}$ $\ldots(i)$

Since, A, B and C lie on the same line, i.e. A, B and C are collinear.

$\therefore$ Slope of $AB =$ Slope of BC

$\Rightarrow$ $\dfrac{1}{2} = \dfrac{k-97}{2010 - 1995}$

$\Rightarrow$ $\dfrac{1}{2} = \dfrac{k-97}{15}$

$\Rightarrow$ $k - 97 = \dfrac{15}{2}$

$\Rightarrow$ $k = 97 + \dfrac{15}{2} = 97 + 7.5 = 104.5$

Hence, slope of $AB = \dfrac{1}{2}$ and population in the year 2010

$= 104.5$ cr

7. Given, point $(-4, 3)$ with slope $-\dfrac{1}{2}$.

As, equation of line $y = mx + c$

Putting value of y, m and x, to find c

$$y = mx + c$$

$$\Rightarrow \quad 3 = \left(-\dfrac{1}{2}\right)(-4) + c$$

So, $\quad c = 1$

Now, putting values of m and c,

then equation of line $y = \left(-\dfrac{1}{2}\right)x + 1$

On solving it, we get

$$x + 2y - 2 = 0$$

8. Given, equation of lines $\quad 2x + y = 5$ ...(i)

and $\qquad\qquad\qquad x + 3y = -8$ ...(ii)

From Eq. (i), $\qquad\qquad y = 5 - 2x$

Now, put the value of y in Eq. (ii), we get

$$x + 3(5 - 2x) = -8$$

$$\Rightarrow \qquad x + 15 - 6x = -8$$

$$\Rightarrow \qquad\qquad -5x = -23$$

$$\Rightarrow \qquad\qquad x = \dfrac{23}{5}$$

Now, $x = \dfrac{23}{5}$ put in Eq. (i), we get

$$y = 5 - \dfrac{46}{5} = \dfrac{25 - 46}{5} = \dfrac{-21}{5}$$

Since, the required line is parallel to the line $3x + 4y = 7$.

So, slope of the line is $m = \dfrac{-3}{4}$.

So, the equation of the line passing through the point $\left(\dfrac{23}{5}, \dfrac{-21}{5}\right)$ having slope $\dfrac{-3}{4}$ is

$$y + \dfrac{21}{5} = \dfrac{-3}{4}\left(x - \dfrac{23}{5}\right)$$

$$\Rightarrow \qquad 4y + \dfrac{84}{5} = -3x + \dfrac{69}{5}$$

$$\Rightarrow \qquad 3x + 4y = \dfrac{84 - 69}{5}$$

$$\Rightarrow \qquad 3x + 4y + \dfrac{15}{5} = 0$$

$$\Rightarrow \qquad 3x + 4y + 3 = 0$$

9. The straight line joining the points $(1, 1)$ and $(2, 3)$ is

$$\dfrac{x - x_1}{x_2 - x_1} = \dfrac{y - 1}{y_2 - y_1}$$

$$\Rightarrow \qquad \dfrac{x - 1}{2 - 1} = \dfrac{y - 1}{3 - 1}$$

$$\Rightarrow \qquad x - 1 = \dfrac{y - 1}{2}$$

$$\Rightarrow \qquad 2x - 2 = y - 1 \Rightarrow 2x - y - 1 = 0$$

10. Given, a line with slope m, then the slope of any line perpendicular to it is

$$m_{\text{perpendicular}} = -\dfrac{1}{m}$$

We know that, $\qquad m = \dfrac{y_2 - y_1}{x_2 - x_1}$

[where, (x_1, y_1) and (x_2, y_2) are coordinate points]

The points are $(x_1, y_1) = (0, 8)$

and $\qquad\qquad (x_2, y_2) = (-5, 2)$

$$\therefore \qquad m = \dfrac{2 - 8}{-5 - 0} = \dfrac{-6}{-5} = \dfrac{6}{5}$$

$$m_{\text{perpendicular}} = \dfrac{-1}{6/5} = \dfrac{-5}{6}$$

11. The equation of line joining the points $(2, 3)$ and $(3, -1)$ is

$$(y + 1) = \dfrac{3 + 1}{2 - 3}(x - 3)$$

$$\left[\because \text{ form } y - y_1 = \dfrac{y_2 - y_1}{x_2 - x_1}(x - x_1)\right]$$

or $\qquad\qquad y + 1 = -4x + 12$

or $\qquad\qquad y + 4x = 11$ ...(i)

Now, the equation of line perpendicular to the line (i) is

$$4x - y = c$$ ...(ii)

Given, the Eq. (ii) passing through $(5, 2)$ then we get, $c = 18$

So, the equation of the line is $4x - y = 18$.

12. Let a and b be the intercepts of the line on X and Y-axes, respectively.

Equation of the line will be $\dfrac{x}{a} + \dfrac{y}{b} = 1$ ...(i)

Given, sum of intercepts, $\quad a + b = 1$ ...(ii)

and product of intercepts, $\quad ab = -6$ ...(iii)

On putting the value of b from Eq. (ii) in Eq. (iii), we get

$$a(1 - a) = -6$$

$$\Rightarrow \qquad a^2 - a - 6 = 0$$

$$\Rightarrow \qquad a^2 - 3a + 2a - 6 = 0$$

$$\Rightarrow \qquad (a - 3)(a + 2) = 0 \Rightarrow a = 3 \text{ or } -2$$

From Eq. (ii), when $a = 3$, $b = -2$ and when $a = -2$, $b = 3$.

On putting the values of a and b in Eq. (i), required equation of the lines are

$$\dfrac{x}{3} + \dfrac{y}{-2} = 1 \text{ and } \dfrac{x}{-2} + \dfrac{y}{3} = 1$$

$$\Rightarrow \quad 2x - 3y - 6 = 0 \text{ and } 3x - 2y + 6 = 0$$

13. Let the equation of line passing through the point of intersection of lines $2x + 3y - 4 = 0$ and $x - 5y - 7 = 0$ is

$$(2x + 3y - 4) + \lambda(x - 5y - 7) = 0$$

where, λ is some constant.

$$\Rightarrow \quad (2 + \lambda)x + (3 - 5\lambda)y - 4 - 7\lambda = 0$$

$$\Rightarrow \quad (2 + \lambda)x + (3 - 5\lambda)y = 4 + 7\lambda$$ ...(i)

$$\Rightarrow \quad \dfrac{x}{\dfrac{4 + 7\lambda}{2 + \lambda}} + \dfrac{y}{\dfrac{4 + 7\lambda}{3 - 5\lambda}} = 1$$

Since, x-intercept of this line is -4.

$$\therefore \qquad \dfrac{4 + 7\lambda}{2 + \lambda} = -4 \Rightarrow 4 + 7\lambda = -8 - 4\lambda$$

$$\Rightarrow \qquad 12 = -11\lambda \Rightarrow \lambda = -\dfrac{12}{11}$$

On putting $\lambda = -\dfrac{12}{11}$ in Eq. (i), we get

$$\left(2 - \frac{12}{11}\right)x + \left(3 + \frac{60}{11}\right)y = 4 + 7\left(-\frac{12}{11}\right)$$

$$\Rightarrow \qquad \frac{10x}{11} + \frac{93y}{11} = \frac{44 - 84}{11}$$

$$\Rightarrow \qquad 10x + 93y + 40 = 0$$

which is the required equation of line.

14. Since, intercepts on the axes are $a, -b$, then equation of the line is $\dfrac{x}{a} - \dfrac{y}{b} = 1$

$$\Rightarrow \qquad \frac{y}{b} = \frac{x}{a} - 1 \Rightarrow y = \frac{bx}{a} - b$$

So, the lope of this line i.e. $m_1 = \dfrac{b}{a}$.

Also, for intercepts on the axes as b and $-a$, then equation of the line is

$$\frac{x}{b} - \frac{y}{a} = 1$$

$$\Rightarrow \qquad \frac{y}{a} = \frac{x}{b} - 1$$

$$\Rightarrow \qquad y = \frac{a}{b}x - a$$

and slope of this line i.e. $m_2 = \dfrac{a}{b}$

$$\therefore \qquad \tan\theta = \frac{\dfrac{b}{a} - \dfrac{a}{b}}{1 + \dfrac{a}{b}\cdot\dfrac{b}{a}}$$

$$= \frac{\dfrac{b^2 - a^2}{ab}}{2} = \frac{b^2 - a^2}{2ab}$$

15. Let the intercept along the axes be a and b.

Given, $a + b = 14 \Rightarrow b = 14 - a$

Now, the equation of line is $\dfrac{x}{a} + \dfrac{y}{b} = 1$ ...(i)

$$\Rightarrow \qquad \frac{x}{a} + \frac{y}{14 - a} = 1$$

Since, the point (3, 4) lies on the line.

$$\therefore \qquad \frac{3}{a} + \frac{4}{14 - a} = 1$$

$$\Rightarrow \qquad \frac{42 - 3a + 4a}{a(14 - a)} = 1$$

$$\Rightarrow \qquad 42 + a = 14a - a^2$$

$$\Rightarrow \qquad a^2 - 13a + 42 = 0$$

$$\Rightarrow \qquad a^2 - 7a - 6a + 42 = 0$$

$$\Rightarrow \qquad a(a - 7) - 6(a - 7) = 0$$

$$\Rightarrow \qquad (a - 7)(a - 6) = 0$$

$$\Rightarrow \qquad a - 7 = 0 \text{ or } a - 6 = 0$$

$$\therefore \qquad a = 7 \text{ or } a = 6$$

When $a = 7$, then $b = 7$

When $a = 6$, then $b = 8$

$\therefore$ The equation of line, when $a = 7$ and $b = 7$ is

$$\frac{x}{7} + \frac{y}{7} = 1$$

$$\Rightarrow \qquad x + y = 7$$

So, the equation of line, when $a = 6$ and $b = 8$ is

$$\frac{x}{6} + \frac{y}{8} = 1$$

16. Line (i) intersect Y-axis at $\left(0, \dfrac{-m+9}{2m+3}\right)$ and line (ii) intersect

Y-axis at $\left(0, -\dfrac{(m-9)}{m-1}\right)$.

Now, for lines to be intersect at a point on Y-axis.

$$-\left(\frac{m+6}{2m+3}\right) = -\left(\frac{m-9}{m-1}\right)$$

$$\Rightarrow \qquad \frac{m+6}{2m+3} = \frac{m-9}{m-1}$$

$$\Rightarrow \qquad m^2 - m + 6m - 6 = 2m^2 + 3m - 18m - 27$$

$$\Rightarrow \qquad m^2 + 5m - 6 = 2m^2 - 15m - 27$$

$$\Rightarrow \qquad m^2 - 20m - 21 = 0$$

$$\Rightarrow \qquad m = -1, 21$$

17. Let the required point be (h, k).

Since, point (h, k) lies on the line $x + y = 4$,

therefore $\qquad\qquad h + k = 4 \qquad\qquad$ ...(i)

Also, the distance of the point (h, k) from the line $4x + 3y = 10$ is

$$\left|\frac{4h + 3k - 10}{\sqrt{16 + 9}}\right| = 1$$

$$\Rightarrow \qquad 4h + 3k - 10 = \pm 5$$

$$\Rightarrow \qquad 4h + 3k = \pm 5 + 10$$

18. We have, point (4, 1) and line $3x - 4y + k = 0$

Now, the length of perpendicular from point on the line is

$$2 = \frac{3 \times 4 - 4 \times 1 + k}{\sqrt{(3)^2 + (4)^2}}$$

$$\left[\because \text{ length of perpendicular } = \frac{ax_1 + by_1 + c}{\sqrt{a^2 + b^2}}\right]$$

$$\Rightarrow \qquad 2 = \frac{12 - 4 + k}{5}$$

$$\Rightarrow \qquad 10 = 8 + k$$

$$\therefore \qquad k = 10 - 8 = 2$$

19. Let the require point be $P(0, a)$. It is given that the length of the perpendicular from $P(0, \alpha)$ on $4x - 3y - 12 = 0$ is 3 units.

$$\therefore \qquad \left|\frac{4 \times 0 - 3\alpha - 12}{\sqrt{(4)^2 + (-3)^2}}\right| = 3$$

$$\Rightarrow \qquad |3\alpha + 12| = 15$$

$$\Rightarrow \qquad |\alpha + 4| = 5$$

$$\Rightarrow \qquad \alpha + 4 = \pm 5 \Rightarrow \alpha = 1, -9$$

Thus, the required points are (0, 1) and (0, -9).

20. Given, inclination angle from X-axis is $45°$.

So, slope of perpendicular line $= \tan\theta = 1 = m_1$

and $m_1 \cdot m_2 = -1$, then $m_2 = -1$.

We know that, $y = mx + c$

$$y = -x + c$$

So, $\left|\dfrac{c}{\sqrt{1+1}}\right| = 4$ [distance from origin $= 4$ units]

$$\Rightarrow \quad \pm\left|\dfrac{c}{2}\right| = 4\sqrt{2}$$

$$\Rightarrow \quad c = \pm 4\sqrt{2}$$

at $c = 4\sqrt{2}$ and at $c = -4\sqrt{2}$

$y = -x + 4\sqrt{2}$ and $y = -x - 4\sqrt{2}$

For positive direction, $y + x + 4\sqrt{2} = 0$

21. Let the required point be $P(a, b)$.

Then, $a + b + 3 = 0$ ...(i)

Also, $\dfrac{|a + 2b + 2|}{\sqrt{(1)^2 + (2)^2}} = \sqrt{5}$

$\Rightarrow \quad |a + 2b + 2| = 5$

$\Rightarrow \quad a + 2b + 2 = 5$ or $a + 2b + 2 = -5$

$\Rightarrow \quad a + 2b = 3$ or $a + 2b = -7$

Thus, $a + 2b = 3$ ...(ii)

or $a + 2b = -7$ ...(iii)

On solving Eqs. (i) and (ii), we get $a = -9$ and $b = 6$.

On solving Eqs. (i) and (iii), we get $a = 1$ and $b = -4$.

Hence, the required points are $(-9, 6)$ and $(1, -4)$.

22. Equation of the line parallel to $3x - 4y + 8 = 0$ is given by

$$3x - 4y + k = 0$$

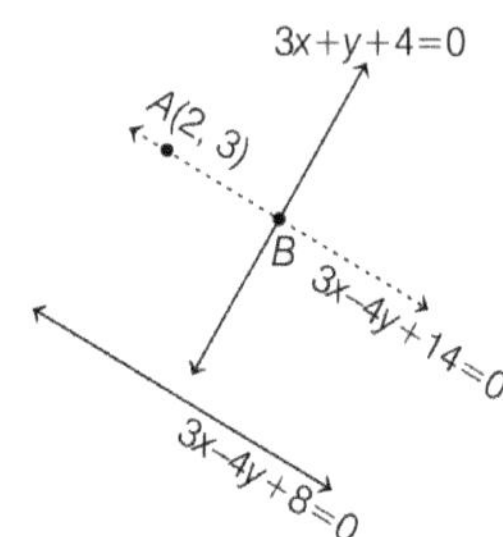

Now, required parallel line should passing through the point $(2, 3)$.

We have, $3(2) - 4(5) + k = 0$

$\Rightarrow \quad k = 20 - 6 = 14$

Thus, distance of the point $(2, 5)$ from the line $3x + y + 4 = 0$ will be measured along the line

$$3x - 4y + 14 = 0$$

Now, solving $3x + y + 4 = 0$ and $3x - 4y + 14 = 0$, we get

$$x = -2 \text{ and } y = 2$$

Thus, the coordinates of B are $(-2, 2)$.

Hence, required distance $=$ length of $AB = 5$ units.

23. Line $3x + 4y + 5 = 0$ divides the distance between the lines

$$3x + 4y + 5 = 0 \text{ and } 3x + 4y - 5 = 0$$

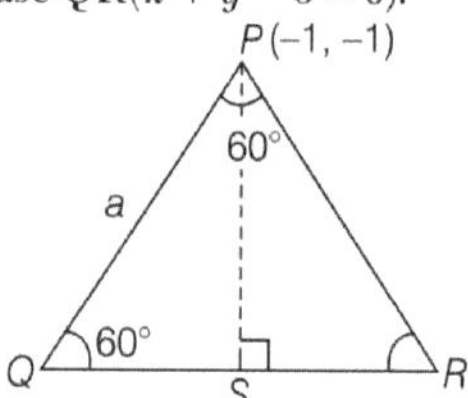

Now, distance between the lines $3x + 4y + 5 = 0$ and $3x + 4y + 2 = 0$ is

$$d_1 = \dfrac{|5 - 2|}{\sqrt{9 + 16}} = \dfrac{3}{5} \text{ unit}$$

and distance between the lines $3x + 4y + 2 = 0$ and $3x + 4y - 5 = 0$ is

$$d_2 = \dfrac{|-5 - 2|}{\sqrt{9 + 16}} = \dfrac{7}{5} \text{ unit}$$

$\therefore$ Required ratio $= \dfrac{\dfrac{3}{5}}{\dfrac{7}{5}} = 3 : 7$

24. Let ΔPQR be an equilateral triangle, having side length a units, with base $QR(x + y - 6 = 0)$.

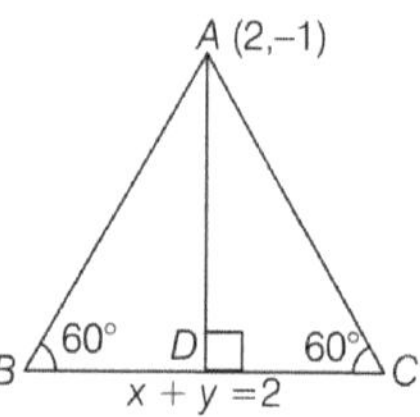

$\therefore$ Vertex $P = (-1, -1)$

Now, from P, draw $PS \perp QR$.

$\therefore \quad PS = \dfrac{|-1 - 1 - 6|}{\sqrt{1^2 + 1^2}} = \dfrac{8}{\sqrt{2}} = 4\sqrt{2}$ units

From right-angled ΔPQS,

$$\sin 60° = \dfrac{PS}{a} \Rightarrow \dfrac{\sqrt{3}}{2} = \dfrac{4\sqrt{2}}{a} \Rightarrow a = \dfrac{8\sqrt{2}}{\sqrt{3}} \text{ units}$$

$\therefore$ Area of $\Delta PQR = \dfrac{\sqrt{3}}{4}\left(\dfrac{8\sqrt{2}}{\sqrt{3}}\right)^2 = \dfrac{32}{\sqrt{3}} = \dfrac{32\sqrt{3}}{3}$ sq units

25. Given that, equilateral ΔABC having equation of base is $x + y = 2$.

In ΔABD, $\sin 60° = \dfrac{AD}{AB}$

$\Rightarrow \quad AD = AB \sin 60° = AB\dfrac{\sqrt{3}}{2}$

$\because \quad AD = AB\dfrac{\sqrt{3}}{2}$ ...(i)

Now, the length of perpendicular from $(2, -1)$ to the line $x + y = 2$ is given by

$$AD = \left| \frac{2 + (-1) - 2}{\sqrt{1^2 + 1^2}} \right| = \frac{1}{\sqrt{2}} \text{ unit}$$

From Eq. (i), $\quad \dfrac{1}{\sqrt{2}} = AB \dfrac{\sqrt{3}}{2}$

$$AB = \sqrt{\frac{2}{3}} \text{ unit}$$

26. Given, equation of lines

$$2x - 3y + 5 = 0 \qquad \qquad ...(i)$$

and $\qquad \qquad 3x + 4y = 0 \qquad \qquad ...(ii)$

From Eq. (ii), put the value of $x = \dfrac{-4y}{3}$ in Eq. (i), we get

$$2\left(\frac{-4y}{3}\right) - 3y + 5 = 0$$

$$\Rightarrow \qquad -8y - 9y + 15 = 0 \;\Rightarrow\; y = \frac{15}{17}$$

From Eq. (ii), $\quad 3x + 4 \cdot \dfrac{15}{17} = 0 \;\Rightarrow\; x = \dfrac{-60}{17 \cdot 3} = \dfrac{-20}{17}$

So, the point of intersection is $\left(\dfrac{-20}{17}, \dfrac{15}{17}\right)$.

$\therefore$ Required distance from the line $5x - 2y = 0$ is,

$$d = \frac{\left|-5 \times \dfrac{20}{17} - 2\left(\dfrac{15}{17}\right)\right|}{\sqrt{25 + 4}} = \frac{\left|\dfrac{-100}{17} - \dfrac{30}{17}\right|}{\sqrt{29}} = \frac{130}{17\sqrt{29}} \text{ units}$$

27. Given, equation of lines are

$$3x + 4y - 9 = 0 \qquad \qquad ...(i)$$

$$\text{Slope} = -\frac{3}{4}$$

and $\qquad \qquad 6x + 8y - 15 = 0 \qquad \qquad ...(ii)$

$$\text{Slope} = -\frac{6}{8} = \frac{-3}{4}$$

$\because$ The slope of line (i) is equal to slope of line (ii).

$\Rightarrow$ The given lines are parallel.

Putting $y = 0$ in Eq. (i), we get

$$x = 3$$

$\Rightarrow (3, 0)$ is a point on line (i).

$\therefore$ Distance between the lines (i) and (ii) is given by

$$= \frac{|6 \times 3 + 8 \times 0 - 15|}{\sqrt{(6)^2 + (8)^2}} = \frac{3}{10} \text{ unit}$$

28. Given, equation of lines are

$$12x - 5y - 3 = 0 \qquad \qquad ...(i)$$
$$12x - 5y + 7 = 0 \qquad \qquad ...(ii)$$
$$12x - 5y - 13 = 0 \qquad \qquad ...(iii)$$

The slope of each of these lines is equal to $\dfrac{12}{5}$.

$\rightarrow$ The given lines are parallel.

Putting $x = 0$ in Eq. (i), we get

$$y = -\frac{3}{5}$$

$\Rightarrow \left(0, \dfrac{-3}{5}\right)$ is a point on Eq. (i).

Now, let d_1 be the distance between Eqs. (i) and (ii)

$$\Rightarrow \quad d_1 = \frac{\left|12 \times 0 - 5 \times \left(\dfrac{-3}{5}\right) + 7\right|}{\sqrt{144 + 25}} = \frac{10}{13} \text{ unit}$$

Again, let d_2 be the distance between Eqs. (i) and (iii)

$$\Rightarrow \quad d_2 = \frac{\left|12 \times 0 - 5 \times \left(\dfrac{-3}{5}\right) - 13\right|}{\sqrt{144 + 25}} = \frac{10}{13} \text{ unit}$$

$\because \qquad d_1 = d_2$

$\Rightarrow$ line (i) is mid-parallel between the other two lines.

29. Let the slope of the other line be m.

It is given that the angle between the two lines is $60°$.

$$\therefore \qquad \tan 60° = \left|\frac{m - 2}{1 + 2m}\right| \qquad \left[\because \tan\theta = \left|\frac{m_2 - m_1}{1 + m_1 m_2}\right|\right]$$

$$\Rightarrow \qquad \sqrt{3} = \left|\frac{m - 2}{1 + 2m}\right|$$

$$\Rightarrow \qquad \frac{m - 2}{1 + 2m} = \pm\sqrt{3}$$

$$\Rightarrow \qquad \frac{m - 2}{1 + 2m} = \sqrt{3} \text{ or } \frac{m - 2}{1 + 2m} = -\sqrt{3}$$

$$\Rightarrow \qquad m - 2 = \sqrt{3} + 2\sqrt{3}\,m \text{ or } m - 2 = -\sqrt{3} - 2\sqrt{3}\,m$$

$$\Rightarrow \quad m(2\sqrt{3} - 1) = -(2 + \sqrt{3}) \text{ or } m(2\sqrt{3} + 1) = 2 - \sqrt{3}$$

$$\Rightarrow \qquad m = -\left(\frac{2 + \sqrt{3}}{2\sqrt{3} - 1}\right) \text{ or } m = \left(\frac{2 - \sqrt{3}}{2\sqrt{3} + 1}\right)$$

On substituting $x_1 = 2$, $y_1 = 3$ and the values of m in $y - y_1 = m(x - x_1)$, we obtain that the equation of the required line is

$$y - 3 = -\frac{2 + \sqrt{3}}{2\sqrt{3} - 1}(x - 2) \text{ or } y - 3 = \frac{2 - \sqrt{3}}{2\sqrt{3} + 1}(x - 2)$$

30. Given point A is $(3, -2)$ and are inclined at $60°$ to the line $\sqrt{3}x + y = 1$.

$$\Rightarrow \qquad y = -\sqrt{3}\,x + 1$$

$\therefore$ Slope, $m_1 = -\sqrt{3}$

Let slope of the required line be m_2.

$$\therefore \qquad \tan\theta = \left|\frac{-\sqrt{3} - m_2}{1 - \sqrt{3}\,m_2}\right| \qquad \left[\because \tan\theta = \left|\frac{m_1 - m_2}{1 + m_1 m_2}\right|\right]$$

$$\Rightarrow \qquad \tan 60° = \pm\left(\frac{-\sqrt{3} - m_2}{1 - \sqrt{3}\,m_2}\right) \qquad \qquad ...(i)$$

$$\Rightarrow \qquad \sqrt{3} = \left(\frac{-\sqrt{3} - m_2}{1 - \sqrt{3}\,m_2}\right) \qquad \text{[taking positive sign]}$$

$$\Rightarrow \quad \sqrt{3} - 3m_2 = -\sqrt{3} - m_2$$

$$\Rightarrow \qquad 2\sqrt{3} = 2m_2$$

$$\Rightarrow \qquad m_2 = \sqrt{3}$$

$\therefore$ Equation of line passing through $(3, -2)$ is

$$y + 2 = \sqrt{3}(x - 3)$$

$$\Rightarrow \qquad y - \sqrt{3}x + 2 + 3\sqrt{3} = 0$$

$\Rightarrow \qquad \sqrt{3}x - y - 2 - 3\sqrt{3} = 0 \qquad \ldots(i)$

$\qquad\qquad$ [taking negative sign from Eq. (i)]

$\Rightarrow \qquad \sqrt{3} - 3m_2 = \sqrt{3} + m_2$

$\Rightarrow \qquad m_2 = 0$

$\therefore$ The equation of line is

$$y + 2 = 0(x - 3)$$

$\Rightarrow \qquad y + 2 = 0 \qquad \ldots(ii)$

So, the required equation of lines are

$$\sqrt{3}\, x - y - 2 - 3\sqrt{3} = 0 \text{ and } y + 2 = 0.$$

31. Since, the given point $P(3, 2)$ and line is $x - 2y = 3$.

Slope of this line is $m_1 = \dfrac{1}{2}$

Let the slope of the required line is m.

Then, $\qquad \tan\theta = \left| \dfrac{m - \dfrac{1}{2}}{1 + \dfrac{1}{2}m} \right|$

$\Rightarrow \qquad 1 = \pm \left(\dfrac{m - \dfrac{1}{2}}{1 + \dfrac{m}{2}} \right) \qquad [\because \tan 45° = 1] \ldots (i)$

Taking positive sign,

$$1 + \frac{m}{2} = m - \frac{1}{2}$$

$\Rightarrow \qquad m - \dfrac{m}{2} = 1 + \dfrac{1}{2}$

$\Rightarrow \qquad \dfrac{m}{2} = \dfrac{3}{2}$

$\Rightarrow \qquad m = 3$

Taking negative sign,

$$1 = -\left(\frac{m - \dfrac{1}{2}}{1 + \dfrac{m}{2}} \right)$$

$\Rightarrow \qquad 1 + \dfrac{m}{2} = -m + \dfrac{1}{2}$

$\Rightarrow \qquad m + \dfrac{m}{2} = \dfrac{1}{2} - 1$

$\Rightarrow \qquad \dfrac{3m}{2} = \dfrac{-1}{2}$

$\Rightarrow \qquad m = \dfrac{-1}{3}$

$\therefore$ First equation of the line is

$$y - 2 = 3(x - 3)$$

$\Rightarrow \qquad 3x - y - 7 = 0$

and second equation of the line is

$$y - 2 = -\frac{1}{3}(x - 3)$$

$\Rightarrow \qquad 3y - 6 = -x + 3$

$\Rightarrow \qquad x + 3y - 9 = 0$

32. Let slope of line AC be m and slope of line BC is $\dfrac{-3}{4}$ and let

angle between line AC and BC be θ.

$\therefore \quad \tan\theta = \left| \dfrac{m + \dfrac{3}{4}}{1 - \dfrac{3m}{4}} \right| \Rightarrow \tan 45° = \pm \left[\dfrac{m + \dfrac{3}{4}}{1 - \dfrac{3m}{4}} \right]$

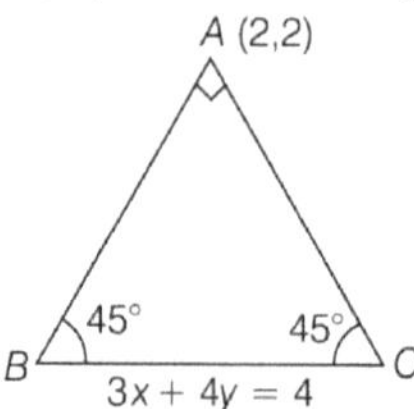

Taking positive sign, $\quad 1 = \dfrac{m + \dfrac{3}{4}}{1 - \dfrac{3m}{4}}$

$\Rightarrow \qquad m + \dfrac{3}{4} = 1 - \dfrac{3m}{4}$

$\Rightarrow \qquad m + \dfrac{3m}{4} = 1 - \dfrac{3}{4}$

$\Rightarrow \qquad \dfrac{7m}{4} = \dfrac{1}{4} \Rightarrow m = \dfrac{1}{7}$

Taking negative sign,

$$1 = -\left(\frac{m + \dfrac{3}{4}}{1 - \dfrac{3m}{4}} \right)$$

$\Rightarrow \qquad 1 - \dfrac{3m}{4} = -m - \dfrac{3}{4}$

$\Rightarrow \qquad m - \dfrac{3m}{4} = -1 - \dfrac{3}{4} \Rightarrow \dfrac{m}{4} = \dfrac{-7}{4} \Rightarrow m = -7$

$\therefore$ Equation of side AC having slope $\left(\dfrac{1}{7}\right)$ is

$$y - 2 = \frac{1}{7}(x - 2)$$

$\Rightarrow \qquad 7y - 14 = x - 2 \Rightarrow x - 7y + 12 = 0$

and equation of side AB having slope (-7) is

$$y - 2 = -7(x - 2)$$

$\Rightarrow \qquad y - 2 = -7x + 14 \Rightarrow 7x + y - 16 = 0$

33. Given, equation of the line is

$$y = 3x + 4 \qquad \ldots(i)$$

$\therefore$ Slope of this line, $m_1 = 3$

So, the slope of line OP is $-\dfrac{1}{3}$ $\qquad [\because \ OP \perp AB]$

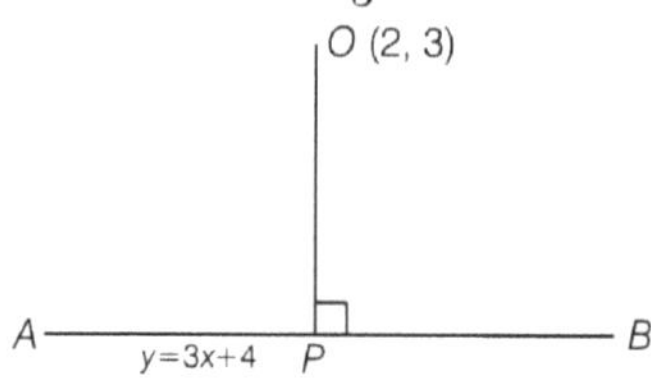

$\therefore$ Equation of line OP is

$$y - 3 = -\frac{1}{3}(x - 2)$$

$\Rightarrow \qquad 3y - 9 = -x + 2$

$\Rightarrow \qquad x + 3y - 11 = 0 \qquad \ldots(ii)$

Using the value of y from Eq. (i) in Eq. (ii), we get

$$x + 3(3x + 4) - 11 = 0$$
$$\Rightarrow \quad x + 9x + 12 - 11 = 0$$
$$\Rightarrow \quad 10x + 1 = 0$$
$$\Rightarrow \quad x = -\frac{1}{10}$$

Put $x = \dfrac{-1}{10}$ in Eq. (i), we get

$$y = \frac{-3}{10} + 4$$
$$= \frac{-3 + 40}{10} = \frac{37}{10}$$

So, the foot of perpendicular is $\left(-\dfrac{1}{10}, \dfrac{37}{10}\right)$.

34. Let $B(m, n)$ be the image of the point $A(3, 8)$ in the line.

$$x + 3y = 7 \qquad \ldots\text{(i)}$$

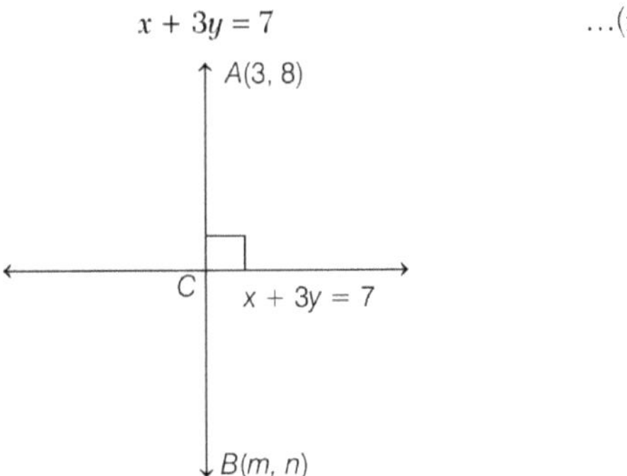

$\because$ The line (i) is assumed to be a plane mirror

$\therefore$ Line (i) is the perpendicular bisector of the segment AB and C is mid-point of the segment AB.

$\therefore$ Slope of $AC = \dfrac{-1}{\text{slope of line(i)}}$

Now, slope of line (i) is $\dfrac{-1}{3}$.

$\therefore$ Slope of $AC = 3$

$\therefore$ Equation of AC is given by $y - 8 = 3(x - 3)$

$$\Rightarrow \quad 3x - y - 1 = 0 \qquad \ldots\text{(ii)}$$

On solving Eqs. (i) and (ii), we get

$$x = 1, y = 2$$
$$\therefore \quad C \equiv (1, 2)$$

$\because C$ is the mid-point of the segment AB.

$$\therefore \quad \frac{m + 3}{2} = 1$$
$$\Rightarrow \quad m = -1$$

and

$$\frac{n + 8}{2} = 2$$
$$\Rightarrow \quad n = -4$$

Hence, the image of point $(3, 8)$ in the given line is $(-1, -4)$.

35. Draw $PS \perp QR$

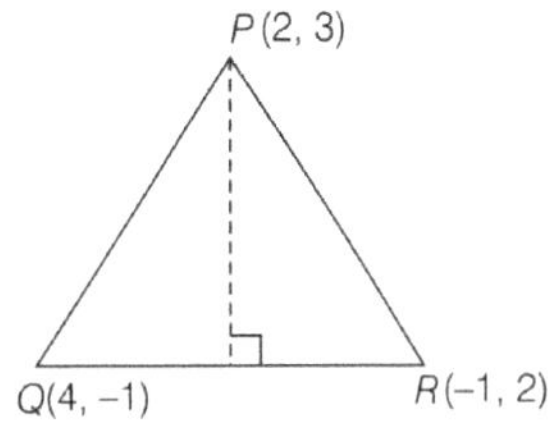

$\therefore$ Slope of $PS = \dfrac{-1}{\text{Slope of } QR}$

Now, slope of $QR = \dfrac{2 + 1}{-1 - 4} = \dfrac{3}{-5} = -\dfrac{3}{5}$

$\therefore$ Slope of $PS = \dfrac{-1}{\left(\dfrac{-3}{5}\right)} = \dfrac{5}{3}$

Now, equation of altitude PS is given by

$$y - 3 = \frac{5}{3}(x - 2)$$
$$\Rightarrow \quad 5x - 3y - 1 = 0$$

Now, equation of QR is

$$y + 1 = -\frac{3}{5}(x - 4)$$
$$\Rightarrow \quad 3x + 5y - 7 = 0$$

$\therefore$ Length of altitude, $PS = \dfrac{|3 \times 2 + 5 \times 3 - 7|}{\sqrt{3^2 + 5^2}} = \dfrac{14}{\sqrt{34}}$ units.

36. Let m be the slope of the required straight line.

$\therefore$ The equation of line passing through the point $(-5, 0)$, having slope x is given by

$$y - 0 = m(x + 5)$$
$$\Rightarrow \quad y = mx + 5m \text{ or } mx - y + 5m = 0 \qquad \ldots\text{(i)}$$

Given, the perpendicular distance of line (i) from origin $(0, 0)$ is 3 units.

$$\therefore \quad \frac{|m \times 0 - 0 + 5m|}{\sqrt{m^2 + (-1)^2}} = 3$$
$$\Rightarrow \quad |5m| = 3\sqrt{m^2 + 1}$$

On squaring both sides, we get

$$25m^2 = 9m^2 + 9$$
$$\Rightarrow \quad 16m^2 = 9 \Rightarrow m = \frac{3}{4} \qquad \left[\because m = \frac{-3}{4} < 0\right]$$

Now, put the value of m in Eq. (i), we get

$$\frac{3}{4}(x) - y + 5\left(\frac{3}{4}\right) = 0$$
$$\Rightarrow \quad 3x - 4y + 15 = 0$$

37. Given equation of lines

$$x - y + 1 = 0 \qquad \ldots\text{(i)}$$
$$\text{and} \quad 2x - 3y + 5 = 0 \qquad \ldots\text{(ii)}$$

From Eq. (i), $\quad x = y - 1$

Now, put the value of x in Eq. (ii), we get

$$2(y - 1) - 3y + 5 = 0$$
$$\Rightarrow \quad 2y - 2 - 3y + 5 = 0$$
$$\Rightarrow \quad 3 - y = 0$$
$$\Rightarrow \quad y = 3$$

Put $y = 3$ in Eq. (i), we get

$$x = 2$$

Since, the point of intersection is $(2, 3)$.

Let slope of the required line be m.

$\therefore$ Equation of line is

$$y - 3 = m\,(x - 2)$$
$$\Rightarrow \quad mx - y + 3 - 2m = 0 \qquad \ldots\text{(iii)}$$

Since, the distance from $(3, 2)$ to line (iii) is $\dfrac{7}{5}$ units.

$$\therefore \quad \frac{7}{5} = \left| \frac{3m - 2 + 3 - 2m}{\sqrt{1 + m^2}} \right|$$
$$\Rightarrow \quad \frac{49}{25} = \frac{(m + 1)^2}{1 + m^2}$$
$$\Rightarrow \quad 49 + 49m^2 = 25\,(m^2 + 2m + 1)$$
$$\Rightarrow \quad 49 + 49m^2 = 25\,m^2 + 50m + 25$$
$$\Rightarrow \quad 24m^2 - 50m + 24 = 0$$
$$\Rightarrow \quad 12m^2 - 25m + 12 = 0$$
$$\therefore \quad m = \frac{25 \pm \sqrt{625 - 4 \cdot 12 \cdot 12}}{24}$$
$$= \frac{25 \pm \sqrt{49}}{24} = \frac{25 \pm 7}{24} = \frac{32}{24} \text{ or } \frac{18}{24} = \frac{4}{3} \text{ or } \frac{3}{4}$$

$\therefore$ First equation of a line is

$$y - 3 = \frac{4}{3}(x - 2)$$
$$\Rightarrow \quad 3y - 9 = 4x - 8$$
$$\Rightarrow \quad 4x - 3y + 1 = 0$$

and second equation of line is

$$y - 3 = \frac{3}{4}(x - 2)$$
$$\Rightarrow \quad 4y - 12 = 3x - 6$$
$$\Rightarrow \quad 3x - 4y + 6 = 0$$

38. Converting each of the given equations to the form $y = mx + C$, we get

$$9x + 6y - 7 = 0$$
$$\Rightarrow \quad y = \frac{-3}{2}x + \frac{7}{6} \qquad \ldots\text{(i)}$$

and

$$3x + 2y + 6 = 0$$
$$\Rightarrow \quad y = \frac{-3}{2}x - 3 \qquad \ldots\text{(ii)}$$

Clearly, the slope of each one of the given lines is $\dfrac{-3}{2}$.

Let the given lines be $y = mx + C_1$ and $y = mx + C_2$.

Then, $\quad m = \dfrac{-3}{2}, C_1 = \dfrac{7}{6}$ and $C_2 = -3$.

Let L be the required line. Then, L is parallel to each one of lines (i) and (ii) and equidistant from each one of them.

$\therefore$ Slope of $L = \dfrac{-3}{2}$

Let the equation of L be $\quad y = \dfrac{-3}{2}x + C \qquad \ldots\text{(iii)}$

Then, distance between lines (i) and (iii) must be equal to the distance between lines (ii) and (iii).

$$\therefore \quad \frac{|C_1 - C|}{\sqrt{1 + m^2}} = \frac{|C_2 - C|}{\sqrt{1 + m^2}}$$
$$\Rightarrow \quad |C_1 - C| = |C_2 - C|$$
$$\Rightarrow \quad \left| \frac{7}{6} - C \right| = |-3 - C|$$
$$\Rightarrow \quad \left| \frac{7}{6} - C \right| = |3 + C|$$
$$\Rightarrow \quad \frac{7}{6} - C = \pm(3 + C)$$
$$\Rightarrow \quad 2C = \frac{-11}{6} \Rightarrow C = \frac{-11}{12}$$

$\therefore$ Equation of L is $y = \dfrac{-3}{2}x - \dfrac{11}{12}$, i.e. $18x + 12y + 11 = 0$

Hence, the line $18x + 12y + 11 = 0$ is midway between the parallel lines $9x + 6y - 7 = 0$ and $3x + 2y + 6 = 0$.

39. Let slope of the line be m.

$\because$ Equation of line passing through $(1, 0)$ is

$$y - 0 = m\,(x - 1)$$
$$\Rightarrow \quad y - mx + m = 0 \qquad \ldots\text{(i)}$$

Since, the distance from origin is $\dfrac{\sqrt{3}}{2}$ unit.

Then, $\quad \dfrac{\sqrt{3}}{2} = \dfrac{0 - 0 + m}{\sqrt{1 + m^2}}$

$$\Rightarrow \quad \frac{\sqrt{3}}{2} = \frac{m}{\sqrt{1 + m^2}}$$
$$\Rightarrow \quad \frac{3}{4} = \frac{m^2}{1 + m^2}$$
$$\Rightarrow \quad 3 + 3m^2 = 4m^2$$
$$\Rightarrow \quad m^2 = 3$$
$$\Rightarrow \quad m = \pm\sqrt{3}$$

So, the first equation of line is

$$y = \sqrt{3}(x - 1) \Rightarrow \sqrt{3}x - y - \sqrt{3} = 0$$

and the second equation of line is

$$y = -\sqrt{3}(x - 1) \Rightarrow \sqrt{3}x + y - \sqrt{3} = 0$$

40. The given equation of lines are

$$4x + 3y + 10 = 0 \qquad \ldots\text{(i)}$$
$$\Rightarrow \quad 5x - 12y + 26 = 0 \qquad \ldots\text{(ii)}$$
$$\Rightarrow \quad 7x + 24y - 50 = 0 \qquad \ldots\text{(iii)}$$

Let the point (h, k) which is equidistant from these lines.

Distance from line (i) $= \dfrac{|4h + 3k + 10|}{\sqrt{16 + 9}}$

Distance from line (ii) $= \dfrac{|5h - 12k + 26|}{\sqrt{25 + 144}}$

Distance from the line (iii) $= \dfrac{|7h + 24k - 50|}{\sqrt{(7)^2 + (24)^2}}$

So, the point (h, k) is equidistant from lines (i), (ii) and (iii).

$\therefore \quad \dfrac{4h + 3k + 10}{\sqrt{16 + 9}} = \dfrac{5h - 12k + 26}{\sqrt{25 + 144}} = \dfrac{7h + 24k - 50}{\sqrt{49 + 576}}$

$\Rightarrow \quad \dfrac{|4h + 3k + 10|}{5} = \dfrac{|5h - 12k + 26|}{13} = \dfrac{|7h + 24k - 50|}{25}$

Clearly, if $h = 0, k = 0$, then $\dfrac{10}{5} = \dfrac{26}{13} = \dfrac{50}{25} = 2$

Hence, the required point is $(0, 0)$.

41. (i) Slope of line $L = \dfrac{-1}{\text{Slope of } 5x - y = 1} = \dfrac{-1}{5}$

(ii) Let line L intersect X-axis at $A(a, 0)$ and Y-axis at $B(0, b)$.

Then, area of $\triangle OAB = \dfrac{1}{2} ab$

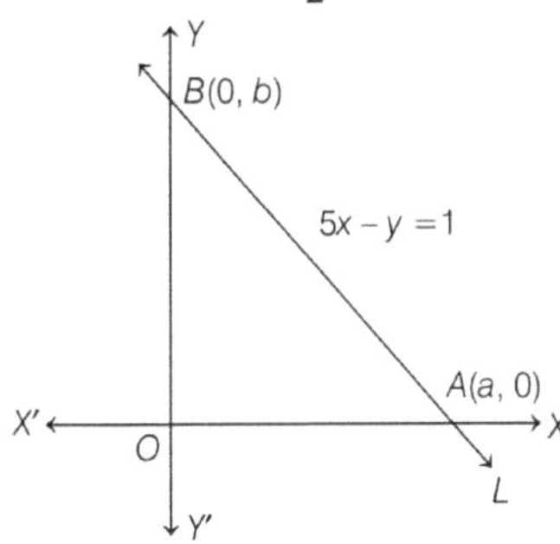

$\Rightarrow \quad \dfrac{1}{2} ab = 5$

$\Rightarrow \quad ab = 10 \text{ sq units} \qquad \ldots(\text{i})$

Also, slope of line $L = \dfrac{-b}{a}$

$\Rightarrow \quad \dfrac{-b}{a} = -\dfrac{1}{5}$

$\Rightarrow \quad b = \dfrac{a}{5} \qquad \ldots(\text{ii})$

On solving Eqs. (i) and (ii) we get

$a = 5\sqrt{2}$ and $b = \sqrt{2}$ or $a = -5\sqrt{2}$ and $b = -\sqrt{2}$

So, $A(5\sqrt{2}, 0)$ and $B(0, \sqrt{2})$

(iii) M is the mid-point of AB.

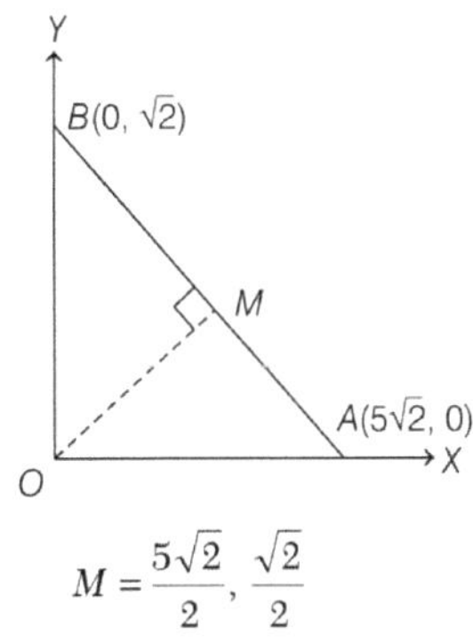

$M = \dfrac{5\sqrt{2}}{2}, \dfrac{\sqrt{2}}{2}$

$OM = \sqrt{\left(\dfrac{5\sqrt{2}}{2}\right)^2 + \left(\dfrac{\sqrt{2}}{2}\right)^2}$

$\qquad = \dfrac{1}{2} \sqrt{50 + 2} = \sqrt{13} \text{ units}$

(iv) Given, parallel lines are

$\qquad 10x - 2y - 7 = 0 \qquad \ldots(\text{i})$

and $\qquad 5x - y = 1 \qquad \ldots(\text{ii})$

On comparing Eqs. (i) and (ii) with $AX + BY + C_1 = 0$ and $AX + BY + C_2 = 0$, we get

$\qquad A = 5, B = -1, C_1 = -1 \text{ and } C_2 = -\dfrac{7}{2}$

$d = \left| \dfrac{C_1 - C_2}{\sqrt{A^2 + B^2}} \right| = \left| \dfrac{-1 + \dfrac{7}{2}}{\sqrt{(5)^2 + (1)^2}} \right|$

$\qquad = \dfrac{1}{2} \left| \dfrac{-2 + 7}{\sqrt{26}} \right| = \dfrac{5}{2\sqrt{26}} \text{ unit}$

(v) Now, the equation of line L is

$\qquad \dfrac{x}{5\sqrt{2}} + \dfrac{y}{\sqrt{2}} = 1 \text{ or } \dfrac{x}{-5\sqrt{2}} + \dfrac{y}{-\sqrt{2}} = 1$

$\Rightarrow \quad x + 5y - 5\sqrt{2} = 0 \text{ or } x + 5y + 5\sqrt{2} = 0$

42. (i) $3x - 2y = 1$

$\qquad y = \dfrac{3}{2} x - \dfrac{1}{2}$

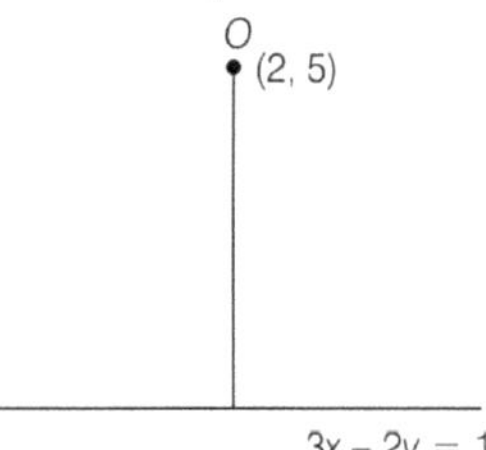

Slope of line, $m = $ Slope of line

$\qquad 3x - 2y = 1$

Slope of line, $m = \dfrac{3}{2}$

$\Rightarrow \quad (y - 2) = \dfrac{3}{2}(x - 1)$

$\Rightarrow \quad 2y - 4 = 3x - 3$

$\Rightarrow \quad 3x - 2y + 1 = 0$

(ii) $d = \left| \dfrac{3 \times 2 - 2 \times 5 - 1}{\sqrt{(3)^2 + (2)^2}} \right| = \left| \dfrac{6 - 10 - 1}{\sqrt{13}} \right| = \dfrac{5}{\sqrt{13}} \text{ units}$

(iii) We know that,

$d = \left| \dfrac{C_1 - C_2}{\sqrt{A^2 + B^2}} \right| = \dfrac{|1 - (-1)|}{\sqrt{(3)^2 + (2)^2}} = \dfrac{2}{\sqrt{13}} \text{ unit}$

Chapter Test

Multiple Choice Questions

1. If the angle between two lines is $\frac{\pi}{4}$ and slope of one of the line is $\frac{1}{2}$, then the slope of the other line is

(a) 3 or $\frac{-1}{3}$

(b) $\frac{1}{3}$ or -3

(c) 3 or $\frac{1}{5}$

(d) $\frac{1}{3}$ or $\frac{1}{6}$

2. A line parallel to the Y-axis at a distance of 6 units to its right, then the equation of line is

(a) $x = -6$

(b) $x = +6$

(c) $x - 12 = 0$

(d) None of these

3. The equation of the line which have slope $\frac{1}{2}$ cut-off an intercept 4 on X-axis.

(a) $x - 2y + 4 = 0$

(b) $x - 2y - 4 = 0$

(c) $x + 2y - 4 = 0$

(d) None of these

4. The equation of the line which cut-off equal and positive intercepts from the axes and passes through the point (α, β) is given by

(a) $x + y = \alpha - \beta$

(b) $x + y = \alpha + \beta$

(c) $x + y = \alpha$

(d) None of these

5. The distance of the point $(2, 3)$ from the line $2x - 3y + 9 = 0$ measured along a line $x - y + 1 = 0$ is

(a) 4 units

(b) $4\sqrt{2}$ units

(c) $4\sqrt{3}$ units

(d) 6 units

6. If the line $\frac{x}{a} + \frac{y}{b} = 1$ passes through the points $(1, -2)$ and $(3, -4)$, the value of (a, b) is

(a) $(-1, 1)$

(b) $(1, 1)$

(c) $(1, -1)$

(d) $(-1, -1)$

7. The length of perpendicular from the point (a, b) to the line $\frac{x}{a} + \frac{y}{b} = 1$ is

(a) $\left(\dfrac{ab}{\sqrt{a^2 + b^2}}\right)$ units

(b) $\left(\dfrac{a^2 b}{\sqrt{a + b}}\right)$ units

(c) $\left(\dfrac{a^2 b^2}{\sqrt{a^2 + b^2}}\right)$ units

(d) $\left(\dfrac{ab}{\sqrt{a + b}}\right)$ units

8. Two sides of a square lie on the lines $x + y = 1$ and $x + y + z = 0$, then area of the square is (in sq units)

(a) 1

(b) $\frac{3}{2}$

(c) $\frac{9}{2}$

(d) $\frac{9}{4}$

Case Based MCQs

9. If P_1, P_2 are points on either of the two lines $y - \sqrt{3}|x| = 2$ at a distance of 5 units from their point of intersection.

Based on the above information answer the following questions.

(i) Angle between the line passing through points P_1 and P_2.

(a) 30°

(b) 60°

(c) 90°

(d) 120°

(ii) The length is $P_1 P_2$ is

(a) 5 units

(b) 10 units

(c) 12 units

(d) None of these

(iii) The length of PM is

(a) 10 units

(b) $\dfrac{5\sqrt{3}}{2}$ units

(c) 12 units

(d) None of these

(iv) The length of OM is

(a) $\left(\dfrac{4 - 5\sqrt{3}}{2}\right)$ units

(b) $\left(\dfrac{5\sqrt{3}}{2}\right)$ units

(c) $\left(\dfrac{4 + 5\sqrt{3}}{2}\right)$ units

(d) None of these

(v) The coordinate M are

(a) $\left(\dfrac{4 + 5\sqrt{3}}{2}, 0\right)$

(b) $\left(\dfrac{5\sqrt{3}}{2}, 0\right)$

(c) $\left(\dfrac{4 - 5\sqrt{3}}{2}, 0\right)$

(d) None of these

Short Answer Type Questions

10. Find the equation of line joining the points $(2, 3)$ and $(3, 5)$.

11. Find the equation of the straight line passing through the origin and bisecting the portion of the line $ax + by + c = 0$ intercepted between the coordinate axes.

12. Find the coordinates of a point on the line $x + y + 3 = 0$, whose distance from the line $x + 2y + 2 = 0$ is $\sqrt{5}$ units.

Long Answer Type Questions

13. Find the points on X-axis whose perpendicular distance from the line $4x + 3y = 12$ is 4 units.

14. Find the area of a square, if two sides of a square are $x + 2y + 3 = 0$ and $x + 2y = 5$.

Answers

1. (a) *2.* (b) *3.* (b) *4.* (b) *5.* (c) *6.* (d) *7.* (a) *8.* (c)

9. (i) (b) (ii) (a) (iii) (b) (iv) (c) (v) (a)

10. $2x - y - 1 = 0$ *11.* $ax - by = 0$ *12.* $(-9, 6)$ and $(1, -4)$

13. $(8, 0)$ and $(-2, 0)$ *14.* $\dfrac{64}{5}$ sq units

For Detailed Solutions

Scan the code

CHAPTER 08

Conic Sections

In this Chapter...

- Circle
- Parabola

Circle

A circle is defined as the locus of a point in a plane, which moves in a plane such that its distance from a fixed point in that plane is always constant.

The fixed point is called the centre of the circle. The constant distance from the centre to a point on the circle, is called **radius**.

Standard Form

Let $C(0, 0)$ be the centre of the circle, $P(x, y)$ be any point on the circumference of the circle and r be the radius of the circle.

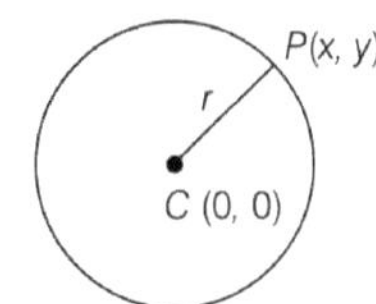

$$\therefore \qquad CP = r$$

$$\Rightarrow \qquad \sqrt{(x-0)^2 + (y-0)^2} = r$$

or $\qquad x^2 + y^2 = r^2$

This is known as standard form.

Central Form

Let $C(h, k)$ be the **centre** of the circle, $P(x, y)$ be any point on the circumference of the circle and r be the **radius** of the circle.

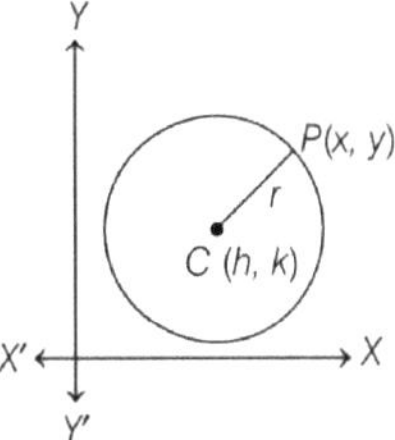

Then, equation of circle in standard form is

$$(x-h)^2 + (y-k)^2 = r^2$$

This equation is also known as central form of the equation of a circle.

Diameter Form

Let (x_1, y_1) and (x_2, y_2) be the end points of the diameter of a circle.

Then, equation of circle drawn on the diameter is

$$(x-x_1)(x-x_2) + (y-y_1)(y-y_2) = 0$$

General Form

We know that, the equation of the circle having centre (h, k) and radius r is

$$(x-h)^2 + (y-k)^2 = r^2$$

$$\Rightarrow \quad x^2 + y^2 - 2hx - 2ky + h^2 + k^2 - r^2 = 0$$

which is of the form

$$x^2 + y^2 + 2gx + 2fy + c = 0$$

where, $g = -h$, $f = -k$ and $c = h^2 + k^2 - r^2$

The above equation of a circle is called the general equation of a circle with centre $(-g, -f)$

and   radius, $r = \sqrt{h^2 + k^2 - c}$

or $r = \sqrt{g^2 + f^2 - c}$

Parabola

A parabola is the locus of a point, which moves in a plane, so that its distance from a fixed point called focus is always equal to its distance from a fixed straight line called directrix in the same plane.

Standard Equations of Parabola

(i) Right handed parabola ($y^2 = 4ax, a > 0$)

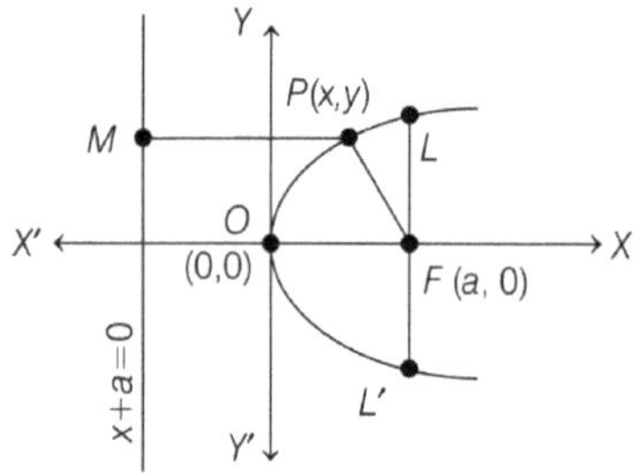

(i) Vertex is $O\,(0, 0)$.

(ii) Axis is the line $y = 0$.

(iii) Focus is $F\,(a, 0)$.

(iv) Directrix is the line $x + a = 0$.

(v) Length of latusrectum $LL' = 4a$

(vi) Coordinates of latusrectum $= (a, \pm 2a)$

(vii) Equation of latusrectum is $x = a$ or $x - a = 0$.

(viii) It is symmetrical about X-axis.

(ii) Left handed parabola ($y^2 = -4ax, a > 0$)

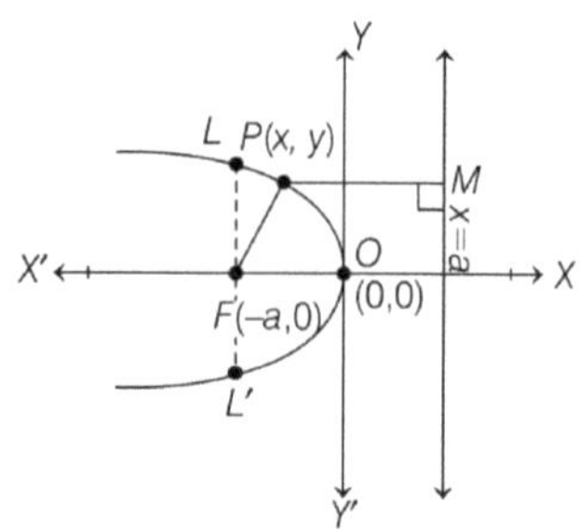

(i) Vertex is $O\,(0, 0)$.

(ii) Axis is the line $y = 0$.

(iii) Focus is $F(-a, 0)$.

(iv) Directrix is the line $x - a = 0$.

(v) Length of the latusrectum is $4a$.

(vi) Coordinates of latusrectum $= (-a, \pm 2a)$

(vii) Equation of latusrectum is $x = -a$ or $x + a = 0$.

(viii) It is symmetrical about X-axis.

(iii) Upward parabola ($x^2 = 4ay, a > 0$)

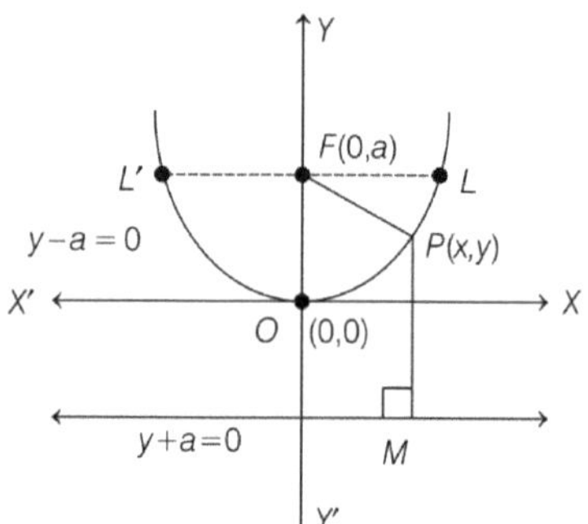

(i) Focus is $F(0, a)$.

(ii) Vertex is $O(0, 0)$.

(iii) Directrix is the line $y + a = 0$.

(iv) Axis is the line $x = 0$.

(v) Length of latusrectum is $4a$.

(vi) Coordinates of latusrectum $= (\pm 2a, a)$

(vii) Equation of latusrectum is $y = a$ or $y - a = 0$.

(viii) It is symmetrical about Y-axis.

Downward Parabola $(x^2 = -4ay, a > 0)$

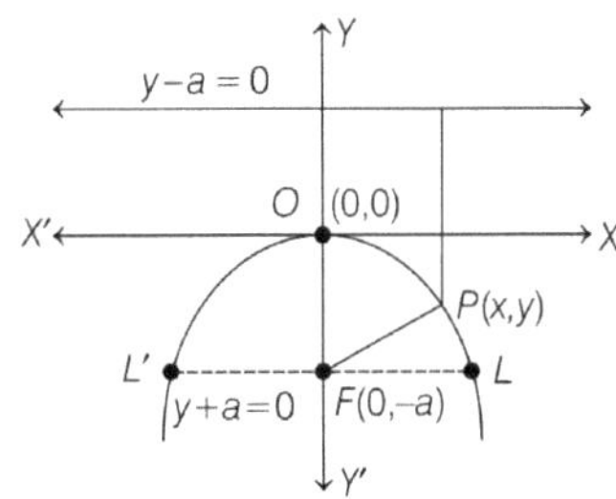

(i) Focus is $F(0, -a)$.

(ii) Vertex is $O(0, 0)$.

(iii) Directrix is the line $y - a = 0$.

(iv) Axis is the line $x = 0$.

(v) Length of latusrectum is $4a$.

(vi) Coordinates of latusrectum $= (\pm 2a, (-a))$

(vii) Equation of latusrectum is $y = -a$ or $y + a = 0$.

(viii) It is symmetrical about Y-axis.

Table for Different Types of Parabola

Parabola	Vertex	Focus	Latusrectum	Coordinates of latusrectum	Axis	Directrix	Symmetry
$y^2 = 4ax$	$(0, 0)$	$(a, 0)$	$4a$	$(a, \pm 2a)$	$y = 0$	$x = -a$	X-axis
$y^2 = -4ax$	$(0, 0)$	$(-a, 0)$	$4a$	$(-a, \pm 2a)$	$y = 0$	$x = a$	X-axis
$x^2 = 4ay$	$(0, 0)$	$(0, a)$	$4a$	$(\pm 2a, a)$	$x = 0$	$y = -a$	Y-axis
$x^2 = -4ay$	$(0, 0)$	$(0, -a)$	$4a$	$(\pm 2a, -a)$	$x = 0$	$y = a$	Y-axis

Solved Examples

Example 1. Find the area of the circle centred at $(1, 2)$ and passing through the point $(4, 6)$.

Sol. Given that, centre of the circle is $(1, 2)$.

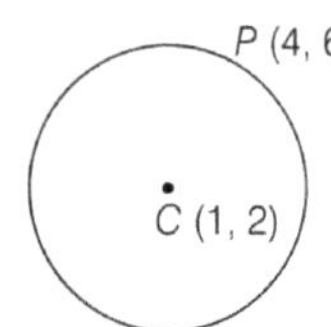

$$\because \qquad CP = \sqrt{(x_2 - x_1)^2 + (y_2 - y_1)^2}$$
$$CP = \sqrt{9 + 16} = 5 \text{ units} = \text{Radius of the circle}$$

$\therefore$ Required area $= \pi r^2 = 25\pi$ sq units

Example 2. Find the equation of the circle concentric with the circle $x^2 + y^2 + 4x + 6y + 11 = 0$ and passing through the point $P(5, 4)$.

Sol. Centre of the required circle is $C(-2, -3)$.

Circle passes through the point $P(5, 4)$.

$$\therefore \text{ Radius} = |CP| = \sqrt{(5 + 2)^2 + (4 + 3)^2}$$
$$= \sqrt{(7)^2 + (7)^2} = 7\sqrt{2} \text{ units}$$

$\therefore$ Required equation of circle is
$$[x - (-2)]^2 + [y - (-3)]^2 = (7\sqrt{2})^2$$
$$\Rightarrow \qquad (x + 2)^2 + (y + 3)^2 = 98,$$

which is the required equation of circle.

Example 3. Find the equation of the circle which touches the lines $x = 0$, $y = 0$ and $3x + 4y = 4$.

Sol. Let centre of circle be (h, k).

Since, it touches both axes, therefore $h = k = a$.
Hence, equation can be $(x - a)^2 + (y - a)^2 = a^2$

But it also touches the line $3x + 4y = 4$.

Therefore, $\dfrac{3a + 4a - 4}{5} = a \Rightarrow a = 2$

Hence, the required equation of circle is
$$x^2 + y^2 - 4x - 4y + 4 = 0$$

Example 4. The centre and radius of the circle $2x^2 + 2y^2 - x = 0$ is (h, k) and r, respectively, Then, find $h - r$.

Sol. Given, equation of circle is
$$2x^2 + 2y^2 - x = 0$$

On dividing by 2, we get
$$x^2 + y^2 - \frac{x}{2} = 0$$

On comparing with $x^2 + y^2 + 2gx + 2fy + c = 0$, we get
$$2g = -\frac{1}{2}, \ 2f = 0 \text{ and } c = 0$$
$$\Rightarrow \qquad g = -\frac{1}{4}, \ f = 0 \text{ and } c = 0$$

$\therefore$ Centre $= (-g, -f) = \left(\dfrac{1}{4}, 0\right)$

and radius $= \sqrt{g^2 + f^2 - c} = \sqrt{\left(\dfrac{1}{4}\right)^2 + 0 - 0}$
$$= \sqrt{\frac{1}{16}} = \frac{1}{4} \text{ unit}$$
$$\Rightarrow \qquad h = \frac{1}{4} \text{ and } r = \frac{1}{4}$$

Now, $h - r = \dfrac{1}{4} - \dfrac{1}{4} = 0$

Example 5. Find the area of the triangle formed by the lines joining the vertex of the parabola $x^2 = 12y$ to the ends of its latusrectum.

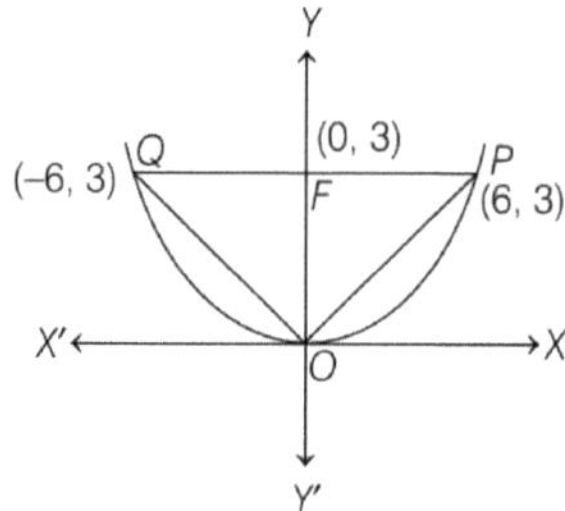

Sol. From the figure, OPQ represents the triangle whose area is to be determined.

Then, area of the triangle $= \dfrac{1}{2} PQ \times OF$
$$= \frac{1}{2}(12 \times 3) = 18 \text{ sq units}$$

Example 6. If the equation of the parabola is $x^2 = -8y$, then find its focus, directrix and length of latusrectum.

Sol. The given equation is of the form $x^2 = -4ay$, where a is positive.

Therefore, the focus is on Y-axis in the negative direction and parabola opens downwards.

On comparing the given equation with standard form, we get
$$a = 2$$

Therefore, the coordinates of the focus are $(0, -2)$ and the the equation of directrix is $y = 2$ and the length of the latusrectum is $4a$, i.e. 8 units.

Chapter Practice

Objective Questions

• Multiple Choice Questions

1. If the equation of circle is $x^2 + y^2 - 2x + 4y - 8 = 0$, then its centre and radius respectively, are
(a) $(-2, 4)$ and $\sqrt{13}$ units
(b) $(-1, 2)$ and $\sqrt{13}$ units
(c) $(1, -2)$ and $\sqrt{13}$ units
(d) $(2, -4)$ and $\sqrt{13}$ units

2. The equation of the circle having centre $(3, -4)$ and touching the line $5x + 12y - 19 = 0$ is
(a) $x^2 + y^2 + 6x + 8y + 9 = 0$
(b) $x^2 + y^2 - 6x - 8y + 9 = 0$
(c) $x^2 + y^2 - 6x + 8y + 9 = 0$
(d) None of the above

3. The centre of the circle $x^2 + y^2 + 8x + 10y - 8 = 0$ is (h, k), then $h - k$ is equal to
(a) 1
(b) 2
(c) -4
(d) -9

4. The equation of the circle having centre at $(3, -4)$ and touching the line $5x + 12y - 12 = 0$ is
(a) $(x - 3)^2 + (y + 4)^2 = \left(\dfrac{45}{13}\right)^2$
(b) $(x - 3)^2 + (y - 4)^2 = \left(\dfrac{45}{13}\right)^2$
(c) $(x + 3)^2 + (y + 4)^2 = \left(\dfrac{45}{13}\right)^2$
(d) None of the above

5. The equation of a circle concentric with the circle $x^2 + y^2 - 6x + 12y + 15 = 0$ and has double its area is
(a) $x^2 + y^2 - 6x + 12y - 15 = 0$
(b) $x^2 + y^2 + 6x - 12y - 15 = 0$
(c) $x^2 + y^2 - 6x - 12y - 15 = 0$
(d) None of the above

6. The equation of a circle with centre $(2, 2)$ which passes through the point $(4, 5)$, is
(a) $x^2 + y^2 + 4x + 4y - 77 = 0$
(b) $x^2 + y^2 - 4x - 4y - 5 = 0$
(c) $x^2 + y^2 + 2x + 2y - 59 = 0$
(d) $x^2 + y^2 - 2x - 2y - 23 = 0$

7. The equation of the circle whose centre is $(1, -3)$ and which touches the line $2x - y - 4 = 0$, is
(a) $5x^2 + 5y^2 - 10x + 30y + 49 = 0$
(b) $5x^2 + 5y^2 + 10x - 30y + 49 = 0$
(c) $5x^2 + 5y^2 - 10x + 30y - 49 = 0$
(d) None of the above

8. The lines $2x - 3y - 5 = 0$ and $3x - 4y = 7$ are the diameters of a circle of area $154 (= 49\pi)$ sq uints, then the equation of circle is
(a) $x^2 + y^2 + 2x - 2y - 62 = 0$
(b) $x^2 + y^2 + 2x - 2y - 47 = 0$
(c) $x^2 + y^2 - 2x + 2y - 47 = 0$
(d) $x^2 + y^2 - 2x + 2y - 62 = 0$

9. The shortest distance from the point $(2, -7)$ to the circle $x^2 + y^2 - 14x - 10y - 151 = 0$ is
(a) 2 units
(b) 5 units
(c) 1 unit
(d) 3 units

10. Equation of the circle with centre on the Y-axis and passing through the origin and the point $(2, 3)$ is
(a) $x^2 + y^2 + 13y = 0$
(b) $3x^2 + 3y^2 + 13x + 3 = 0$
(c) $6x^2 + 6y^2 - 13y = 0$
(d) $x^2 + y^2 + 13x + 3 = 0$

11. If the equation of circle is $x^2 + y^2 - 4x - 8y - 45 = 0$, then its centre and radius respectively, are
(a) $(2, 4)$ and $\sqrt{65}$ units
(b) $(4, 2)$ and $\sqrt{65}$ units
(c) $(2, 4)$ and $\sqrt{48}$ units
(d) None of these

12. The equation of circle is $(x - 5)(x - 1) + (y - 7)(y - 4) = 0$, then its radius is
(a) 3 units
(b) 4 units
(c) $\dfrac{5}{2}$ units
(d) $\dfrac{7}{2}$ units

13. The equation of the circle whose end points of a diameter are $A(1, 5)$ and $B(-1, 3)$, is given by

(a) $x^2 + y^2 - 8y + 14 = 0$ (b) $x^2 + y^2 + 8y - 14 = 0$

(c) $x^2 - y^2 - 8y + 14 = 0$ (d) None of these

14. The equation of the circle, if the end points of whose diameter are the centres of the circles $x^2 + y^2 + 6x - 14y - 1 = 0$ and $x^2 + y^2 - 4x + 10y - 2 = 0$ is

(a) $x^2 + y^2 + x - 2y + 41 = 0$ (b) $x^2 + y^2 + x - 2y - 41 = 0$

(c) $x^2 + y^2 - x - 2y - 41 = 0$ (d) None of these

15. If the equation of parabola is $y^2 = 12x$, then

(a) focus $= (3, 0)$

(b) length of latusrectum $= 12$ units

(c) directrix is $x = -3$ and axis of symmetry is X-axis

(d) All of the above

16. If the parabola $y^2 = 4ax$ passes through the point $(3, 2)$, then the length of its latusrectum is

(a) $\dfrac{4}{3}$ units   (b) $\dfrac{3}{4}$ unit

(c) 1 unit   (d) 4 units

17. If parabola is passing through $(2, 3)$, vertex $(0, 0)$ and axis is along X-axis, then the equation of parabola is

(a) $y^2 = \dfrac{9}{2}x$ (b) $x^2 = \dfrac{9}{2}y$

(c) $y^2 = \dfrac{3}{2}x$ (d) $x^2 = \dfrac{3}{2}y$

18. The focal distance of a point on the parabola $y^2 = 12x$ is 4 units. Then, the abscissa of this point is

(a) 1   (b) 2

(c) 3   (d) -1

19. If parabola is passing through $(5, 2)$, vertex $(0, 0)$ and symmetric with respect to Y-axis, then the equation of parabola is

(a) $y^2 = \dfrac{25}{2}x$ (b) $x^2 = \dfrac{25}{2}y$

(c) $y^2 = \dfrac{5}{2}x$ (d) $x^2 = \dfrac{5}{2}y$

20. If the focus of a parabola is $(0, -3)$ and its directrix is $y = 3$, then its equation is

(a) $x^2 = -12y$ (b) $x^2 = 12y$

(c) $y^2 = -12x$ (d) $y^2 = 12x$

21. The equation of the parabola which is symmetric about the Y-axis and passes through the point $(2, -3)$ is given by

(a) $3x^2 = -4y$ (b) $3x^2 = 4y$

(c) $4x^2 = 3y$ (d) $4x^2 = -3y$

• Case Based MCQs

22. The equation of the circle having centre (h, k) and radius r is

$$(x - h)^2 + (y - k)^2 = r^2$$

$$\Rightarrow x^2 + y^2 - 2hx - 2ky + h^2 + k^2 - r^2 = 0$$

which is of the form

$$x^2 + y^2 + 2gx + 2fy + c = 0$$

where, $g = -h$, $f = -k$

and $c = h^2 + k^2 - r^2$

The above equation of a circle is called the general equation of a circle with centre $(-g, -f)$

and radius, $r = \sqrt{h^2 + k^2 - c}$ or $r = \sqrt{g^2 + f^2 - c}$.

On the basis of above information, answer the following questions

(i) If the equation of circle is $x^2 + y^2 + 8x - 16y - 1 = 0$, then its radius is

(a) 9 units   (b) 1 unit

(c) 4 units   (d) 8 units

(ii) If the equation of circle is $x^2 + y^2 + 2x + 2y + 5 = 0$, then its centre is

(a) $(1, 1)$ (b) $(-1, -1)$

(c) $(-1, 1)$ (d) $(1, -1)$

(iii) If the equation of circle is $x^2 + y^2 + 2x - 2y - 5 = 0$, then its radius is

(a) $\sqrt{7}$ units   (b) $\sqrt{8}$ units

(c) 3 units   (d) 1 unit

(iv) If centre of the circle $2x^2 + 2y^2 + 8x - 4y + 16 = 0$ is (h, k), then $k - h$ is equal to

(a) 3   (b) 2   (c) 1   (d) -1

(v) If radius of circle $x^2 + y^2 + 4x - 10y + 4 = 0$ is r_1 and radius of circle $x^2 + y^2 + 4x + 2y + 1 = 0$ is r_2, then $r_1 - r_2$ is equal to

(a) 2   (b) 1   (c) 3   (d) 0

23. The cable of a uniformly loaded suspension bridge hangs in the form of a parabola. The roadway which is horizontal and 100 m long is supported by vertical wires attached to the cable, the longest wire being 30 m and the shortest being 6 m.

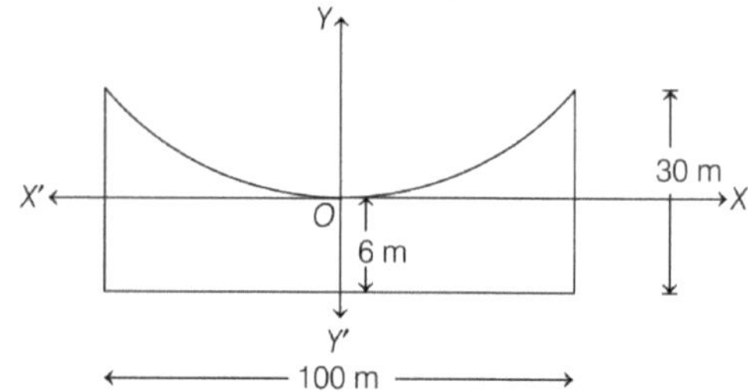

On the basis of above information, answer the following questions.

(i) The equation of parabola is

(a) $6x^2 = 625y$ (b) $6x^2 = -625y$

(c) $6x^2 = 2500y$ (d) $x^2 = 625y$

(ii) The coordinates of focus of the parabola are

(a) $\left(0, \dfrac{24}{625}\right)$ (b) $\left(0, \dfrac{625}{24}\right)$

(c) $\left(\dfrac{625}{24}, 0\right)$ (d) $\left(\dfrac{2500}{24}, 0\right)$

(iii) The equation of directrix of the parabola is

(a) $24y - 625 = 0$ (b) $24y = -500$

(c) $24y + 625 = 0$ (d) $y = -625$

(iv) Length of latusrectum of parabola is

(a) $\dfrac{625}{24}$ m   (b) $\dfrac{625}{6}$ m

(c) $\dfrac{2500}{3}$ m   (d) $\dfrac{6}{625}$ m

(v) The length of a supporting wire attached to the roadway 18 m from the middle is

(a) 7.5 m   (b) 9.11 m

(c) 1.5 m   (d) 3.67 m

PART 2
Subjective Questions

• Short Answer Type Questions

1. Find the equation of the circle which touches X-axis and whose centre is $(1, 2)$.

2. Find the equation of a circle of radius 5 units which is touching another circle $x^2 + y^2 - 2x - 4y - 20 = 0$ at $(5, 5)$.

3. Show that the point (x, y) given by $x = \dfrac{2at}{1 + t^2}$ and

$y = \dfrac{a(1 - t^2)}{1 + t^2}$ lies on a circle.

4. If the lines $3x + 4y + 4 = 0$ and $6x - 8y - 7 = 0$ are tangents to a circle, then find the radius of the circle.

5. Find the equation of the circle passing through the point $(2, 4)$ and having its centre at the intersection of the lines $x - y = 4$ and $2x + 3y + 7 = 0$.

6. Find the equation of the circle which touches both the axes and whose radius is 5 units.

7. Find the equation of the circle whose centre is (a, b) and passes through the origin.

8. Find the equation of the circle of radius 5 units, whose centre lies on X-axis and passes through the point $(2, 3)$.

9. Circle of radius 5 units touches the coordinate axes in the first quadrant. If the circle makes one complete roll on X-axis along the positive direction of X-axis. Find its equation in the new position.

10. A circle of radius 2 units lies in the first quadrant and touches both the axes of coordinates. Find the equation of the circle with centre at $(6, 5)$ and touching the above circle externally.

11. Find the equation of the circle with centre is $\left(\dfrac{1}{2}, \dfrac{1}{4}\right)$ and radius is $\dfrac{1}{12}$ unit.

12. Find the equation of the circle with centre is $(a\cos\theta, a\sin\theta)$ and radius is a units.

13. Find the equation of the circle passing through two points on Y-axis at distances 3 units from the origin and having radius 5 units.

14. Find the equation of the circle, whose centre is $(2, -3)$ and passing through the intersection of the lines $3x - 2y = 1$ and $4x + y = 27$.

15. Find the equation of a circle which passes through $(3, 6)$ and touches the axes.

16. If one end of a diameter of the circle $x^2 + y^2 - 4x - 6y + 11 = 0$ is $(3, 4)$, then find the coordinates of the other end of the diameter.

17. Find the equation of the circle having $(1, -2)$ as its centre and passing through $3x + y = 14$ and $2x + 5y = 18$.

18. Find the equation of a circle whose centre is $(3, -1)$ and which cuts off a chord of length 6 units on the line $2x - 5y + 18 = 0$.

19. Show that the centres of three circles $x^2 + y^2 - 4x - 6y - 14 = 0$, $x^2 + y^2 + 2x + 4y - 5 = 0$ and $x^2 + y^2 - 10x - 16y + 7 = 0$ are collinear.

20. Find the coordinates of the middle point of the chord which the circle $x^2 + y^2 + 4x - 2y - 3 = 0$ cuts off on the line $x - y + 2 = 0$.

21. Find the length of the line segment joining the vertex of the parabola $y^2 = 4ax$ and a point on the parabola, where the line segment makes an angle θ to the X-axis.

22. For the parabola $y^2 = 36x$, find the coordinates of vertex, coordinates of focus, equation of directrix, axis of the parabola and length of the latusrectum.

23. Equilateral triangle is inscribed in the parabola $y^2 = 16x$, whose one vertex is at the vertex of the parabola. Find the length of the side of the triangle.

24. A double ordinate of the parabola $y^2 = 4ax$ is of length $8a$ units. Prove that the lines from the vertex to its ends are at right angles.

25. Find the equation of the parabola with vertex at the origin, the axis along the X-axis and passing through the point $(2, 3)$.

26. Find the area of the triangle formed by the lines joining the vertex of the parabola $x^2 = -36y$ to the ends of the latusrectum.

27. Find the equation of the parabola with vertex at origin, symmetric with respect to Y-axis and passing through $(2, -3)$.

28. Find the coordinates of focus, the equation of directrix and the length of latusrectum of the parabola $5x^2 = -12y$.

29. For the parabola $4x^2 = -9y$. Find the coordinates of vertex, coordinates of focus, equation of directrix, axis of the parabola and length of the latusrectum.

30. Find the equation of the parabola with focus $(6, 0)$ and directrix $x = -6$. Also, find the length of latusrectum.

• Long Answer Type Questions

31. Find the equation of a circle which touches both the axes and the line $3x - 4y + 8 = 0$ and lies in the third quadrant.

32. If the circle passes through the point $(2,3)$, then find the equation of the circle whose radius is 5 units and centre lies on X-axis.

33. Find the equation of a circle passing through the point $(7, 3)$ having radius 3 units and whose centre lies on the line $y = x - 1$.

34. Find the equation of the circle which passes through the points $(2, 3)$ and $(4, 5)$ and the centre lies on the straight line $y - 4x + 3 = 0$.

35. Show that the points $(5, 5)$, $(6, 4)$, $(-2, 4)$ and $(7, 1)$ are concyclic, i.e. all lie on the same circle. Find the equation, centre and radius of this circle.

36. Find the equation of the circle circumscribing the triangle whose sides are the lines $y = x + 2$, $3y = 4x$ and $2y = 3x$.

37. Find the summation of radius of the circles $x^2 + y^2 = 1$, $x^2 + y^2 - 2x - 6y = 6$ and $x^2 + y^2 - 4x - 12y = 9$.

38. Find the equation of a circle passing through the points $(2, -6)$, $(6, 4)$ and $(-3, 1)$.

39. Find the equation of the circle passing through the vertices of a triangle whose sides are represented by the equations $x + y = 2$, $3x - 4y = 6$ and $x - y = 0$.

40. In each of the following questions, find the coordinates of the focus, axis of the parabola, the equation of the directrix and the length of the latusrectum.

(i) $y^2 = -8x$ (ii) $y^2 = 10x$ (iii) $x^2 = -9y$

41. In each of the following questions, find the coordinates of the focus, axis of the parabola, the equation of the directrix and the length of the latus rectum.

(i) $5y^2 = -16x$ (ii) $x^2 = 10y$ (iii) $3x^2 = 8y$

42. An arch is in the form of a parabola with its axis vertical. The arch is 10 m high and 5 m wide at the base. How wide it is 2 m from the vertex of the parabola?

• Case Based Questions

43. A parabola is the locus of a point, which moves in a plane such that its distance from a fixed point is always equal to its distance from a fixed straight line in the same plane.

If parabola opens towards right side, then it is called right handed parabola. The equation of right handed parabola is of the form $y^2 = 4ax, a > 0$.

Some important terms related to this parabola are

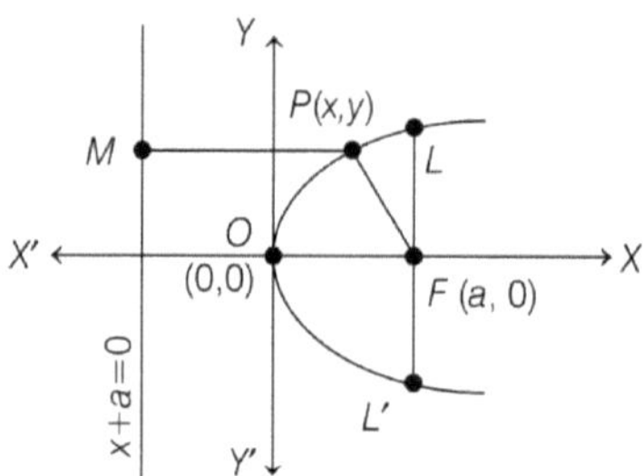

• Vertex is $O\,(0, 0)$.

• Axis is the line $y = 0$.

- Focus is $F(a, 0)$.
- Directrix is the line $x + a = 0$.
- Length of latusrectum $LL' = 4a$.
- Coordinates of latusrectum $= (a, \pm 2a)$
- Equation of latusrectum is $x = a$ or $x - a = 0$.
- It is symmetrical about X-axis.

On the basis of above information, answer the following questions.

(i) For the parabola $y^2 = 11x$, find its vertex, axis, focus, directrix, length of latusrectum, coordinates of latusrectum and equation of latus rectum.

(ii) For the parabola $3y^2 = x$, find its vertex, axis, focus, directrix, length of latus rectum, coordinates of latusrectum and equation of latusrectum.

(iii) If a parabolic reflector is 20 cm in diameter and 5 cm deep. Find the focus.

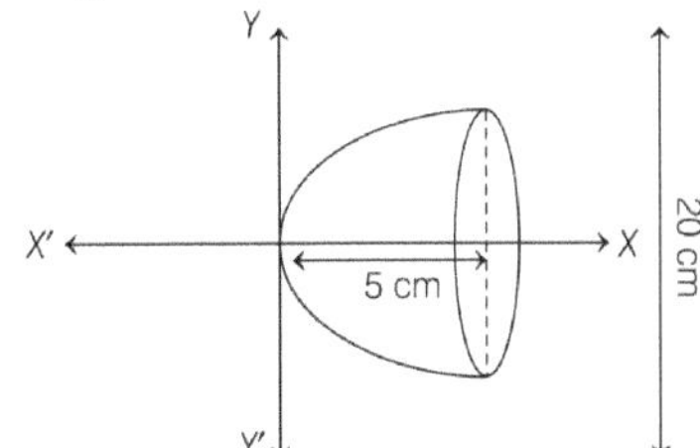

SOLUTIONS

Objective Questions

1. (c) We write the given equation in the standard form as
$$(x^2 - 2x) + (y^2 + 4y) = 8$$
Now, completing the squares, we get
$$(x^2 - 2x + 1) + (y^2 + 4y + 4) = 8 + 1 + 4$$
$$[\because \text{ adding 1 and 4 on both sides}]$$
$$(x - 1)^2 + (y + 2)^2 = 13$$

Comparing it with the standard form of the equation of the circle, we see that the centre of the circle is $(1, -2)$ and radius is $\sqrt{13}$ units.

2. (c) Centre of circle $= (3, -4)$

$\therefore$ Radius of circle = Perpendicular distance of line
$5x + 12y - 19 = 0$ from $(3, -4)$.
$$= \left| \frac{5(3) + 12(-4) - 19}{\sqrt{25 + 144}} \right|$$
$$= \left| \frac{-52}{13} \right| = 4 \text{ units}$$

$\therefore$ Required equation of circle is
$$(x - 3)^2 + (y + 4)^2 = (4)^2$$
$$\Rightarrow x^2 + 9 - 6x + y^2 + 16 + 8y = 16$$
$$\Rightarrow \qquad x^2 + y^2 - 6x + 8y + 9 = 0$$

3. (a) The given equation is
$$(x^2 + 8x) + (y^2 + 10y) = 8$$
Now, completing the squares within the parenthesis, we get
$$(x^2 + 8x + 16) + (y^2 + 10y + 25) = 8 + 16 + 25$$
i.e. $$(x + 4)^2 + (y + 5)^2 = 49$$
i.e. $$\{x - (-4)\}^2 + \{y - (-5)\}^2 = (7)^2$$
Comparing it with the standard form of the equation
$(x - h)^2 + (y - k)^2 = (r)^2$.
We see that, the centre of the circle is $(-4, -5)$
$$\Rightarrow \qquad h = -4 \text{ and } k = -5$$
Now, $$h - k = -4 - (-5)$$
$$= -4 + 5 = 1$$

4. (a) The perpendicular distance from centre $(3, -4)$ to the line $5x + 12y - 12 = 0$ is
$$d = \left| \frac{15 - 48 - 12}{\sqrt{25 + 144}} \right|$$
$$= \frac{45}{13} \text{ units}$$

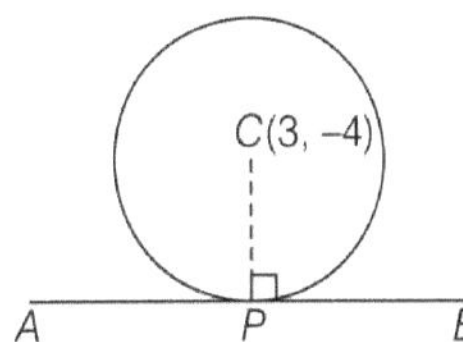

So, the required equations of the circle is
$$(x - 3)^2 + (y + 4)^2 = \left(\frac{45}{13} \right)^2$$

5. (a) Given, equation of the circle is
$$x^2 + y^2 - 6x + 12y + 15 = 0$$
Centre of this circle $= (3, -6)$
Radius of this circle $= \sqrt{9 + 36 - 15}$
$$= \sqrt{30} \text{ units}$$
The required circle is concentric to the given circle.
$\therefore$ Its centre is also coincide.

So, its centre is $(3, -6)$.
Let r be the radius of the required circle.
Then, according to the question,
$$\pi r^2 = 2 \times \pi (\sqrt{30})^2$$
$$\Rightarrow \qquad r^2 = 60$$
Hence, the required equation of the circle is
$$(x - 3)^2 + (y + 6)^2 = 60$$
or $$x^2 + y^2 - 6x + 12y - 15 = 0$$

6. (b) Here, centre $(h, k) = (2, 2)$ and point on the circle
$P(x, y) = (4, 5)$

$$\therefore \quad r = \sqrt{(2 - 4)^2 + (2 - 5)^2} = \sqrt{4 + 9} = \sqrt{13} \text{ units}$$

$$[\because r = \sqrt{(x - h)^2 + (y - k)^2}]$$

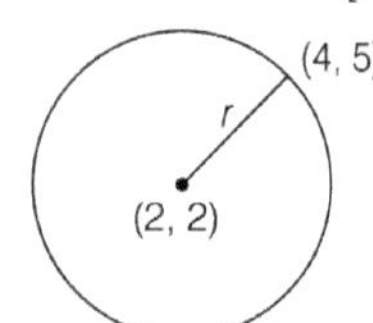

$\therefore$ Required equation of circle is
$$(x - h)^2 + (y - k)^2 = r^2$$
$$\therefore \quad (x - 2)^2 + (y - 2)^2 = (\sqrt{13})^2$$
$$[\text{given}, (h, k) = (2, 2) \text{ and } r = \sqrt{13}]$$
$$\Rightarrow \quad x^2 + 4 - 4x + y^2 + 4 - 4y = 13$$
$$\Rightarrow \quad x^2 + y^2 - 4x - 4y - 5 = 0$$

7. (a) Since, the circle with centre $(1, -3)$ touches the line
$2x - y - 4 = 0$.

Therefore, radius of circle is $\left| \dfrac{2 + 3 - 4}{\sqrt{5}} \right| = \dfrac{1}{\sqrt{5}}$ unit

Therefore, equation is $(x - 1)^2 + (y + 3)^2 = \dfrac{1}{5}$

or $\quad x^2 + y^2 - 2x + 6y + 1 + 9 = \dfrac{1}{5}$

or $\quad 5x^2 + 5y^2 - 10x + 30y + 49 = 0$

8. (c) The centre of the required circle lies at the intersection
of $2x - 3y - 5 = 0$ and $3x - 4y - 7 = 0$.
Thus, the coordinates of the centre are $(1, -1)$.
Let r be the radius of the circle.
Then, by hypothesis, we have
$$\pi r^2 = 154$$
$$\Rightarrow \quad \frac{22}{7} r^2 = 154$$
$$\Rightarrow \quad r = 7$$
Hence, the required equation of the circle is
$$(x - 1)^2 + (y + 1)^2 = (7)^2$$
$$\Rightarrow \quad x^2 + y^2 - 2x + 2y - 47 = 0$$

9. (a) Given circle is $x^2 + y^2 - 14x - 10y - 151 = 0$.

$\therefore \quad$ Centre $= (7, 5)$
and radius $= \sqrt{49 + 25 + 151}$
$$= \sqrt{225} = 15 \text{ units}$$
So, the distance between the point $(2, -7)$ and centre of the
circle is given by
$$d_1 = \sqrt{(2 - 7)^2 + (-7 - 5)^2}$$
$$= \sqrt{25 + 144}$$
$$= \sqrt{169} = 13 \text{ units}$$
$\therefore$ Shortest distance, $d = |13 - 15|$
$$= 2 \text{ units}$$

10. (c) Let general equation of the circle is
$x^2 + y^2 + 2gx + 2fy + c = 0$.

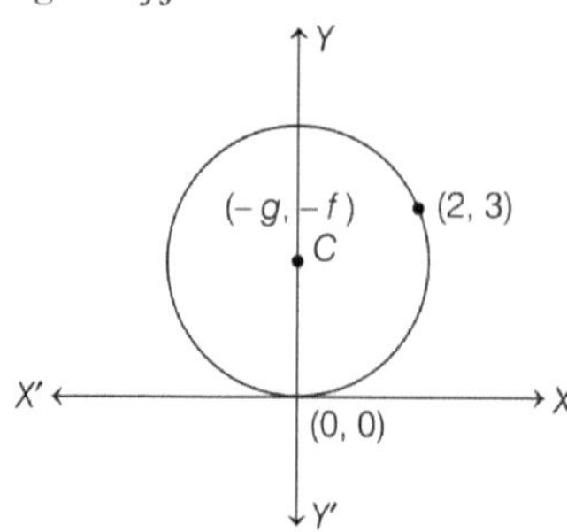

Since, the point $(0, 0)$ and $(2, 3)$ lie on it $c = 0$.
$$\therefore \quad 4 + 9 + 4g + 6f = 0$$
$$\Rightarrow \quad 2g + 3f = -13/2$$
Since, the centre lie on Y-axis, then $g = 0$.
$$\therefore \quad 3f = -13/2$$
$$\Rightarrow \quad f = -13/6$$
So, the equation of circle is
$$x^2 + y^2 - \frac{13y}{6} = 0$$
$$\Rightarrow \quad 6x^2 + 6y^2 - 13y = 0$$

11. (a) Given, equation of circle is
$$x^2 + y^2 - 4x - 8y - 45 = 0$$
On comparing it with $x^2 + y^2 + 2gx + 2fy + c = 0$, we get
$$2g = -4, 2f = -8 \text{ and } c = -45$$
$$\Rightarrow \quad g = -2, f = -4 \text{ and } c = -45$$
$\because$ Centre and radius of circle $x^2 + y^2 + 2gx + 2fy + c = 0$
are respectively
$$C(-g, -f) \quad \text{and} \quad r = \sqrt{g^2 + f^2 - c}$$
$\therefore$ Centre $= (-g, -f) = (2, 4)$
and radius $= \sqrt{g^2 + f^2 - c} = \sqrt{(2)^2 + (4)^2 - (-45)}$
$$= \sqrt{4 + 16 + 45} = \sqrt{65} \text{ units}$$

12. (c) Extremities of diameter are $(5, 7)$ and $(1, 4)$ and radius
is half of the distance between them.
$\therefore \quad$ Radius $= \dfrac{1}{2}\sqrt{(4)^2 + (3)^2} = \dfrac{1}{2}\sqrt{16 + 9} = \dfrac{5}{2}$ units

13. (a) Given, end points of a diameter are $A(1, 5)$ and $B(-1, 3)$.

We know that, the equation of circle, the end points of one
of whose diameter are (x_1, y_1) and (x_2, y_2) is given by
$$(x - x_1)(x - x_2) + (y - y_1)(y - y_2) = 0$$
Hence, the required equation of circle is
$$(x - 1)(x + 1) + (y - 5)(y - 3) = 0$$
$$\Rightarrow \quad x^2 - 1 + y^2 - 8y + 15 = 0$$
$$\Rightarrow \quad x^2 + y^2 - 8y + 14 = 0$$

14. (b) Given circles are
$$x^2 + y^2 + 6x - 14y - 1 = 0$$
and $\quad x^2 + y^2 - 4x + 10y - 2 = 0$

On comparing the above equation with
$x^2 + y^2 + 2gx + 2fy + c = 0$ one-by-one, we get the centres
of given circles $(-3, 7)$ and $(2, -5)$, respectively.

Since, the points $(-3, 7)$ and $(2, -5)$ are end points of the
diameter of the required circle.

Hence, the required equation of circle is
$$(x + 3)(x - 2) + (y - 7)(y + 5) = 0$$
$$\Rightarrow \quad x^2 + y^2 + x - 2y - 41 = 0$$

15. (d) Given, equation of parabola is $y^2 = 12x$,

which is of the form $y^2 = 4ax$

i.e. focus lies on the positive direction of X-axis.

Here, $\quad 4a = 12$
$$\Rightarrow \quad a = 3$$
$$\text{Focus} = (a, 0) = (3, 0)$$
$$\text{Axis} = X\text{-axis}$$

Directrix, $x = -a \Rightarrow x = -3$

Length of latusrectum $= 4a = 4 \times 3 = 12$ units

16. (a) Parabola $y^2 = 4ax$ passes through the point $(3, 2)$.
$$\therefore \quad (2)^2 = 4a(3)$$
$$\Rightarrow \quad a = \frac{1}{3}$$

Then, length of latusrectum $= 4a$
$$= \frac{4}{3} \text{ units}$$

17. (a) Given, vertex $= (0, 0)$

Point $= (2, 3)$ and axis $= X$-axis

Since, point $(2, 3)$ lies in first quadrant and axis is X-axis.
Hence, equation of parabola will be of the form $y^2 = 4ax$,
which passes through $(2, 3)$ i.e.

Put $\quad x = 2$ and $y = 3$ in $y^2 = 4ax$
$$\therefore \quad (3)^2 = 4a \times (2)$$
$$\Rightarrow \quad a = \frac{9}{8}$$

Hence, required equation of parabola is
$$y^2 = 4\left(\frac{9}{8}\right)x$$
$$\Rightarrow \quad y^2 = \frac{9}{2}x$$

18. (a) Given parabola is $y^2 = 12x$.

Here, $\quad 4a = 12$
$$\Rightarrow \quad a = 3$$
$$\therefore \quad \text{Focus}: F = (3, 0)$$

Let $P(x, y)$ be any point on the parabola, then $PF = 4$
$$\Rightarrow \quad (x - 3)^2 + (y - 0)^2 = (4)^2$$
$$\Rightarrow \quad x^2 + 9 - 6x + 12x = 16 \qquad [\because y^2 = 12x]$$
$$\Rightarrow \quad x^2 + 6x - 7 = 0$$
$$\Rightarrow \quad x = 1 \qquad [\because x \neq -7]$$

19. (b) Given, vertex $= (0, 0)$

Point $= (5, 2)$

Since, point $(5, 2)$ lies in first quadrant and axis is Y-axis.
Therefore, parabola is symmetric with respect to Y-axis.
Hence, equation of parabola will be of the form $x^2 = 4ay$,
which passes through $(5, 2)$ i.e.

Put $x = 5$ and $y = 2$ in $x^2 = 4ay$
$$\therefore \quad (5)^2 = 4a \times 2$$
$$\Rightarrow \quad a = \frac{25}{8}$$

Hence, required equation of parabola is
$$x^2 = 4 \times \frac{25}{8} y \Rightarrow x^2 = \frac{25}{2}y$$

20. (a) Given that, focus of parabola at $F(0, -3)$ and equation of
directrix is $y = 3$.

Let any point on the parabola is $P(x, y)$.

Then, $\qquad PF = |y - 3|$
$$\Rightarrow \quad \sqrt{(x - 0)^2 + (y + 3)^2} = |y - 3|$$
$$\Rightarrow \quad x^2 + y^2 + 6y + 9 = y^2 - 6y + 9$$
$$\Rightarrow \quad x^2 + 12y = 0 \Rightarrow x^2 = -12y$$

21. (a) Parabola is symmetrical about Y-axis and passes through
$(2, -3)$.

So, equation of parabola is of the form $x^2 = -4ay$.

On putting $x = 2, y = -3$, we get
$$4 = -4a(-3) \Rightarrow a = \frac{1}{3}$$

$\therefore$ Required equation of parabola is
$$x^2 = -4\left(\frac{1}{3}\right)y \Rightarrow 3x^2 = -4y$$

22. (i) (a) Given, circle is $x^2 + y^2 + 8x - 16y - 1 = 0$

On comparing with $x^2 + y^2 + 2gx + 2fy + c = 0$,
we get
$$g = 4, f = -8 \text{ and } c = -1$$
$\therefore$ Radius $= \sqrt{16 + 64 + 1}$
$$= \sqrt{81} = 9 \text{ units} \qquad [\because r = \sqrt{g^2 + f^2 - c}]$$

(ii) (b) Given, circle is $x^2 + y^2 + 2x + 2y + 5 = 0$

On comparing with $x^2 + y^2 + 2gx + 2fy + c = 0$,
we get
$$g = 1 \text{ and } f = 1$$
$\therefore$ Centre $\equiv (-1, -1)$

(iii) (a) Given, circle is $x^2 + y^2 + 2x - 2y - 5 = 0$

On comparing with $x^2 + y^2 + 2gx + 2fy + c = 0$,
we get
$$g = 1, f = -1 \text{ and } c = -5$$
$\therefore$ Radius $= \sqrt{1 + 1 + 5}$
$$= \sqrt{7} \text{ units} \qquad [\because r = \sqrt{g^2 + f^2 - c}]$$

(iv) (a) Given, circle is $2x^2 + 2y^2 + 8x - 4y + 16 = 0$

or $\qquad x^2 + y^2 + 4x - 2y + 8 = 0$

On comparing with $x^2 + y^2 + 2gx + 2fy + c = 0$, we get

$$g = 2 \text{ and } f = -1$$

$\therefore$ Centre $\equiv (-2, 1)$

$\Rightarrow \qquad h = -2 \text{ and } k = 1$

$\therefore \quad k - h = 1 - (-2) = 3$

(v) (c) Given, circles are $x^2 + y^2 + 4x - 10y + 4 = 0$ ...(i)

and $\qquad x^2 + y^2 + 4x + 2y + 1 = 0$ ...(ii)

General equation of circle is

$$x^2 + y^2 + 2gx + 2fy + c = 0 \quad ...(iii)$$

On comparing Eq. (i) with Eq. (iii), we get

$$g = 2 \text{ and } f = -5 \text{ and } c = 4$$

$\therefore \qquad r_1 = \sqrt{4 + 25 - 4} = 5$ units

On comparing Eq. (ii) with Eq. (iii), we get

$$g = 2, f = 1 \text{ and } c = 1$$

$\therefore \qquad r_2 = \sqrt{4 + 1 - 1} = 2$ units

$\therefore \qquad r_1 - r_2 = 5 - 2 = 3$

23.

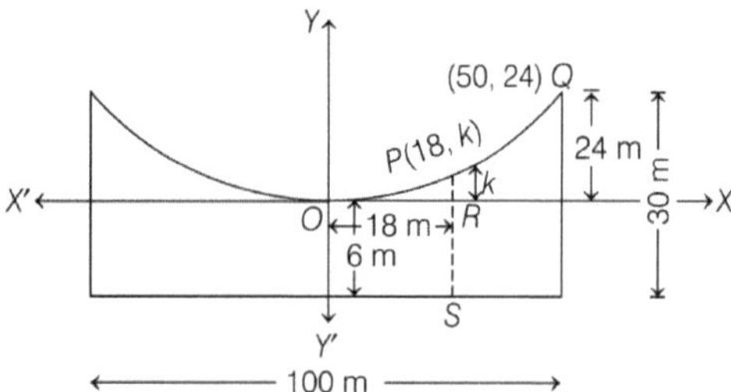

(i) (a) Take the vertex O of the parabola as origin and the axis of the parabola as Y-axis.

$\therefore$ The given parabola is of the form

$$x^2 = 4ay, a > 0 \qquad ...(i)$$

Clearly, the coordinates of $Q(50, 24)$ will satisfy Eq. (i).

$\therefore \qquad (50)^2 = 4a \times 24$

$\Rightarrow \qquad 2500 = 96a \Rightarrow a = \dfrac{2500}{96}$

Hence, from Eq. (i), $x^2 = 4 \times \dfrac{2500}{96} y$

$\Rightarrow \qquad x^2 = \dfrac{2500}{24} y$

$\Rightarrow \qquad x^2 = \dfrac{625}{6} y \Rightarrow 6x^2 = 625y$

(ii) (b) For parabola $x^2 = \dfrac{625}{6} y$

$$4a = \dfrac{625}{6}$$

$\Rightarrow \qquad a = \dfrac{625}{24} \qquad$ [from Eq. (i)]

So, focus of the parabola is $\left(0, \dfrac{625}{24}\right)$.

(iii) (c) We know that, the equation of the directrix of the parabola $x^2 = 4ay$ is $y = -a$.

So, the equation of directrix is

$$y = -\dfrac{625}{24}$$

$\Rightarrow \qquad 24y = -625 \Rightarrow 24y + 625 = 0$

(iv) (b) Length of latusrectum of the parabola

$$= 4a = 4\left(\dfrac{625}{24}\right) = \dfrac{625}{6} \text{ m}$$

(v) (b) Let $PR = k$ m

Then, point $P(18, k)$ will satisfy the equation of parabola.

$\therefore$ From Eq. (i), $(18)^2 = \dfrac{2500}{24} \times k$

$\Rightarrow \qquad 324 = \dfrac{2500}{24} k$

$\Rightarrow \qquad k = \dfrac{324 \times 24}{2500} = \dfrac{324 \times 6}{625} = \dfrac{1944}{625}$

$\Rightarrow \qquad k = 3.11$

$\therefore$ Required length $= 6 + k = 6 + 3.11 + 9.11$ m (approx.)

Subjective Questions

1. Given that, centre of the circle is $(1, 2)$.

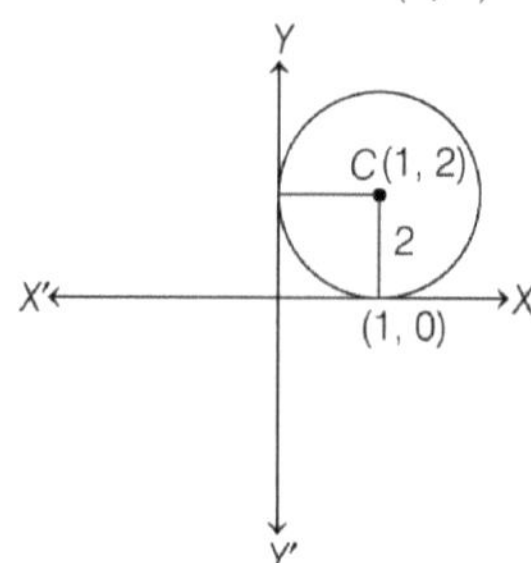

$\because$ Radius $= 2$ units

So, the equation of circle is

$$(x - 1)^2 + (y - 2)^2 = 2^2$$

$\Rightarrow \qquad x^2 - 2x + 1 + y^2 - 4y + 4 = 4$

$\Rightarrow \qquad x^2 - 2x + y^2 - 4y + 1 = 0$

$\Rightarrow \qquad x^2 + y^2 - 2x - 4y + 1 = 0$

2. Let the coordinates of centre of the required circle are (h, k), then the centre of another circle is $(1, 2)$.

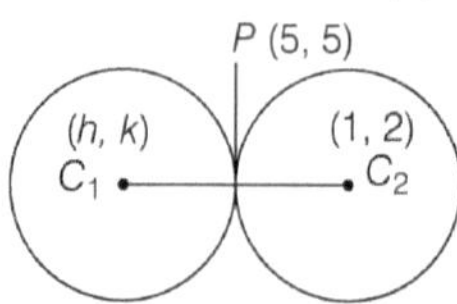

Radius $= \sqrt{1 + 4 + 20} = 5$ units $\qquad [\because r = \sqrt{g^2 + f^2 - c}]$

So, it is clear that P is the mid-point of $C_1 C_2$.

$\therefore \qquad 5 = \dfrac{1 + h}{2} \Rightarrow h = 9$

and $\qquad 5 = \dfrac{2 + k}{2} \Rightarrow k = 8$

So, the required equation of circle is
$$(x-9)^2 + (y-8)^2 = (5)^2$$
$$\Rightarrow \quad x^2 - 18x + 81 + y^2 - 16y + 64 = 25$$
$$\Rightarrow \quad x^2 + y^2 - 18x - 16y + 120 = 0$$

3. Given points are
$$x = \frac{2at}{1+t^2} \text{ and } y = \frac{a(1-t^2)}{1+t^2}.$$
$$\because \quad x^2 + y^2 = \frac{4a^2 t^2}{(1+t^2)^2} + \frac{a^2(1-t^2)^2}{(1+t^2)^2}$$
$$\Rightarrow \quad \frac{1}{a^2}(x^2+y^2) = \frac{4t^2 + 1 + t^4 - 2t^2}{(1+t^2)^2}$$
$$\Rightarrow \quad \frac{1}{a^2}(x^2+y^2) = \frac{t^4 + 2t^2 + 1}{(1+t^2)^2}$$
$$\Rightarrow \quad \frac{1}{a^2}(x^2+y^2) = \frac{(1+t^2)^2}{(1+t^2)^2}$$
$$\Rightarrow \quad x^2 + y^2 = a^2, \text{ which is a required circle.}$$

4. Given lines, $\quad 3x + 4y + 4 = 0 \quad\quad$ ...(i)
$$6x - 8y - 7 = 0$$
or $\quad\quad 3x - 4y - 7/2 = 0 \quad\quad$ ...(ii)

It is clear that lines (i) and (ii) parallel.

Now, distance between them

i.e. $\quad d = \left| \dfrac{4 + 7/2}{\sqrt{9+16}} \right| = \left| \dfrac{\dfrac{8+7}{2}}{5} \right| = \dfrac{3}{2}$ units

∴ Distance between these line = Diameter of these circle

∴ Diameter of the circle $= \dfrac{3}{2}$ units

and radius of the circle $= \dfrac{3}{4}$ unit

5. Given, equation of lines are $x - y = 4$ and $2x + 3y + 7 = 0$.

On solving these equations, we get
$$x = 1 \text{ and } y = -3$$

Also, the point of intersection of the given lines is centre.

∴ Coordinates of centre is $(1, -3)$.

Now, the circle passes through the point $(2, 4)$.

∴ Radius of circle $= \sqrt{(1-2)^2 + (-3-4)^2}$
$$= \sqrt{(-1)^2 + (-7)^2}$$
$$= \sqrt{1 + 49}$$
$$= \sqrt{50} \text{ units} \quad\quad \text{[by distance formula]}$$

Hence, the required equation of circle whose centre is $(1, -3)$ and radius is $\sqrt{50}$, is
$$(x-1)^2 + (y+3)^2 = (\sqrt{50})^2$$
$$\Rightarrow \quad x^2 + 1 - 2x + y^2 + 9 + 6y = 50$$
$$\Rightarrow \quad x^2 + y^2 - 2x + 6y - 40 = 0$$

6. Given, radius $= 5$ units and circle touches both the axes.

So, circle may lies in anyone of the four quadrants.

∴ Centre of circle is $(\pm 5, \pm 5)$.

Hence, the required equation of circle is
$$(x \mp 5)^2 + (y \mp 5)^2 = (5)^2$$
$$\Rightarrow \quad x^2 + 25 \mp 10x + y^2 + 25 \mp 10y = 25$$
$$\Rightarrow \quad x^2 + y^2 \mp 10x \mp 10y + 25 = 0$$

7. We know that, circle passes through the origin, so radius of circle will be equal to the distance between point (a, b) and origin.

∴ Radius of circle = Distance between points $(0, 0)$ and (a, b)
$$= \sqrt{(0-a)^2 + (0-b)^2}$$
$$= \sqrt{a^2 + b^2} \text{ units} \quad\quad \text{[by distance formula]}$$
$$\because \quad\quad \text{Centre} = (h, k) = (a, b)$$

On putting these values in equation of circle
$(x-h)^2 + (y-k)^2 = r^2$, we get
$$(x-a)^2 + (y-b)^2 = (\sqrt{a^2+b^2})^2$$
$$\Rightarrow x^2 + a^2 - 2ax + y^2 + b^2 - 2by = a^2 + b^2$$
$$[\because (A-B)^2 = A^2 - 2AB + B^2]$$
$$\Rightarrow \quad x^2 + y^2 - 2ax - 2by = 0$$

which is the required equation of circle.

8. Let $C(k, 0)$ be the centre of the circle.

∵ Radius of the circle $= 5$ units

∴ Equation of the required circle is given by
$$(x-k)^2 + (y-0)^2 = (5)^2 \quad\quad \text{...(i)}$$
$$(x-k)^2 + y^2 = 25$$

∵ Circle (i) passes through $(2, 3)$, we get
$$(2-k)^2 + 9 = 25$$
$$\Rightarrow \quad (2-k)^2 = 16$$
$$\Rightarrow \quad 2 - k = \pm 4 \Rightarrow k = -2, 6$$

∴ From Eq. (i), required equation of circles are
$$(x+2)^2 + y^2 = 25$$
and $\quad\quad (x-6)^2 + y^2 = 25$

9. Let C be the centre of the circle in its initial position.

∴ $\quad\quad\quad C \equiv (5, 5)$

Now, centre of the circle in the new position will have its x-coordinate equal to $5 + 2\pi(5)$.

∴ Centre of the circle in the new position is $(5 + 10\pi, 5)$ and its radius is 5 units.

∴ Its equation will be
$$(x - 5 - 10\pi)^2 + (y-5)^2 = (5)^2$$
$$\Rightarrow x^2 + 25 + 100\pi^2 + 100\pi - 10x - 20\pi x + y^2 + 25 - 10y = 25$$
$$\Rightarrow x^2 + y^2 - 10(2\pi + 1)x - 10y + 100\pi^2 + 100\pi + 25 = 0$$

10. Given, $\quad\quad AM = AL = AC = 2$

and $\quad$ points $A \equiv (2, 2)$ and $B \equiv (6, 5)$

∴ $\quad$ Distance $AB = \sqrt{(2-6)^2 + (2-5)^2}$
$$= \sqrt{(-4)^2 + (-3)^2}$$
$$= \sqrt{16 + 9}$$
$$= \sqrt{25} = 5 \text{ units}$$

Then, distance $BC = AB - AC = 5 - 2 = 3$

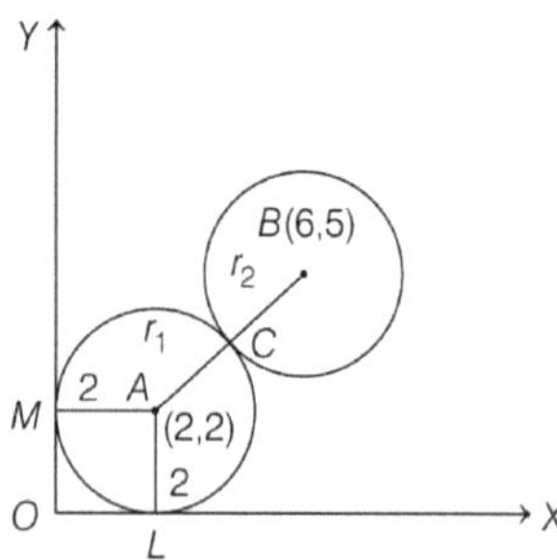

Hence, the equation of required circle whose centre is $(6, 5)$ and radius is 3 units will be

$$(x - 6)^2 + (y - 5)^2 = (3)^2$$
$$\Rightarrow \quad x^2 + y^2 - 12x - 10y + 52 = 0$$

11. Given, centre is $\left(\dfrac{1}{2}, \dfrac{1}{4}\right)$.

$$\therefore \quad h = \dfrac{1}{2}, k = \dfrac{1}{4}$$

and radius $(r) = \dfrac{1}{12}$ unit

On putting these values in equation of circle $(x - h)^2 + (y - k)^2 = r^2$, we get

$$\left(x - \dfrac{1}{2}\right)^2 + \left(y - \dfrac{1}{4}\right)^2 = \left(\dfrac{1}{12}\right)^2$$

$$\Rightarrow \quad x^2 + \dfrac{1}{4} - x + y^2 + \dfrac{1}{16} - \dfrac{y}{2} = \dfrac{1}{144}$$

$$\Rightarrow \quad x^2 + y^2 - x - \dfrac{y}{2} + \dfrac{1}{4} + \dfrac{1}{16} - \dfrac{1}{144} = 0$$

$$\Rightarrow \quad x^2 + y^2 - x - \dfrac{y}{2} + \dfrac{11}{36} = 0$$

$$\Rightarrow \quad 36x^2 + 36y^2 - 36x - 18y + 11 = 0$$

$$\text{[multiplying both sides by 36]}$$

which is the required equation of circle.

12. Given, centre is $(a\cos\theta, a\sin\theta)$.

$\therefore \ h = a\cos\theta, k = a\sin\theta$ and radius $(r) = a$

On putting these values in equation of circle $(x - h)^2 + (y - k)^2 = r^2$, we get

$$(x - a\cos\theta)^2 + (y - a\sin\theta)^2 = a^2$$

$$\Rightarrow x^2 + a^2\cos^2\theta - 2ax\cos\theta + y^2 + a^2\sin^2\theta - 2ay\sin\theta = a^2$$

$$\Rightarrow x^2 + y^2 - 2ax\cos\theta - 2ay\sin\theta + a^2(\sin^2\theta + \cos^2\theta) = a^2$$

$$\Rightarrow x^2 + y^2 - 2a(x\cos\theta + y\sin\theta) + a^2 = a^2$$

$$[\because \ \sin^2 A + \cos^2 A = 1]$$

$$\therefore \quad x^2 + y^2 - 2a(x\cos\theta + y\sin\theta) = 0$$

which is the required equation of circle.

13. Let coordinates of points on Y-axis be $A \equiv (0, 3)$ and $B \equiv (0, -3)$, respectively.

Given, circle passes through points A and B, therefore its centre will be on the perpendicular bisector of AB.

Clearly, two such circles are possible.

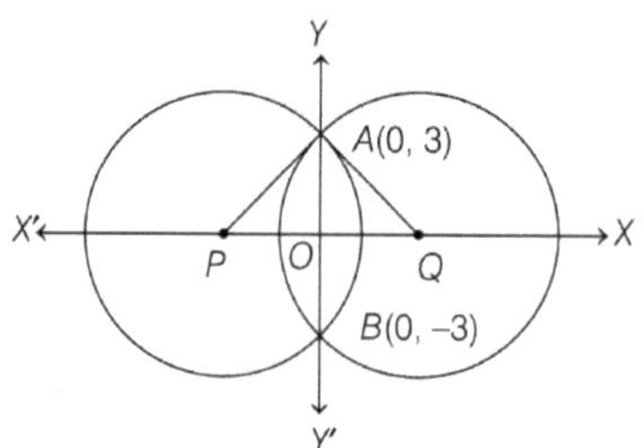

Let points P and Q be the centres of such circles.

Given, $AP = AQ = 5$ and $OA = 3$

$$\Rightarrow \quad OP = OQ = \sqrt{(5)^2 - (3)^2} = \sqrt{25 - 9} = \sqrt{16} = 4\,\text{units}$$

Then, centres $P = (-4, 0)$ and $Q = (4, 0)$

Thus, centres of the required circles are $P(-4, 0)$ and $Q(4, 0)$ and their radii are 5 units.

$\therefore$ Required equation of the circles will be

$$(x + 4)^2 + (y - 0)^2 = 5^2 \ \text{ i.e. } x^2 + y^2 + 8x - 9 = 0$$

and $(x - 4)^2 + (y - 0)^2 = 5^2$ i.e. $x^2 + y^2 - 8x - 9 = 0$

14. Let $P(x, y)$ be the point of intersection of the lines,

$$3x - 2y = 1 \qquad \qquad \text{...(i)}$$

and $\qquad \qquad 4x + y = 27 \qquad \qquad \text{...(ii)}$

On solving Eqs. (i) and (ii), we get

$$x = 5 \text{ and } y = 7$$

So, the coordinates of P are $(5, \ 7)$.

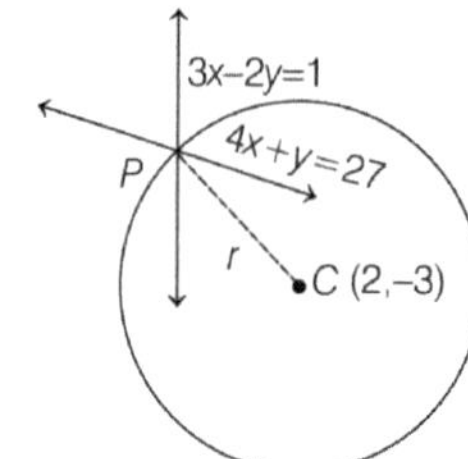

Given, coordinates of centre C are $(2, -3)$.

$\therefore \qquad \qquad CP = \text{Radius}$

$$\Rightarrow \sqrt{(5 - 2)^2 + (7 + 3)^2} = r \ \Rightarrow \ \sqrt{(3)^2 + (10)^2} = r$$

$$\Rightarrow \qquad \sqrt{9 + 100} = r \ \Rightarrow \ r = \sqrt{109}\,\text{units}$$

Hence, the required equation of circle is

$$(x - 2)^2 + (y + 3)^2 = (\sqrt{109})^2$$

$$\Rightarrow \quad x^2 - 4x + 4 + y^2 + 6y + 9 = 109$$

$$\Rightarrow \quad x^2 + y^2 - 4x + 6y - 96 = 0$$

15. Let centre of the circle be (a, a), then equation of the circle is $(x - a)^2 + (y - a)^2 = a^2$.

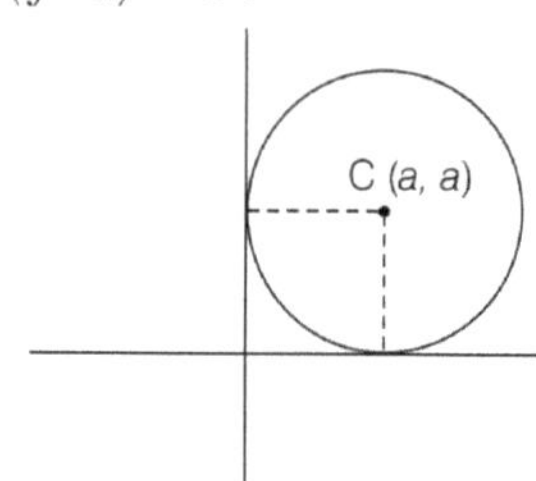

Since, the point (3, 6) lies on this circle, then
$$(3 - a)^2 + (6 - a)^2 = (a)^2$$
$$\Rightarrow \quad a^2 + 9 - 6a + 36 - 12a + a^2 = a^2$$
$$\Rightarrow \quad a^2 - 18a + 45 = 0$$
$$\Rightarrow \quad a^2 - 15a - 3a + 45 = 0$$
$$\Rightarrow \quad a(a - 15) - 3(a - 15) = 0$$
$$\Rightarrow \quad (a - 3)(a - 15) = 0$$
$$\Rightarrow \quad a = 3 \text{ or } 15$$
So, the required equation of circle is
$$(x - 3)^2 + (y - 3)^2 = (3)^2$$
$$\Rightarrow \quad x^2 - 6x + 9 + y^2 - 6y + 9 = 9$$
$$\Rightarrow \quad x^2 + y^2 - 6x - 6y + 9 = 0$$

16. Given, equation of the circle is

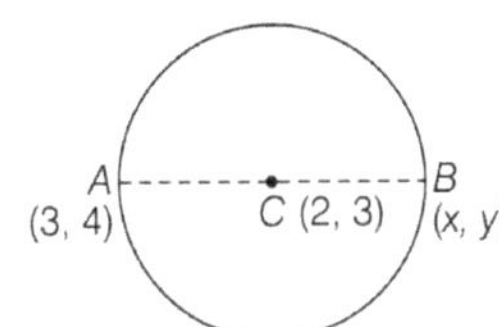

$$x^2 + y^2 - 4x - 6y + 11 = 0.$$
$$\therefore \qquad 2g = -4 \text{ and } 2f = -6$$
So, the centre of the circle is $(-g, -f)$ i.e. $(2, 3)$.
Since, the mid-point of AB is $(2, 3)$.

Then, $\qquad 2 = \dfrac{3 + x_1}{2} \Rightarrow 4 = 3 + x_1$

$\therefore \qquad x_1 = 1$

and $\qquad 3 = \dfrac{4 + y_1}{2}$

$\Rightarrow \qquad 6 = 4 + y_1 \Rightarrow y_1 = 2$

So, the coordinates of other end of the diameter will be $(1, 2)$.

17. Given that, centre of the circle is $(1, -2)$ and the circle passing through the lines
$$3x + y = 14 \qquad \qquad \text{... (i)}$$
and $\qquad 2x + 5y = 18 \qquad \qquad \text{...(ii)}$
From Eq. (i) $y = 14 - 3x$ put in Eq. (ii), we get
$$2x + 70 - 15x = 18$$
$$\Rightarrow \qquad -13x = -52 \Rightarrow x = 4$$
Now, $x = 4$ put in Eq. (i), we get
$$12 + y = 14$$
$$\Rightarrow \qquad y = 2$$
Since, point $(4, 2)$ lie on these lines also lies on the circle.

$\therefore$ Radius of the circle $= \sqrt{(4-1)^2 + (2+2)^2}$

$\qquad\qquad = \sqrt{(3)^2 + (4)^2}$ [by distance formula]

$\qquad\qquad = \sqrt{9 + 16} = 5$ units

Now, the required equation of the circle is
$$(x - 1)^2 + (y + 2)^2 = (5)^2$$
$$\Rightarrow \quad x^2 - 2x + 1 + y^2 + 4y + 4 = 25$$
$$\Rightarrow \quad x^2 + y^2 - 2x + 4y - 20 = 0$$

18. Given, centre of the circle is $(3, -1)$.

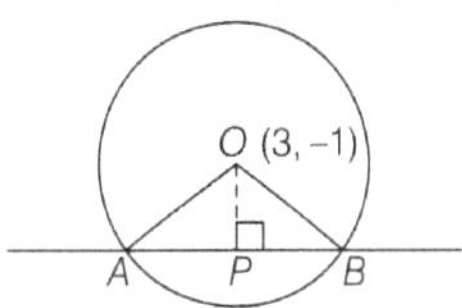

Now, $\qquad OP = \left| \dfrac{6 + 5 + 18}{\sqrt{4 + 25}} \right| = \dfrac{29}{\sqrt{29}} = \sqrt{29}$

In $\triangle OPB$, $OB^2 = OP^2 + PB^2$ [by pythagoras theorem]
$$\Rightarrow \qquad OB^2 = 29 + 9 \qquad [\because AB = 6 \Rightarrow PB = 3]$$
$$\Rightarrow \qquad OB^2 = 38$$
So, the radius of circle is $\sqrt{38}$ units.

$\therefore$ Equation of the circle with radius $r = \sqrt{38}$ and centre $(3, -1)$ is
$$(x - 3)^2 + (y + 1)^2 = (\sqrt{38})^2$$
$$\Rightarrow \quad x^2 - 6x + 9 + y^2 + 2y + 1 = 38$$
$$\Rightarrow \quad x^2 + y^2 - 6x + 2y = 28$$
which is the required equation of circle.

19. We know that, general equation of a circle is
$$x^2 + y^2 + 2gx + 2fy + c = 0 \qquad \text{...(i)}$$
Now, the equation of the given circles are
$$x^2 + y^2 - 4x - 6y - 14 = 0 \qquad \text{...(ii)}$$
$$x^2 + y^2 + 2x + 4y - 5 = 0 \qquad \text{...(iii)}$$
$$x^2 + y^2 - 10x - 16y + 7 = 0 \qquad \text{...(iv)}$$
On comparing Eq. (ii) with Eq. (i), we get
$$g = -2 \text{ and } f = -3$$
$\therefore$ Centre of the circle (ii) is $A(2, 3)$.
Similarly, centre of the circle (iii) is $B(-1, -2)$ and the centre of the circle (iv) is $C(5, 8)$.
Hence, equation of the line passing through A and B is
$$y - 3 = \dfrac{-2 - 3}{-1 - 2}(x - 2) \text{ or } y - 3 = \dfrac{5}{3}(x - 2)$$
$$\Rightarrow 5x - 3y - 1 = 0 \qquad \text{...(v)}$$
On putting point $C(5, 8)$ in Eq. (v), we get
$$5(5) - 3(8) - 1 = 25 - 25 = 0$$
$\because$ It satisfies Eq. (v)
$\therefore$ The centres of the given circles are collinear.

20. Given, circle is $x^2 + y^2 + 4x - 2y - 3 = 0$ $\qquad$ ...(i)

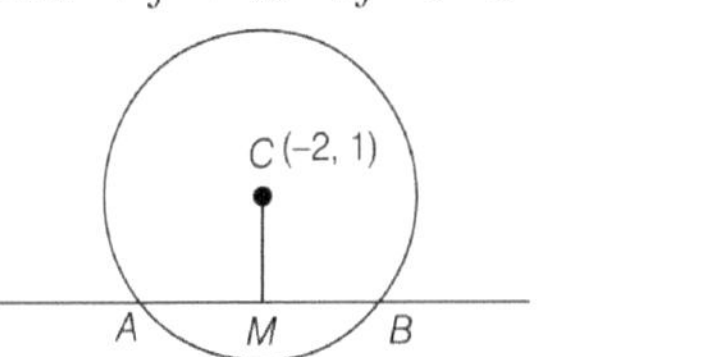

Given line AB is $x - y + 2 = 0$ $\qquad\qquad$ ...(ii)
Let C be the centre of the circle (i).
$\therefore \qquad\qquad C = (-2, 1)$
Let M be the middle point of chord AB.
$\because \qquad\qquad MC \perp AB$
$\therefore$ Slope of $MC \times$ Slope of $AB = -1$

$\therefore$ Slope of $MC = \dfrac{-1}{\text{Slope of } AB} = \dfrac{-1}{1} = -1$

Now, equation of MC is given by

$$y - 1 = -(x + 2) \Rightarrow x + y + 1 = 0 \qquad \ldots(iii)$$

Solving Eqs. (ii) and (iii), we get

$$x = -\frac{3}{2}$$

$$\therefore \qquad y = \frac{-3}{2} + 2 = \frac{1}{2}$$

$\therefore$ Coordinates of M is $\left(-\dfrac{3}{2}, \dfrac{1}{2}\right)$.

21. Let equation of parabola be

$$y^2 = 4ax \qquad \ldots(i)$$

and its vertex is $(0, 0)$.

Again, let any point on the parabola be $P(h, k)$.

On putting the values $x = h$ and $y = k$ in Eq. (i), we get

$$k^2 = 4ah \qquad \ldots(ii)$$

Let $OP(=l)$ be the line segment joining the vertex and point P. Also, it makes an angle θ with the X-axis.

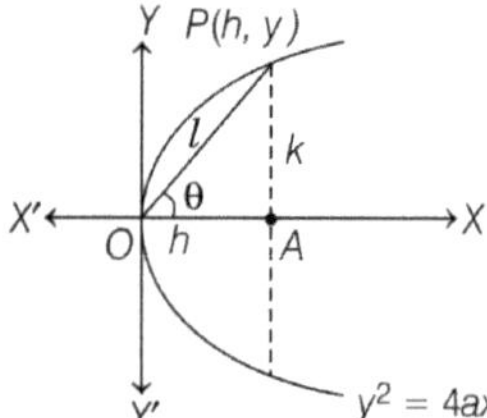

In right-angled ΔOAP,

$$\sin \theta = \frac{PA}{OP} \Rightarrow \sin \theta = \frac{k}{l} \Rightarrow k = l \sin \theta$$

and $\quad \cos \theta = \dfrac{OA}{OP} \Rightarrow \cos \theta = \dfrac{h}{l} \Rightarrow h = \cos \theta$

On substituting the values of h and k in Eq. (ii), we get

$$l^2 \sin^2 \theta = 4al \cos \theta \Rightarrow l = \frac{4a \cos \theta}{\sin^2 \theta}$$

which is the required length.

22. Given, equation of the parabola is $y^2 = 36x$,

which is of the form $y^2 = 4ax$.

Here, $4a = 36 \Rightarrow a = 9$

$\therefore \qquad$ Vertex $= V(0, 0)$

$\qquad$ Focus $= F(a, 0) = (9, 0)$

$\qquad$ Directrix, $x = -a \Rightarrow x = -9$

$\qquad$ Axis $= X$-axis

$\therefore$ Length of latusrectum $= 4a = 4 \times 9 = 36$ units

23. Given, equation of the parabola is $y^2 = 16x \qquad \ldots(i)$

$\therefore$ Its vertex $P \equiv (0, 0)$

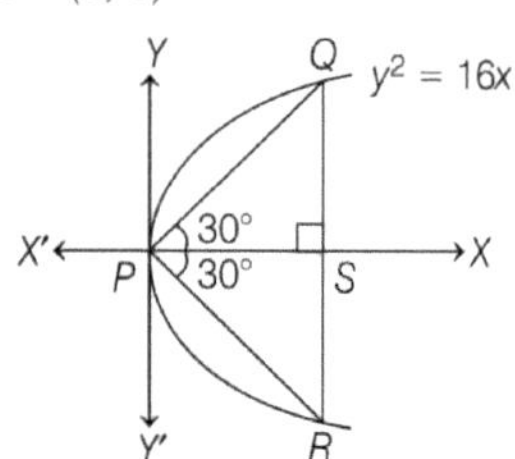

Let PQR be the inscribed equilateral triangle.

$\therefore \angle QPS = 30°$ and $\angle PSQ = 90°$

Let side $PQ = a$

Now, consider ΔPSQ

$$\therefore \quad \cos 30° = \frac{PS}{PQ} \text{ and } \sin 30° = \frac{QS}{PQ}$$

$$\Rightarrow \qquad PS = \frac{l\sqrt{3}}{2} \text{ and } QS = \frac{l}{2}$$

$$\Rightarrow \qquad Q \equiv \left(\frac{\sqrt{3}l}{2}, \frac{l}{2}\right)$$

$\because$ The point Q lie on parabola.

$\therefore$ From Eq. (i),

$$\left(\frac{l}{2}\right)^2 = \frac{16\sqrt{3}l}{2} \Rightarrow l = 32\sqrt{3}$$

Hence, the required length is $32\sqrt{3}$ units.

24. Let AB be the double ordinate of length $8a$ units of the parabola $y^2 = 4ax$.

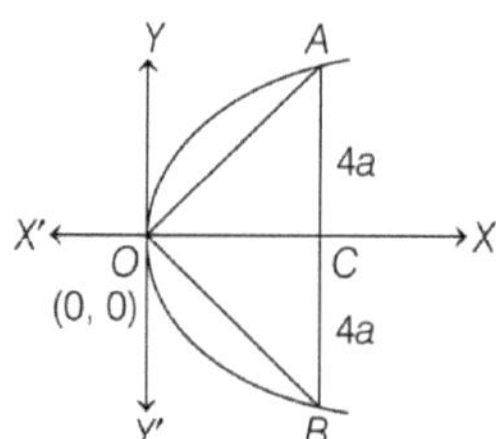

Let AB meet X-axis at the point C, then

$$CA = CB = 4a$$

Now, let $OC = k$

$\therefore A \equiv (k, 4a)$ and $B \equiv (k, -4a)$

$\because A(k, 4a)$ lies on the parabola $y^2 = 4ax$.

$$\Rightarrow \qquad 16a^2 = 4ak$$

$$\Rightarrow \qquad k = 4a$$

Slope of $OA = m_1 = \dfrac{4a - 0}{k - 0} = \dfrac{4a}{4a} = 1$

Slope of $OB = m_2 = \dfrac{-4a - 0}{k - 0} = \dfrac{-4a}{4a} = -1$

$$\therefore \quad m_1 m_2 = 1(-1) = -1 \Rightarrow OA \perp OB$$

25. Equation of the parabola with vertex at the origin, the axis along the X-axis is

$$y^2 = 4ax \qquad \ldots(i)$$

Since, parabola (i) passes through $(2, 3)$.

$\therefore \qquad 9 = 4 \times a \times 2 \qquad$ [from Eq. (i)]

$$\Rightarrow \qquad 9 = 8a$$

$$\Rightarrow \qquad a = \frac{9}{8}$$

On putting $a = \dfrac{9}{8}$ in Eq. (i), we get

$$y^2 = 4 \times \frac{9}{8}x = \frac{9}{2}x$$

Hence, the required equation of parabola is $y^2 = \dfrac{9}{2}x$.

26. Given, equation of parabola is $x^2 = -36y \Rightarrow x^2 = -4(9y)$

Here, $a = 9$

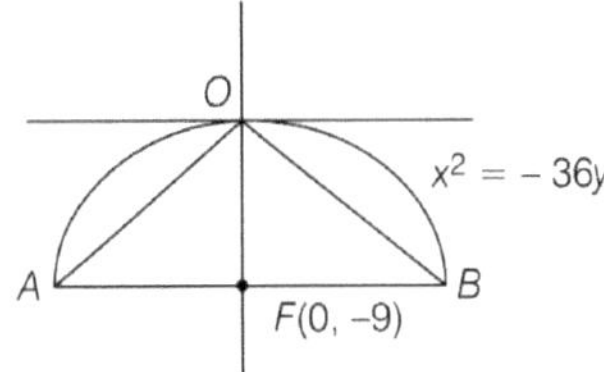

Focus $\equiv (0, -a) = (0, -9)$

Let AB be the latusrectum.

$\therefore \qquad y = -9$, then $x^2 = -36(-9)$

$\Rightarrow \qquad x = \pm 18$

So, the coordinates of A and B are $(-18, -9)$ and $(18, 9)$, respectively.

$\therefore \quad$ Area of $\Delta AOB = 2 \times$ Area of ΔOFB

$$= 2 \times \left(\frac{1}{2} \times 18 \times 9\right) = 162 \text{ sq units}$$

27. Given, the vertex of the parabola is at origin and it is symmetric with respect to Y-axis, also it passes through $(2, -3)$ a point in the fourth quadrant.

$\therefore$ Required parabola is of the form

$$x^2 = -4ay \qquad \qquad \dots(i)$$

Now, put $(2, -3)$ in Eq. (i), we get

$$4 = 12a \Rightarrow a = \frac{1}{3} \qquad \dots(ii)$$

$\therefore$ From Eqs. (i) and (ii),

The equation of the parabola is

$$x^2 = -4\left(\frac{1}{3}\right)y \Rightarrow x^2 = -\frac{4}{3}y \Rightarrow 3x^2 = -4y$$

28. Given, equation of parabola is $5x^2 = -12y$ or $x^2 = \frac{-12}{5}y$,

which is of the form $x^2 = -4ay$.

Here, $\quad 4a = \frac{12}{5} \Rightarrow a = \frac{3}{5}$

$\therefore \qquad$ Focus $= (0, -a) = \left(0, \frac{-3}{5}\right)$

Directrix, $y = a \Rightarrow y = \frac{3}{5}$

$\therefore$ Length of latusrectum $= 4a = 4 \times \frac{3}{5} = \frac{12}{5}$ units

29. Given, equation of the parabola is $4x^2 = -9y$

or $x^2 = -\frac{9}{4}y$, which is of the form $x^2 = -4ay$.

Here, $\quad 4a = \frac{9}{4} \Rightarrow a = \frac{9}{16}$

$\therefore \qquad$ Vertex $= V(0, 0)$

$$\text{Focus} = F(0, -a) = F\left(0 - \frac{9}{16}\right)$$

Directrix, $y = a \Rightarrow y = \frac{9}{16}$

$\qquad$ Axis $= Y$-axis

$\therefore$ Length of latusrectum $= 4a = 4 \times \frac{9}{16} = \frac{9}{4}$ units

30. Given, focus of the parabola $F(6, 0)$ and directrix, $x = -6$

Now, let $P(x, y)$ be any point on the parabola and MP be the perpendicular distance from P to the directrix.

$\Rightarrow \qquad\qquad FP = MP$

$\therefore \sqrt{(x-6)^2 + (y-0)^2} = \dfrac{|x+6|}{1}$

$\Rightarrow \quad x^2 - 12x + 36 + y^2 = x^2 + 12x + 36$

$\Rightarrow \qquad\qquad y^2 = 24x$

Above equation is of the form $y^2 = 4ax \Rightarrow 4a = 24$

$\therefore$ Length of latusrectum $= 4a = 24$ units

31. Let a be the radius of the circle. Then, the coordinates of the circle are $(-a, -a)$.

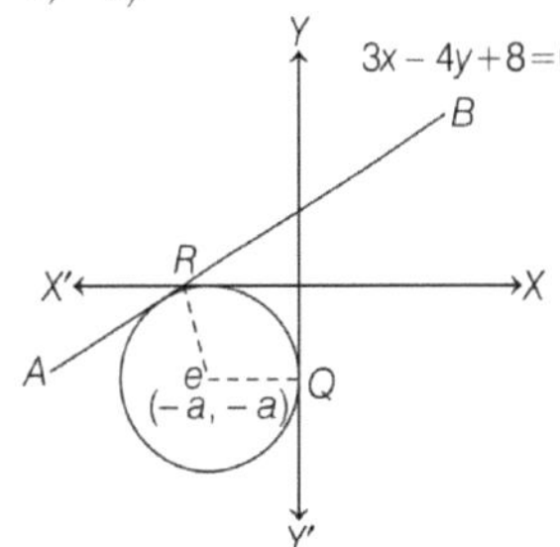

Now, perpendicular distance from C to the line AB = Radius of the circle

$$d = \left|\frac{-3a + 4a + 8}{\sqrt{9 + 16}}\right| = \left|\frac{a + 8}{5}\right|$$

$\because \qquad\qquad a = \pm\left(\dfrac{a+8}{5}\right)$

Taking positive sign,

$$a = \frac{a+8}{5} \Rightarrow 5a = a + 8$$

$\Rightarrow \qquad\qquad 4a = 8 \Rightarrow a = 2$

Taking negative sign,

$$a = \frac{-a-8}{5} \Rightarrow 5a = -a - 8$$

$\Rightarrow \qquad\qquad 6a = -8 \Rightarrow a = -\frac{4}{3}$

But $\qquad\qquad a \neq -\frac{4}{3}$

$\because \qquad\qquad a = 2$

So, the required equation of circle is

$$(x+2)^2 + (y+2)^2 = (2)^2 \qquad [\because a = 2]$$

$\Rightarrow \qquad x^2 + 4x + 4 + y^2 + 4y + 4 = 4$

$\Rightarrow \qquad x^2 + y^2 + 4x + 4y + 4 = 0$

32. Given, radius, $r = 5$ units, point lies on circle $= (2, 3)$ and centre of circle is on X-axis.

$\therefore$ Its y-coordinate will be zero.

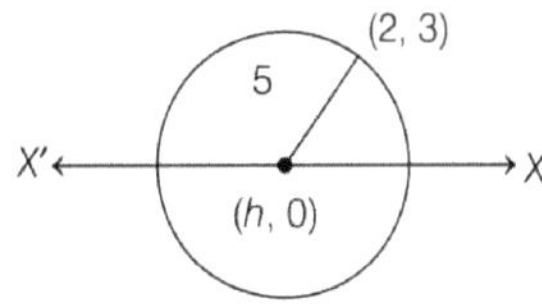

Let centre of circle $= (h, 0)$

Now, distance from the centre to a point on the circle

$$= \text{Radius of circle}$$

$$\therefore \quad \sqrt{(h-2)^2 + (0-3)^2} = 5 \quad \text{[by distance formula]}$$

$$\Rightarrow \quad \sqrt{h^2 + 4 - 4h + 9} = 5 \quad [\because (a-b)^2 = a^2 + b^2 - 2ab]$$

$$\Rightarrow \quad h^2 + 4 - 4h + 9 = 25 \quad \text{[squaring on both sides]}$$

$$\Rightarrow \quad h^2 - 4h + 13 - 25 = 0$$

$$\Rightarrow \quad h^2 - 4h - 12 = 0$$

$$\Rightarrow \quad h^2 - 6h + 2h - 12 = 0$$

$$\Rightarrow \quad h(h-6) + 2(h-6) = 0$$

$$\Rightarrow \quad (h-6)(h+2) = 0$$

$$\Rightarrow \quad h - 6 = 0 \text{ or } h + 2 = 0$$

$$\Rightarrow \quad h = 6 \text{ or } -2$$

So, the centre of circle is $(6, 0)$ or $(-2, 0)$.

When centre $(h, k) = (6, 0)$ and radius $(r) = 5$, then the equation of circle is

$$(x-6)^2 + (y-0)^2 = (5)^2 \quad [\because (x-h)^2 + (y-k)^2 = r^2]$$

$$\Rightarrow \quad x^2 + 36 - 12x + y^2 = 25 \quad [\because (a-b)^2 = a^2 - 2ab + b^2]$$

$$\Rightarrow \quad x^2 + y^2 - 12x + 11 = 0$$

When centre $(h, k) = (-2, 0)$ and radius $(r) = 5$, then the equation of circle is

$$(x+2)^2 + (y-0)^2 = (5)^2 \quad [\because (x-h)^2 + (y-k)^2 = r^2]$$

$$\Rightarrow \quad x^2 + 4 + 4x + y^2 = 25$$

$$\Rightarrow \quad x^2 + y^2 + 4x + 4 - 25 = 0$$

$$\Rightarrow \quad x^2 + y^2 + 4x - 21 = 0$$

Hence, the required equations of circle are

$x^2 + y^2 - 12x + 11 = 0$ and $x^2 + y^2 + 4x - 21 = 0$.

33. Let equation of circle be

$$(x-h)^2 + (y-k)^2 = r^2$$

$$\Rightarrow \quad (x-h)^2 + (y-k)^2 = (3)^2 \quad \text{...(i)}$$

Given that, centre (h, k) lies on the line

$$y = x - 1 \text{ i.e. } k = h - 1 \quad \text{...(ii)}$$

Now, the circle passes through the point $(7, 3)$.

$$\therefore \quad (7-h)^2 + (3-k)^2 = (3)^2$$

$$\Rightarrow \quad 49 - 14h + h^2 + 9 - 6k + k^2 = 9$$

$$\Rightarrow \quad h^2 + k^2 - 14h - 6k + 49 = 0 \quad \text{...(iii)}$$

On putting $k = h - 1$ in Eq. (iii), we get

$$h^2 + (h-1)^2 - 14h - 6(h-1) + 49 = 0$$

$$\Rightarrow \quad h^2 + h^2 - 2h + 1 - 14h - 6h + 6 + 49 = 0$$

$$\Rightarrow \quad 2h^2 - 22h + 56 = 0$$

$$\Rightarrow \quad h^2 - 11h + 28 = 0$$

$$\Rightarrow \quad h^2 - 7h - 4h + 28 = 0$$

$$\Rightarrow \quad h(h-7) - 4(h-7) = 0$$

$$\Rightarrow \quad (h-7)(h-4) = 0$$

$$\therefore \quad h = 4, 7$$

When $h = 7$, then $k = 7 - 1 = 6$

$$\therefore \text{ Centre} = (7, 6)$$

When $h = 4$, then $k = 3$

$$\therefore \text{ Centre} = (4, 3)$$

So, the required equation of circle when centre $(7, 6)$, is

$$(x-7)^2 + (y-6)^2 = (3)^2$$

$$\Rightarrow \quad x^2 - 14x + 49 + y^2 - 12y + 36 = 9$$

$$\Rightarrow \quad x^2 + y^2 - 14x - 12y + 76 = 0$$

When centre $(4, 3)$, then the equation of the circle is

$$(x-4)^2 + (y-3)^2 = 9$$

$$\Rightarrow \quad x^2 - 8x + 16 + y^2 - 6y + 9 = 9$$

$$\Rightarrow \quad x^2 + y^2 - 8x - 6y + 16 = 0$$

34. Let the general equation of the circle is

$$x^2 + y^2 + 2gx + 2fy + c = 0 \quad \text{...(i)}$$

Since, this circle passes through the points $(2, 3)$ and $(4, 5)$.

$$\therefore \quad 4 + 9 + 4g + 6f + c = 0$$

$$\Rightarrow \quad 4g + 6f + c = -13 \quad \text{...(ii)}$$

$$\text{and} \quad 16 + 25 + 8g + 10f + c = 0$$

$$\Rightarrow \quad 8g + 10f + c = -41 \quad \text{...(iii)}$$

Since, the centre of the circle $(-g, -f)$ lies on the straight line $y - 4x + 3 = 0$

$$\text{i.e.} \quad 4g - f + 3 = 0 \quad \text{...(iv)}$$

From Eq. (iv), $\quad 4g = f - 3$

On putting $4g = f - 3$ in Eq. (ii), we get

$$f - 3 + 6f + c = -13$$

$$\Rightarrow \quad 7f + c = 10 \quad \text{... (v)}$$

From Eqs. (ii) and (iii),

$$8g + 12f + 2c = -26$$

$$8g + 10f + c = -41$$

$$\underline{- \quad - \qquad - \quad\quad +}$$

$$2f + c = 15 \quad \text{...(vi)}$$

From Eqs. (ii) and (vi),

$$7f + c = -10$$

$$2f + c = 15$$

$$\underline{- \quad - \quad -}$$

$$5f = -25$$

$$\therefore \quad f = -5$$

Now, $c = 10 + 15 = 25$

From Eq. (iv), $4g + 5 + 3 = 0 \Rightarrow g = -2$

From Eq. (i), required equation of the circle is

$$x^2 + y^2 - 4x - 10y + 25 = 0$$

35. Let the equation of the circle passing through the points $(5, 5)$, $(6, 4)$ and $(7, 1)$ be given by

$$x^2 + y^2 + 2gx + 2fy + c = 0 \quad \text{...(i)}$$

Then, each of these points must satisfies Eq. (i).

$$\therefore \quad 25 + 25 + 10g + 10f + c = 0$$

$$\Rightarrow \quad 10g + 10f + c = -50 \quad \text{...(ii)}$$

$$\Rightarrow \quad 36 + 16 + 12g + 8f + c = 0$$

$$\Rightarrow \quad 12g + 8f + c = -52 \quad \text{...(iii)}$$

$$\text{and} \quad 49 + 1 + 14g + 2f + c = 0$$

$$\Rightarrow \quad 14g + 2f + c = -50 \quad \text{...(iv)}$$

On solving Eqs. (ii), (iii) and (iv) simultaneously, we get

$$g = -2, f = -1 \text{ and } c = -20$$

On putting the values of g, f and c in Eq. (i), we get
$$x^2 + y^2 - 4x - 2y - 20 = 0$$
On putting $x = -2$ and $y = 4$ in the above circle, we get
$$4 + 16 + 8 - 8 - 20 = 0$$
This shows that the point $(-2, 4)$ also lies on the circle.
Hence, the points $(5, 5)$, $(6, 4)$, $(-2, 4)$ and $(7, 1)$ are concyclic and equation of this circle is
$$x^2 + y^2 - 4x - 2y - 20 = 0$$
Its centre is $(-g, -f) = (2, 1)$
and radius $= \sqrt{g^2 + f^2 - c} = \sqrt{4 + 1 + 20} = 5$ units

36. Given, equations of line are
$$y = x + 2 \qquad \text{...(i)}$$
$$3y = 4x \qquad \text{...(ii)}$$
$$2y = 3x \qquad \text{...(iii)}$$
From Eqs. (i) and (ii),
$$\frac{4x}{3} = x + 2 \implies 4x = 3x + 6 \implies x = 6$$
On putting $x = 6$ in Eq. (i), we get
$$y = 8$$
$\therefore$ Point $A = (6, 8)$
From Eqs. (i) and (iii),
$$\frac{3x}{2} = x + 2 \implies 3x = 2x + 4 \implies x = 4$$
When $x = 4$, then $y = 6$
$\therefore$ Point $B = (4, 6)$
From Eqs. (ii) and (iii),
$$x_1 = 0 \text{ and } y_1 = 0$$
Now, $C = (0, 0)$
Let the equation of circle is
$$x^2 + y^2 + 2gx + 2fy + c = 0$$
Since, the points $A(6, 8)$, $B(4, 6)$ and $C(0, 0)$ lie on this circle.
$$36 + 64 + 12g + 16f + c = 0$$
$\implies$ $12g + 16f + c = -100 \qquad \text{...(iv)}$
and $16 + 36 + 8g + 12f + c = 0$
$\implies$ $8g + 12f + c = -52 \qquad \text{...(v)}$
$\implies$ $c = 0 \qquad \text{...(vi)}$
From Eqs. (iv), (v) and (vi),
$$12g + 16f = -100 \implies 3g + 4f + 25 = 0$$
or $8g + 12f = -52 \implies 2g + 3f + 13 = 0$
$\implies$ $\dfrac{g}{52 - 75} = \dfrac{f}{50 - 39} = \dfrac{1}{9 - 8}$
$\implies$ $\dfrac{g}{-23} = \dfrac{f}{11} = \dfrac{1}{1}$
$\implies$ $g = -23$ and $f = 11$
So, the equation of circle is
$$x^2 + y^2 - 46x + 22y + 0 = 0$$
$\implies$ $x^2 + y^2 - 46x + 22y = 0$

37. Given circles are $x^2 + y^2 - 1 = 0 \qquad \text{...(i)}$
$$x^2 + y^2 - 2x - 6y - 6 = 0 \qquad \text{...(ii)}$$
and $x^2 + y^2 - 4x - 12y - 9 = 0 \qquad \text{...(iii)}$

Let r_1, r_2 and r_3 be the radii of circles (i), (ii) and (iii), respectively.
We know that, the general form of the circle is
$$x^2 + y^2 + 2gx + 2fy + c = 0 \qquad \text{...(iv)}$$
Now, comparing Eq. (i) with Eq. (iv), we get
$$2g = 0 \implies g = 0 \text{ and } 2f = 0$$
$\implies$ $f = 0$ and $c = -1$
$\therefore$ Radius $(r_1) = \sqrt{g^2 + f^2 - c} = \sqrt{0^2 - 0^2 - (-1)} = 1$ unit
On comparing Eq. (ii) with Eq. (iv), we get
$$2g = -2 \implies g = -1 \text{ and } 2f = -6$$
$\implies$ $f = -3$ and $c = -6$
$\therefore$ Radius $(r_2) = \sqrt{g^2 + f^2 - c} = \sqrt{(-1)^2 + (-3)^2 + 6}$
$$= \sqrt{1 + 9 + 6} = \sqrt{16} = 4 \text{ units}$$
Again, comparing Eq. (iii) with Eq. (iv), we get
$$2g = -4 \implies g = -2$$
$$2f = -12 \implies f = -6 \text{ and } c = -9$$
$\therefore$ Radius $(r_3) = \sqrt{g^2 + f^2 - c} = \sqrt{(-2)^2 + (-6)^2 - (-9)}$
$$= \sqrt{4 + 36 + 9} = \sqrt{49} = 7 \text{ units}$$
Now, the required sum $= r_1 + r_2 + r_3 = 1 + 4 + 7 = 12$ units

38. Let equation of the circle passing through the given points be
$$x^2 + y^2 + 2gx + 2fy + c = 0 \qquad \text{...(i)}$$
Since, the circle passes through the point $(2, -6)$.
On, putting $x = 2$ and $y = -6$ in Eq. (i), we get
$$4 + 36 + 4g - 12f + c = 0$$
$\implies$ $4g - 12f + c = -40 \qquad \text{...(ii)}$
Also, the circle passes through the point $(6, 4)$.
On, putting $x = 6$ and $y = 4$ in Eq. (i), we get
$$36 + 16 + 12g + 8f + c = 0$$
$\implies$ $12g + 8f + c = -52 \qquad \text{...(iii)}$
Also, the circle passes through the point $(-3, 1)$.
On putting $x = -3$ and $y = 1$ in Eq. (i), we get
$$9 + 1 - 6g + 2f + c = 0$$
$\implies$ $-6g + 2f + c = -10 \qquad \text{...(iv)}$
On subtracting Eq. (iii) from Eq. (ii), we get
$$-8g - 20f = 12 \qquad \text{...(v)}$$
On subtracting Eq. (iv) from Eq. (iii), we get
$$18g + 6f = -42 \qquad \text{...(vi)}$$
On solving Eqs. (v) and (vi) for g and f, we get
$$g = -\frac{32}{13} \text{ and } f = \frac{5}{13}$$
On putting the values of g and f in Eq. (ii), we get
$$c = -\frac{332}{13}$$
Now, putting $g = -\dfrac{32}{13}$ and $f = \dfrac{5}{13}$ and $c = -\dfrac{332}{13}$ in Eq. (i),
we get
$$x^2 + y^2 - \frac{64}{13}x + \frac{10}{13}y - \frac{332}{13} = 0$$
$\implies$ $13x^2 + 13y^2 - 64x + 10y - 332 = 0$
which is the required equation of circle.

39. Let the sides AB, BC and CA of $\triangle ABC$ be represented by the equations $x + y = 2$, $3x - 4y = 6$ and $x - y = 0$, respectively.

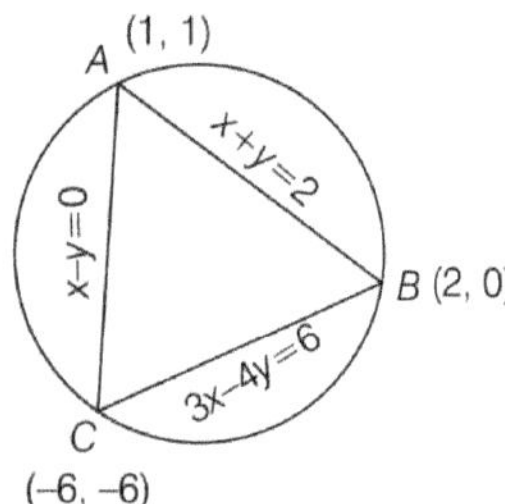

On solving $x + y = 2$ and $3x - 4y = 6$, we get $B(2, 0)$

On solving $3x - 4y = 6$ and $x - y = 0$, we get $C(- 6, - 6)$

On solving $x + y = 2$ and $x - y = 0$, we get $A(1, 1)$

Let the required equation of the circle be

$$x^2 + y^2 + 2gx + 2fy + c = 0 \qquad \ldots(i)$$

Since, it passes through $A(1, 1)$, $B(2, 0)$ and $C(- 6, - 6)$, so each of these points satisfy Eq. (i).

$\therefore \qquad (1)^2 + (1)^2 + 2g + 2f + c = 0$

$\Rightarrow \qquad\qquad 2g + 2f + c = - 2 \qquad \ldots(ii)$

$\Rightarrow \qquad 2^2 + 0^2 + 4g + c = 0$

$\Rightarrow \qquad\qquad 4g + c + 4 = 0 \qquad \ldots(iii)$

and $\quad (- 6)^2 + (- 6)^2 - 12g - 12f + c = 0$

$\Rightarrow \qquad\qquad 12g + 12f - c = 72 \qquad \ldots(iv)$

On subtracting Eqs. (ii) from (iii), we get

$$2g - 2f + 2 = 0 \Rightarrow g - f = - 1 \qquad \ldots(v)$$

On adding Eq. (iv) and Eq. (iii), we get

$$16g + 12f - 68 = 0 \Rightarrow 4g + 3f = 17 \qquad \ldots(vi)$$

On solving Eqs. (v) and (vi), we get $g = 2$ and $f = 3$

On putting $g = 2$ in Eq. (iii), we get $c = - 12$

Hence, the required equation of circle is

$$x^2 + y^2 + 4x + 6y - 12 = 0$$

40. (i) Given, equation of parabola is $y^2 = 12x$

which is of the form, $y^2 = 4ax$ i.e focus lies on the positive direction of X-axis.

Here, $\quad 4a = 12 \Rightarrow a = 3$

$\therefore \qquad$ Focus $= (a, 0) = (3, 0)$

Axis $= X$-axis

Directrix, $x = - a \Rightarrow x = - 3$

and length of latusrectum $= 4a = 4 \times 3 = 12$ units

(ii) Given, equation of parabola is $y^2 = - 8x$ which is of the form $y^2 = - 4ax$ i.e. focus lies on the negative direction of X-axis.

Here, $\quad 4a = 8 \Rightarrow a = 2$

$\therefore \qquad$ Focus $= (- a, 0) = (- 2, 0)$

Axis $= X$-axis

Directrix, $x = a \Rightarrow x = 2$

and length of latusrectum $= 4a = 4 \times 2 = 8$ units

(iii) Given, equation of parabola is $y^2 = 10x$, which is of the form $y^2 = 4ax$ i.e. focus lies on the positive direction of X-axis.

Here, $\quad 4a = 10 \Rightarrow a = \dfrac{5}{2}$

$\therefore \qquad$ Focus $= (a, 0) = \left(\dfrac{5}{2}, 0\right)$

Axis $= X$-axis

Directrix, $x = - a \Rightarrow x = -\dfrac{5}{2}$

and length of latusrectum $= 4a = 4 \times \dfrac{5}{2} = 10$ units

(iv) Given, equation of parabola is $x^2 = - 9y$, which is of the form $x^2 = - 4ay$ i.e. focus lies on the negative direction of Y-axis.

Here, $\quad 4a = 9 \Rightarrow a = \dfrac{9}{4}$

$\therefore \qquad$ Focus $= (0, - a) = \left(0, -\dfrac{9}{4}\right)$

Axis $= Y$-axis

Directrix, $y = a \Rightarrow y = \dfrac{9}{4}$

and length of latusrectum $= 4a = 4 \times \dfrac{9}{4} = 9$ units

41. (i) Given, equation of parabola is $5y^2 = - 16x$

or $y^2 = - \dfrac{16}{5}x$, which is of the form $y^2 = - 4ax$.

Here, $\quad 4a = \dfrac{16}{5}$

$\Rightarrow \qquad a = \dfrac{4}{5}$

$\therefore \qquad$ Focus $= (- a, 0) = \left(-\dfrac{4}{5}, 0\right)$

Axis $= X$-axis

Directrix, $x = a$

$\Rightarrow \qquad x = \dfrac{4}{5}$

and length of latusrectum $= 4a$

$$= 4 \times \dfrac{4}{5} = \dfrac{16}{5} \text{ units}$$

(ii) Given, equation of parabola is $x^2 = 10y$, which is of the form $x^2 = 4ay$.

Here, $\quad 4a = 10$

$\Rightarrow \qquad a = \dfrac{5}{2}$

$\therefore \qquad$ Focus $= (0, a) = \left(0, \dfrac{5}{2}\right)$

Axis $= Y$-axis

Directrix, $y = - a$

$\Rightarrow \qquad y = -\dfrac{5}{2}$

and length of latusrectum $= 4a$

$$= 4 \times \dfrac{5}{2}$$

$$= 10 \text{ units}$$

(iii) Given, equation of parabola is $3x^2 = 8y$ or $x^2 = \dfrac{8}{3}y$, which is of the form $x^2 = 4ay$.

Here, $\quad 4a = \dfrac{8}{3}$

$\Rightarrow \qquad a = \dfrac{2}{3}$

$\therefore \quad$ Focus $= (0, a) = \left(0, \dfrac{2}{3}\right)$

$\qquad$ Axis $= Y$-axis

Directrix, $y = -a$

$\Rightarrow \qquad y = -\dfrac{2}{3}$

and length of latusrectum $= 4a = 4 \times \dfrac{2}{3} = \dfrac{8}{3}$ units

42. Here, axis is vertical, so let arch of parabola is in the form

$$x^2 = 4ay \qquad \qquad \dots(i)$$

Given, $\quad OB = 10\,$m

and $\qquad AC = 5\,$m

$\Rightarrow \qquad AB = \dfrac{5}{2}\,$m $\qquad \left[\because AB = BC = \dfrac{BC}{2}\right]$

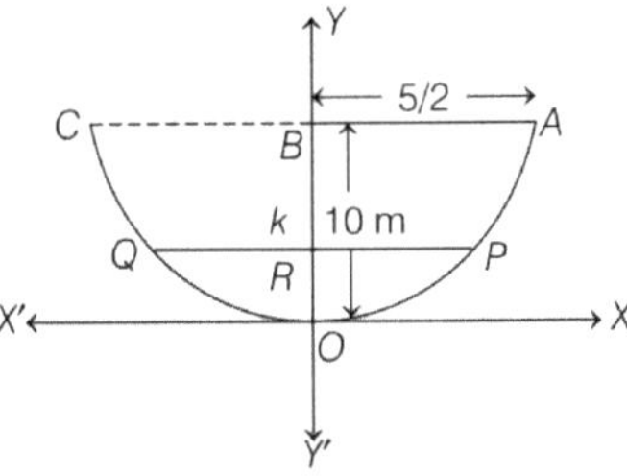

Hence, coordinates of $A = \left(\dfrac{5}{2}, 10\right)$ will satisfy Eq. (i).

i.e. $\qquad \left(\dfrac{5}{2}\right)^2 = 4a \times 10$

$\Rightarrow \qquad \dfrac{25}{4} = 40a$

$\Rightarrow \qquad a = \dfrac{5}{32}$

From Eq. (i), $\quad x^2 = 4 \times \dfrac{5}{32}\,y$

$\Rightarrow \qquad x^2 = \dfrac{5}{8}\,y$

Now, let $\quad OR = 2$ and $PQ = k$

$\Rightarrow \qquad RP = \dfrac{k}{2}$

Therefore, $P = \left(\dfrac{k}{2}, 2\right)$ will lie on parabola.

$\therefore \qquad \left(\dfrac{k}{2}\right)^2 = \dfrac{5}{8} \times 2$

$\Rightarrow \qquad \dfrac{k^2}{4} = \dfrac{5}{4}$

$\Rightarrow \qquad k = \sqrt{5} = 2.23\,$m (approx.)

43. (i) Given, equation of the parabola is $y^2 = 11x$, which is of the form $y^2 = 4ax$.

Here, $\quad 4a = 11 \Rightarrow a = \dfrac{11}{4}$

$\therefore \quad$ Vertex $= V(0, 0)$

$\qquad$ Axis $= X$-axis

$\qquad$ Focus $= F(a, 0) = F\left(\dfrac{11}{4}, 0\right)$

Directrix, $x = -a \Rightarrow x = -\dfrac{11}{4}$

Length of latusrectum $= 4a = 4\left(\dfrac{11}{4}\right) = 11$ units

Coordinates of latusrectum $= (a, \pm 2a) = \left(\dfrac{11}{4}, \pm \dfrac{11}{2}\right)$

Equation of latusrectum, $x = a \Rightarrow x = \dfrac{11}{4}$

(ii) Given, equation of the parabola is $3y^2 = x$ or $y^2 = \dfrac{1}{3}x$, which is of the form $y^2 = 4ax$.

Here, $\quad 4a = \dfrac{1}{3} \Rightarrow a = \dfrac{1}{12}$

$\therefore \quad$ Vertex $= V(0, 0)$

$\qquad$ Axis $= X$-axis

$\qquad$ Focus $= F(a, 0) = F\left(\dfrac{1}{12}, 0\right)$

Directrix, $x = -a \Rightarrow x = -\dfrac{1}{12}$

Length of latusrectum $= 4a = 4\left(\dfrac{1}{12}\right) = \dfrac{1}{3}$ units

Coordinates of latusrectum $= (a, \pm 2a) = \left(\dfrac{1}{3}, \pm \dfrac{2}{3}\right)$

Equation of latusrectum, $x = a \Rightarrow x = \dfrac{1}{12}$

(iii) Let POQ be the parabolic reflector which is 20 cm in diameter and 5 cm deep.

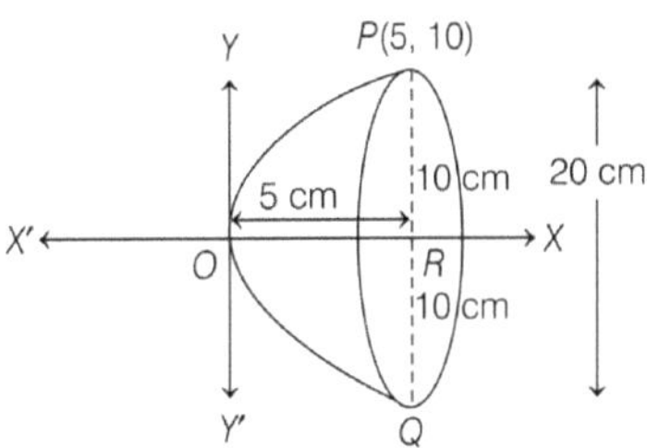

Then, $PQ = 20\,$cm and $OR = 5\,$cm, where R is the mid-point of PQ. We take OX as X-axis and OY as Y-axis.

The equation of parabola may be taken as $y^2 = 4ax$.

Since, the point $P(5, 10)$ lies on the parabola.

$\therefore \qquad 10^2 = 4a(5) \Rightarrow a = 5$

Therefore, the coordinate of the focus are $(a, 0)$ i.e. $(5, 0)$.

Hence, the focus is the mid-point of the given diameter.

Chapter Test

Multiple Choice Questions

1. The centre and radius of a circle
$x^2 + y^2 + 4x + 4y - 1 = 0$ is
(a) 3 units   (b) 4 units   (c) 6 units   (d) 9 units

2. The centre of the circle $x^2 + y^2 + 16x + 8y + 15 = 0$ is
(h, k), then the value of $k - h$ is
(a) 8   (b) 4   (c) 12   (d) 0

3. If the equation of circle is $x^2 + y^2 - 10x + 16y + 50 = 0$,
then its centre and radius respectively, are
(a) (2, 4) and $\sqrt{65}$ units   (b) (5, – 8) and $\sqrt{39}$ units
(c) (–8, 5) and $\sqrt{39}$ units   (d) (– 5, – 8) and $\sqrt{65}$ units

4. The equation of the circle, whose end points of a
diameter are $A(1, 2)$ and $B(3, -1)$, is given by
(a) $x^2 + y^2 + 4x + y - 1 = 0$ (b) $x^2 + y^2 - 4x - y + 1 = 0$
(c) $x^2 + y^2 - 4x - y - 1 = 0$ (d) None of these

5. If the parabola $y^2 = 4ax$ passes through the point $(8, 3)$,
then the length of its latusrectum is
(a) $\dfrac{1}{4}$ unit   (b) $\dfrac{9}{4}$ units   (c) $\dfrac{9}{32}$ unit   (d) $\dfrac{9}{8}$ units

Case Based MCQs

6. A beam is supported at its ends by supports which are
10 m apart. Since, the load is concentrated at the
centre, there is a deflection of 2 cm at the centre and
the deflected beam is the shape of a parabola.

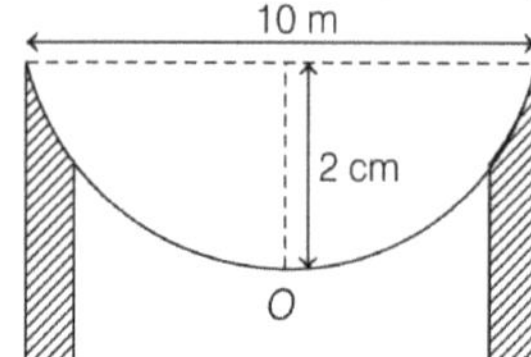

Based on the above information, answer the following
questions.

(i) The equation of parabola is
(a) $x^2 = -1250y$ (b) $x^2 = 1250y$
(c) $y^2 = 1250x$ (d) $y^2 = -1250x$

(ii) The coordinates of focus of the parabola are
(a) (0, 1250)   (b) $\left(\dfrac{625}{2}, 0\right)$
(c) $\left(0, \dfrac{625}{2}\right)$ (d) (1250, 0)

(iii) The equation of directrix of the parabola is
(a) $2y + 625 = 0$ (b) $2y - 625 = 0$
(c) $y = 625$ (d) $y = -500$

(iv) Length of latusrectum of the parabola is
(a) 550 m   (b) 600 m
(c) 625 m   (d) 1250 m

(v) The equation of circle with centre at focus of the
parabola and radius equal to the length of latusrectum
is

(a) $(x - 0)^2 + \left(y - \dfrac{625}{2}\right)^2 = (1250)^2$

(b) $(x - 0)^2 + \left(y + \dfrac{625}{2}\right)^2 = (1250)^2$

(c) $(x - 0)^2 + (y - 625)^2 = (1200)^2$

(d) None of the above

Short Answer Type Questions

7. Find the equation of the circle having $(-2, 1)$ as its
centre and passing through $3x + y = 10$ and $x + y = 6$.

8. Find the equation of the circle passing through the
point (4, 1) and having its centre at the intersection of
the lines $2x + y = 1$ and $x + 3y = 8$.

9. A circle of radius 1 unit touches the coordinate axes in
the first quadrant. If the circle makes one complete roll
on X-axis along the positive direction of X-axis. Find its
equation in the new position.

10. If one end of a diameter of the circle
$x^2 + y^2 + 4x + 8y + 15 = 0$ is (1, 2), then find the
coordinates of the other end of the diameter.

11. Find the coordinates of a point on the parabola
$y^2 = 8x$, whose focal distance is 4 units.

12. For the parabola $y^2 = -20x$, find the coordinates of
vertex, coordinates of focus, equation of directrix, axis
of the parabola and length of the latusrectum.

Long Answer Type Questions

13. Find the equation of a circle passing through the point
(7, 3) having radius 3 units and whose centre lies on
the line $y = x - 1$.

14. In each of the following questions, find the coordinates
of the focus, axis of the parabola, the equation of the
directrix and the length of the latusrectum.
(i) $y^2 = 8x$ (ii) $y^2 = -16x$ (iii) $x^2 = -16y$ (iv) $x^2 = 36y$

Answers

1. (a)   *2.* (b)   *3.* (b)   *4.* (b)   *5.* (d)

6. (i) (b)   (ii) (c)   (iii) (a)   (iv) (d)   (v) (a)

7. $x^2 + y^2 + 4x - 2y - 20 = 0$ *8.* $x^2 + y^2 + 2x - 6y - 19 = 0$

9. $x^2 + y^2 - 2x(1 + 2\pi) - 2y + 4\pi^2 + 4\pi + 1 = 0$ *10.* $(-5, -10)$

11. $(2, 4)$ and $(2, -4)$

12. Vertex $= (0, 0)$, Focus $= (-5, 0)$, Directrix $= 5$, Axis $= X$-axis and
Length of latusrectum $= 20$ units

13. $x^2 + y^2 - 8x - 6y + 16 = 0$

14. (i) Focus $= (2, 0)$, Axis $= X$-axis, Directrix $= -2$,
and Length of latusrectum $= 8$ units

(ii) Focus $= (-4, 0)$, Axis $= X$-axis, Directrix $= 4$,
and Length of latusrectum $= 16$ units

(iii) Focus $= (0, -4)$, Axis $= Y$-axis, Directrix $= 4$,
and Length of latusrectum $= 16$ units

(iv) Focus $= (0, 9)$, Axis $= Y$-axis, Directrix $= -9$,
and Length of latusrectum $= 36$ units

For Detailed Solutions

Scan the code

CBSE Term II
Applied
Mathemtics XI

Practice Papers
1-3

Practice Paper 1*
(Solved)

Instructions

- Time : 2 Hr
- Max. Marks : 40

1. The question paper contains three sections A, B and C.
2. Section A has 5 questions with 3 internal choices.
3. Section B has 4 questions with 3 internal choices.
4. Section C has 1 Case Based MCQs comprises of 5 MCQs.
5. There is no negative marking.

As exact Blue-print and Pattern for CBSE Term II exams is not released yet. So the pattern of this paper is designed by the author on the basis of trend of past CBSE Papers. Students are advised not to consider the pattern of this paper as official.

Section A
(3 Marks Each)

This section consists of 5 questions of Short Answer Type.

1. If $P(A) = \dfrac{6}{11}$, $P(B) = \dfrac{5}{11}$ and $P(A \cup B) = \dfrac{7}{11}$, then find

    (i) $P(A \cap B)$ (ii) $P(A/B)$ (iii) $P(B/A)$.

    Or

    A bag contains 19 tickets, numbered from 1 to 19. A ticket is drawn and then another ticket is drawn without replacement. Find the probability that both tickets will show even numbers.

2. If $\dfrac{n!}{2!(n-2)!}$ and $\dfrac{n!}{4!(n-4)!}$ are in the ratio $2:1$, then find the value of n.

3. How many words, with or without meaning, can be formed using all the letters of the word EQUATION at a time so that the vowels and consonant occurs together?

    Or

    We wish to select 6 persons from 8 but, if the person A is chosen, then B must be chosen. In how many ways, can the selection be made?

4. Evaluate the left hand and right hand limits of the following function at $x = 2$.

$$f(x) = \begin{cases} 2x + 3, & \text{if } x \leq 2 \\ x + 5, & \text{if } x > 2 \end{cases}$$

    Does $\lim\limits_{x \to 2} f(x)$ exist?

Or

If $y = \dfrac{x}{x+5}$, then prove that $x\,\dfrac{dy}{dx} = y\,(1-y)$.

5. The compound interest is ₹ 6.40 more than the simple interest, if a sum is lent for 2 yr at 8% compound interest. Find the sum.

Section B
(5 Marks Each)

This section consists of 4 questions of Long Answer Type.

6. Differentiate $\dfrac{x^2 + 3x - 9}{x^2 - 9x + 3}$ w.r.t. x.

Or

If $f(x) = \begin{cases} |x|+1 & , & x < 0 \\ 0 & , & x = 0, \\ |x|-1 & , & x > 0 \end{cases}$ for what value(s) of a does $\lim\limits_{x \to a} f(x)$ exist?

7. The line through the points $(h, 3)$ and $(4, 1)$ intersects the line $7x - 9y - 19 = 0$ at right angle. Find the value of h.

Or

Find the equation of the circle passing through the vertices of a triangle whose sides are represented by the equations $x + y = 2$, $3x - 4y = 6$ and $x - y = 0$.

8. A retailer buys a TV set for ₹ 40000 from a wholesaler at a discount of 20% on the printed price and sells it to a consumer at the printed price. If the sales are intra-state and the rate of GST is 12%, find
  (i) the price, including GST, at which TV set was bought by the retailer.
 (ii) the price at which the consumer bought the TV set.
(iii) the GST paid by the retailer.

9. (i) Find the compound interest on ₹ 2000 at 15% per annum for 2 yr 4 months compounded annually.
  (ii) If person wants to accumulate ₹ 50000 by making equal payments at the end of each quarter for the next 5 yr, what will be the size of these investments, if money is worth 6% converted quarterly? (given $(1.015)^{20} = 1.343$)

Or

Find the amount and present value of an annuity due of ₹ 500 per quarter for 8 yr and 9 months at 6% compounded quarterly.

Section C
(1 Mark Each)

This section consists of 1 Case Based comprises of 5 MCQs.

10. In a school, teacher ask a question to three students Ravi, Mohit and Sonia. The probability of solving the question by Ravi, Mohit and Sonia are 30%, 25% and 45% respectively. The probability of making error by Ravi, Mohit and Sonia are 1%, 1.2% and 2% respectively.

Based on the above information, answer the following questions.

(i) The conditional probability that an error is committed in solving question given that question is solved by Sonia, is

    (a) 0.001   (b) 0.012
    (c) 0.02   (d) 0.027

(ii) The probability that Sonia solved the question and committed an error is

    (a) 0.008   (b) 0.009
    (c) 0.010   (d) 0.011

(iii) The total probability of committing an error in solving the question is

    (a) 0.15   (b) 0.10
    (c) 0.05   (d) 0.01

(iv) If the solution of question is checked by teacher and has some error, then the probability that the question is not solved by Ravi is

    (a) 0.02   (b) 0.98
    (c) 0.04   (d) 0.96

(v) Let A be the event of committing an error in solving the question and let E_1, E_2 and E_3 be the events that Ravi, Mohit and Sonia solved the question. The value of $\sum_{i=1}^{3} P(E_i / A)$ is

    (a) 3   (b) 5
    (c) 1   (d) 9

Solutions

1. Given, $P(A) = \dfrac{6}{11}$, $P(B) = \dfrac{5}{11}$ and $P(A \cup B) = \dfrac{7}{11}$

(i) $P(A \cup B) = P(A) + P(B) - P(A \cap B)$

$\Rightarrow \quad \dfrac{7}{11} = \dfrac{6}{11} + \dfrac{5}{11} - P(A \cap B)$

$\Rightarrow \quad P(A \cap B) = \dfrac{6}{11} + \dfrac{5}{11} - \dfrac{7}{11} = \dfrac{4}{11}$

$\therefore \quad P(A \cap B) = \dfrac{4}{11}$

(ii) $P\left(\dfrac{A}{B}\right) = \dfrac{P(A \cap B)}{P(B)} = \dfrac{4/11}{5/11} = \dfrac{4}{5}$

(iii) $P\left(\dfrac{B}{A}\right) = \dfrac{P(A \cap B)}{P(A)} = \dfrac{4/11}{6/11} = \dfrac{4}{6} = \dfrac{2}{3}$

Or

Let A be the event of drawing an even numbered ticket in first draw and B be the event of drawing an even numbered ticket in the second draw.

Then, required probability $= P(A \cap B)$

$$= P(A) \cdot P(B/A) \qquad \ldots(i)$$

Since, there are 19 tickets numbered 1 to 19 in the bag, out of which 9 are even numbered *viz.* 2, 4, 6, 8, 10, 12, 14, 16 and 18.

Therefore, $\quad P(A) = \dfrac{9}{19}$

Since, the ticket drawn in the first draw is not replaced, therefore second ticket drawn is from the remaining 18 tickets, out of which 8 are even numbered.

$\therefore \qquad P\left(\dfrac{B}{A}\right) = \dfrac{8}{18} = \dfrac{4}{9}$

Hence, required probability $= P(A \cap B)$

$$= P(A) \cdot P(B/A) \ \text{[from Eq. (i)]}$$
$$= \dfrac{9}{19} \times \dfrac{4}{9} = \dfrac{4}{19}$$

2. We have, $\quad \dfrac{n!}{2!\,(n-2)!} : \dfrac{n!}{4!\,(n-4)!} = 2 : 1$

$\Rightarrow \quad \dfrac{n!}{2!\,(n-2)!} \times \dfrac{4!\,(n-4)!}{n!} = \dfrac{2}{1} \Rightarrow \dfrac{4!\,(n-4)!}{2!\,(n-2)!} = 2$

$\Rightarrow \quad \dfrac{4 \times 3 \times 2! \times (n-4)!}{2! \times (n-2)(n-3)(n-4)!} = 2$

$\Rightarrow \quad \dfrac{12}{(n-2)(n-3)} = 2$

$\Rightarrow \quad 12 = 2(n-2)(n-3)$

$\Rightarrow \quad 12 = 2(n^2 - 5n + 6)$

$\Rightarrow \quad 6 = n^2 - 5n + 6$

$\Rightarrow \quad n^2 - 5n = 0$

$\Rightarrow \quad n(n-5) = 0$

$\Rightarrow \quad n = 0 \text{ or } 5$

When $n = 0$, then $(n-2)!$ and $(n-4)!$ are not defined, so rejecting $n = 0$.

$\therefore \qquad n = 5$

3. There 8 distinct letters in the word EQUATION, out of which 5 are vowels, namely A, E, I, O, U and 3 are consonants namely Q, T, N.

Now, let us take all vowels together as one object and all consonants together as another object.

(A, E, I, O, U) (Q, T, N)

Clearly, these objects can be arranged in $2! = 2$ ways.

Again, all vowels taken together can be arranged in $5! = 120$ ways and all consonants taken together can be arranged in $3! = 6$ ways.

Hence, by fundamental principle of multiplication required number of words $= 2 \times 5! \times 3!$

$$= 2 \times 120 \times 6 = 1440$$

Or

Let us make the following cases and find the number of possible selection in each case.

Case I When A is chosen

In this case B must be chosen also. So, we have to choose 4 persons out of 6 persons. This can be done in

$$^6C_4 = {}^6C_2 = \dfrac{6 \times 5}{2 \times 1} = 15 \text{ ways.}$$

Case II When A is not chosen

In this case, we have to choose 6 persons out of 7 persons. This can be done in $^7C_6 = {}^7C_1 = 7$ ways.

Hence, total number of ways of selecting 6 persons

$$= 15 + 7 = 22$$

4. Given, $f(x) = \begin{cases} 2x + 3, & \text{if } x \le 2 \\ x + 5, & \text{if } x > 2 \end{cases}$

$\text{LHL} = \lim\limits_{x \to 2^-} f(x) = \lim\limits_{x \to 2^-} 2x + 3$

$$[\because f(x) = 2x + 3, \text{ if } x \le 2]$$

$$= \lim\limits_{h \to 0} [2(2-h) + 3] = 2(2-0) + 3$$

$$[\text{putting } x = 2 - h \text{ and when } x \to 2^-, \text{ then } h \to 0]$$

$$= 4 + 3 = 7$$

and $\quad \text{RHL} = \lim\limits_{x \to 2^+} f(x)$

$$= \lim\limits_{x \to 2^+} (x + 5) \qquad [\because f(x) = x + 5, \text{ if } x > 2]$$

$$= \lim\limits_{h \to 0} (2 + h + 5)$$

$$= 2 + 0 + 5 = 7$$

$$[\text{putting } x = 2 + h \text{ and } x \to 2^+, \text{ then } h \to 0]$$

$\because$ LHL of f (at $x = 2$) = RHL of f (at $x = 2$)

$\therefore \lim\limits_{x \to 2} f(x)$ exists and it is equal to 7.

Or

We have, $\quad y = \dfrac{x}{x+5} \qquad \ldots(i)$

On differentiating both sides of Eq. (i) w.r.t. x, we get

$$\dfrac{dy}{dx} = \dfrac{d}{dx}\left(\dfrac{x}{x+5}\right)$$

$$= \frac{(x+5)\dfrac{d}{dx}x - x\dfrac{d}{dx}(x+5)}{(x+5)^2}$$

$$\left[\because \frac{d}{dx}\left(\frac{u}{v}\right) = \frac{v\dfrac{du}{dx} - u\dfrac{dv}{dx}}{v^2}\right]$$

$$= \frac{(x+5)(1) - x(1+0)}{(x+5)^2} = \frac{x+5-x}{(x+5)^2}$$

$$\Rightarrow \quad \frac{dy}{dx} = \frac{5}{(x+5)^2}$$

Now, $\quad$ LHS $= x\dfrac{dy}{dx} = \dfrac{5x}{(x+5)^2}$ $\qquad$ ...(ii)

and $\quad$ RHS $= y(1-y) = \dfrac{x}{x+5}\left(1 - \dfrac{x}{x+5}\right)$

$$= \frac{x}{x+5}\left(\frac{x+5-x}{x+5}\right) = \frac{5x}{(x+5)^2} \qquad \text{...(iii)}$$

From Eqs. (ii) and (iii), we get

$$x\frac{dy}{dx} = y(1-y) \qquad \textbf{Hence proved.}$$

5. Given, CI $-$ SI $= ₹\,6.40$, $t = 2$ yr and $r = 8\%$

$$\Rightarrow \quad P\left[\left(1+\frac{r}{100}\right)^t - 1\right] - \frac{P \times r \times t}{100} = 6.40$$

$$\Rightarrow \quad P\left[\left(1+\frac{8}{100}\right)^2 - 1\right] - \frac{P \times 8 \times 2}{100} = 6.40$$

$$\Rightarrow \quad P\left[\left(\frac{27}{25}\right)^2 - 1\right] - \frac{16P}{100} = 6.40$$

$$\Rightarrow \quad P\left[\frac{(27)^2 - (25)^2}{625}\right] - \frac{16P}{100} = 6.40$$

$$\Rightarrow \quad \frac{104P}{625} - \frac{16P}{100} = 6.40$$

$$\Rightarrow \quad \frac{416P - 400P}{2500} = 6.40$$

$$\Rightarrow \quad 16P = 6.40 \times 2500$$

$$\Rightarrow \quad P = \frac{6.40 \times 2500}{16} = ₹\,1000$$

6. Let $y = \dfrac{x^2 + 3x - 9}{x^2 - 9x + 3}$

On differentiating both sides w.r.t. x, we get

$$\frac{dy}{dx} = \frac{d}{dx}\left[\frac{x^2 + 3x - 9}{x^2 - 9x + 3}\right]$$

$$= \frac{\left\{(x^2 - 9x + 3)\left[\dfrac{d}{dx}(x^2 + 3x - 9)\right] - (x^2 + 3x - 9)\dfrac{d}{dx}(x^2 - 9x + 3)\right\}}{(x^2 - 9x + 3)^2}$$

[using quotient rule of derivative]

$$= \frac{\left[(x^2 - 9x + 3)(2x + 3 - 0) - (x^2 + 3x - 9) \times (2x - 9 + 0)\right]}{(x^2 - 9x + 3)^2}$$

$$= \frac{[(x^2 - 9x + 3)(2x + 3) - (x^2 + 3x - 9)(2x - 9)]}{(x^2 - 9x + 3)^2}$$

$$= \frac{\left[2x(x^2 - 9x + 3) + 3(x^2 - 9x + 3) - 2x(x^2 + 3x - 9) + 9(x^2 + 3x - 9)\right]}{(x^2 - 9x + 3)^2}$$

$$= \frac{\left[2x(x^2 - 9x + 3 - x^2 - 3x + 9) + (3x^2 - 27x + 9 + 9x^2 + 27x - 81)\right]}{(x^2 - 9x + 3)^2}$$

$$= \frac{2x(-12x + 12) + (12x^2 - 72)}{(x^2 - 9x + 3)^2}$$

$$= \frac{-24x^2 + 24x + 12x^2 - 72}{(x^2 - 9x + 3)^2}$$

$$= \frac{-12x^2 + 24x - 72}{(x^2 - 9x + 3)^2} = \frac{-12(x^2 - 2x + 6)}{(x^2 - 9x + 3)^2}$$

Or

We have, $f(x) = \begin{cases} -x+1, & x < 0 \\ 0, & x = 0 \\ x-1, & x > 0 \end{cases}$ $\qquad \left[\because |x| = \begin{cases} x, & \text{if } x \geq 0 \\ -x, & \text{if } x < 0 \end{cases}\right]$

Case I When $a = 0$

In this case,

$$\text{LHL} = \lim_{h \to 0^-} f(x) = \lim_{h \to 0} f(0 - h)$$

$$= \lim_{h \to 0} -(0 - h) + 1$$

$$[\because \text{for } x < 0, \ f(x) = -x + 1]$$

$$= \lim_{h \to 0}(h + 1) = \lim_{h \to 0} h + \lim_{h \to 0} 1$$

$$= 0 + 1 = 1$$

and $\text{RHL} = \lim_{x \to 0^+} f(x) = \lim_{h \to 0} f(0 + h)$

$$= \lim_{h \to 0} f(0 + h) - 1 = -1 \quad [\because \text{for } x > 0, f(x) = x - 1]$$

$\therefore \quad$ LHL $\neq$ RHL

$\because$ For $a = 0$, $\lim\limits_{x \to a} f(x)$ does not exists.

Case II When $a < 0$

In this case, $\lim\limits_{x \to a} f(x) = \lim\limits_{x \to a}(-x + 1)$

$$[\because \text{for } x < 0, \ f(x) = -x + 1]$$

$$= -a + 1, \text{ which is a fixed real number.}$$

$\therefore$ For $a < 0$, $\lim\limits_{x \to a} f(x)$ exists.

Case III When $a > 0$

In this case, $\lim\limits_{x \to a} f(x) = \lim\limits_{x \to a}(x - 1)$

$$[\because \text{for } x > 0, f(x) = x - 1]$$

$$= a - 1, \text{ which is a fixed real number.}$$

$\therefore$ For $a > 0$, $\lim\limits_{x \to a} f(x)$ exists.

Hence, from case I, II and III, we conclude that $\lim\limits_{x \to a} f(x)$ exists for all $a \neq 0$.

7. Equation of line through $(h, 3)$ and $(4, 1)$ is given by

$$y - y_1 = \frac{y_2 - y_1}{x_2 - x_1}(x - x_1)$$

$$\Rightarrow \quad y - 3 = \frac{1 - 3}{4 - h}(x - h)$$

$$[\because x_1 = h, y_1 = 3, x_2 = 4 \text{ and } y_2 = 1]$$

$$\Rightarrow \quad y - 3 = \frac{-2}{4 - h}(x - h)$$

$$\Rightarrow \quad y - 3 = -\frac{2x}{4 - h} + \frac{2h}{4 - h}$$

$$\Rightarrow \quad y = -\frac{2x}{4 - h} + \left(3 + \frac{2h}{4 - h}\right) \qquad \ldots(i)$$

Given, equation of line is

$$7x - 9y - 19 = 0$$

$$\Rightarrow \quad y = \frac{7}{9}x - \frac{19}{9} \qquad \ldots(ii)$$

On comparing Eqs. (i) and (ii) with $y = mx + c$, we get

$$m_1 = -\frac{2}{4 - h}$$

and $\qquad m_2 = \frac{7}{9}$

$\because$ Lines (i) and (ii) are perpendicular to each other

$\therefore$ Slope of line (i) $\times$ Slope of line (ii) $= -1$

i.e. $\qquad m_1 m_2 = -1$

$$\Rightarrow \quad -\frac{2}{4 - h} \times \frac{7}{9} = -1$$

$$\Rightarrow \quad 14 = 9(4 - h)$$

$$\Rightarrow \quad 14 = 36 - 9h$$

$$\Rightarrow \quad 9h = 22$$

$$\Rightarrow \quad h = \frac{22}{9}$$

Or

Let the sides AB, BC and CA of $\triangle ABC$ be represented by the equations $x + y = 2$, $3x - 4y = 6$ and $x - y = 0$, respectively.

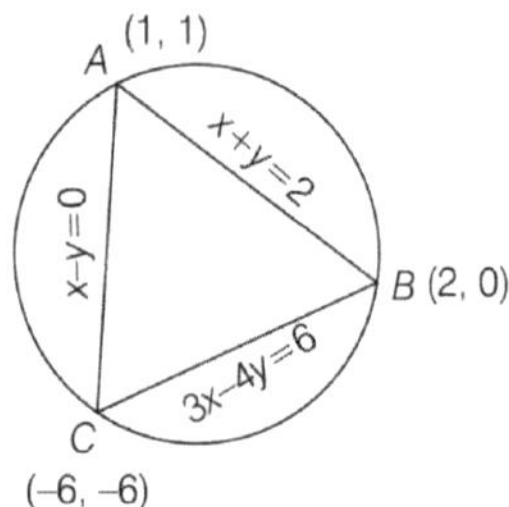

On solving $x + y = 2$ and $3x - 4y = 6$, we get $B(2, 0)$

On solving $3x - 4y = 6$ and $x - y = 0$, we get $C(-6, -6)$

On solving $x + y = 2$ and $x - y = 0$, we get $A(1, 1)$

Let the required equation of the circle be

$$x^2 + y^2 + 2gx + 2fy + c = 0 \qquad \ldots(i)$$

Since, it passes through $A(1, 1)$, $B(2, 0)$ and $C(-6, -6)$, so each of these points satisfy Eq. (i).

$\therefore \qquad (1)^2 + (1)^2 + 2g + 2f + c = 0$

$$\Rightarrow \quad 2g + 2f + c = -2 \qquad \ldots(ii)$$

$$(2)^2 + (0)^2 + 4g + c = 0$$

$$\Rightarrow \quad 4g + c + 4 = 0 \qquad \ldots(iii)$$

and $(-6)^2 + (-6)^2 - 12g - 12f + c = 0$

$$\Rightarrow \quad 12g + 12f - c = 72 \qquad \ldots(iv)$$

On subtracting Eq. (ii) from Eq. (iii), we get

$$2g - 2f + 2 = 0$$

$$\Rightarrow \quad g - f = -1 \qquad \ldots(v)$$

On adding Eq. (iv) and Eq. (iii), we get

$$16g + 12f - 68 = 0 \Rightarrow 4g + 3f = 17 \qquad \ldots(vi)$$

On solving Eqs. (v) and (vi), we get

$$g = 2 \text{ and } f = 3$$

On putting $g = 2$ in Eq. (iii), we get

$$c = -12$$

Hence, the required equation of circle is

$$x^2 + y^2 + 4x + 6y - 12 = 0$$

8. (i) Here, discount $= ₹\left(\dfrac{20}{100} \times 40000\right) = ₹\, 8000$

Net price of TV set $= ₹\,(40000 - 8000) = ₹\, 32000$

SGST paid by the retailer to the wholesaler

$$= ₹\left(\frac{6}{100} \times 32000\right) = ₹\, 1920$$

CGST paid by the retailer to the wholesaler

$$= ₹\left(\frac{6}{100} \times 32000\right) = ₹\, 1920$$

GST paid by the retailer (or Input GST of retailer)

$$= \text{SGST} + \text{CGST}$$

$$= ₹\,(1920 + 1920) = ₹\, 3840$$

$\therefore$ Price at which TV set was bought by the retailer

$$= \text{Net price of TV set} + \text{GST}$$

$$= ₹\,(32000 + 3840) = ₹\, 35840$$

(ii) $\therefore$ SGST paid by consumer to the retailer

$$= 6\% \text{ of } ₹\, 40000$$

$$= ₹\left(\frac{6}{100} \times 40000\right)$$

$$= ₹\, 2400$$

and CGST paid by the consumer to the retailer

$$= 6\% \text{ of } ₹\, 40000$$

$$= ₹\left(\frac{6}{100} \times 40000\right) = ₹\, 2400$$

GST paid by the consumer to the retailer (or Output CGST of retailer)

$$= \text{SGST} + \text{CGST}$$

$$= ₹\,(2400 + 2400)$$

$$= ₹\, 4800$$

Price at which the consumer bought the TV set

$$= \text{SP of TV set} + \text{GST}$$

$$= ₹\,(40000 + 4800)$$

$$= ₹\, 44800$$

(iii) GST paid by the retailer to the government

$$= \text{Output GST of retailer} - \text{Input GST of retailer}$$

$$= ₹\,(4800 - 3840) = ₹\, 960$$

9. (i) Given that, $P = ₹\,2000$, $n = 2$, $\dfrac{a}{b} = \dfrac{4}{12} = \dfrac{1}{3}$ and $r = 15\%$

Now, according to the formula,

$$\therefore \text{ Amount} = P\left(1 + \frac{r}{100}\right)^n \times \left(1 + \frac{\frac{a}{b}\,r}{100}\right)$$

$$= \left[2000\left(1 + \frac{15}{100}\right)^2 \times \left(1 + \frac{\frac{1}{3} \times 15}{100}\right)\right]$$

$$= 2000 \times \frac{23}{20} \times \frac{23}{20} \times \frac{21}{20} = \frac{11109}{4} = 2777.25$$

$$\therefore \quad \text{CI} = ₹\,(2777.25 - 2000) = ₹\,777.25$$

(ii) Let the size of each payment be $₹\,R$. Then, the amount S is given.

We have, $S = ₹\,50000$, $i = \dfrac{6}{4 \times 100} = 0.015$

and $\quad n = 5 \times 4 = 20$

We know that, $S = R\left\{\dfrac{(1 + i)^n - 1}{i}\right\}$, where i is the interest per period.

$$\therefore 50000 = R\left\{\frac{(1 + 0.015)^{20} - 1}{0.015}\right\}$$

$$\Rightarrow \quad R = \frac{50000 \times 0.015}{(1.015)^{20} - 1} = \frac{750}{1.343 - 1}$$

$$= \frac{750}{0.343} = 2186.58$$

Hence, the size of equal payments is $₹\,2186.58$.

Or

We have, $R = ₹\,500$, $i = \dfrac{6}{400} = 0.015$

and $\quad n = 8 \times 4 + 3 = 35$

We know that,

$$A = R(1 + i)\left[\frac{(1 + i)^n - 1}{i}\right]$$

$$\Rightarrow \quad A = 500(1 + 0.015)\left[\frac{(1.015)^{35} - 1}{0.015}\right]$$

$$\Rightarrow \quad A = 500\,(1.015)\left[\frac{(1.015)^{35} - 1}{0.015}\right] \qquad \ldots\text{(i)}$$

Here, let $x = (1.015)^{35}$

Taking log on both sides, we get

$\Rightarrow \quad \log x = 35\log 1.015 = 35 \times 0.0064 = 0.224$

$\Rightarrow \quad x = \text{antilog}\,0.224$

$\Rightarrow \quad x = 1.675$

$$A = 500(1.015)\left[\frac{1.675 - 1}{0.015}\right] \qquad \text{[from Eq. (i)]}$$

$$= 5075 \times \frac{0.675}{0.015} = 22837.50$$

Hence, amount of annuity due is $₹\,22837.50$.

We know that, $P = R(1 + i)\left[\dfrac{1 - (1 + i)^{-n}}{i}\right]$

$$\therefore \quad P = 500\,(1.015)\left[\frac{1 - (1.015)^{-35}}{0.015}\right] \qquad \ldots\text{(ii)}$$

Here, let $x = (1.015)^{-35}$

$\Rightarrow \quad \log x = -35\log 1.015 = -35 \times 0.0064 = -0.224$

$\Rightarrow \quad x = \text{antilog}\,(-0.224) = \text{antilog}\,(\overline{1}.7760)$

$\Rightarrow \quad x = 0.5970$

$$P = 500 \times (1.015)\left[\frac{1 - 0.5970}{0.015}\right] \qquad \text{[from Eq. (i)]}$$

$$\Rightarrow \quad P = 507.50 \times \frac{0.4030}{0.015} = 13634.83$$

Hence, present value of annuity due is $₹\,13634.83$.

10. Let

$\quad A$: The event that question has some error

$\quad E_1$: The event that question is solved by Ravi

$\quad E_2$: The event that question is solved by Mohit

$\quad E_3$: The event that question is solved by Sonia

Then, we have

$$P(E_1) = \frac{30}{100},\ P(E_2) = \frac{25}{100},\ P(E_3) = \frac{45}{100},$$

$$P(A/E_1) = \frac{1}{100},\ P(A/E_2) = \frac{1.2}{100}\ \text{and}\ P(A/E_3) = \frac{2}{100}$$

(i) (c) $\therefore$ Required probability $= P(A/E_3) = \dfrac{2}{100} = 0.02$

(ii) (b) $\therefore$ Required probability $= P(E_3 \cap A) = P(A \cap E_3)$

$$= P(E_3)\,P(A/E_3)$$

$$= \frac{45}{100} \times \frac{2}{100} = \frac{90}{10000} = 0.009$$

(iii) (a) $\therefore$ Required probability $= P(A)$

$$= \sum_{i=1}^{3} P(E_i)\,P(A/E_i)$$

$$= P(E_1)\,P(A/E_1) + P(E_2)\,P(A/E_2) + P(E_3)\,P(A/E_3)$$

$$= \frac{30}{100} \times \frac{1}{100} + \frac{25}{100} \times \frac{1.2}{100} + \frac{45}{100} \times \frac{2}{100}$$

$$= 0.003 + 0.003 + 0.009 = 0.15$$

(iv) (b) $\therefore$ Required probability $= P(\overline{E}_1/A) = 1 - P(E_1/A)$

$$= 1 - \left[\frac{P(E_1)\,P(A/E_1)}{P(E_1)\,P(A/E_1) + P(E_2)\,P(A/E_2) + P(E_3)\,P(A/E_3)}\right]$$

$$= 1 - \left[\frac{\dfrac{30}{100} \times \dfrac{1}{100}}{\dfrac{30}{100} \times \dfrac{1}{100} + \dfrac{25}{100} \times \dfrac{1.2}{100} + \dfrac{45}{100} \times \dfrac{2}{100}}\right]$$

$$= 1 - \frac{0.003}{0.15} = 1 - 0.02 = 0.98$$

(v) (c) $\displaystyle\sum_{i=1}^{3} P(E_i/A) = \sum_{i=1}^{3} \frac{P(E_i)P(A/E_i)}{P(A)}$

where, $\quad P(A) = \displaystyle\sum_{i=1}^{3} P(E_i)\,P\left(\dfrac{A}{E_i}\right) = \dfrac{P(A)}{P(A)} = 1$

Practice Paper 2*
(Unsolved)

Instructions

■ Time : 2 Hr
■ Max. Marks : 40

1. The question paper contains three sections A, B and C.
2. Section A has 5 questions with 3 internal choices.
3. Section B has 4 questions with 3 internal choices.
4. Section C has 1 Case Based MCQs comprises of 5 MCQs.
5. There is no negative marking.

As exact Blue-print and Pattern for CBSE Term II exams is not released yet. So the pattern of this paper is designed by the author on the basis of trend of past CBSE Papers. Students are advised not to consider the pattern of this paper as official.

Section A

(3 Marks Each)

This section consists of 5 questions of Short Answer Type.

1. Find the relationship between a and b so that the function f defined by $f(x) = \begin{cases} ax + 1, & \text{if } x \le 3 \\ bx + 3, & \text{if } x > 3 \end{cases}$.

Or

If $(x^2 + y^2)^2 = xy$, find $\dfrac{dy}{dx}$.

2. Two cards are drawn at random and without replacement from a pack of 52 playing cards. Find the probability that both the cards are black.

Or

Bag I contains 3 black and 2 white balls, bag II contains 2 black and 4 white balls. A bag and a ball is selected at random. Determine the probability of selecting a black a ball.

3. Find the coordinates of a point on the line $x + y + 3 = 0$, whose distance from the line $x + 2y + 2 = 0$ is $\sqrt{5}$.

Or

Find the equation of the circle passing through two points on Y-axis at distance 3 from the origin and having radius 5.

4. Find the equation of the parabola whose vertex is at $(2, 1)$ and the directrix is $x - y + 1 = 0$.

5. What sum invested for $1\dfrac{1}{2}$ years compounded half-yearly at the rate of 4%. p.a. will amount to ₹ 132651?

Section B

(5 Marks Each)

This section consists of 4 questions of Long Answer Type.

6. Find all points of discontinuity of f, where f is defined by $f(x) = \begin{cases} |x| + 3, & \text{if } x \leq -3 \\ -2x, & \text{if } -3 < x < 3 \\ 6x + 2, & \text{if } x \geq 3 \end{cases}$.

Or

If $e^x + e^y = e^{x+y}$, then prove that $\dfrac{dy}{dx} + \dfrac{e^x (e^y - 1)}{e^y (e^x - 1)} = 0$.

7. Find the amount of an ordinary annuity, if payment of ₹ 500 is made at the end of every quarter for 10 yr at the rate of 8% per-year compounded quarterly.

Or

(i) The difference between CI and SI for 3 yr at the rate of 20% per annum is ₹ 152. What is the principal lent?

(ii) Find the compound interest on ₹ 5000 in 2 yr at 4% per annum, if the interest being compounded half-yearly.

8. Bag 1 contains 3 red and 4 black balls and bag II contains 4 red and 5 black balls. One ball is transferred from bag I to bag II and then ball is drawn from bag II. The ball so drawn is found to be red in colour. Find the probability that the transferred ball is black.

Or

A man is known to speak the truth 3 out of 5 times. He throws a die and reports that it is 1. Find the probability that it is actually 1.

9. A Shopkeeper in Tamil Nadu buys an bullet bike at the printed price of ₹ 40000 from a wholesaler in West Bengal. The shopkeeper sells the bullet bike to a consumer in Tamil Nadu at a profit of 25% on the basic cost price. If the rate of GST is 18%, find

(i) the price of the bullet bike inclusive of tax (under GST) in which the shopkeeper bought it.

(ii) the amount of tax (under GST) paid by the shopkeeper to the Central Government?

(iii) the amount of tax (under GST) received by West Bengal Government.

(iv) the amount of tax (under GST) received by Central Government.

(v) the amount which the consumer pays for the bullet bike.

Section C

(1 Mark Each)

This section consists of 1 Case Based comprises of 5 MCQs.

10. Five students Ajay, Shyam, Yojana, Rahul and Akansha are sitting in a play ground in a line.

Based on the above information answer the following questions.

(i) Total number of ways of sitting arrangement of five students is
   (a) 120
   (b) 60
   (c) 24
   (d) None of these

(ii) Total number of arrangement of sitting if Ajay and Yojana sit together is
   (a) 60
   (b) 48
   (c) 72
   (d) 120

(iii) Total number of arrangement Yojana and Rahul sitting at extreme position is
   (a) 24
   (b) 36
   (c) 48
   (d) 12

(iv) Total number of arrangement if Shyam is sitting in the middle is
   (a) 24
   (b) 12
   (c) 6
   (d) 36

(v) Total number of arrangement sitting Yojana and Rahul not sit together, is
   (a) 72
   (b) 120
   (c) 60
   (d) 144

Answers

1. $a = b + \dfrac{2}{3}$ *Or* $\dfrac{dy}{dx} = -\dfrac{[y - 4x(x^2 + y^2)]}{[x - 4y(x^2 + y^2)]}$

2. $\dfrac{25}{102}$ *Or* $\dfrac{7}{15}$

3. *(–9, 6) and (1, – 4) Or* $x^2 + y^2 - 8x - 9 = 0$

4. $x^2 + y^2 + 2xy - 14x + 2y + 17 = 0$

5. *₹ 125000*

6. *Point of discontinuity is* $x = 3$

7. *₹ 30200 Or (i) ₹ 1187.5 (ii) ₹ 412.16*

8. $\dfrac{16}{31}$ *Or* $\dfrac{3}{13}$

9. *(i) ₹ 47200 (ii) ₹ 1800 (iii) Nil (iv) ₹ 7200 (v) ₹ 59000*

10. *(i) (a) (ii) (b) (iii) (d) (iv) (a) (v) (a)*

Practice Paper 3*
(Unsolved)

Instructions

1. The question paper contains three sections A, B and C.
2. Section A has 5 questions with 3 internal choices.
3. Section B has 4 questions with 3 internal choices.
4. Section C has 1 Case Based MCQs comprises of 5 MCQs.
5. There is no negative marking.

■ Time : 2 Hr
■ Max. Marks : 40

As exact Blue-print and Pattern for CBSE Term II exams is not released yet. So the pattern of this paper is designed by the author on the basis of trend of past CBSE Papers. Students are advised not to consider the pattern of this paper as official.

Section A
(3 Marks Each)

This section consists of 5 questions of Short Answer Type.

1. How many words can be formed out of the letters of the word 'OBEDIENCE' so that vowels and consonants occur together?

Or

How many natural numbers less than 1000 can be formed with the digits 1, 2, 3, 4 and 5, if repetition of digits is allowed?

2. Find $\lim\limits_{x \to 0} f(x)$ and $\lim\limits_{x \to 1} f(x)$, where $f(x) = \begin{cases} 2x + 3, & x \leq 0 \\ 3(x + 1), & x > 0 \end{cases}$.

Or

Find k so that $\lim\limits_{x \to 2} f(x)$ may exists, where $f(x) = \begin{cases} 4x - 5, & x \leq 2 \\ x - k, & x > 2 \end{cases}$.

3. A and B are two candidates seeking admission in a college. The probability that A is selected is 0.7 and the probability that exactly one of them is selected is 0.6. Find the probability that B is selected.

Or

Probabilities of solving a specific problem independently by A and B are $\dfrac{1}{2}$ and $\dfrac{1}{3}$ respectively. If both try to solve the problem independently, find the probability that

(i) the problem is solved

(ii) exactly one of them solves the problem

4. A sum of money lent at compound interest for 2 yr at 20% per annum would fetch ₹ 964 more, if the interest was payable half-yearly, then if it was payable annually. What is the sum?

5. A man wants to have ₹ 12000 in his account after 10 yr. He deposits annual payments in an account that pays 4% rate of interest compounded annually. How much should be deposite each year?

Section B
(5 Marks Each)

This section consists of 4 questions of Long Answer Type.

6. Differentiate $\sqrt{\dfrac{(x-3)(x^2+4)}{3x^2+4x+5}}$ with respect to x.

Or

For what value of λ is the function $f(x) = \begin{cases} \lambda(x^2 - 2x), & \text{if } x \leq 0 \\ 4x + 1, & \text{if } x > 0 \end{cases}$ continuous at $x = 0$? What about its continuity at $x = \pm 1$?

7. An urn contains 3 red and 5 black balls. A ball is drawn at random, its colour is noted and returned to the urn. Moreover, 2 additional balls of the colour noted down, are put into the urn and then two balls are drawn at random (without replacement) from the urn. Find the probability that both the balls drawn are of red colour.

Or

The reliability of a HIV test is specified as follows:

Of people having HIV, 90% of the tests detect the disease but 10% undetected. Of people free of HIV, 99% of the tests are judged negative but 1% are wrongly diagnosed as HIV + ve. In a city having only 0.1% have HIV, one person is randomly chosen, given the HIV test and is diagnosed as HIV + ve. What is the probability that the person actually has HIV?

8. Find the equation of the parabola whose focus is $(1, -1)$ and vertex is $(2, 1)$.

Or

Find the equation of the line passing through the point $(1, 0)$ and at a distance $\dfrac{\sqrt{3}}{2}$ from the origin.

9. Sekharkant monthly salary is ₹ 225000 with HRA at the rate of 20%. He donates ₹ 5000 per month towards P.M.'s relief fund getting a relief of 100% on the donation. Calculate the income tax payable by Sekharkant.

Section C
(1 Mark Each)

This section consists of 1 Case Based comprises of 5 MCQs.

10. The printed price of a washing machine is ₹ 40000. A wholesaler in Chhattisgarh buys the washing machine from a manufacturer in Delhi at a discount of 10% on the printed price. The wholesaler sells the washing machine to a retailer in Haryana at 5% above the printed price. If the rate of GST on the washing machine is 18%, find

(i) the amount inclusive of tax (under GST) paid by the wholesaler for the washing machine is

    (a) ₹ 42480   (b) ₹ 30400

    (c) ₹ 51300   (d) ₹ 35150

(ii) the amount inclusive of tax (under GST) paid by the retailer for the washing machine is

    (a) ₹ 31390   (b) ₹ 29300

    (c) ₹ 49560   (d) ₹ 53064

(iii) the amount of tax retailer pays to wholesaler is
    (a) ₹ 7560   (b) ₹ 8600
    (c) ₹ 9230   (d) ₹ 8760

(iv) the amount of tax (under GST) paid by the wholesaler to the Central Government is
    (a) ₹ 2330   (b) ₹ 1080
    (c) ₹ 950   (d) ₹ 1160

(v) the amount of tax (under GST) received by the Central Government is
    (a) ₹ 5675   (b) ₹ 4930
    (c) ₹ 7830   (d) ₹ 7560

Answers

1. *960 Or 155*

2. *3 and 6 Or −1*

3. $\dfrac{1}{4}$ *Or (i)* $\dfrac{2}{3}$ *(ii)* $\dfrac{1}{2}$

4. *₹ 40000*

5. *₹ 1002.08*

6. $\dfrac{1}{2}\sqrt{\dfrac{(x-3)(x^2+4)}{(3x^2+4x+5)}}\left[\dfrac{1}{x-3}+\dfrac{2x}{x^2+4}-\dfrac{6x+4}{3x^2+4x+5}\right]$

   Or No value of λ *can make given function continuous at at* $x=0$ *and at* $x=\pm 1$, *given function is continuous for all values of* λ.

7. $\dfrac{1}{8}$ *Or* $\dfrac{99}{1089}$

8. $4x^2+y^2-4xy+8x+46y-71=0$ *Or* $\sqrt{3}x-y-\sqrt{3}=0$ *and* $\sqrt{3}x+y-\sqrt{3}=0$

9. *₹ 1027485*

10. *(i) (a) (ii) (c) (iii) (a) (iv) (b) (v) (d)*

Printed by Libri Plureos GmbH in Hamburg,
Germany